RECLAIMING
THE JESUS
OF HISTORY

Books by A. Roy Eckardt

Christianity and the Children of Israel

The Surge of Piety in America

Elder and Younger Brothers

The Theologian at Work (editor)

Christianity in Israel (editor)

Your People, My People

Jews and Christians

For Righteousness' Sake

Black-Woman-Jew

Reclaiming the Jesus of History

Sitting in the Earth and Laughing

By Alice L. Eckardt and A. Roy Eckardt

Encounter With Israel

Long Night's Journey into Day: A Revised
Retrospective on the Holocaust

RECLAIMING THE JESUS OF HISTORY

Christology Today

A. Roy Eckardt

Fortress Press · Minneapolis

For
Marion and Elie Wiesel

RECLAIMING THE JESUS OF HISTORY
Christology Today

Scripture quotations, unless otherwise noted, are from the Revised Standard Version of the Bible, copyright © 1952, 1946 by the Division of Christian Education of the National Council of the Churches of Christ in the United States of America.

Library of Congress Cataloging-in-Publication Data

Eckardt, A. Roy (Arthur Roy), 1918–
    Reclaiming the Jesus of history : Christology today / A. Roy Eckardt.
      p. cm.
    Includes bibliographical references and index.
    ISBN 0-8006-2513-7 (alk. paper)
    1. Jesus Christ—Person and offices.   2. Jesus Christ—Jewishness.
  I. Title.
  BT202.E26   1992
  232—dc20
                                 91-35746
                                 CIP

The paper used in this publication meets the minimum requirements of American National Standard for Information Sciences—Permanence of Paper for Printed Library Materials, ANSI Z329.48–1984. ∞™

Manufactured in the U.S.A.   AF 1–2514

96   95   94   93   92   1   2   3   4   5   6   7   8   9   10

The doctrine that God is hidden is probably the most pertinent Christian witness about God for our time.... The nature of God's presence is that God is so solely and completely God in his presence that he cannot but remain hidden.... For transcendence does not mean God is so far away that he is hidden but rather he is so near that he is hidden.

—*Carl Michalson*

And from there [Jesus] arose and went away to the region of Tyre and Sidon. And he entered a house, and would not have any one know it; yet he could not be hid.

—*Mark 7:24*

Let the children come to me, and do not hinder them; for to such belongs the kingdom of heaven.

—*Matt. 19:14*

What really matters is the children.

—*John Fitzgerald Kennedy*

Contents

Preface

Through years of research and published work, I have wandered in sundry directions: the piety of Americans, how theologians operate, political theory, social ethics, the encounter of Christians and Jews, Christian moral philosophy, Black and Latin American liberation thinking, the women's movement, and the interpretation of humor. This is not to pin roses on myself; on the contrary, it is usually the "specialist" (in medicine, law, theology, biblical studies, etc.) who occupies higher storeys of the professional totem pole. I simply seem to be curious (intellectually, morally, aesthetically) about a number of subjects—perhaps inordinately so. My only spiritual excuse is to be a pilgrim in the company of pilgrims (Heb. 11:13-14).

The question of Christology has lain implicit in my various efforts to date, but until now I have not quite had the presumption to reckon with that question intensively. Age takes certain liberties. I am hardly expert in this area, yet I have here worked out a procedure that may be of some interest and have some consequence: Let a cadre of today's professionals have their say, and let me simply chime in here and there as an amateur whose warrant is that of a believing Christian who has been around long enough at least to have ruminated over some of the more salient and real-life christological challenges.

I seek to address general readers, students, and scholars. And I hope to have something to say to non-Christian inquirers as well as to Christians. The book describes and assesses certain aspects of current historical science (historiography). Of course, if it is to be true to history, such historiography will try to catch as many glimpses as it can of the Jesus of the first century. The ideal consequence will be a conversation between our century and what we may seek to uncover from the first century. Let us, at any rate, see how the schema works out.

I express gratefulness to my wife Alice Eliza, to David Patterson of the University of Oxford, and in the United States to colleagues of the Christian Study Group on Judaism and the Jewish People. I am appreciative as well of the expert guidance of Kyle J. Halverson, Charles Puskas, and Julie Odland, editors at Fortress Press.

A. Roy Eckardt
Oxford Centre for
Postgraduate Hebrew Studies

PART
1
Preliminaries

CHAPTER

1

Journey into
the Apostolic Past

Construed broadly, Christology is the interpretation of Jesus Christ.[1] The full title of this book, *Reclaiming the Jesus of History: Christology Today,* suggests that for all its expressed support of historical work, the study cannot be exclusively historical in character or intention. For to resolve to "do" Christology with the aid of history and historiography is itself to propound a normative judgment rather than a strictly historical judgment. In this last respect, the present volume is representative of Christian moral philosophy.

THREE CHRISTOLOGICAL ASSUMPTIONS

Christologies come and go with the times and seasons. Today, along with other constant and competing interpretations, we are met by certain christological views that are perhaps unitive enough to be treated under the one rubric. The overall approach I have in mind is marked by three characteristics, not always easily reconcilable yet often found together.

(1) In varied and often divergent ways, the point of view represents and conserves, or at least assumes, the historical-moral-theological distinctiveness and validity or integrity of the Christian faith. Accordingly, such endeavor is consonant with personal support of the life and work of the Christian community.

(2) Many adherents of the christological outlooks we shall review try nonetheless to keep themselves and Christology as a whole free of traditionalist imperialism, triumphalism, or elitism vis-à-vis other faiths or life-views.

3

Where this *Anschauung* is not given positive voice, it is at least implicit. Minimally speaking, triumphalist impulses or assumptions are not accentuated.

(3) Most exigent of all is a developing, insistent stress upon the historical Jesus as a preeminent factor, subject, or theme in christological effort and assertion, together with the implied corollary that the use of historical-critical method is justified and essential within christological endeavor. That is to say, that Jesus of history—what he said, what he did, how he lived, how he died—is identified as a primary foundation of any tenable Christology. There comes to the fore what James H. Charlesworth calls "Jesus Research."[2] The great British historian James Parkes used to warn repeatedly, "Bad history cannot be the foundation for good theology." To put the point a bit more circumspectly: Suspicion is present—tacit or expressed—concerning christological affirmations that cannot be sustained by or reconciled to historical findings.[3]

The third emphasis is linked to, and is perhaps consequential of, today's Christian "return into history" (see my *For Righteousness' Sake,* chaps. 10–13), a move that not only parallels but is often influenced by a comparable trend in Jewish quarters (see Emil L. Fackenheim's *The Jewish Return into History,* one of that philosopher's more influential volumes).[4]

Speaking of our colleague Fackenheim, I recall his assertion that philosophic historicism "fails to philosophize about itself; it asserts the historical relativity of all things, those philosophical included; yet it claims or implies that it is itself exempt."[5] The "historicism" that underlies the present inquiry is quite different; it is self-critical or strives to be. Furthermore, its self-critical character is made possible and underwritten by its theocentrism.[6]

A Christian historicism—by which I mean no more than Christian historicalness, a stress upon history—that is joined to the history and life of Israel has as its foundation and incentive the Jew, Jesus of Nazareth: his outlook, his message, his behavior. In and through the event of Jesus there is manifest the essential historicity that marries the Christian community to Israel, a flesh-and-blood authorization and confession that historical Israel is the root that sustains the church (Rom. 11:18). In this connection, Luke Timothy Johnson points out that "in the most proper sense, the New Testament remains always a commentary upon the Torah," the Hebrew Bible.[7]

In principle, the third characteristic of the new or fresh christological outlook, while never claiming that history can demonstrate faith, nevertheless differs sharply from any *Tendenz* to focus Christology exclusively upon "the Christ of faith" or upon, even more extremely, the Second Person of the Trinity.

At least four qualifications upon, or elaborations of, the third characteristic may be indicated.

(a) Since Christology is itself interpretive rather than purely historical, any given Christology will perforce involve itself in a dialectical relation between the historical Jesus as we seek to know of him and certain religious, social, and theological responses to that figure. One consequence of this state of affairs may be the counterbalancing and perhaps even the nourishing of history by faith. For while neither historical research nor analytic study provides a final basis or ultimate justification of faith, such procedures may yet be of help in clarifying or understanding the dimension of faith. And if there is no way to do Christology without entering upon historical questions,[8] so, too, there is no way to deal with the history or story of Jesus without entering upon theological and moral questions.

The two sides of the dialectic spill over upon each other: To some extent, faith is itself treatable as a historical phenomenon (i.e., it operates and expresses itself within human experience), and historical data may themselves gain meaning under the impetus and inspiration of various affirmations of faith. If faith ties the Judeo-Christian tradition to human history in ways that do not always apply with other religions[9] — in Judaism and Christianity alike history is the stage upon which the drama of revelation and redemption is reputedly enacted — it is also the case that history (including the history of faith) exerts an influence upon faith. And "if it is so that humankind's distinctive quality is its historicalness — identified as the recognition and acceptance of history as the determining condition and opportunity of all human life — the endeavor to characterize and to cope with Jesus of Nazareth in all his historicity thereby gains human and moral sanction"[10] — this quite apart from fealty to a particular faith.

All in all, neither history nor faith is independent of the other. In this respect, we have to say that no Christology is superior to or independent of the history of Jesus. But the other side completes the paradox: No history of Jesus is possible apart from some expression of Christology.

(b) To reckon with the historical Jesus is to combine disinterested objectivity and interested subjectivity. There is much to ponder in the words of Leonardo Boff:

> No text and no investigation, however objective it may seek and pose to be, can fail to be structured around some horizon of interest. To know is always to interpret. The hermeneutic structure of all knowledge and science means that the subject — with his or her models, paradigms, and categories — always enters into the composition of the experience of the object, mediated by a language. The subject is not a pure reason; he or she is immersed in history, in a sociopolitical context, and is motivated by personal and group interests. Hence a purely disinterested cognition free of ideology does not exist.[11]

(c) We are limited in what we can finally know concerning Jesus as a figure of history. As examples: Jesus wrote nothing; we have no chronology of his life (hence we cannot offer a comprehensive historical biography); and we have no way to reckon with the states of his mind (Michael L. Cook).[12] More-over, historical research, even when "working with optimum sources and employing the finest methodologies, is capable of producing only probabilities" (James H. Charlesworth).[13] Again, "no matter how cautious, critical, and self-conscious our methods and modest our claims when attempting to recover him, this 'historical Jesus' is but an image, at best a coherent set of inferences from historical knowledge" (Paula Fredriksen).[14] Yet were we to turn away from such questions as Jesus' intention or intentions, we would run the danger of losing contact with the available history in its fullness.

(d) Scholars in the field provide counsel of great use in the work of restoring the historical Jesus. Naturally, the counsel varies from expert to expert. Marcus J. Borg contends that we can know as much about Jesus as we can of any person in the ancient world. E. P. Sanders concludes that "the dominant view today seems to be that we can know pretty well what Jesus was out to accomplish, that we can know a lot about what he said, and that those two things make sense within the world of first-century Judaism." The method that is more and more followed, and the one that seems necessary to follow, is to construct hypotheses about Jesus that, on the one hand, "rest on material generally considered reliable without, on the other hand, being totally dependent on the authenticity of any given pericope [cutting or extract]." It is, of course, well known that the Gospel writers were not simply composing objective history. They wrote as Christian believers (cf. John 20:31: What the evangelist says is written "that you may believe that Jesus is the Christ . . . "). With respect to the purposes of the Synoptics, Johnson suggests that an older and rather simple explanation of their occasion and aim may well be "the human desire to remember Jesus and preserve the memory accurately" for generations to come.[15]

In *Jesus and Judaism* Sanders lists eight "almost indisputable facts" about Jesus:

1. Jesus was baptized by John the Baptist.
2. Jesus was a Galilean who preached and healed.
3. Jesus called disciples and spoke of their being twelve.
4. Jesus confined his activity to Israel.
5. Jesus engaged in a controversy about the temple.
6. Jesus was crucified outside Jerusalem by the Roman authorities.
7. After his death Jesus' followers continued as an identifiable movement.
8. At least some Jews persecuted at least parts of the new movement (Gal. 1:13, 22; Phil. 3:6), and it appears that this persecution endured at least to a time near the end of Paul's career (2 Cor. 11:24; Gal. 5:11; 6:12; cf. Matt. 10:17; 23:34).

Toward the end of his study Sanders divides the available data about Jesus into six categories: *certain or virtually certain* (e.g., Jesus shared the worldview of

Jewish restoration eschatology); *highly probable* (e.g., his disciples thought of Jesus as "king"); *probable* (e.g., he did not emphasize the national character of the kingdom of God); *possible* (e.g., he may have spoken of the kingdom as a present reality into which people enter one by one); *conceivable* (e.g., he may have given his death martyrological significance); and *incredible* (e.g., as a Jew he was rare in believing in love, mercy, grace, repentance, and forgiveness).[16]

In *Jesus Within Judaism* Charlesworth arranges under seven headings his assessment of where we are today, methodologically and perceptively speaking, with regard to the gospel tradition and its transmission. First, while the Gospels come from a generation after Jesus, they are nevertheless informed by eyewitnesses. Sometimes, oral tradition "is more reliable than the written word." Second, although the Gospels and other Christian documents reflect church needs, the Christian community also functioned as a source for the faithful remembrance of Jesus. Third, while the Gospels do contain legendary and mythical elements, the basic story of Jesus "derives from authentic and very early traditions." Fourth, although Matthew obviously "expands and often allegorizes Mark and Q,[17] a lost source known only because Matthew and Luke inherit portions of it," it in no way follows that Matthew is ahistorical. Fifth, inauthentic words of Jesus may nevertheless preserve accurately the Nazarene's real intention. "Our task sometimes is not so much to recover Jesus' own words (the so-called *ipsissima verba Jesu*) as to grasp . . . Jesus' own purpose." Sixth, while it is so that Matthew and Luke altered certain sayings of Jesus and that Mark, too, exercised the same exegetical freedom, it remains "obvious from comparing Mark with Q and Jesus' sayings found only in Matthew with those only in Luke, that many of Jesus' sayings date long before 70.[18] It simply is not true that Jesus' sayings were created by the earliest Christians or invented by the evangelists." And seventh, even though Rom. 1:3-4 and other early traditions tend to say that the followers of Jesus affirmed him as "the Christ" only after his resurrection, it does not follow from this that Christology "begins only after Easter, or that the cross and the resurrection were the only important aspects of Jesus' life. The claim that the Gospels are post-Easter confessionals is essentially true, but to contend that they are *only* post-Easter confessionals also fails to do justice to the abundance of pre-Easter data and traditions that are preserved, perhaps almost always in an edited form, in the New Testament."[19]

In *From Jesus to Christ* Paula Fredriksen enumerates basic criteria that have been formulated by scholars for aid in testing the authenticity of Gospel passages: *dissimilarity* (authenticity *may* turn upon whether "a saying or story differs in emphasis from a characteristic teaching or concern both of contemporary Judaism and of the early church"); *coherence* ("If material from the earlier strata of tradition is consonant with other material already established as probably authentic, then it too is probably authentic"); *multiple attestation* ("if material appears in a number of different sources and literary contexts, . . . it may be authentic"); and *linguistic suitability* ("material with a claim to authenticity should be susceptible of Aramaic rendering, since Jesus did not teach in Greek, the language of the documents").[20]

Much controversy surrounds the principle of dissimilarity, particularly in recent years. The notion that the "authentic" teaching of Jesus must be "unique" is often contradicted by the consideration that his ideas and sayings would naturally reflect the milieu in which he lived. Much depends upon how seriously we take "the proposition that Jesus of Nazareth was a Jew."[21] A comparison of two titles of recent books helps to illustrate this issue: E. P. Sanders's *Jesus and Judaism* and James H. Charlesworth's *Jesus Within Judaism.* The *and* and the *within* may point up fundamentally different approaches and methodologies. Charlesworth testifies, "My study of the Jesus tradition has led me to the conclusion that a considerable amount of that tradition which is discontinuous with needs and concerns of the earliest Christians places Jesus squarely in the midst of Early Judaism, and that is precisely where one would expect to find a first-century Palestinian Jew. . . . Without becoming guilty of [a] distorting philosemitism, we must struggle to see not Jesus *and* Judaism, as if we are confronted in some ways with an antithesis, but Jesus *within* Judaism."[22]

I am aware that when taken together the characteristics I submit at the start of this section of the chapter embrace a rather wide area of Christian writing and thought, a large segment that contains its own conflicts and differences. Some readers may come to feel that it is oversimple to speak of the general point of view before us as a single christological orientation. Sometimes two or only one rather than three of the characteristics I have listed are discernible. But overall I do find more elements of continuity than of discontinuity, of agreement than of disagreement, within these christological efforts. Let us at least see how the latter premise works out. At any rate, I try in this study to give voice to the three characteristics—in part through reporting upon the work of other scholars and in part through presenting my own position. (By no means all the scholars I shall cite represent the stated point of view.) To respect the honesty that is due every reader: The three characteristics comprise this writer's own goals.

FOUR NEGATIONS

An alternate means of identifying the threefold position I have introduced is to ask what it is that many of the scholars and writers in question are replacing, either deliberately or perhaps just tacitly. I think that at least four such historical-moral phenomena qualify for notice, sometimes even serving as foils: a modernism that in its theological dimension sought to assimilate religious faith to the norms and attainments of the modern world;[23] a neoorthodoxy that sought to prosper the univocal, severe transcendence of God and to take into account the ravaging sinfulness of humankind; androcentric dominance; and the ecclesiastical-theological triumphalism of a pre-Holocaust (pre-*Shoah*)[24] mentality and ideology. In one or more ways these new Christologies reflect a postmodernist,[25] post-neoorthodox, postpatriarchal,[26] and post-*Shoah*[27] universe of discourse and understanding. Sometimes, of course, one or another of these four critical outlooks will prevail at the expense of the others. Yet all four of them are united willy-nilly through shared participation in a particular epoch: the late twentieth century.

I venture a brief interjection upon the concept of postmodernity. Calvin O. Shrag enumerates as general features of the postmodern frame of mind "the plurality of narratives, the multiplicity of language games, the heterogeneity of social practices, and the diversity of forms of knowledge." Yet Harvey Cox writes that while "no one is quite sure just what the postmodern era will be like, . . . one thing seems clear. Rather than an age of rampant secularization and religious decline, it appears to be more of an era of religious revival and the return of the sacral. . . . [The] task of a postmodern [Christian] theology is to interpret the Christian message at a time when the rebirth of religion, rather than its disappearance, poses the most serious questions."[28]

To bring together the contentions of Shrag and Cox: A postmodern Christology is obliged to come to terms at one and the same time with a pluralist social and intellectual order *and* a burgeoning or hearty religiousness.

A few illustrations from within the twin contexts of post-*Shoah* thinking and feminist thinking may help to point up the growing christological orientation that I am reporting on and in a way advocating. (Mary Daly contends that patriarchal gynocide is "the root and paradigm for genocide.")[29] The Catholic theologian Johann Baptist Metz of the University of Münster provides one watchword for the movement at hand, as originally directed to his students: "Ask yourselves if the theology you are learning is such that it could remain unchanged before and after Auschwitz. If this is the case, be on your guard."[30] Fresh American denominational, moral-theologic testimony extends to a declaration of the United Church of Christ (30 June 1987), which, within and through its very (traditionally normative) stance of asking for "God's forgiveness through our Lord Jesus Christ," yet asserts that "Judaism has not been superseded by Christianity"—an assertion that calls into question major parts of Christian Scripture. The American Catholic theologian Michael McGarry has identified supersessionism—the claim that Christianity has taken the place of Judaism—as nothing less than a Christian heresy.[31] Coherent with some other contemporary Christian feminist expression, Elisabeth Schüssler Fiorenza's *In Memory of Her* furnishes an essential historical and moral corrective to any effort to cut Jesus off from his Jewishness or from the Jewish community. Beverly Wildung Harrison adjudges that it is fitting to characterize Jesus' teaching as political, for "he was engaging people in an effort to change their lifestyles, their social relationships, and the ethos of their culture."[32] And for Tom F. Driver theology, when profoundly conceived, is itself politics, "because it has to do with the actions and values of the children of God during their life upon earth."[33]

Additional exemplification of the mode of thinking under analysis is provided by reference to other names. The list that follows is not exhaustive, but it is representative: Marcus J. Borg, James H. Charlesworth, Harvey Cox, Alice L. Eckardt, A. Roy Eckardt, Robert A. Everett, Monika K. Hellwig, Isabel Carter Heyward, John Hick, Luke Timothy Johnson, Paul F. Knitter, John T. Pawlikowski, Sharon H. Ringe, Letty M. Russell, E. P. Sanders, Marjorie Hewitt Suchocki, Leonard Swidler, John T. Townsend, Paul M. van Buren, and Clark M. Williamson.

HISTORY-TRUTH-REASON

To bring together and conclude this preliminary schema, I offer three interrelated points upon the general problem of how the events or phenomena of human history may be read and assessed.

(1) It is my assumption (not proved, perhaps not provable) that the way human events are rendered (described and evaluated) tends to be a function of the understanding that accompanies differing human roles and interests. (This means that the rendering of events, at least in part, does not surmount ideology.)[34] Take, for example, "the crossing of the Red Sea" by the children of Israel (Exod. 14:15—15:19). The theologian, as partisan of a given faith, may naturally identify that event as a special "act of God." (Attention to such acts will perforce assume God's hiddenness as well; this is the case with any ostensible historical revelation of God.) But a natural scientist looking at the *very same event* may approach it in a quite different frame of reference and frame of mind—for example, that of climatology. A sociologist or psychologist or historian will marshal yet other ways of apprehending the event. It is important to note that the individual observer often occupies more than one role and nourishes more than the one interest (the natural scientist who is a believing Jew, the historian who is a Christian, the psychologist who is a Muslim, etc.). This means that the one persuasion will often be counteracted or supplemented by another—and sometimes within the very same person or group. Judgments and interpretations of events vary with human roles and with the ideas and in-

terests that attend given roles. And to come to the point, christological endeavor does not escape this condition.[35] (It is not alone the devil who quotes Scripture for his purposes. Nondevilish, relatively innocent people do the very same thing. Indeed, anybody and everybody quote anything and everything for any and every purpose.)

The viewpoint expressed here contrasts sharply with the virtual acceptance of a splitting of reality through assuming that nonreligious explanations are quite sufficient for most events, but that in those (few) cases where such explanations may not suffice, it is permitted to muster up God (cf. the "God of the gaps"). The affirmation I support (viz., a faith in the presence of God hidden behind any or all events)[36] contradicts any such reductionist representation of God. An old Jewish tale thus explains the life story of all blades of grass: Each and every blade is attended by an angel who whispers, "Grow."

The principle of role/interest applies, of course, to this volume and to its author (a Christian moral and political philosopher and historian) as much as it does elsewhere. Michael L. Cook puts the matter simply, and he puts it well: "Christology is inextricably intertwined with discipleship." And Marcus J. Borg points out that what Jesus was like "provides the context of what following him means."[37]

(2) There is an allied way to conceptualize the opportunities and limits within various truth-claims. Following Karl Mannheim, Arnold Nash has spoken of a "relationist" means of trying to face up to the problem of truth. Relationism falls between extreme absolutism and extreme relativism. The extreme absolutist maintains that his view of truth and his contentions respecting "reality" are unreservedly correct; they are wholly independent of and immune to historical contingency or the drag of historical contexts. Contrariwise, the extreme relativist holds, in effect, that there is no such thing as objective truth, no truth "out there." In his view, differing assertions about "truth" are equally arbitrary. Against both these extremes, the relationist argues that the human mind has the capacity to achieve *some kind* of relation to truth, even though it cannot express or possess truth absolutely or without distortion and ambiguity. Nash illustrates the three positions "through the figure of a steeple jack inspecting a church building. An extreme relativist and skeptic will claim that, because the church looks so different from various positions, all statements about the building are no more than equally true and hence equally false. Indeed, there may not be a church present at all! The extreme absolutist holds that the steeple jack need simply say 'I see the church.' The relationist insists that the more correct or authentic description would be, 'I see the church *from the steeple,* or 'I see the church *from the roof.*' "[38]

The relationist rejects the absolutist's contention that there is only one truth, that the absolutist is in possession of it, and hence that the only way others can get to see or appreciate the truth is to come and stand in the place where the absolutist stands. But the relationist also rejects the (lachrymose?) conclusion of the extreme relativist or skeptic for whom no truth-claim can really partake of the truth or for whom it is impossible to reach any valid historical or moral position from among conflicting truth-claims.

My own orientation is toward relationism, the assumption that human beings are capable of achieving partial glimpses of truth from particular, limited standpoints.

(3) In his *Essay Concerning Human Understanding* John Locke distinguishes among propositions that are (a) according to reason; (b) above reason; and (c) contrary to reason. Although I dissent from much in Locke's overall moral-philosophic position, I agree with him that sensible or legitimate historical and theological affirmations may be either themselves reasonable or above and beyond reason (reason transcending itself) but not in contradiction of reason.

Taken together, the foregoing philosophic and methodological assumptions suggest that there is no such thing as *the* point of view that makes other points of view wholly false. The influence of these assumptions is of much importance whenever one seeks to wrestle with the phenomenon of the historical Jesus and with christological assertion as a whole.

THE WAY OF HISTORICALNESS

Different references and tributes to Jesus today involve diverse reactions, understandings, and life-decisions.[39] Really to speak of Jesus, however, is to announce to everyone (not excluding skeptics, cynics, and detached observers) that Christianity is a historicist faith, a way of historicalness. For the foundation of the church, the foundation reared upon Israel, is an event: the birth, life, and fate of a particular human being. At this vital juncture the Christian historian dedicates herself or himself to "the quest of the historical Jesus," since that quest's basic concern is, in Michael L. Cook's wording, "the decisive importance of the historical Jesus for Christian faith."[40]

Yet the historical-existential sources of Christianity reach infinitely deeper than the life of one individual by himself. For what is the history of a human being apart from his life with his people?[41] A house rests upon a foundation, but the foundation is in turn supported by the earth beneath, perhaps even by bedrock. The foundation of the Christian church's foundation is a certain historical collectivity together with its highly diverse societal ways, its politics, its fortunes, its faith, its betrayals of faith. This foundation of the Christian foundation is Jewishness, which means historical peoplehood (*laos*), a laic reality.

The rudiments of the Christian story thus come to focus in a dialectic additional to and supplementing the dialectic of history (Jesus) and faith (Christianity). This other dialectic is the one between Jesus of Nazareth and the people from whom he came and to whom he ministered. This dialectic provides a resource for meeting the question, Why does the Christian affirmation and reaffirmation of Jewishness mean a "return into history"?[42] The link is found within the reality of Jewishness itself, a reality that forever breaks out of religiousness into the great social world (today's preeminent case being the State of Israel). Before this fact the religion called Christianity may itself come to be, paradoxically, redeemed from "pure" religiousness. In and through the presence of a historicist Israel the Christian church is empowered to implement and sanctify its worldly obligations and to be saved from falling into otherworldly spirituality and spiritualization. For the Jewish *laos* is wholly "secular" in a determining respect: A people wholly of the world (*saeculum*) is here among us. The Jewish life-phenomenon is epitomized in a characterization by James Parkes: The Jewish people are a *natural community*.[43] A fundamental moral-theological challenge to the contemporary church is to recognize and celebrate its link to Jewishness as at the same time it is not reducing itself to a version of Judaism.

To end these short remarks upon a Christian historicism that traces itself to Jesus and the Jewish people as its foundation: Jürgen Moltmann has lamented the churchly pretension of attempting through the device of impartiality to realize a universalist potential. He has written: "Only in and through the dialectic of taking sides does the universalism of the Crucified become a reality in this world. The phony universalism of the church is something very different. It is a premature and untimely anticipation of the *Kingdom* of God."[44] A "taking of sides" with the people Israel constitutes a discrete, historical application of a fundamental principle of the contemporary theology of liberation —as in the now famous watchword, "a preferential option for the poor." This particular commitment, however, means not alone self-transcendence but also self-fulfillment. Through love of the neighbor who is not a Christian neighbor, the ideological taint of Christian self-concentration is fought. But insofar as Christians are returning, in and through the reality of Israel, to their own ancestral home and family, they may fulfill themselves. (Here is suggested the ultimate foundation of Christian unity.)

2

Synoptic Titles

Our appropriated history of Jesus is ruled by the fact or datum that he is a Galilean Jewish man from the village of Nazareth who from first to last gives of himself to the God of Israel, to his Jewish neighbors and friends, and to the Jewish nation as a whole.[1] Jesus lived and died a faithful Jew. To speak of Jesus as other than a Jew of *that time* and *that place* is no longer to speak of him. As Gerard S. Sloyan declares, to be faithful to Jesus as Christian Scripture witnesses to him "is to be in full continuity with him in his Jewishness."[2] The Jewishness of Christianity is grounded in the historical truth that Jesus is a Jew. One defect in much Christian scholarship has been its tendency to separate Jesus from his Jewishness and his Judaism on behalf of one or another kind of trans-Jewish or even anti-Jewish Christology. (For at least four decades—c.e. 30 to 70—the followers of Jesus were a group within Judaism.)

The historical authorization of the foregoing paragraph is that such data concerning Jesus as are referred to therein dominate the earlier strata of the Apostolic Writings, and these are the materials that constitute the primary and authoritative sources of whatever we may know of Jesus. Accordingly, the Jesus whom we may wish to reclaim, or at least to re-present, is the person partially described in the previous paragraph.[3]

JESUS' TITLES AND JESUS' IDENTITY

This chapter concerns itself with the way in which Jesus' identity may be addressed, at least prolegomenously, through titles imputed to him in the Synoptic Gospels.[4] However interpretive these writings are of Jesus, they are the closest we have to historical documents about him. The Fourth Gospel represents a later and different class; the Synoptics are recognized as more authentic upon historical matters, as they are upon aspects of Christology that build upon their history. Nevertheless, the Gospel of John is today adjudged to be somewhat more helpful or reliable historically than was the case at earlier stages of scholarship (for example, concerning Jesus' original discipleship under John the Baptist). Furthermore, Jewish, extra-Christian sources are more and more coming into their own in our understanding of Jesus' time and thereby of Jesus himself.[5]

One assumption of this inquiry is that the message, mission, and ultimate fate of Jesus are rather more difficult to handle, and hence more controversial, than is his identity as at least *partly* represented or disclosed in the Synoptic titles. This explains why I deal with these titles first and in fairly brief and unoriginal fashion. I include this chapter under introductory materials because of its relatively less argumentative or debatable quality. Subsequent chapters will involve us in much greater historical, theological, and moral controversy.

Within the oldest recoverable layers of apostolic confession several titles are associated with Jesus, and some help is provided therein upon the perplexing question of his own self-understanding.[6] These sources help to throw light upon Jesus' personhood as such.

PROPHET

Jesus is identified as a prophet, and he appears to accept that appellation.[7]

When subjected to serious questioning in his local synagogue, Jesus responds, "A prophet is not without honor, except in his own country, and among his own kin, and in his own house" (Mark 6:4; cf. Luke 4:24; John 4:44).[8] Later on he declares: "It cannot be that a prophet should perish away from Jerusalem" (Luke 13:33). Of much greater import, although more obliquely so, as Michael L. Cook writes, "Jesus acted as one having authority (*exousia*) which is certainly a prophetic trait." In the biblical tradition, the justification of a prophet's authority is possession by the Spirit of God. When Jesus' family and others worry that he is beside himself or has perhaps been afflicted by demons, he answers by celebrating the presence of the Holy Spirit and the will of God (Mark 3:21-35). For Jesus is identified not only as a prophet but as an eschatological prophet, one who proclaims God's *telos* (ultimate purpose) and *finis* (ultimate end) and who brings to bear "the definitive salvific activity of God for his people. . . . Jesus did not simply proclaim the Kingdom of God and call for a response of faith but he laid his own life on the line for the truth of his message. It is this total commitment to one's message that gives prophetic utterance its true authority. It is on this level that we can profitably speak in historical terms of Jesus' own awareness of his mission."[9]

Two additional factors present themselves. First, for Jesus and his followers, "prophet" is evidently synonymous with "miracle-worker." Fittingly, therefore, Jesus performs many healings of various illnesses, especially demon possession. He is a thaumaturge. E. P. Sanders concludes that Jesus "gained fame" from his miracles.[10] Second, with other prophets Jesus manifests special concerns for the outcast, the suffering, the lowly,[11] concerns that are emphasized in today's theology of liberation.[12] In his description of Jesus before the time of the "theologization" of Christianity, Albert Nolan writes, "The people to whom Jesus turned his attention are referred to in the Gospels by a variety of terms: the poor, the blind, the lame, the crippled, the lepers, the hungry, the miserable (those who weep), sinners, prostitutes, tax collectors, demoniacs (those possessed by unclean spirits), the persecuted, the downtrodden, the captives, all who labour and are overburdened, the rabble who know nothing of the law, the crowds, the little ones, the least, the last and the babes or the lost sheep of the house of Israel." It is to these that Jesus proclaims the good news of the kingdom of God.[13]

LORD

Jesus is often named as *lord* (*kyrios*).

When Christians of today attest that "Jesus is Lord," they are probably testifying to him as the sine qua non of the Christian faith, the one who is their way, their truth, their life (John 14:6), the one through whom they believe themselves to be reconciled to the God of Israel (2 Cor. 5:18-20). In contrast to the appellation *prophet,* however, the Synoptic Gospels present Jesus as refusing to make lordly claims. Furthermore, in Jewish Aramaic (Jesus' own language), *(the) lord* has a variety of meanings (as it does in English today). It may refer to God himself. It may also be applied to social or political dignitaries, to respected teachers, or to people (including miracle workers) known for their spiritual power. Mark and Matthew characteristically link Jesus as *lord* to his ability to perform miracles. For Luke, Jesus' lordship becomes associated with his role as teacher and religious leader. *Lord* is the typical way the disciples either allude to Jesus or address him directly. In general, the title *lord* links Jesus fundamentally "to his dual role of charismatic[14] Hasid [holy person] and teacher [sage], and if the stress is greater in the earlier strata of the tradition," this accords with "the fact that his impact as a holy man preceded that of teacher and founder of a religious community" within Judaism and Jewish life.[15]

MESSIAH

There is the title *Messiah* (*Mashiach*).

Geza Vermes makes clear the centrality of this description:

> Whatever significance is ultimately ascribed to the title "the Christ," "the Anointed," one fact is at least certain: the identification of Jesus, not just with *a* Messiah, but with *the* awaited Messiah of Judaism, belonged to the heart and kernel of the earliest phase of Christian belief. So central and vital was this designation in the life of the primitive Church that within a generation of the crucifixion a Greek neologism, "Christian," could be coined in the Judeo-Hellenistic community of Antioch in Syria. . . . Indeed, the original style, "Jesus the Christ," or "the Christ Jesus," became so generally employed and so much part of everyday language that in the Gentile circles evangelized by Paul it contracted into the double-barrelled "Jesus Christ" and even the shortened "Christ." From indicating a function, it was thus transformed into a personal name.[16]

What was this messianic function? By the time of Jesus, the social conviction of the Messiah's role, the understanding of what he was to do, had become more or less crystallized and remained stable, at least for a time: A son of David (i.e., a king of Davidic lineage) was anticipated and prayed for.[17] The Messiah was to be a royal, holy figure who would be associated with victory over gentile oppressors, with saving and restoring Israel, and with establishing the reign of God's righteousness and justice. Ancient Jewish prayers and biblical interpretation together demonstrate that, if during the intertestamental period "a man claimed, or was proclaimed, to be 'the Messiah,' his listeners would as a matter of course have expected to find before them a person endowed with the combined talents of soldierly prowess, righteousness, and holiness."[18]

Even though the phrase *Jesus Christ* is rare in the Synoptics, the centering of messianic hope upon Jesus is made plain. Probably the most salient passage is the report of an episode on the road to Caesarea Philippi when Jesus asks his disciples, "Who do you say that I am?" Peter confesses, "You are the Christ" (Mark 8:27-29; Matt. 16:13-16; Luke 9:18-20). Again, the centering of messianic hope upon Jesus is evident in the request of James and John to Jesus, "Grant us to sit, one at your right hand, and one at your left, in your glory" (Mark 10:35-37).[19]

This Synoptic stress upon the Messiahship of Jesus is counterbalanced by seeming doubt on the part of Jesus himself respecting the application to him of the title *Messiah*—a doubt that is as striking as, or more striking than, his refusal to make lordly claims for himself. Thus, we have his response to Peter's confession: His disciples were "to tell no one about him" (Mark 8:30). And he informs James and John that they do not know what they are asking (Mark 10:38; Matt. 20:22). It is pointed out that the single authentic literary context "in which Jesus is treated as a self-proclaimed King Messiah" is the account of his appearance before Pontius Pilate along with the sequel to that appearance—although the most that Jesus answers, in the face of Pilate's question of whether he is "King of the Jews," is "You have said so" (Mark 15:2; Matt. 27:11; Luke 23:3). "All in all, great doubt is expressed that Jesus ever maintained, directly or spontaneously, that he was a promised Messiah."[20]

This confronts us with the prodigious question of how on earth Jesus gets to be put to death as "King of the Jews." We must return to this formidable problem.[21]

In *For Righteousness' Sake* I pay some attention to the phrase *Son of Man,* following Vermes's long discourse on the subject.[22] I have decided to omit that item here on the grounds of Donald J. Goergen's exhaustive analysis of *Son of Man* (= "the human one," the "son of humanity")[23] and of Vermes's careful argument that *Son of Man* is not, in fact, a title. Yet some debate remains concerning that conclusion. The term is used in clearly Jewish, pre–c.e. 70 documents.[24]

SON OF GOD

We come to the most signal description, *Son of God.*[25]

The Apostolic Writings bestow this title upon Jesus in a number of places (e.g., Matt. 11:27; 27:54; John 3:16; Gal. 4:6; Heb. 1:2; 1 John 4:9-10, 15; 2 John 1:3). But objectively speaking, the title is somewhat reminiscent of *lord* in that it can represent a variety of designations. Within Palestinian-Jewish thinking, "son of God could refer, in an ascending order, to any of the children of Israel; or to a good Jew; or to a charismatic holy Jew; or to the king of Israel; or in particular to the royal Messiah; and finally, in a different sense, to an angelic or heavenly being. In other words 'son of God' was always understood metaphorically in Jewish circles. In Jewish sources, its use never implies participation by the person so named in the divine nature."[26]

As is the case with *prophet* and perhaps with *lord,* the early application to Jesus of the title *Son of God* appears to be linked to two factors: his life as a charismatic miracle worker and exorcist, and his consciousness (as a *hasid*) of being in a special relationship with God, his heavenly Father.[27] To pursue Jesus' identity, however, within the metaphorical frame of reference of family relationships (son/Father) makes, I think, for a fundamental difficulty. For this metaphor can take us in diametrically opposite directions. If Richard Gordon is Stacy's father, we say that Stacy must be "a Gordon." By the same token, if God is Jesus' Father, must not Jesus be God? The line of reasoning opposite to this is expressed in the following passage:

Although our religious conditioning (including especially the lingering power of

Hellenism, even in the late twentieth century) makes almost irresistible the assumption that when the evangelists refer to Jesus as *son of God* they must be making him in a real way equal to God—as if he possessed or were claiming *divine* sonship (divinity or Godness)—the actual historical morphology of the earliest New Testament record demands quite an opposite position. This opposite view is required by everything we know of Jesus' own conviction and behavior, his "special filial consciousness." Precisely because, in an especially intimate way, he accepts and worships God as his very own Father . . . his awareness of sonship is thereby intensified. This fact rules out the view that by calling God "his own Father," Jesus makes himself "equal with God" (John 1:18). On the contrary, the fatherhood of God means that Jesus is *un*equal to the Father, since he is not the father. . . . Jesus can thus ask, *sans façon,* "Why do you call me good? No one is good but God alone" (Luke 18:19). All this is in sharp contradistinction to the Hellenistic *son of God*/"divine man" hypothesis that was waiting to be superimposed upon Palestinian–Jewish Gospel belief and terminology.[28]

In *Jesus the Jew* Vermes concludes that there is "no reason to contest the possibility, and even the great probability, that already during his life Jesus was spoken of and addressed by admiring believers as *son of God.*" Could Jesus also have considered *himself* Son of God? "The answer must be that he could"— even were we to take the extreme position that the surviving *son* sayings of the Gospels may not be genuine.[29] In later years, of course, theological revisionism will assert itself, as in John 1:14: "the Word became flesh and dwelt among us, full of grace and truth; we have beheld his glory, glory as of the only Son from the Father." Yet this very affirmation makes more than a little astonishing the Fourth Gospel's subsequent refutation in behalf of Jesus of the charge that he has made himself equal to God: Jesus is not only "recorded as having endorsed the standard Jewish confession of monotheism (Mark 12:29) and accepted the prohibition which this implied of any moral comparison between himself and God (Mark 10:18), [but] in the Fourth Gospel he is made to deny vigorously the accusation that he set himself up as a being equal to and independent of God." The reference is to the alleged confrontation recorded in John 10:31-38, wherein, as A. E. Harvey points out, the burden of Jesus' reply is that "far from being a second or rival god, he is totally dependent on and united with the Father."[30] Thus are we returned to the living ambiguity that is present within christological attempts to utilize metaphors taken from the human family.

Marcus J. Borg sums up the titular question of Jesus as Son of God:

> If "Son of God" is used in the special Christian sense which emerges in the rest of the New Testament (by the time of Paul and John, preexistent with God from before creation; by the time of Matthew and Luke, conceived by the Spirit and born of a virgin), then almost certainly Jesus did not think of himself as *the* Son of God. But if "son of God" is given the meaning that it carried within Judaism at the time of Jesus, then it is possible he did. There, "son of God" was used in three different contexts to refer to three different entities, though with a common nuance of

meaning. In the Hebrew Bible, it referred to Israel as a whole or to the king of Israel. Contemporary with Jesus, the image of God as father and a particular person as God's son was used . . . in stories about Jewish charismatic holy men. All three uses have one element in common. All designate a relationship of special intimacy with God—Israel as the chosen people, the king as the adopted son, the charismatic as one who knows and is known by God.[31]

This rounds out our brief and preliminary review upon the identity of Jesus as grounded in titles assigned to him in the oldest recoverable layers of the Gospel tradition.

PART

2
Five
Historical
Images

3

The Judaism of
Jesus, Countercultural
Spiritualizer

We come now to matters rather more controversial than those ventured and reviewed thus far. Varying levels of disputation will be present through the remainder of the book, along with much objective exposition.

Part Two is made up of five major historical images of Jesus (chaps. 3–7). This chapter centers in the scholarly contribution and claims of Marcus J. Borg together with some appraisal of his point of view. The chapter following this one will concentrate upon certain aspects of E. P. Sanders's understanding of Jesus and his life. In chapter 5 I will present something of my own position—noticeably different from that of Borg and that of Sanders yet in some continuity with them. Chapter 6 will develop interpretations of Jesus put forward within the theology of liberation, and chapter 7 will represent feminist christological positions. Some readers will perhaps prefer exemplifications different from the ones I use.

A NEW VISION OF JESUS

In two different studies Professor Borg reckons with many of the most significant and persisting questions respecting the Jesus of history: *Conflict, Holiness and Politics in the Teachings of Jesus* (1984) and *Jesus, A New Vision* (1987). The emphasis in my analysis is upon the development of the later volume's argument.[1]

For Borg, "Christianity has very little to do with believing forty-nine impossible things before breakfast—as the late Bishop John Robinson puckishly described the impression that people commonly have of what it means to be a Christian; but it has everything to do with taking seriously what Jesus took seriously." In this declaration the primacy of the historical Jesus for Christian faith is set forth as unqualified. At the same time, "the 'new vision' of Jesus—an image of what can be known about him, as well as his own vision of life—radically calls into question our most common way of being and invites us to see differently." For the scholarly case that Borg wishes to build entails "a particular image of the historical Jesus that is considerably at variance with the dominant scholarly image." Moreover, for Borg the trouble with the scholarly image is paralleled in "the popular image" of Jesus as a divine or semidivine figure who saw himself as a godly savior, "whose purpose it was to die for the sins of the world, and whose life and death open up the possibility of eternal life." The answers that the popular image provides to the salient questions of Jesus' identity, purpose, and message are very clear: Jesus, as the divinely begotten Son of God, "was sent into the world for the purpose of dying on the cross as a means of reconciliation between God and humankind, and his message consisted primarily of inviting his hearers to believe that what he said about himself and his role in salvation was true."

The difficulty with this popular image is a fateful one: It "is not *historically* true."[2]

Implied in Borg's approach is a persuasion that the Christian church simply must not fall into double standards respecting truth/falsity. For what is false historically cannot be true theologically or morally. (To express this matter in Lockean language: Legitimate theological affirmation can either be reasonable or go beyond reason. In the second case, theological affirmation may become independent of reason. But such affirmation can never be permitted to contradict reason.)

Borg's historical Christology may be treated under his own headings of Jesus and the Spirit, and Jesus and culture.

JESUS AND THE SPIRIT

Jesus had "an intensely vivid relationship to the world of Spirit," a reality affirmed and known in just about every society prior to modern times, but very often lost in the modern world. This "other reality" is spoken of variously as the sacred, the holy, or simply God. Jesus' relation to that dimension, a dimension beyond the visible world of ordinary, material experience, "was the source of his power and teaching, his freedom, courage, and compassion, and of his urgent mission to the culture of his day."[3]

The key to who and what Jesus was is his life as "a Spirit-filled person in the charismatic stream of Judaism" that extends back to Moses and the other prophets. Charismatics are "people who know the world of Spirit firsthand," and who are thereby able to bridge the two worlds. Accordingly, "to try to understand the Jewish tradition and Jesus while simultaneously dismissing the notion of another world [that continually impinges ontologically upon our world] or immediately reducing it to a merely psychological realm is to fail to see the phenomena, to fail to take seriously what these charismatic mediators experienced and reported."[4]

The visions Jesus had—e.g., "I saw Satan fall like lightning from heaven" (Luke 10:18)—are paralleled in the rest of the Apostolic Writings, which suggests that the early church experienced reality in the same Spirit-filled way as Jesus. The "strange episode" of the Transfiguration thus signifies not alone Jesus' connection with the world of Spirit but also (some of) his disciples' place in that experience: " . . . Jesus took with him Peter and James and John, and led them up a high mountain apart by themselves; and he was transfigured before them, and his garments became glistening, intensely white. . . . And there appeared to them Elijah with Moses; and they were talking to Jesus" (Mark 9:2-4; cf. Matt. 17:1-3; Luke 9:28-32). In sum, "from [Jesus'] baptism onward, through his ordeal in the wilderness, and continuing throughout his ministry, his life and mission were marked by an intense experiential relationship to the Spirit."[5]

This internal experience of the Spirit was matched in Jesus' public life through the impressions he made on other people, his claims to authority, and the style of his speech. Thus does the Gospel of Mark convey "the cloud of the *numinous*" that surrounded Jesus: "And they were on the road, going up to Jerusalem, and Jesus was walking ahead of them; and they were amazed, and those who followed were filled with awe" (Mark 10:32). Jesus was quite aware of possessing this power of the Spirit; it was what made possible his claims to authority. When queried by some religious leaders about his authority, he responded, "I will ask you a question; answer me, and I will tell you by what authority I do these things. Was the baptism of John from heaven or from men?" (Mark 11:29-30). Implicitly, Jesus was here claiming the same authority as John the Baptist, an authority "grounded neither in institution nor tradition but in the Spirit." The Gospel of Mark has people exclaim, "With *authority* he commands even the unclean spirits, and they obey him" (1:27). This means that it is from "the mouth of the *Gevurah* (Spirit)" that Jesus casts out demons. Furthermore, Jesus' linguistic practice, "You have heard that it was said . . . but I say to you" (as recorded in Matthew 5), embodied a contrast with tradition in behalf of Spirit. Again, the fact that Jesus should call disciples exemplified and implemented his sense of charismatic authority. As Peter exclaimed, "we have *left everything* to follow you" (Mark 10:28). All in all, Jesus' relationship to Spirit constituted the source and the energy of his mission, and it provides the key for understanding "the central dimensions of his ministry: as healer, sage, revitalization movement founder, and prophet."[6]

It is the category of Spirit-power that enables us to grasp the "mighty deeds" of Jesus. Indeed, such phenomena as possession and exorcism *presuppose* a Spirit-world that interacts with the visible world. The mighty deeds "were understood by the gospel writers and Jesus himself as *powers* from *the Power*." This is how Borg concludes his analysis of Jesus' miracles:

> In their historical context, the miracles of Jesus do not "prove" that he was divine. [For in] the tradition in which he stood . . . the healings and exorcisms reported of him were not unique. Yet though the historical study of the miracles results in the loss of their uniqueness, it produces a gain in their credibility. Contrary to the modern notion that such events are impossible, we must grant that the historical evidence that Jesus stood in the stream of Jewish charismatic healers is very strong.
>
> . . . Not only did he come out of such a stream, but others followed in his wake. According to the gospels, he commissioned his twelve disciples to be charismatic healers [Mark 6:7-13; Matt. 10:5-8; Luke 10:8-9]. His two most important first-century followers, Peter and Paul, were also charismatic holy men. . . . Though foreign to our experience and way of thinking in the modern world, the world of spirits and God was, for Jesus and his predecessors and followers in the Jewish-Christian tradition, very real—not simply as an element of belief, but of experience.[7]

JESUS AND CULTURE

Jesus versus the politics of holiness.   The historic Christian tendency (or temptation) to deny any religious significance to culture or society would have made no sense to Jesus. In this respect, he was a good Jew, a typical Jew. He was passionately engaged with the culture of his day; he "sought the transformation of his social world." He was spiritual in that, as we have seen, the central reality of his life was his relation to the Spirit. And he was political in the identical way that the mainstream of his Jewish tradition was political: "concerned about creating a community within history whose corporate life reflected faithfulness to God."[8] Accordingly, Jesus "radically criticized" his human world, warning it of the consequences of its present ways and seeking "its transformation in accord with an alternative vision." His deep involvement in sociopolitical life distinguished him, for the most part, from many other Jewish charismatics. For Jesus "became a national figure who undertook a mission to his own people in the midst of a cultural crisis, climaxing in a final journey to Jerusalem, the very center of their cultural life."[9]

For all his denials, Borg's accounting is strongly reminiscent of much in our "scholarly" tradition. Thus, according to him the Jewish social world had become "increasingly structured around the polarities of *holiness as separa-*

tion: clean and unclean, purity and defilement, sacred and profane, Jew and Gentile, righteous and sinner." For Borg, these forms of holiness—understood as "separation from everything impure"—became "the paradigm by which the Torah was interpreted. The portions of the law [*sic*][10] which emphasized the separateness of the Jewish people from other peoples, and which stressed separation from everything impure within Israel, became dominant. Holiness became the *Zeitgeist,* the 'spirit of the age,' shaping the development of the Jewish social world in the centuries leading up to the time of Jesus, providing the particular content of the Jewish ethos or way of life. Increasingly, the ethos of holiness became the politics of holiness." Within the quest for holiness, undergirded as it was by the twin institutions of Torah and Temple, we uncover "the source of Israel's resistance to Rome and a context for understanding the politics of Jesus."[11]

In keeping with the foregoing claim, and as we might now expect from the thrust of his position, Borg offers the almost inevitable, even stereotypical proposition: The Pharisees "were the most visible manifestation of the politics of holiness."[12] Having fabricated his idea of the Jewish politics of holiness—for other earlier and comparable scholars the parallel terms were "Jewish legalism" or "Pharisaism" or even *"Spät judentum"*[13]—Borg enables himself to install Jesus as the sworn enemy of that tradition. Jesus becomes countercultural spiritualizer. We shall return to the question of Jesus and the Pharisees.

According to Borg, all renewal movements of Jesus' day (excepting, of course, Jesus' own) tried to preserve the Jewish world "by shaping it increasingly in accord with the politics of holiness." Moreover, this politics was practiced by many people who were not actually part of any particular movement. It was, after all, conventional Torah wisdom that "enshrined the ethos of holiness. . . . [All] of them—the renewal movements as well as the people not identified with any movement—were committed to the politics of holiness, for that was . . . the cultural dynamic shaping the society as a whole."[14]

Jesus versus conventional wisdom.   We are advised that the prophet Jesus called his people to something other than the politics of holiness. He "founded a renewal movement whose purpose was to embody what Israel was meant to be." The teaching of Jesus "involved a radical criticism of the conventional wisdom that lay at the core of the first-century Jewish social world." What distinguished Jesus from "most of his contemporaries" and from "the dominant consciousness of his day"—it is as though Professor Borg has somehow managed to travel back to the first century and to conduct a definitive public opinion poll—was Jesus' "vivid sense that reality was ultimately gracious and compassionate." In accordance with this conviction, the graciousness of God "emerges everywhere in his teaching."[15] (Query: Why is the phenomenon of Jesus not utilized by Borg to suggest Jesus' typicality, or at least to suggest the wider presence in society of persons of Jesus' religious views?)

The persuasion of God's graciousness lay behind a striking feature of Jesus' ministry: his meals with "sinners" and "outcasts." ("Sinners" were those who failed to follow "the ways of the fathers as spelled out by the Torah wisdom of the sages." But the worst of the nonobservant were "outcasts," the "notori-ously 'wicked' [murderers, extortioners, prostitutes, and the like], as well as members of certain occupational groups, membership in which made one as a 'non-Jew.' ") Jesus engaged in the extraordinary practice of sharing meals with these rejected people. Many of his parables defended this practice. In the Pal-estine of the day, to share a meal with anyone was to signify social and moral acceptance of that person. Since Jesus "spoke from the mouth of the Spirit," his own acceptance of sinners and outcasts would be perceived as a claim that God accepted them, too. "Implicit in the action is an understanding of God as gracious and compassionate, embracing even the outcasts," in direct contrast to "conventional wisdom." Jesus' practice "radically threatened the social world of his opponents, and was thus a cultural as well as religious challenge. For a charismatic person to say, with both his teaching and behavior, that the outcasts were accepted by God was to challenge and threaten the central or-dering principle of the Jewish social world: the division between purity and impurity, holy and not-holy, righteous and wicked. The table fellowship of Jesus called into question the politics of holiness as the cultural dynamic of the society." Again, for Jesus—we are told—conventional wisdom, "with its focus on the securities and identities offered by culture, even though sanctioned by Scripture and hallowed by practice," was "the chief rival to centering in God." Thus, in the parable of the Pharisee and the tax collector (Luke 18:9-14), the Pharisee's fault was neither hypocrisy nor immodesty but resting his security in those very genuine religious accomplishments that had become the center of his life. By contrast, the outcast tax collector rested his security in God alone, making no claim to righteousness: "God, be merciful to me a sinner."[16]

It appears hard to grasp Marcus Borg's argumentation here apart from the evident influence upon him of the later issue of "faith and works." Leonard Swidler's conclusion stands in basic contrast: Various false dichotomies—law and grace, justice and love, faith and works—"run absolutely counter to the teaching and life of Rabbi Yeshua."[17]

We are advised by Borg that the cure for the moral and spiritual problems created by conventional wisdom with its focus on externals is "the narrow way of transformation." People need a "new heart." The heart "as the fundamental determinant of both being and behavior" was central in Jesus' thinking and ac-tion. A tension between a correct adherence to tradition and the importance of the inner self was "a central theme" of Jesus' message. "About some of the practitioners of tradition in his day, Jesus said, 'This people honors God with their lips, but their *heart* is far from God' [Mark 7:6, quoted from Isaiah]. That is, they said (and to a large extent did) the right things, but the inner self remained far away. . . . Jesus consistently radicalized the Torah by applying it to the inner self rather than simply to behavior." The stress upon a new heart was not peculiar to Jesus, however:

> To speak of radically centering in God is central to the tradition in which Jesus stood. It is the "radical monotheism" of the Old Testament, crystalized in the *Shema* which was recited twice daily by faithful Jews in the time of Jesus: "Hear, O Israel: The Lord our God is one Lord; and you shall love the Lord your God with all your heart, and with all your soul, and with all your might" [Deut. 6:4-5]. Indeed, Jesus himself stated that the *Shema* was the "great commandment."[18] To say that "centering in God" was the essence of the tradition was thus commonplace; but deliberately to contrast "centering in God" to the centers legitimated by conventional wisdom, indeed to conventional wisdom itself, was radical. Yet this is precisely what Jesus did. The central concerns of the conventional wisdom of his day—family, wealth, honor, and religion—were all seen as rival centers. His criticism of them was to call to center in Spirit, and not culture.[19]

The way that the inner transformation to a new heart takes place is not simply by an act of will, or by deciding to "believe" something, or by resolving to be "good." Instead, it happens via the "way of death." This means, on the one hand, "a dying of the self as the center of its own concern," and, on the other hand, "a dying to the world as the center of security and identity." The second of these transformations is often misinterpreted. It is not that form of world denial grounded in a dualism of matter as evil and spirit as good. Nor is it a total rejection of tradition. Instead, it must be kept "within the framework of [Jesus'] perception of reality as gracious and compassionate. His challenge must not be seen as a new *requirement*; when it is, his teaching becomes another form of conventional wisdom, sometimes a very severe one. Rather, his challenge is an *invitation* to see things as they really are—namely, at the heart of everything is a reality that is in love with us."[20]

Professor Borg's reasoning here carries forward the affirmation of First John: "We love, because he [God] first loved us" (4:19). The reasoning is further reminiscent of H. Richard Niebuhr's "ethic of response": The Christian life is, or at least ought to be, essentially a response of gratitude to the prior love of God for us. All in all, Jesus "taught an alternative way of being and an alternative consciousness shaped by the relationship to Spirit. . . . He was thus not only a subversive sage but a transformative sage."[21]

Jesus as founder of a renewal movement. "Just as [Jesus] challenged the conventional wisdom at the heart of his social world, so he also challenged the politics of holiness as the dynamic shaping his people's corporate life." He did not, of course, found a new religion; instead he created a charismatic "sectarian revitalization movement within Israel."[22] In scholarly circles his endeavor has become known as the "Jesus movement," with its purpose of transforming the Jewish social world.[23] For "one of the most certain facts of Jesus' ministry" was its restriction to Israel, as epitomized in Matthew: "Go nowhere among the Gentiles, and enter no town of the Samaritans, but rather to the lost sheep of the house of Israel" (10:5-6).[24]

The itinerant Jesus movement was exceptional in including in its numbers both outcasts and women. The life of this joyous group "embodied a different vision of what Israel was to be, a different ethos for the people of God." Jesus expressed that ethos as an *imitatio dei,* but whereas the ethos of first-century Judaism centered primarily in imitating the *holiness* of God—so Borg insists—Jesus' ethos focused primarily upon the *compassion* of God. Borg's argumentation concerning the uniqueness of this focus loses some of its force in light of the traditional and living prophetic stress upon the pathos of God, including tenderness and compassion, as Borg himself has to grant. The outcome is a sort of relativist compromise: "First-century Judaism could also speak of the compassion of God, and Jesus never denied that God was holy. The issue was not whether God was compassionate or holy, but concerned which of these was to be the central paradigm for imaging God and for portraying the life of the faithful community." Be this as it may, "the *pathos* of God *as compassion* was to be the ethos of the Jesus movement and, ideally, of Israel."[25]

The ethos of compassion led to a politics of compassion.[26] "The 'shape' of the alternative community or 'counterculture' was visible in the constituency of its membership which stood in sharp contrast to the relatively rigid social boundaries of the Jewish social world: boundaries between righteous and outcast, men and women, rich and poor, Jew and Gentile.[27] These boundaries, established by the politics of holiness and embodied in the culture as a whole and in varying forms in other renewal movements, were negated by the Jesus movement. The negation pointed to a much more inclusive understanding of the community of Israel."[28] (Query: Why are we to believe that the inclusiveness of a community must do something to make it superior to another ethos? In this connection, Jesus' restriction of his own movement to Israel was hardly an inclusivist act.)

A further quality of the Jesus movement—so we are told—is that it was the "peace party." "In the same context where Jesus spoke of the *imitatio dei* as compassion, he also spoke of loving one's enemies: 'You have heard that it was said, "Love your neighbor," but I say to you, Love your enemies' [Matt. 5:43-44; Luke 6:27]. The quoted words, 'Love your neighbor,' come from the holiness code [Leviticus 17–26] and were understood within contemporary Judaism to mean, 'Love your fellow member of the covenant,' that is, your fellow Israelite or compatriot. In this context, the opposite of neighbor is clearly 'non-Israelite,' and so loving one's enemy must mean, 'Love the non-Israelite enemy,' including the Gentile occupiers."[29] Furthermore, in "the same immediate context as the saying about loving one's enemies, Jesus said, 'If anyone strikes you, turn the other cheek' and added 'If any one forces you to go one mile, go with him two miles' [Matt. 5:39, 41], which referred to the right of a Roman soldier to require a civilian to carry his gear for one mile. ... Elsewhere he said, 'Blessed are the peacemakers, for they shall be called children of God,' and 'All who live by the sword will perish by the sword' [Matt. 5:9; 26:52]." It is Borg's conviction that the Jesus movement completely rejected violent resistance to Rome[30]—a viewpoint that is contradicted by such other scholars as S. G. F. Brandon, John T. Townsend, and Hyam Maccoby.

The source of Jesus' radical relativizing of cultural and class distinctions and separations lay—so Borg maintains—in the Nazarene's charismatic experience of the divine grace and compassion as extending to all children of God. "The intense experience of the Spirit generated a new way of seeing and being that stood in sharp contrast to the boundaries and rivalries created by culture." The overall category utilized by our author in his attempt to show that the Jesus movement "shattered the norms of the Jewish social world" is *spiritualization,* "the claim that what truly matters is not the external practice or reality, but the internal or spiritual reality to which the external points." Borg's psychocentrism and individualism reach a climax in these passages. "True purity was internal, not dependent upon the ability to measure up to standards of purity as defined by conventional wisdom. ... What mattered was an internal transformation, 'purity of heart,' which was possible even for those whom the social world placed beyond the pale. Similarly, the notion of righteousness was internalized."[31]

For Borg, Jesus went so far as to spiritualize the very idea of Israel. Membership in God's people meant much more than mere physical or laic descent. Yet "Jesus remained deeply Jewish, even as he radicalized Judaism. He neither advocated the social world of the Gentiles, nor dissolved Judaism in the name of a more universal vision. His movement was concerned with what it meant to be Israel." In sum, Jesus' "politics of compassion addressed the two central issues generated by the crisis in the Jewish social world: the growing internal division within Jewish society, and the deepening of the conflict with Rome."[32] The die was cast between a politics of holiness and a politics of compassion.

The prophet and a world in crisis.   Jesus stood squarely in the tradition of the great prophets of Israel. With them, his outlook was dominated by urgency and crisis. And with them, he indicted his people for having violated their covenant with God, warned of future destruction unless they mended their ways, and summoned them to change lest the judgment of God fall upon them. At this point, Borg somewhat tempers the internalizing or subjectivist interpretation noted above: For Jesus as prophet "the issue was not individual sinfulness, but allegiance to a cultural dynamic that was leading to historical catastrophe. . . . The Israel of [Jesus'] generation, living by the ethos of holiness, ʾwas no longer what it was meant to be—the vineyard of God yielding fruit, the faithful servant of God, the light to the nations."[33]

Borg zeros in on "the Pharisees"—here and there in *Jesus* but at much greater length and throughout his earlier work *Conflict, Holiness and Politics in the Teachings of Jesus,* wherein his attack upon this grouping, ostensibly on behalf of Jesus, is much more severe and much more intense. Borg claims that most of Jesus' conflicts were with the Pharisees for their equating of holiness with separation. Instead, genuine holiness means justice, mercy, compassion, and faithfulness (cf. the parable of the good Samaritan [Luke 10:29-37]).[34] "From Jesus' point of view, the Pharisees, far from being a social religious grouping bringing Israel to holiness, were the very opposite; he described their influence on those around them as pernicious, as a defiling rather than hallow- ing contagion, as one about which Israel needed to be warned in the strongest terms."[35] Yet even in his later book, *Jesus, A New Vision,* Borg is not exactly on good terms with "the Pharisees." The trouble with them was not hypocrisy or insincerity but rather *"what they were sincere about:* the ethos and politics of holiness," which they intended that *all* Israel must practice. Jesus is reputed by Borg to have attacked them for their concerns with purity and tithing. Purity is not a matter of externals but is of the heart (Mark 7:1-23; Luke 11:38-41; Matt. 23:25-26). And as for tithing: "Woe to you Pharisees! for you tithe mint and rue and every herb, and neglect justice and the love of God; these you ought to have done without neglecting the others" (Luke 11:42).[36]

Along with such earlier prophets as Jeremiah and Ezekiel, Jesus warned that unless Israel changed its direction, military destruction would be visited upon Jerusalem and the temple (Luke 13:34-35; Matt. 23:37-39; Luke 21:20, 23-24; 19:42-44; Mark 13:1-2). Together with Jeremiah, Jesus would not have his hearers join in Jerusalem's defense. Instead, the people were to flee to the mountains (Luke 21:21; Mark 13:14). (Query: If the people Jesus was lambast- ing were in fact guilty of sin, ought he not have told them to remain and accept their just punishment?) All need not be lost, however. There was still time to change; indeed, that possibility was presupposed in Jesus' message. He de- manded repentance, not only of individuals but at the collective level: "Israel itself was being called to change in the face of a future that was still contingent. . . . Two paths lay before the people to whom Jesus spoke, the broad way of conventional wisdom and its loyalties, and the narrow way of transformation to an alternative way of being. The broad way led to destruction, the narrow way to life [cf. Matt. 7:13-14]."[37] (Query: How is it ever possible to predict or calculate that invading armies will behave in one way if their [potential] victims are "good" and another way if the victims are "evil"? The idea is, on the face of it, absurd.)

The end and the End.[38]   This haunting passage in Luke is attributed to Jesus: "I must go on my way today and tomorrow and the day following; for it cannot be that a prophet should perish away from Jerusalem. O Jerusalem, Jerusalem, killing the prophets and stoning those who are sent to you! How often would I have gathered your children together as a hen gathers her brood under her wings, and you would not!'" (13:33-34).

In a climactic chapter of *Jesus,* Marcus Borg hypothesizes that even though the outcome of Jesus' journey to Jerusalem was to be his death, such was not the purpose of that journey. Instead, "as the climax of his prophetic mission and call to renewal, [Jesus] went there to make a final appeal to his people at the center of their national and religious life," and at a time of the year when the city would be filled with pilgrims.[39]

As understood by Borg, Jesus' entry into Jerusalem upon a donkey's colt, allegedly cheered by followers and sympathizers, was a calculated symbolic act on the Nazarene's part to indicate that the kingdom he represented was a kingdom of peace rather than of war. Among other scholars this reading is not accepted. For example, E. P. Sanders more or less dismisses the "triumphal entry" (if it took place at all) as a small occurrence that went unnoticed.[40]

Professor Borg's interpretation of "the prophetic act in the Temple," viz., the expulsion of "the moneychangers and sellers of sacrificial birds," puts us on equally or even more controversial ground. It also entangles us in what is perhaps the most practically decisive question of all historical Christology: whether Jesus' own viewpoint was eschatological (e.g., E. P. Sanders) or noneschatological (e.g., Marcus J. Borg).[41] It is particularly significant that Sanders should place the so-called cleansing of the temple at the very beginning, procedurally speaking, of his own study *Jesus and Judaism,* regarding that event as "the surest starting point" for such an investigation.[42] (This is my adopted rationale for paying extra attention at this juncture to Jesus' *Aktion* in the temple. The allusion also serves to anticipate chap. 4.)

The older understanding of the temple event maintains that Jesus was indeed *cleansing* the temple, in a fully religious or spiritual sense, due to its profanation or contamination through the conduct of trade there. This view is reaffirmed in Borg's own apprehension of Jesus' behavior—as we would now fully anticipate: The moneychangers and sellers of birds "were there in service of the ethos of holiness." For Borg, Jesus' act was that of a prophet but an act that was "limited in area, intent, and duration, done for the sake of the message it conveyed. As often with prophetic acts, the action was accompanied by a pronouncement which interpreted its meaning: 'Is it not written, "My house shall be called a house of prayer for all nations"? But you have made it a den of robbers [Mark 11:17; cf. Matt. 21:13; Luke 19:46; John 2:13-16].' "[43]

E. P. Sanders rejects the understanding of the "cleansing" of the temple that is found in many Christian scholars; now we can include Marcus Borg among these. The view that Jesus was opposing externals on behalf of authentic religious interiority has, of course, been pervasive. Sanders remarks that this outlook owes more to the nineteenth-century notion that what is external is bad than it does to any first-century Jewish view. (At this point, Borg's argumentation comes straight out of the nineteenth century.) Sanders writes, more positively,

> In the view of Jesus and his contemporaries, the requirement to sacrifice must always have involved the supply of sacrificial animals, their inspection, and the changing of money. Thus one may wonder what scholars have in mind who talk about Jesus' desire to stop this "particular use" of the temple. Just what would be left of the service if the supposedly corrupting externalism of sacrifices, and the trade necessary to them, were purged? Here as often we see a failure to think concretely and a preference for vague religious abstractions. . . . Everyone agreed that sacrifices were integral to the function of the temple. . . . The notion that the temple should serve some function other than sacrifice would seem to be extremely remote from the thinking of a first-century Jew.
>
> But could the sacrifices continue without the changing of money and the selling of birds? It is hard to see how. . . . The buyers and sellers were . . . required for the maintenance of the temple service, and they provided a convenient service for pilgrims. . . . The business arrangements around the temple were *necessary* if [God's] commandments were to be obeyed. An attack upon what is necessary is not an attack on "present practice." . . . [We] should drop the discussion of Jesus' action as one concerned with purifying the worship of God.

There is no evidence at all that Jesus' act was in criticism of the priests and Levites and their conduct of the temple.[44] Accordingly, we must look elsewhere for an accounting of Jesus' act. We are required to do this because the conflict concerning the temple is deeply implanted in the early Christian tradition, "and that there was such a conflict would seem to be indisputable." I need not or at least cannot enter here into the many issues and unanswered questions that Sanders addresses. Most scholars reject Mark 11:17, deeming it a later addition. Nevertheless, it is Sanders's contention that Jesus did predict or threaten the destruction of the temple: "The threat of destruction appears in too many strata [of the tradition] and coheres too well with the 'cleansing' of the temple to be denied to Jesus."[45]

Constructively speaking, the *Aktion* of Jesus "is to be regarded as a symbolic demonstration. . . . We should suppose that Jesus *knew what he was doing*. . . . [But on] what conceivable grounds could Jesus have undertaken to attack—and symbolize the destruction of—what was ordained by God? The obvious answer is that destruction, in turn, looks to restoration." This is best seen through considering Jesus' sayings about the temple's destruction, which Jesus most probably predicted (Mark 13:2; cf. 14:58; Matt. 26:61), together with his promises for the future. But if it is so that "Jesus either threatened or predicted the destruction of the temple [together with its rebuilding], . . . that is, if the saying in any of its forms is even approximately authentic, his meaning would be luminously clear: he predicted the imminent appearance of the judgment and the new age." We may conclude that Jesus' prediction or threat was shaped by his expectation of the eschaton, "that he probably also expected a new temple to be given by God from heaven, and that he made a demonstration which prophetically symbolized this coming event."[46]

We see, then, the essential conflict between Borg and Sanders respecting their apprehension of the crucial episode in the temple: a noneschatological or extra-eschatological "attack" upon the "politics of holiness" (Borg) versus eschatological understanding that does not depend upon this or any other politics (Sanders). Jesus does not take the stance that Borg attributes to him.

To return to Borg's own presentation: In contradiction of the view of E. P. Sanders that Jesus' behavior in Jerusalem (as elsewhere) was predicated upon his conviction of a coming, eschatological divine intervention and judgment, Borg argues on the basis of the Synoptic tradition that Jesus faced his hearers, not with "the imminent and inevitable end of the world, but [with] the imminent and yet contingent destruction of Israel" due to the sin of a politics and piety of holiness. " . . . Jesus warned in the most solemn terms, using language that echoed the prophetic strand of the [Hebrew Bible], of the destruction of Jerusalem and the temple by an invading military force. . . . Thus the end to which he *clearly* referred, the last hour that he *certainly* announced, concerned the threat of historical catastrophe for his people." (None of this analysis by Borg denies that Jesus also believed in a *final* divine judgment.) In Jerusalem, center of the Jewish world, Jesus continued on with his mission and message. He indicted the leaders of the people as responsible for Israel's current moral plight. He spoke of Jerusalem's impending destruction (Mark 12:9; 13:2, 14; Luke 19:41-44; 21:20-24). During what was to be the last week of his life, the Nazarene primarily filled the role of prophet, urging his people to change. Borg reminds readers that "despite the fact that Jesus' mode of death reflects a Roman execution, the stories of his death emphasized Jewish responsibility. Indeed, this emphasis led to a progressive shifting of responsibility from the Romans to the Jews, a tendency perhaps intensified by the early church's concern to claim that they were not a rebellious group within the Empire, despite their founder's having been executed by the Romans as a rebel." For Borg, we may say that Jesus died for a crime of which he was innocent (cf. chap. 5 wherein I argue that Jesus was by no means innocent of the charge that was to mean his death). "In another sense, he was guilty, for he did not give his ultimate allegiance to Rome or to any other kingdom of the world." Also—we are told—there was in all probability collaboration with Rome on the part of the "circle of Jewish religious figures and aristocracy." (Query: Why identify them as Jewish? The people of Palestine were Jews, including Jesus.) But there is added affront in Borg's attempt to fabricate much greater "Jewish" culpability than is found in other contemporary scholars. This state of affairs derives from his persisting effort to establish massive conflict between Jesus and his "social world":

> To a large extent, it was the conventional wisdom of the time . . . that was responsible for the death of Jesus. . . . [The] dominant consciousness of conventional wisdom [was] threatened by the voice of an alternative consciousness. . . . The politics of holiness also played a role. It accounted for much of the resistance to [Jesus'] message and movement. The Pharisees, the embodiment of the politics of holiness in an intensified form, were the most vocal verbal critics during the ministry, though they do not seem to have been involved in the arrest and trial of Jesus. But the politics of holiness was in the culture as a whole, not just in the Pharisees. In this less intense form, it shaped the lives of ordinary people (even the outcasts) as well as the lives of the accommodationist ruling class. . . . [The] politics of holiness found the politics of compassion both unorthodox and threatening. . . . Jesus was killed because he sought, in the name and power of the Spirit, the transformation of his own culture.[47]

The effect of Borg's attempt to establish or at least retain "Jewish" responsibility for Jesus' death can only be a lessening of responsibility for those who were in truth to blame, the Roman authorities, and to broaden and deepen the "sin" of "the Jews." Such is the consequence once a wedge is driven between Jesus and his own people.

Additional critical commentary upon Borg's christological endeavors is found in the final section of this chapter.

ASSESSMENT OF MARCUS BORG

Several questions may be posed respecting the contribution of Marcus J. Borg, beyond those already suggested.

(1) *The issue of newness.* I put this question first because of the claim that the title *Jesus, A New Vision* embodies. The issue has two aspects to it, Borg's newness and Jesus' newness. That is to say, it is assumed here that the "new vision" applies both *on behalf of* Jesus and *to* Jesus.

First, Borg stands in the line of such figures as Wilhelm Bousset, Rudolf Bultmann, Günther Bornkamm, Martin Dibelius, E. Käsemann, W. G. Kümmel, Eduard Schweizer, C. F. D. Moule, C. H. Dodd, Joachim Jeremias, John Bowker, and Wolfhart Pannenberg (a lineage apart from which it is not possible to understand Borg) in depicting Jesus as in fundamental opposition to decisive elements in the Judaism and among the religious authorities of his time.[48] It is as though we are being forced again and again to listen to the highly dubious finding of Jeremias, "The supreme religious duty" in the Judaism of Jesus' day "was to keep away from sinners."[49]

Second, at the same time that he is setting Jesus in essential conflict with his social world, Borg readily concedes—as a responsible scholar—that there was already in effect a whole tradition that supported Jesus and that (upon Borg's own rendering of the data) makes Jesus out as not terribly new:

> [The] emphasis upon a clean heart is not new to the Jewish tradition. The author of the fifty-first psalm petitioned God for a clean heart, in words which have been prayed and sung by Jews and Christians for centuries: "Create in me a *clean heart*, O God." Jeremiah spoke of a new covenant which would be *within, written upon the heart.* Hence the struggle between Jesus and the wisdom of his time was not a struggle between a new religion (Christianity) and an old religion (Judaism), but a struggle between two ways of being religious that run through Judaism and Christianity alike. The conflict was between a way of being religious that depended upon observance of externals (the way of conventional wisdom) and a way of being religious that depended upon inner transformation.
>
> Jesus was not the first in Jewish history to criticize conventional wisdom. In the Hebrew Bible, the authors of Ecclesiastes and Job protested against the conventional wisdom represented by the Book of Proverbs, that easy confidence that the righteous would prosper and the wicked wither. They were *subversive* sages who challenged and subverted the popular wisdom of their day.
>
> Jesus stood in this tradition of subversive wisdom. . . . It was a conflict within the tradition itself, between a version of the tradition that had hardened into conventional wisdom under the pressure of historical circumstances, and an alternative version that was freshly in touch with the Spirit.[50]

By implication, the vision of Jesus is here being identified as not new at all. Ostensibly, people like the authors of the Psalms, Ecclesiastes, and Job could have written the same kind of commendatory report concerning Jesus that Borg provides. More broadly and significantly, the question arises, If Jesus was not in fact original or singular in his teaching, why are we to make such a fuss over him and particularly over his reputed conflicts with other parties? At the center of this difficulty is that in the very nature of the case—Borg's allegations that "most of Jesus' contemporaries" and "the dominant consciousness of his day" differed from Jesus are woefully conjectural—we simply do not know, and probably have no way of knowing, where "the people" of Jesus' day prevailingly stood. This creates a serious problem for Borg: His purposefully *histori-*

cal Christology is highly limited and subject to error amidst its very effort to furnish historical authentication for itself.

(2) *The issue of supersessionism.* For all Borg's avowal of Jesus' conflict with the Judaism of his time, our author satisfies the three characteristics listed in chapter 1 for the genre of Christology that is reviewed in this book: the distinctive validity of Christianity; opposition to religious imperialism and supersessionism; and the centrality of the historical Jesus for Christian faith. Questions, however, here arise concerning the second characteristic.

As we have noted, Professor Borg is careful to make plain that the conflict between Jesus and his social world is a conflict wholly *within* Judaism:

> Oftentimes Jesus' criticism of his social world is seen as an indictment of Judaism itself. But it was not. Not only does such an attitude affect one's assessment of Judaism today, but it also ignores the fact that Jesus (like his prophetic predecessors) was the voice of an alternative consciousness *within* Judaism calling his Jewish hearers to a transformed understanding of their own tradition. It was not Judaism itself which he saw as unfruitful, any more than the prophets of the Old Testament were "anti-Jewish." Rather, it was the current direction of his social world that he saw as blind and misguided. The conflict between Jesus and his contemporaries was not about the adequacy of Judaism or the Torah, or about the importance of being "good" rather than "bad," but was about two different versions of what it meant to be a people centered in God. Both visions flowed out of the Torah: a people living in the ethos and politics of holiness, or a people living by the ethos and politics of compassion.[51]

Here is the basis for entitling the present chapter of this book "The *Judaism* of Jesus, Countercultural Spiritualizer." Unlike those who utilize Jesus' reputed conflict with the Judaism of his day as material justification for Christian supersessionism vis-à-vis Judaism, Borg refrains from this. What evidently saves him from supersessionist imperialism is very important: his faithfulness to historical analysis. However much he makes Jesus over into a countercultural spiritualizer, he cannot violate, and has no wish to violate, the simple but stern historical truth that Jesus never once betrays the Judaism in which he was reared and never once implies that his friends and compatriots require a new religion. Even in Borg's presentation of Jesus' (alleged) conflict with "the Pharisees," he does not at all separate Jesus from Judaism; on the contrary, he makes Jesus a representative of the highest in Judaism. All in all, the Jesus movement was a renewal movement and not a replacement movement.

Why, then, do I include in my critique the issue of supersessionism? The practical problem is that, all unintentionally, Borg provides ammunition for Christian supersessionists who are all too eager (as they have been in the past) to apply such a dichotomy as *politics of holiness/politics of compassion* to the Judaism/Christianity antithesis. (The older dichotomy of law/love was saying much the same thing.) Unfortunately, there appears to be no way to prevent

Borg's dichotomy from fueling the fires of anti-Judaism and antisemitism. Much in his argumentation and exegesis can be easily utilized in the service of super-sessionism, most especially his egregiously oversimple antithesis between "ho-liness" and "compassion." His claim to a dominating conflict between Jesus and first-century Judaism tends, on balance, to ally Borg with anti-Jewish ele-ments within Christian scholarship much more than it connects him with the scholarship that receives Jesus as primarily in solidarity with his people and its faith.

This is in no way to imply or suggest that Borg is not entitled to describe or assess the history as he sees it. It is only to point up a contemporary problem with which all Christian scholars have to wrestle, in the presence of theological antisemitism and under the shadow of the Holocaust.

(3) *The issue of "the Pharisees."* Borg fails to pay sufficient attention to elements of today's scholarship that do three things: deny that Jewish materials contemporary with Jesus reveal a predominantly legalistic, externalistic, sepa-ratist Judaism that Jesus is supposed to have criticized or fought;[52] recognize Jesus as a full and convinced member of, or at least sympathizer with, the Phar-isee grouping; and point out that "the harsh portraits of the Pharisees [in the Gospels] reflect not so much Jesus' time as the clashes between the Christians and the Pharisees after 70 c.e."[53]

E. P. Sanders "doubts that there were any substantial points of opposition between Jesus and the Pharisees. . . . " All the scenes of debate "have more than a slight air of artificiality." There was no real conflict between Jesus and the Pharisees "with regard to Sabbath, food, and purity laws."[54]

(a) Clark M. Williamson writes, "There has been a veritable revolution in our understanding of who the Pharisees were and what they did. The Pharisees constituted a revolution within the religious tradition of Judaism—a successful and radical revolution. Their innovations resulted in the emergence of a new sensitivity within Judaism and, subsequently, within Christianity. Jesus partici-pated in that transformation and expressed this sensitivity in ways closely akin to, if perhaps more radical than, those of the Pharisees." The Pharisees stood for the oral Torah as equally authoritative with the written *Tanak.* Thus, one of their typical expressions was, "You have heard that it was said, . . . but I say to you," an antithesis also resorted to by Jesus (cf. Matt. 5:21, 27-28, 31-34, 38-39, 43-44). We read in Jesus' Sermon on the Mount, "if you love those who love you, what reward have you?" This teaching comes from the Pharisees, who "stressed love for its own sake, regardless of compensation. The rabbis seized upon this idea—that we should love our fellow human beings as ourselves—as context and foundation for all the Mosaic teachings. For them, love took pre-cedence over fear of God (awe) as the basis for loving action. To love our fel-low human beings, who are as fallible as we, was the [Pharisee][55] expression of our solidarity with all people." In addition, the Pharisees taught that the elect of God can be justified or accepted only by God's grace and compassion; that God's power is necessary for moral living; that God is ever near to, and full of mercy for, *every* individual; that we must seek to overcome evil with good; that the way to serve God is through individual and social responsibility; that there is a resurrection from the dead;[56] and that the Torah is to be internalized. "Passionately advocating the kingdom of God within, 'they were the grand internalizers.' God sees into the heart of each person and looks at actions in the light of motivation."[57]

John T. Pawlikowski states, "What is clear from [the Pharisee] concern with the oral Torah is the necessity for religious persons committed to the ideals of the Exodus covenant to move beyond mere nominal generalizations to concrete programs that would correct the injustices being perpetuated by existing social structures. The [Pharisee] rabbis were convinced that religious men and woman had to offer concrete and detailed plans for changing unjust practices in a society. Only thus could they truly fulfill their role as co-creators [with God]. Only thus would the Messianic Kingdom of peace and justice be brought closer to realization."[58]

Jesus was a great Pharisee teacher.[59]

(b) Perhaps the major historical error in trying to transmute Jesus into a foe of "the Pharisees" is that it contradicts the insistence of Professor Borg himself that Jesus was the friend of evil tax collectors, sinners, and outcasts—which means all kinds of "reprehensible" people. Once we posit that Jesus was a sensible and just man who knew what he was doing, a man "who did not make entrance into the kingdom dependent on being better at Pharisaism than the Pharisees themselves,"[60] it becomes impossible for him not to be friend as well of the (supposedly reprehensible) Pharisees. If Jesus' reputed way of "compassion" was in fact selective and *did not extend to practitioners of "holiness" and "separateness,"* then his "compassion" was either phony or a merely sometime thing or not present at all. It is inconceivable that the man whom Borg portrays as summoning his followers to love of all enemies would somehow exclude "the Pharisees"—or anyone else—from such love. Borg forces himself into an analytic-historical-scholarly split between Jesus' reputed prophetic denunciations and his reputed compassion.

Perhaps an ultimate irony for Borg is that he, who makes so much of Jesus' table fellowship with sinners, must face the fact that Jesus *partakes of dinner with the Pharisees themselves* (Luke 14:1-14). There could hardly be a more forceful witness to the inclusion of the Pharisees within members (i.e., sinners) of the kingdom of God.

(c) On Borg's argument that the Judaism and the social world of Jesus' time had degenerated into a miasma of false "holiness" (else ostensibly Jesus would have had no reason to try to revolutionize it so urgently and so radically), we are left in the impossible situation of having to apprehend and treat the development of postbiblical, rabbinic Judaism, with its great themes of human compassion, justice, and human responsibility, as having come to pass wholly *ex nihilo*. On the contrary, rabbinic Judaism was made possible by the ethos and morality of a revolutionary Pharisee Judaism of which Jesus was himself a devoted spokesperson.[61]

The above points are coherent with a twofold summarization by Clark M. Williamson: "First, the Pharisees were highly self-critical, and the criticisms found in the Gospels cannot be said to exceed those found in Pharisaic literature itself. Second, the church of the later first century wrote the Gospels. That church was in direct conflict with the Pharisees who were the leaders of synagogue-Judaism after the fall of the Temple in the year 70. The clash is reflected in the Gospels, retrojected into the life of Jesus." Because much of the teaching of Jesus is couched in the form of criticizing "the Pharisees," it follows that every misunderstanding of this group contributes to misconceptions of Jesus' own message and mission.[62]

(4) *The issue of eschatology.* Borg places the onus for the transformation of Israel primarily upon the shoulders of Israel. A more balanced approach may be found in the message of Jesus himself, a message that is synergist in conception and application: To be sure, Jesus calls upon his people to act, but that summons is undergirded and is to be supported by the imminent power and action of God. As E. P. Sanders writes, the evidence "points towards Jewish eschatology as the general framework of Jesus' ministry."[63] (In my own use of the term *eschatology,* I tend to go along with what appears to be Borg's preference: as characterizing "a decisive act of God in history, whereby something new enters and decisively changes history, even though it may have continuity with the past and does not obviate an historical future.")[64] The difficulty in Borg is his tendency to deeschatologize Jesus, his message, and his mission in the sense that any truly revolutionary act of God in history gets downplayed. The stress falls instead upon Jesus' demand for human conversion. In this regard, it is to be noted that Borg pays relatively minor attention to the messianic question in its relation to Jesus.[65]

EXCURSUS: CAN THERE BE A
HOLY SECULARITY?

The dictionary identifies an excursus as an "incidental digression." A final bit of commentary upon Marcus Borg's work is not directly upon the subject of the message or mission of Jesus, although it does bear upon that subject as it also bears upon the analysis and substance of religion or faith in general. The issue is an ontological one.

Borg observes that in the history of Israel as of other cultures *some people* "become channels through which healing power flowed from the world of Spirit into the visible world."[66] We are advised that, sadly, this awareness of truly spiritual or charismatic activity has been pretty much lost in our modern world. We occupy an essentially flat universe that makes no real allowance for the domain of the invisible, the world of the Spirit. In the final resort, *everything becomes the same.* The world that surrounds us has been desanctified, and with the loss of the sacred—which stands in contrast to the profane—there is the specter of meaninglessness.

I suggest that there may be a third alternative and therefore that there may be hope for us. As against *some things are different* (the premodern apprehension), but also against *everything is the same* (the modern temptation or conclusion), it is possible for us to affirm that *everything is different* (a postmodern eventuality). Perhaps the problem with the first alternative (some things are different) is its essential conservatism together with its implicit arrogance. To maintain that only *some* people are charismatic (or beautiful or great or especially talented, etc.) is a rather *timid* thing to say. (It occurs to me that arrogance and timidity are blood relatives.) To attest that *everything* is different (e.g., all people are differently beautiful) is in one sense to return to the first stage of provision for the Spirit, but it is also to transcend that stage in a revolutionary way. A *holy secularity* can now be declared—what Irving Greenberg has spoken of as "the sacred significance of the secular" as such. For this is the only way that the essential elitism of the primordial spirit world described by Borg can be vanquished.

Perhaps our world had first to be desanctified before it could become the utensil that proclaims unqualified sacredness. Only once everything had become profane could everything become sacred. Now, at last and for the first time, we may celebrate "*all* creatures, great and small."

I return at the end to the old Jewish tale of one angel per blade of grass: In effect, the original worldview made only some blades of grass sacred. All the others were profane; they didn't really count. The modern world came along and made no blade of grass sacred; every blade of grass is the same as every other blade. Thereby was lost the marvel of grass. The postmodern opportunity is to sanctify each and every blade of grass— for each has been assigned its special angel. (Query: Without the Spirit hidden behind *all* phenomena, rather than behind only *some* phenomena, how could we ever escape superstition?)

4

The Judaism of Jesus, Rejected Advocate of Israel's Restoration

---

We have already been introduced to E. P. Sanders's magnum opus, *Jesus and Judaism.* In that volume stress falls upon ostensibly "unassailable facts about Jesus, their possible significance in his own time, and the outcome of his life and work." Following Joseph Klausner, Sanders maintains that any defensible hypothesis respecting Jesus' intention and his relation to Judaism ought to satisfy the twofold test of situating Jesus believably within Judaism and of explaining why the Jesus movement eventually broke with Judaism. Such a hypothesis must also show a connection between Jesus' activity and his death.[1]

JEWISH RESTORATION ESCHATOLOGY

Professor Sanders holds that most of the things we can with certainty know about Jesus place him under the rubric of Jewish restoration eschatology. For from within a frame of reference of imminent-eschatological expectations, Jesus sought to restore or renew the people of Israel. Sanders provides a jussive guideline: "In general terms it may be said that 'Jewish eschatology' and 'the restoration of Israel' are almost synonymous." We have reviewed his contention that the so-called cleansing of the temple is "the surest starting point" for investigating Jesus' message and mission. Sanders asserts, as we reported, that Jesus' demonstration in the temple was intended as symbolic of a future divine destruction to be followed by a restoration in and through an imminent judgment and new age. It is simply wrongheaded to suppose that the man from Nazareth "intended something different when he 'cleansed' the Temple from what he intended to achieve by his teaching. . . . The kingdom was at hand, and one of the things which that meant was that the old Temple would be replaced by a new." A new Jerusalem implied a new temple.[2]

There is also the Nazarene's selection of the Twelve as close disciples. First-century Jewish hopes for the future extended to the restoration of Israel's twelve tribes. It is against this background that we may "understand the motif of the twelve disciples in the Gospels. . . . [The] expectation of the reassembly of Israel was so widespread, and the memory of the twelve tribes remained so acute, that 'twelve' *would necessarily mean 'restoration.'*" The notion of "twelve" was a fixed part of the pre-Pauline tradition. As we read in Matt. 19:28, "In the new world, . . . you who have followed me will also sit on twelve thrones, judging the twelve tribes of Israel." It appears "virtually certain that the conception of 'the twelve' goes back to Jesus himself. . . . His use of the conception 'twelve' points towards his understanding of his own mission. He was engaged in a task which would include the restoration of Israel."[3]

Jewish restoration eschatology contains as well the theme of repentance. I have called attention to Marcus Borg's emphasis, or overemphasis, upon that eventuality. As Sanders points out, much Jewish thought upon end-time salvation focuses on God's action rather than humankind's. Thus, we "cannot say of repentance, as we said of the twelve, that the theme itself signals the redemption of the end-time." But "it would be very surprising for a herald of the eschaton not to invoke the mighty theme of the nation's need to turn to God." Were this "combined with the prediction of God's coming to cleanse, purify, and heal, both sides of the repentance/cleansing scheme would be present." This suggests, I submit once again, that Jesus was a thoroughgoing synergist. On the other hand, as Sanders says, there is very little evidence—contra Borg—to link Jesus explicitly with a call for *national* repentance (in light of the coming *eschaton*). Gospel materials on Jesus and repentance that are connected to the nearness of the kingdom of God are slight. Beyond Mark 1:15—a questionable summary—there are only the rather dubious passages (Matt. 11:21-24/Luke 10:13-15; Matt. 12:38-42/Luke 11:29-32; and Luke 13:1-5). Sanders is "arguing (1) that there is no firm tradition which shows that [Jesus] issued a call for national repentance in view of the coming end, as did John the Baptist;[4] (2) that 'forgiveness' in the message of Jesus does not take on the tone of eschatological restoration;[5] (3) but that, if Jesus had called for national repentance, or if he had promised national forgiveness, he would fit quite comfortably into the category of a prophet of Jewish restoration." All this means that the materials under survey contain something *very surprising*:

> The gathering of the twelve, the start under John the Baptist, the post-resurrection activity of the apostles, and the action in and saying about the Temple clearly point

to the well-known eschatological expectation that God would renew his worship, save those who turned to him, and reassemble Israel. One would have expected, accompanying these clear signs, an emphatic call to all Israel to repent in view of the coming end and the explicit promise that God's forgiving mercy would be extended in saving and restoring his people. But the emphatic call and the explicit promise are missing. New Testament scholars have not, I think, sufficiently registered surprise over this situation. Most, in fact, would deny that it exists. But there it is. The great themes of national repentance and God's forgiveness, shown in restoring his repentant people, are prominent in all the literature which looks toward Jewish restoration. Jesus fits *somehow* into that view of God, the world and his people; but his message curiously lacks emphasis on one of the most important themes in the overall scheme.[6]

Finally, Sanders adds to the foregoing enigma the problem of divine judgment: It is surprising that "the evidence for a *message* about the coming judgment of Israel is so slight." Surely, "Jesus was not opposed to the idea of judgment. He expected there to be a selection, which implies a judgment. He did not, however, address a message to Israel to the effect that at the end there would be a great assize at which Israel would be vindicated and the nations rebuked and destroyed; and it seems that he did not make thematic the message that Israel should repent and mend their ways so as to escape punishment at the judgment." Instead, we are met by a very strange state of affairs: If no explicit information is forthcoming that Jesus preached national repentance, "our discussion of judgment points in [exactly] the same direction. . . . [There] is no explicit teaching material about a judgment which would weed out the unworthy from Israel." At this juncture, Sanders gives voice to a measure of bafflement: "[The] authentic sayings which imply judgment raise questions about Jesus as a prophet of the eschatological restoration of Israel, the same question which is raised by the study of repentance. We find, as we would expect, the theme of judgment, but we do not find teaching or proclamation which depicts or predicts the impending judgment of the nation of Israel. We would have expected such a message to accompany the expectation that Israel would be restored."[7]

Chapter 5 will seek to show, or at least to intimate, that a possible way out of the above double maze (repentance; judgment) is found in Jesus' theocentricity: "Fear not, little flock, for it is your father's good pleasure to give you the kingdom" (Luke 12:32). In the meantime, it would appear that Marcus Borg's castigation, reputedly in behalf of Jesus, of a politics of holiness is subject to very serious criticism.

E. P. Sanders concludes Part One of *Jesus and Judaism,* "The Restoration of Israel," with these lines:

> I have argued that the themes of *national* repentance, forgiveness and judgment are largely absent from [Jesus'] sayings material. I do not, however, take it that this

proves that Jesus opposed Jewish nationalism. There are, on the contrary, clear and undeniable indications that he expected the restoration *of Israel*; temple and twelve are national symbols. In this context it is noteworthy that his message largely omits the typical *means* for the achievement of restoration. That Jesus did not think that national restoration would be achieved by arms is not especially surprising. What is surprising is that, while looking for the restoration of Israel, he did not follow the majority and urge the traditional means towards that end: repentance and a return to observance of the law.[8]

THE KINGDOM OF GOD

In Part Two of *Jesus and Judaism* Professor Sanders addresses himself to the overall theme of the kingdom of God, treated under these successive headings: Jesus' sayings; miracles and crowds; the sinners; the Gentiles; and the nature of the kingdom.

The sayings. Sanders employs the comprehensive term *sayings material* to include sayings proper (*logia*), parables, other forms of teaching, and proclamation. But he is nonetheless quite skeptical, or at least cautious: "I regard most of the exegetical efforts of the last decades as proving a negative: analysis of the sayings material does not succeed in giving us a picture of Jesus which is convincing and which answers historically important questions." There are severe limitations in the method of attempting to explain Jesus through interpreting the sayings. Decisive here is Sanders's pronounced restriction upon what historical method is able to do: "How can one argue historically that a certain attitude or conception is unique?" On the other hand, we can all agree that the concept *kingdom* means at its core "the 'sphere' (whether geographical, temporal or spiritual) where God exercises his [ruling] power." Sanders here applies his certainty/uncertainty continuum: It is certain that Jesus proclaimed the kingdom of God and that he regarded his own career as significantly connected to that kingdom. But it is no more than possible that Jesus looked upon the kingdom as "breaking in" through his own praxis. And it is only "conceivable" that his interpretation of his work is conveyed by the wording, "if it is by the Spirit of God that I cast out demons, then the kingdom of God has come upon you" (Matt. 12:28/Luke 11:20; cf. Matt. 11:5-6).[9]

We are presented with a sixfold categorization of the "kingdom" sayings: (a) Kingdom in the sense of covenant (e.g., "Not every one who says to me, 'Lord, Lord,' shall enter the kingdom of heaven, but he who does the will of my Father who is in heaven" [Matt. 7:21]). (b) The kingdom as still to be fully established (e.g., "Thy kingdom come" [Matt. 6:10]). (c) The kingdom as coming in the form of an otherworldly, unexpected event, at which time the righteous and the wicked will be separated (e.g., Matt. 13:40-42). "[It] would be rash to deny to Jesus this complex of ideas." (d) The kingdom as a decisive future event resulting in "a recognizable social order involving Jesus' disciples and presumably Jesus himself" (e.g., the disciples as judges of the twelve tribes; Matt. 19:28). (e) The kingdom as seemingly present in Jesus' own words and deeds (e.g., Matt. 12:28, discussed by Sanders at considerable length). (f) The kingdom described in quite definite terms (e.g., most of the parables).[10]

Sanders devotes much attention to the problem of the kingdom as present/future. He finds no difficulty in this double ascription as such; rather for him the surprising thing is that the same word should be used to cover a great range of meanings, as is the case in the Synoptics. If in the matter of the kingdom a choice must be made between "present" and "future," current scholarly evidence puts the emphasis upon the latter: the kingdom as "immediately future." (This fits Sanders's understanding of eschatology as referring "to the expectation of an imminent end to the current order.") There are several reasons for this choice of "future": Jesus' early association with John the Baptist; the behavior of the apostles as indicating their expectation of an imminent dramatic event; the prediction of the temple's destruction; and the grounding of an expected kingdom in the Judaism of Jesus' day.[11]

What happens, then, to the claim, as in C. H. Dodd, that "Jesus thought that the kingdom was present in some *extraordinary sense,* in its *full end-time power*"? Sanders replies that the available passages are not clear enough "to allow us to think that Jesus claimed that the kingdom which was present was the same as the kingdom which he expected to come"—even though it is beyond doubt that he saw the kingdom as at once imminent and "intimately tied to himself and his work," and also that he believed that the power of God was active in him as God's spokesman: "Blessed are the eyes which see what you see!"; "Behold, something greater than Jonah is here" (Luke 10:23; 11:32).

In summary: "Jesus expected the kingdom in the near future, he awaited the rebuilding of the Temple, he called 'twelve' to symbolize the restoration of Israel, and his disciples thought about the kingdom concretely enough to ask about their place in it." All this means that we are forbidden to "shift the normal expectations of Jewish restoration theology to the periphery."[12]

Miracles and crowds.   Most scholars agree that Jesus' miracles and his inclusion of sinners are tied to his conception of the kingdom and his own mission. But the opinions that explain the meaning of miracles in Jesus' career and the offer of the kingdom to sinners have been so successful that they have tended to inhibit further exploration. There are four such opinions: (a) In Jesus' time exorcisms were received as signs of the kingdom. (b) Forgiveness of sinners was also looked upon as among the promises of the end time. (c) Jesus saw his exorcisms and healings as showing the inbreaking of the kingdom, or at least its imminence. (d) Jesus was basically a teacher and preacher. As crowds would flock to hear him, he would heal some among them.

Sanders regards the first two of these opinions as quite erroneous. The third "is possible but not provable," and the fourth "is uncertain and in need of examination." Sanders denies that Jesus can be considered simply a teacher. In the course of the chapter under review our author raises and answers four questions: (1) Does the fact of the miracles teach us anything about Jesus' self-understanding and his followers' understanding of him? Answer: "We do not learn with certainty what Jesus thought of himself, although it is reasonable to think that he, as well as his followers, saw his miracles as testifying to his being a true messenger from or agent of God." It is very hard to assess Jesus' motives for the healings (contra A. E. Harvey); the miracles simply do not tell us what Jesus had in mind. It "seems to be that Jesus found that he could heal; that he thus attracted crowds and special followers; that he complemented his healing of the needy in Galilee by promising the kingdom to the poor and the outcasts." It is probably wrong to say that he healed simply on compassionate grounds (cf. Borg).

(2) Can we be apprised of anything important for apprehending the outcome of Jesus' career? Answer: The miracles "doubtless contributed greatly to his ability to gather crowds, and they thus help explain why he was executed." That he attracted attention and commotion was challenging to the authorities. (Queries: How so? And which authorities?)

(3) How was Jesus seen by people who were not his followers? Answer: " 'Outsiders' probably regarded Jesus as a charlatan, a magician." However, "whether or not he offered his miracles as signs that he spoke for God, they convinced some that he did so, and they considered him a special figure in God's plan."

(4) Does Jesus fit a general social and religious type? Answer: "The miracles do not require us to think that he was an eschatological prophet, but they are compatible with that view. ... There is nothing about miracles which would trigger, in the first-century Jewish world, the expectation that the end was at hand. ... [There] is other evidence which leads us to think of Jesus as an eschatological prophet, not because the miracles make him one. ... [It] is entirely reasonable to assume that Jesus' following, and perhaps Jesus himself, saw [the miracles] as evidencing his status as true spokesman for God, since that sort of inference was common in the Mediterranean."[13]

The "sinners": Who is to be included in the kingdom? The phrasing of the question that I here add to the subheading is meant to convey something of the cruciality of the next issue, an issue that warrants extra space.

One distinctive note that "we may be certain marked Jesus' teaching" is that the kingdom of God extends to "sinners" or "the wicked." Even though such summary statements as Matt. 9:11-13//Mark 2:16-17//Luke 5:30-32 were probably fashioned by the early church, the church "would not have created . . . Jesus' proclamation as being directed toward 'sinners' " (since that church soon developed heavy intolerance of such people). At this juncture, Sanders "can happily join the consensus and agree that Jesus associated with the wicked [meaning those who disobeyed the law] and was criticized for it." (Impurity must never be confused with sin; purity was *not* the issue between Jesus and his critics.) "Jesus saw his mission as being to 'the lost' and the 'sinners': that is, to the wicked. He was doubtless also concerned with the poor, the meek and the downtrodden, and in all probability he had a following among them. But the *charge* against him was not that he loved the *'amme ha-arets,* the common people. If there was a conflict, it centered in the status of the *wicked. It is a mistake to think that the Pharisees were upset because he ministered to the ordinarily pious common people and the economically impoverished."* Observance "of the biblical purity laws was not a special concern of the Pharisees." What Jesus was actually accused of was associating with, and offering the kingdom to, people who were "wicked" by *normal* religious standards.

We are up against a "dearly cherished view"—but a wholly false one—that the Pharisees, who (reputedly yet not in fact) dominated Judaism, "excluded everyone but themselves from salvation," while Jesus "let the common people in." Sanders provides a lengthy, fivefold refutation of the incredible but widespread notion that Jesus believed in grace and forgiveness while his "Jewish" and "Pharisaic" detractors did not.[14]

Sanders's positive though circumspect proposal is that Jesus may (N.B.) have offered certain people "inclusion in the kingdom not only *while they were still sinners* but also *without* requiring repentance as normally understood, and therefore he could have been accused of being a friend of people who indefinitely *remained* sinners.[15] Here at last we see the full implication of the repeated observation that Jesus did not issue a call for repentance. . . . " In other words, the trouble with Jesus lay in the fact that he was, in a sense, "immoral" in his message. Evidently, John the Baptist was "the spokesman for *repentance and righteousness ordinarily understood* [cf., e.g., Matt. 21:32], whereas Jesus, equally convinced that the end was at hand, proclaimed the *inclusion of the wicked who heeded him."* Additional passages point in the same direction: the call of the publican Levi (Matt. 9:9-13//Mark 2:13-17//Luke 5:27-32); the question about fasting (Matt. 9:14-17//Mark 2:18-22//Luke 5:33-39); and the story of the would-be follower who wanted to bury his father

(Matt. 8:21-22; Luke 9:59-60), the last of which "puts following Jesus above obeying the fifth commandment."[16]

Sanders is proposing, then,

> that the novelty and offense of Jesus' message was that the wicked who heeded him would be included in the kingdom even though they did not repent as it was universally understood—that is, even though they did not make restitution, sacrifice, and turn to obedience to the law. . . . If Jesus added to this such statements as that the tax collectors and prostitutes would enter the kingdom before the righteous (Matt. 21:31), the offense would be increased. The implied self-claim, to know whom God would include and not, and the equally implied downgrading of the normal machinery of righteousness, would push Jesus' stance close to, or over, the border which separates individual charisma from impiety. . . . Putting the matter this way explains the connection between tax collectors and sinners in the Gospels (complete outsiders), attributes to Jesus a distinctive view of his own mission and the nature of the kingdom, and offers an explanation of what in Jesus' message was offensive to normal piety—not just to trivial, externalistic super-piety.

Sanders freely concedes that his proposal is speculative. Yet he considers its validity to be much more likely than the popular but thoroughly false notion that mainline Judaism, opposed to repentance and forgiveness, and therefore to Jesus' call to sinners to repent, resolved to kill him.[17]

I have to say that our author's admittedly speculative hypothesis does not finally convince me. That certain people heeded Jesus at all carried in itself, I should think, a *sort* of "repentance." Otherwise, what is the content of "heed"? Did not the very heeding of Jesus' call point to a life-and-death transformation? It is very hard to picture these people simply going out and celebrating in an entirely phony way, "Goody, goody. We are about to be saved, and we don't have to do a damn thing about it!" People possessed of that kind of self-righteousness would scarcely be worrying about the state of their souls in the first place. Why would such people bother to listen to Jesus? Did not their actual acceptance of Jesus' call—with its stress (we cannot forget) on the need to *get ready* for the kingdom—signal in itself the presence of *some* form of repentance (*metanoia*)? To be sure, Jesus' "Jewish opponents"—were there any such—may not have found the "repentance" to be genuine, but it seems more than a little gratuitous to identify that state of affairs as finally capable of bringing about Jesus' death. Later in his study, Sanders himself accentuates Jesus' demand "that his followers observe the highest of moral standards." For that matter, "the Jesus of Matthew 5, 6 and 23 is not depicted as relaxing" *external* requirements. "His disciples are still to tithe mint, dill and cummin (23:23) and to fast (6:16-18)." Matthew 5:21—6:18 and 23:1-36 portray Jesus as "preaching a super-piety which is even more rigorous than that of the scribes and Pharisees." Sanders inclines to reject part of this material, Matt. 5:17—6:18 but not the Lord's Prayer (6:9-13) with its petition for *forgiveness*.[18]

Sanders has shown that the major traditional and alleged conflict between Jesus and the religious authorities and teachers never existed. The question is whether his own substitute hypothesis is strong enough historically to account for Jesus' death. He himself concedes that Jesus' "characterization of the kingdom as including a 'reversal of values' and his inclusion of the sinners might have been offensive to some of the pious, but they do not explain the Roman execution. The call to follow him at great cost and to love one's neighbor does not lead us to see him as a threat to the established order." And there is a further very important admission, italicized in the text: "Some form of 'other-worldliness' must be attributed to Jesus and his disciples even before the crucifixion, and it would appear that neither the Jerusalem aristocracy nor the Romans understood Jesus' hope differently."[19] In any event and as is to be expected, Sanders's general conclusion contrasts sharply with Borg's position. The prevalent view

> that Jesus was criticized by the Pharisees for breaking their purity code by eating with common people and for offering them forgiveness, and that the common people responded with joy to his readmission of them to Judaism, from which their ritual impurity had cut them off ... is against all the evidence: (1) The term "wicked" or "sinners" does not include the common people [the *'amme ha-arets*]. Neither the *haberim* [lay people who accepted special purity rules][20] nor the Pharisees considered the ordinary people to be condemned sinners. (2) Jesus' going to the wicked did not have primarily to do with his willingness to break purity laws. Most forms of impurity do not result from sin, nor is wickedness primarily a state of impurity—though it is also that. (3) In any case Jesus' eating with sinners[21] probably did not involve him in a dispute with a super-scrupulous group (whether called *haberim* or Pharisees). (4) Even if it had, it would not have thrown him into conflict with the leading powers in Judaism. The *haberim,* even if the same as the Pharisees [Sanders does not accept any such identity.—A.R.E.],[22] did not control Judaism. Neither the common people nor the priests [controllers of the temple] accepted the special rules of the *haberim.* Had Jesus opposed them, he would simply have sided with the majority and with commonly accepted practice. (5) It is incorrect to say that the issue was *readmission* to Judaism. (6) The offense was not that Jesus favored repentance and forgiveness.[23]

Marcus Borg's "descriptions" of Jesus' "conflicts" with the "religious authorities," and more especially with "the Pharisees," are shown by historical analysis to be incorrect. But as we shall see, Sanders by no means denies a discrete form of conflict between Jesus and the religious authorities. The question remains whether Sanders's exposition of that conflict is convincing or is instead subject to difficulties parallel or equal to those in Borg. In any event, the "politics of holiness" did not in truth exist as a socially and religiously *dominating* reality in the Palestine of Jesus' time.

The Gentiles.   At this point in E. P. Sanders's investigation a paradox presents itself. On the one hand, a telling proof that Jesus' career falls "within the general context of Jewish eschatological expectation" is that the movement he initiated also "spawned a Gentile mission."[24] On the other hand, there is no necessity to "think that Jesus imparted to his disciples any view at all about the Gentiles and the kingdom." Even Matt. 8:11—"many will come from east and west"—"need not push Jesus' message beyond the framework of Jewish restoration. The hope of restoration generally included the theme of the inclusion of the Gentiles."

We are obligated to reject the "stark good-bad-good pattern" propagated by Joachim Jeremias, John Riches, et al., a pattern that only serves special ideological (theological) interests: biblical-prophetic religion was "good"; "Spät judentum" was "bad"; Jesus came and reformed "late Judaism," to a large extent by returning to the prophetic tradition. Contra such nonsense, the apostle Paul was very likely representing a common view in believing that, while Gentiles were sinners in their everyday life, "at the end many of them would turn to God from idols (I Thess. 1:9) and conform their behavior to the normal requirements of the law (Rom. 13:8-10)."

What, then, may we conclude? Information is available from the disciples' postresurrection activity and especially from the Epistle to the Galatians:

> The leaders among Jesus' own followers (Peter and John, plus James the Lord's brother) were conducting a mission to prepare Israel for the coming of the kingdom. They were not engaged in the Gentile mission, but they regarded it as an entirely appropriate activity. . . . [No] Christian group objected to the Gentile mission; they disagreed only as to its terms and conditions. . . . [The] overwhelming impression is that Jesus started a movement which *came to see the Gentile mission as a logical extension of itself.* . . . [The early disciples reflect what is probably] the common Jewish view: in the last days the Gentiles can be admitted to the kingdom on some condition or other. . . . We understand the debates in early Christianity best if we attribute to Jesus no explicit viewpoint. . . . [25]

The nature of the kingdom.[26]   We have already been apprised of a good deal of Sanders's interpretation and findings upon the kingdom. But the whatness of the kingdom helps to complete and make concrete its thatness.

Sanders discerns that Jesus was expecting imminently "an otherworldly-earthly kingdom," which would involve a transformed social order with evil and evildoers eliminated, the building of a new, glorious temple, "the reassembly of Israel with himself and his disciples as leading figures in it," and a place for "sinners." Indeed, "his special mission was to promise inclusion in the coming kingdom to the outsiders, the wicked, if they heeded his call." The eschatological renewal is to include "known social elements and institutions" but it "cannot be achieved without a direct intervention of God which actually changes things. . . . It is like the present world—it has a king, leaders, a temple, and twelve tribes—but it is not just a rearrangement of the present world."[27]

With respect to the disciples, the issue of the kingdom was to be transmogrified yet also complicated by Jesus' (asserted) resurrection following upon his death. Before the crucifixion, Jesus' disciples could think of the kingdom as a transformed earth; with the resurrection, that hope was shifted to "in the air." That is to say, the disciples "almost immediately started a movement which (1) was identifiable as a separate entity within Judaism; (2) [newly?] regarded Jesus as the Messiah; (3) expected him to establish a kingdom on a different plane from those of this world. We must also bear in mind (4) the apolitical nature of Jesus' work as healer and preacher.[28] *It would be hard to account for these facts if the original expectation were fundamentally different from the post-Easter one.*" Sanders thinks then

> that we must grant an element of continuity between what Jesus expected and what the disciples expected after the crucifixion and resurrection. It appears that the latter originally expected something which was *transformed* by the resurrection appearances, but which was not as completely different as is often thought. The resurrection did not change political, military, and nationalistic hopes (based on misunderstanding) into spiritual, heavenly ones, but otherworldly-earthly hopes into otherworldly-heavenly. What the disciples originally expected, I propose, was a kingdom which did not involve a military revolt, but which was a good deal more concrete than either a collection of nice thoughts about grace and forgiveness, or a *message* about God's love for sinners and his being near. . . . If [the disciples] had always expected an eschatological miracle, it is easy to understand the role of the resurrection appearances in the creation of Christian belief in a heavenly kingdom.[29]

Finally, we cannot fail to refer to the (affirmed) second advent (*parousia*) of the Lord. "The Christian movement was differentiated from the rest of Judaism by the conviction that the Lord would soon return"; for Sanders, "this is to be seen as a transformation of Jesus' view that the kingdom of God was near." This state of affairs is coherent with the identification of Jesus as Messiah. For "the disciples already thought of Jesus as 'king'—or, better, as viceroy under the true king, God. If Jesus taught his disciples that there would be a kingdom and that *they* would have a role in it, he certainly, at least by implication, gave himself a role also. . . . As long as they expected him to return and establish 'his' kingdom (Matt. 20:21), the disciples could think of Jesus as Messiah."[30]

JESUS: CONFLICT AND DEATH

We are left with "Conflict and Death," Part Three of the Sanders study. Including as it does analyses of the law, opposition and opponents, and Jesus' execution, the section provides further comparisons and contrasts with other scholars.

The law.   The Synoptic materials hardly justify the notion that Jesus changed or avoided the law (a traditional way, among other ways, of trying to account for Jesus' death). The fact that the postresurrection Christian community debated the status of the law helps support the asseveration that Jesus could not have taken an unambiguously negative stance toward the law. Evidence is conspicuously absent for the view that Jesus deliberately challenged the Mosaic dispensation (which is not the same as acting to make that dispensation final).[31]

Sanders does grant that the dictum to a would-be disciple whose father had died, "Follow me, and leave the dead to bury their own dead" (Matt. 8:22 / /Luke 9:60), shows that "at least once Jesus was willing to say that following him superseded the requirements of piety and the Torah." Again, there is the matter of divorce (Matt. 5:31-32; Luke 16:18; cf. Matt. 19:3-9/ /Mark 10:2-12); the passages on that subject "are determined by the view that divorce leads to adultery." Nevertheless, Jesus does not here "directly defy the Mosaic law," for it is an accepted principle "that greater stringency than the law requires is not illegal." Thus, to accept Jesus' prohibition of divorce could not make one a transgressor of the law. The most we could say is that at this point the Mosaic dispensation is inadequate.[32] Such passages as these are probably best explained "by appealing to Jesus' expectation of the eschaton." Because he looked to a new age, he could view "the institutions of this age as not final. . . . He was not, however, a reformer. We find no criticism of the law which would allow us to speak of his opposing or rejecting it."[33]

Opposition and opponents.   In my view it is easy, even tempting, to overstate the place of "Jewish opposition" to Jesus as a historical personage or for that matter as Lord of the church. Indeed, I am not sure that the general category of "opposition" is all that vital to an objective and truthful understanding of Jesus. His mission and message were, after all, pervasively theocentric. Again, I tend to think that it is historically not the case that Jesus "came into fundamental conflict" with Judaism (cf. the citation from Sanders below)—this in vital, determining, and most pertinent contrast with his conflict with the Romans. The cruciality or lesson of the latter conflict may be said to lie in the ongoing struggle between Yahweh and Caesar, between the one God and all-destructive human idolatry. Historically speaking, I believe that James Charlesworth's concept "Jesus *within* Judaism" is infinitely more congruous than E. P. Sanders's implied dichotomy "Jesus *and* Judaism." Sanders is clearly of a different persuasion, however, as evidenced by his full and semiclimactic chapter

"Opposition and Opponents," and our first responsibility here is to chronicle his position. I will treat that position under four points.

(1) There follows part of Sanders's summary of what he has been arguing with special reference to the temple:

> Jesus did come into fundamental conflict with "Judaism"; that is, with views, opinions, and convictions that were probably shared by most. He made a threatening gesture, and added a threatening statement, against the Temple. He was doubtless seen as having attacked it. . . . [Not] just the priests, but most Jews, probably even those only marginally observant, would have been deeply offended. . . . [We] surely cannot think that a thrust against the Temple would have been offensive only to the priestly hierarchy. . . . The Temple was the pride and joy of Jewry, both at home and abroad. . . . The Temple was ordained by God, and any threat against it would have been deeply offensive.[34]

The above passage points to the appropriateness of the second part of the title of the present chapter of this book: Jesus as "rejected advocate of Israel's restoration."

(2) Sanders discerns three kinds of probable opponents of Jesus: the pious, the leaders, and the populace. But within the second group, the priestly aristocracy were "the prime movers behind Jesus' execution."[35]

(3) According to Sanders, a central and widely offensive aspect of Jesus' message was, as we have seen, the claim that sinners would have a place in the kingdom, and this without having "to make restitution and to indicate their repentance by offering sacrifice." Jesus' own association with "tax collectors and sinners" was probably offensive. He "was probably seen as having challenged the adequacy of the Mosaic covenant, not because there was some part which he explicitly opposed, but because he thought that its requirements could be waived for whose who accepted him." Jesus was displaying an egocentricity that "must have struck many of his contemporaries as impious." And "anyone even normally pious might have been offended at his saying that tax collectors and harlots would precede the righteous in the kingdom."[36]

(4) In earlier pages we have made extended reference to the alleged controversy between Jesus and the Pharisees. A few additional comments from Sanders's chapter "Opposition and Opponents" may here suffice: We know "of no substantial dispute about the law, nor of any substantial conflict with the Pharisees." The refrain, "scribes and Pharisees, hypocrites," and the saying in Matt. 23:23 "show that somebody accused the Pharisees of hypocrisy and legalism, but it was not, I think, Jesus. . . . [The] Jesus of Matt. 23:5-7, 23-26 is not the historical Jesus. He is one who objects to the Pharisees because they are not righteous enough, and he favors a higher righteousness according to the law, while not denying any of the law, even its minutiae. . . . " As Sanders makes clear, the attempt to place a "legalist Pharisaism" in conflict with Jesus reflects

an ideological-theological orientation or campaign that is insupportable by historical investigation and historical truth. "Did Jesus oppose self-righteousness at all? I think that he had his mind on other things than the interior religious attitudes of the righteous. . . . His message in general was about God and the kingdom, and it was not a critique of problems which develop within a religious community, such as self-righteousness. . . . [And] the opposition to him did not spring from his criticism of self-righteousness. Those who need texts on which to base criticism of religious hypocrisy and self-righteousness still have them. . . . [But such texts do not] serve to explain Jesus' conflict with Judaism."[37]

Jesus' execution.   As already implied, it is Sanders's basic conviction that "an internal conflict within Judaism" was "the principal cause of Jesus' death." This does not mean an acritical rendering of the Synoptic materials. For example, Sanders presents no less than seven difficulties with Jesus' "trial" and concludes that "the trial scene is unlikely on all counts." Again, any charge of "blasphemy" is highly unlikely. For that matter, Jesus' stance toward the wicked "does not linger in the Gospels as having had anything to do with his death." The "one point that will not go away is the attack (both by word and deed) against the Temple." But yet Sanders is perfectly assured that Jesus was executed by the Romans "for sedition or treason, as would-be king."[38] A line of thought that he rejects unreservedly is that Jesus intended to die for others. But he finds a "serious historical possibility" that Jesus died for his own "self-claim."[39]

At this juncture I shift temporarily to another of E. P. Sanders's writings. In his brief contribution to a recent symposium, "Who Killed Jesus? And Why?" Sanders fully acknowledges that the Gospels "have the intention of shifting responsibility from the Romans to the Jews,[40] and they go out of their way, especially Matthew and John, to make Pilate insist on Jesus' innocence, though he is coerced by the crowd, which is inspired by the chief priests, into executing Jesus." Nevertheless, Sanders finds two things wrong with the explanation that since Jesus "was executed by Rome as a rebel, he really was a rebel" and that "the Gospels try to obscure this fact in order to avoid Roman wrath in their own time": (1) The explanation "makes nonsense of the teaching material ascribed to Jesus and requires that most of it be attributed to subsequent Christian invention." I think that Sanders is being extreme here and, in fact, begs the question. For the extent to which Jesus' teachings actually involved him in conflicts with his religious compatriots remains very debatable territory and is continually at issue. Furthermore, in his work *Jesus and Judaism,* Sanders himself attests again and again to the continuity between Jesus and his followers. To give four among many possible examples: (a) That Jesus' followers "worked

within the framework of Jewish eschatological expectation is indisputable."
(Of course, not too many years afterward the Jesus movement was to be seized
by a spiritualization process.) (b) "The Pauline letters show us that the apostles
and brothers of the Lord (I Cor. 9:5) were acting as leaders of a Jewish eschatological movement." (c) "After his crucifixion Jesus' followers constituted
a sect or a semi-sectarian group within Judaism. There is every reason to
attribute to them the same degree of intentionality which we can attribute to
the ḥaberim and the Dead Sea community. Their program, as it emerges for
example in Paul's letters, was clear and straightforward, and it determined their
activities." In other words, they were not behaving like meek little lambs. (d)
After Jesus' death, his disciples fully "expected him to return to establish the
kingdom."[41]

(2) To Sanders, the explanation alluded to near the beginning of the previous paragraph "does not account for the fact that the disciples, after Jesus'
death, were not rounded up and killed."[42] In subsequent years they lived in
Jerusalem, "never troubled by the Romans, and on the whole protected by
them."[43] I think there are logical difficulties here. These difficulties are associated with the consideration that historical phenomena are so often amenable
to more than a single explanation. Again, as Sanders concedes elsewhere, "a
negative cannot be proved."[44] In the present case I suggest that the phenomenon at hand can be as readily accounted for by the proposition that the Romans were content *for a time* to have silenced the ringleader of a disruptive
and troublesome movement. (But the Roman persecution of Christians was not
long in coming. Sanders himself limits the period of nonpersecution to "the
next thirty years or so" after Jesus' execution.)[45]

Within a frame of reference of the "Jewish responsibility" for the Nazarene's death that Sanders postulates, he is left with two alternatives: to assume
essential *continuity* between the message and work of Jesus and his followers
or to advocate essential *discontinuity* between them. On the first possibility
(continuity) Sanders's historical claim that the Roman nonpersecution of Jesus'
followers demonstrates diminished or only partial Roman blame for the death
of Jesus does not make sense. For the Romans ought to have pursued the followers along with the ringleader. And there is an additional problem. Sanders
has earlier contended that the expectation among Jesus and the disciples that
the coming kingdom is *otherworldly* explains all the following facts: Jesus was
executed by the Romans, his followers were not pursued and killed, and subsequently the followers "did not expect a legion of heavenly warriors."[46] The
difficulty here is that the characterization of otherworldliness explains too
much. For if it was their otherworldliness that enabled the disciples to escape
persecution, the same should have applied to a proposedly otherworldly Jesus.

On the second possibility (discontinuity between Jesus and his disciples), Sanders's historical claim becomes no more than a truism. Naturally, the Romans would go after Jesus and him alone.

Lastly, Sanders may have undermined part of his own case through his (historically convincing) attestation that—as we have seen—Jesus did not stress either the necessity of national acts of repentance or the threat of a coming divine judgment. I suggest that this twofold negative datum may cut in two different directions. On the one hand, it could conceivably compound opposition among those Jews who were standing for the praxis of repentance (although I fail to see how such a state of affairs could bring about the killing of Jesus). On the other hand, Jesus' stance could serve to reduce or negate opposition to him, particularly within a conservative or quisling religious establishment that was tacitly united against any such possibility of overt repentance. Relevant as well is Sanders's *rejection* of any idea that Jesus had "gained truly massive support from the populace and . . . was executed because he posed a real threat to the Jerusalem leaders."[47]

The most formidable of Sanders's problems, shared with all interpreters who strive to fabricate "Jewish" complicity in the death of Jesus, is how to construct the pathway, which becomes absolutely obligatory, from "Jewish" attitudes and behavior to an exclusively Roman form of execution, the cross. (Thus, had Jesus "blasphemed"—he had not—the method of execution would have been stoning.) In one place in his conclusion—in the context of reviewing the temple episode—Sanders makes an astonishing admission the implications of which he may not realize: "*No one* could think that the wandering charismatic posed an actual threat to the Jewish government (centered around the high priest), and certainly not to the Roman Empire."[48] More broadly and of equal or greater formidableness: Insofar as Jesus was the apostle of a restored Israel, as Sanders claims for him, how can this factor be reconciled with the "Jewish" opposition that was ostensibly to mean Jesus' death? The fact of Jesus as a signal figure of positive Jewish restoration is much more coherent with Roman opposition than with Jewish opposition.

A way out of Sanders's historiographical predicament is the orientation, increasingly documented in biblical-historical scholarship, that Jesus' execution had little or nothing of substance to do with "the Jews" but was Roman business from start to finish. The historical tendentiousness of the Gospels is here given all due weight. In this view, the dialectic of continuity/discontinuity between Jesus and his compatriots loses any substantive necessity or decisiveness respecting actual moral-historical responsibility (*Strafbarkeit*, culpability) for his death. Distinctively, Jesus was a seditionary, a pretender king "of the Jews"—in obvious and complete discontinuity with his followers—and from the standpoint of the Roman overlords and occupation, he had to be put out of the way. In Hyam Maccoby's words, "Jesus was crucified by the Romans for the same reason that so many other Jews were crucified during the same period— because he was the leader of a messianic movement aiming at the liberation of the Jews from Roman rule."[49]

This way of reading the history is developed in chapter 5.

5

The Judaism
of Jesus, Champion
of Israel

This chapter comprises a review and analysis of certain of my own ruminations upon the historical Jesus. I shall do my best to link the discussion to the presentations in chapters 3 and 4.

Four comments may lay the groundwork of the exposition: (1) Contra Marcus J. Borg, I think we may question whether the most adequate interpretation of the Jesus of history is countercultural spiritualizer. (2) Contra E. P. Sanders, I believe we may question the rendering of Jesus as rejected prophet of Israel's restoration. (3) In the presence of the all-decisive eschatological question, I think I stand somewhere between Borg and Sanders. This is not to pretend that my view comprises a "synthesis" of and beyond the one scholar as "thesis" and the other scholar as "antithesis." Instead, all I mean is agreement that the eschatological dimension of Jesus' message and mission is central, yet further that this dimension is not (from Jesus' apparent standpoint) transhistorical but is instead this-worldly in a revolutionary sense. (4) I suggest that the most adequate way to encapsulate the message and mission of the historical Jesus is to identify him as a champion of his people Israel.[1]

GETTING READY FOR THE KINGDOM

Near the beginning of the Gospel of Mark, Jesus is cited: "The time is fulfilled, and the kingdom of God is at hand; repent and believe in the gospel" (1:14). This announcement and its accompanying demand by Jesus have often been deemed the core of his message. These early words ally the man from Nazareth with the Qumran or Essene (Dead Sea) sect and also with John the Baptist (Matt. 3:1-2; Luke 16:16),[2] and they awaken as well memories of the classical prophets of Israel.[3] Further, they plunge us right away into the political arena, since *kingdom* or *reign* is a thoroughly political concept.[4]

Jesus assures his hearers: "Truly, I say to you, there are some standing here who will not taste death before they see that the kingdom of God has come with power" (Mark 9:1; cf. Matt. 16:28; Luke 9:27). Peter, James, John, and Andrew are targets of a stern admonition: "Take heed, watch; for you do not know when the time will come. It is like a man going on a journey, when he leaves home and puts his servants in charge, each with his work, and commands the doorkeeper to be on the watch. Watch therefore—for you do not know when the master of the house will come, in the evening, or at midnight, or at cock-crow, or in the morning—lest he come suddenly and find you asleep. And what I say to you I say to all: Watch" (Mark 13:33-37; cf. Matt. 24:42-44). God is the master of the house. And Jesus instructs all twelve disciples to pray "like this":

> Our Father who art in heaven,
> Hallowed be thy name.
> Thy kingdom come,
> Thy will be done,
> On earth as it is in heaven. ...
>   (Matt. 6:9-10)

Of late, doubts have been raised respecting the authenticity of this "Lord's Prayer." Perhaps only the word *Father*—when rendered *Abba,* as in the Gospel of Luke—can be directly linked to Jesus.[5] But as a matter of fact, we already knew that the "Our Father" form of address is found in the Pharisee liturgy.[6]

Jesus calls for the cessation of worldly hostilities and contentiousness, for turning "the other cheek," and for the practice of unalloyed love. These demands are not so much motivated by what we would today call pacifism, or even by gentleness or sympathy (though Jesus does manifest great compassion; see, e.g., Mark 6:34), but overridingly by the importance of preparing for and gaining entrance to the kingdom that is surely coming. It is out of the question to treat literalistically the prescription to "turn the other cheek" (Matt. 5:39; Luke 6:29), any more than we could do so with a different and equally well-known set of demands upon would-be disciples, namely, "If any one comes to me and does not hate his own father and mother and wife and children and brothers and sisters, yes, and even his own life, he cannot be my disciple" (Luke 14:26).[7] Geza Vermes reminds us that the independent passion account in the Fourth Gospel portrays Jesus as himself performing the opposite of cheek-turning: "If I have spoken wrongly, bear witness to the wrong; but if I have spoken rightly, why do you strike me?" (John 18:23).[8]

In Matt. 5:43-45 the motivation to gain entrance to God's kingdom may be somewhat qualified; the goal behind love for enemies and persecutors becomes "that you may be sons [*sic*] of your Father who is in heaven." We have here a parallel to the Pharisee teaching that love is to be engaged in for its own sake, quite apart from hope of reward or compensation.[9] But I do not see any ultimate conflict between a loving preparation for entry into the kingdom and love on behalf of sonship. For as Jesus pronounces elsewhere, "Whoever seeks to gain his life will lose it, but whoever loses his life will preserve it" (Luke 17:33; cf. Luke 9:24; Matt. 10:39; 16:25; Mark 8:35). Admission to the kingdom of God, "the one and only aim that is worth pursuing," the pearl of great price (Matt. 13:45), is contingent upon an openness and humility like unto that of little children: "At that time the disciples came to Jesus, saying, 'Who is the greatest in the kingdom of heaven?' And calling to him a child, he put him in the midst of them, and said, 'Truly, I say to you, unless you turn and become like children, you will never enter the kingdom of heaven. Whoever humbles himself like this child, he is the greatest in the kingdom of heaven' " (Matt. 18:1-4). People who would get themselves ready to enter the kingdom have to do a complete about-face (*metanoia*); they have to show their backs to "this world" and turn instead to God, which means a complete change of heart, mind, and soul.[10]

For some time there has been widespread agreement that the kingdom of God is the thematic core of Jesus' praxis.[11] For James H. Charlesworth, Jesus "was obsessed with the need to proclaim to all Israel the approaching nearness and importance of God's Kingdom." Donald J. Goergen writes, "The reign of God was central to the consciousness, ministry, preaching and teaching of Jesus. . . . There is no denying the centrality of God's reign as the prominent element in the authentic sayings of Jesus, in the parables, in the Beatitudes and in the prayer he taught."[12] In recent years, however, significant questioning has been raised respecting that theme as reputedly *the* key to or center of Jesus' teaching. Thus, Marcus J. Borg comments that North American historical-Jesus scholars *as a consensus* no longer tend to identify their man as an apocalypticist messenger of the imminent end of the world. In this connection, the "coming Son of Man" sayings are increasingly understood as nonauthentic, i.e., as not from Jesus. Together with this, the centrality given to the eschatological kingdom of God "as the primary motif of Jesus' message" is challenged. More positively put, Borg finds that as a charismatic who was also sage, prophet, and renewal-movement founder, "Jesus sought a transformation in the historical shape and direction of his *social world*," calling his hearers "to ground their lives in the Spirit of God, rather than in the securities and identities offered by culture." For although Jesus "did speak of a last judgment, there is no reason to believe that he thought it was imminent. Instead, like the predestruction prophets before him, the crisis he announced was the threat of historical crisis for his society." And to "follow after" Jesus is "to take seriously what he took seriously: life in the Spirit, and life in history." Indeed, what Jesus was like "provides the content of what following him means."[13]

I do not find that the conflict between the argumentation of Borg et al. and earlier understandings is essential or fateful. For one thing, the concept *eschatological* has been, as Borg himself indicates, employed variously— sometimes "as a nuanced synonym for 'decisive,' or as 'world-shattering,' or to point to the *telos* of history entering history but not in such a way as to end history."[14] Again, within the eschatological thinking of Jesus' time the advent of the kingdom of God did not have to mean a catastrophic end to all things earthly; it could instead refer to a revolutionary transformation of the world itself, whereby the righteous and beneficent will of God comes to reign. We cannot forget that the Lord's Prayer asks that God's kingdom come and his will be done *on earth* just as is already the case in heaven. Donald J. Goergen finds that Jesus' eschatology "did not frame itself in terms of *either* this world *or* another world but rather that God's future for God's people and Israel's future involved *both* this world *and* another world that would co-exist with greater harmony. *God would now reign on earth,* and this reign was about to begin. Jesus' eschatological consciousness was essentially a God-consciousness, that of a prophet to Israel."[15]

My own christological interpretation is not at substantive odds with this latest understanding, as I shall make plain. I do, however, differ with Professor Borg at the twin points of Jesus' methods and strategies, including the allegation that Jesus founded a "peace party within Palestine."[16] Furthermore, Borg gives voice to a significant complication that cannot be passed over: It is now "commonplace to locate the origin of the church's eschatological expectation in the Easter event. It was the conviction that Jesus had been raised from the dead (for resurrection was an event associated with the end of time) that led some in the early church to believe that they were living in the 'end times.' "[17] While I think that to remove the imminent kingdom of God from a central place in the Nazarene's (preresurrection) message is extreme, it is yet incumbent upon me to come back to the question of Jesus' resurrection (cf. chap. 11 of this book). On the other hand, Borg's findings are coherent with many known facts: Jesus' magnificent obsession in behalf of the Torah of God; his critical place within Pharisee life and conviction;[18] his calling as an itinerant Galilean *hasid*; his charismatic-prophetic role (inclusive of his "feminism," which, as Leonard Swidler shows, is strictly assimilable to moral implications and lessons within the Jewish prophetic tradition);[19] Jesus' protorabbinic vocation (as emphasized by Phillip Sigal, Clark M. Williamson, et al.);[20] and his

God-wrought resurrection as integrally commensurate with one *Tendenz* within Jewish witness and spirituality.

To return to the specific issue of the kingdom of God: Jesus the peripatetic *hasid* is apparently convinced that in certain ways that kingdom is already here.[21] This is made evident in connection with some of his "mighty works," as his miracles are characterized (Mark 6:1-2; Matt. 13:54; Luke 19:37). Thus, upon healing "a blind and dumb demoniac," Jesus says, "if it is by the Spirit of God that I cast out demons, then the kingdom of God has come upon you" (Matt. 12:22, 28). Again, after healing ten lepers Jesus declares, according to Luke, "the kingdom of God is in the midst of you" (17:11-21). Along with his attacks upon Satan and with his nature wonders, Jesus' healings are treated as at once, in Michael Grant's phrasing, "symbols and events in the dawning of the kingdom of God"—all of which makes noteworthy and even strange the fact that Jesus does not always appear to comprehend his "mighty works" and indeed that, as A. E. Harvey expresses it, the Synoptics "record a very striking reserve on the part of Jesus towards his own miracles." Thus, there was a certain woman "who had had a flow of blood for twelve years, and who had suffered much under many physicians, and had spent all that she had, and was no better but rather grew worse." She resolved that if she could but touch Jesus' garments, she would be made well.[22] And by that very act, she *was* made well! "Jesus, perceiving in himself that power had gone forth from him, immediately turned about in the crowd, and said, 'Who touched my garments?' " (Mark 5:25-30; cf. Luke 8:43-46). Upon occasion neither do Jesus' disciples appear to understand everything that is going on (Mark 8:17-21). When John the Baptist asks whether Jesus is "he who is to come," however, the answer that is forthcoming is resolute: "Go and tell John what you hear and see: the blind receive their sight and the lame walk, lepers are cleansed and the deaf hear, and the dead are raised up, and the poor have good news preached to them" (Matt. 11:2-5). Even Borg agrees that these words seem to refer to more than healings; Jesus' "use of them identifies his time as a time of deliverance."[23]

In one place Matthew fittingly ties together three elements: Jesus' teaching of Judaism, his proclamation of the kingdom, and his healings. He goes "about all the cities and villages, teaching in their synagogues and preaching the gospel of the kingdom and healing every disease and every infirmity. When he saw the crowds, he had compassion for them, because they were harassed and helpless, like sheep without a shepherd" (Matt. 9:35-36).[24] When these several elements are combined with John the Baptist's messianic question, we are met by a fundamental convergence, a singular blend: teaching—healing—a measure of messianic expectation—compassion—signs (anticipations) of the kingdom of God—and with it all a marked reserve.

The parables of Jesus comprise an additional vehicle for his representation of the kingdom of God.[25] Many of them speak for themselves. To reproduce several examples, as assembled by Matthew:

> The kingdom of heaven is like a grain of mustard seed which a man took and sowed in his field; it is the smallest of all seeds, but when it has grown it is the greatest of shrubs and becomes a tree, so that the birds of the air come and make nests in its branches.
>
> ... The kingdom of heaven is like leaven which a woman took and hid in three measures of flour, till it was all leavened.
>
> The kingdom of heaven is like treasure hidden in a field, which a man found and covered up; then in his joy he goes and sells all that he has and buys that field.
>
> Again, the kingdom of heaven is like a merchant in search of fine pearls, who, on finding one pearl of great value, went and sold all that he had and bought it.
>
> Again, the kingdom of heaven is like a net which was thrown into the sea and gathered fish of every kind; when it was full, men drew it ashore and sat down and sorted the good into vessels but threw away the bad. So it will be at the close of the age. The angels will come out and separate the evil from the righteous, and throw them into the furnace of fire; there men will weep and gnash their teeth. (Matt. 13:31-33, 44-50)

Finally, a poignant relation obtains between people who are suffering and the kingdom of God. Vermes writes, "The prophets spoke on behalf of the honest poor, and defended the widows and the fatherless, those oppressed and exploited by the wicked, rich and powerful. Jesus went farther. In addition to proclaiming these blessed, he actually took his stand among the pariahs of his world, those despised by the respectable. Sinners were his table-companions and the ostracised tax-collectors and prostitutes his friends."[26] (We know that the Pharisees champion the cause of the oppressed.) Jesus proclaims,

> Blessed are you poor, for yours is the kingdom of God.
> Blessed are you that hunger now, for you shall be satisfied.
> Blessed are you that weep now, for you shall laugh.
> Blessed are you when men hate you, and when they exclude you and revile
>   you, and cast out your name as evil, on account of the Son of man! Rejoice
>   in that day, and leap for joy, for behold, your reward is great in heaven; for so
>   their fathers did to the prophets.
> But woe to you that are rich, for you have received your consolation.
> Woe to you that are full now, for you shall hunger.
> Woe to you that laugh now, for you shall mourn and weep.
> Woe to you, when all men speak well of you, for so their fathers did to the false
>   prophets.
>
> (Luke 6:20-26)[27]

"When God rules on earth there will be neither hunger nor tears."[28] Michael Grant brings together the parables, the praxis of "mighty works," the present/future of the downtrodden and the suffering, and the sense of crisis and urgency that is so "acute and pressing":

> It is imperative for all men and women to define their position, *both* because of what is happening now *and* because of what is going to happen shortly. The teaching of Jesus dwells on both these aspects at length. First, the present dawning: the strong man is disarmed, the forces of evil are in retreat, the physician comes to the sick, the lepers are cleansed, the great debt is wiped out, the lost sheep is brought home, the door of the father's house stands open, the poor and the beggars are summoned to the banquet, a master pays full wages to a man who does not deserve it, a great joy fills all hearts. The hour of fulfillment has come. It has come, or rather it has *begun* to come: its full realization still lies in the future, and this, too, is equally stressed in Jesus' utterances. That is the reason for all this insistence upon alertness: do not be caught asleep; be ready to render your account. The Kingdom is with us, but not all of it is with us yet. Himself on the battlefield, Jesus struck Satan down and "watched how he fell like lightning from the sky." Nevertheless, the *final* battle still remains to be fought.[29]

We are here driven into a severe crisis of life and thought. This crisis is born out of the fact that, on the basis of the record, Jesus' message appears, ultimately, to be set upon a kind of collision course with his mission. For the "cataclysmic eruption of God into history" never occurs.[30] A *kind* of battle is going to take place all right—between Jesus and his Roman foes—but few are they who will witness it or even know it is transpiring. Our crisis is caused by "a historical paradox that taxes belief. On the one hand, when it comes to the imminent arrival of the kingdom of God, the Jesus of the oldest recoverable layers of the Apostolic Writings is so aggressive, so intolerant, so assured, even oracular. On the other hand, when it comes to his own place (as potential Messiah) in God's future, he is so nonbelligerent, so reticent, so diffident, even at times psychically withdrawn."[31]

How are we to live with this incongruity, this conflict?

THE KINGDOM AND THE KING

If we are effectively to confront the recorded, life-and-death conflict between Jesus' aggressiveness and his reticence we have little choice but to take into account the silences (intended? unintended?) of the Apostolic Writings—not to mention all the fabrications and all the wondrously or at least obstinately authentic materials therein—since, as I shall delineate, much of the real story is cloaked within those silences. I know that "arguments from silence" can be arbitrary and even perilous. But in this instance, what is the alternative?

One of our several difficulties is that, according to the available record, Jesus speaks so sparingly of himself. But there are problems more serious than this—at least three in number. First, implicitly as well as explicitly, the Apostolic Writings minimize the stark truth that the *Eretz Yisrael* (Land of Israel) of the time is under tyrannical foreign occupation, a tyranny that the Jewish people are, in fact, greatly resisting and a situation that is productive of much popular unrest. The Jewish resistance to Roman oppression, centering in Jerusalem and Judea, extends across all segments of society. The Pharisees are often in the forefront, but the priesthood is involved as well. There are conditions of constant crisis. Thousands are slaughtered.[32] Jesus' cross is one of hundreds, perhaps thousands. Second is the marked tendentiousness of the Apostolic Writings, especially in the matter of Jesus' trial and death.[33] The Gospels were put together in their present form a full generation and more after the death of Jesus. They reflect apologetic interests and missionary designs vis-à-vis the people and even sometimes the leaders of the Roman Empire. A serious consequence of this situation is that the Gospels underplay the conflict that is raging between Rome and the people of Jesus, and they overplay and even distort contentions between the nascent church and the Jewish community. Third and most serious of all, the accounts of Jesus' last days contain historical falsehoods. The Christian evangelists, with their great concern to foster good relations with the Romans, do their best to establish the Jewish (*sic*) "rejection" of Jesus and to set "the Jews" and their leaders against Jesus. Joel Carmichael is probably right that the Gospel writers *intend* to blame "the Jews."[34] The efforts in the Apostolic Writings to shift culpability from the Romans to "the Jews" are held to be unhistorical within modern scholarship.[35]

I am going to propose a historical-phenomenological hypothesis. As background for this I reproduce a negative finding of Geza Vermes: "There is little evidence in the Gospels of a kingdom of God to be established by force. There was no plan for Jesus to reconquer Jerusalem, or any indication that he intended to challenge the power even of Herod, let alone that of the emperor of Rome." While this finding correctly reflects the written record,[36] it also helps to point up our problem. With respect to Jesus' attitude to the use of force, the Synoptic tradition is not conclusive either way; the recorded praxis appears to condone both "pacifism" and "nonpacifism."[37] (But cf. Pawlikowski: The data in the Apostolic Writings do not produce sufficient evidence for any absolute rejection of violence "in the quest for justice.")[38] To concentrate upon the question of whether Jesus' focus is upon *human* violence or *human* nonviolence does not take us very far. For his primary concern appears to lie elsewhere: with God's active intervention in history. Vermes's negative finding is thus more descriptive of what was to be the written (= literary) fate of Jesus' story than it is of Jesus' history qua history. For the nagging question does not let us go: *How is it that Jesus comes to be executed?* This question yet persists even after careful analyses by such scholars as Borg, Sanders, and Charlesworth. I remain not quite convinced by their arguments and conjectures. In this connection, no justification is forthcoming for rejecting the "strict definition of 'Messiah' as a valorous, holy, just and mighty Davidic king of the end of time."[39] Note that the "religious" domain and the "political" domain here live together.

This is my hypothesis: For Jesus, during the months or days when in his spiritual, wracking solitude he is striving to face up to the nature and demands of his own calling, "kingdom of God" somehow comes to converge upon "King Messiah," and "King Messiah" somehow comes to converge upon "kingdom of God." (The best that we can do respecting Jesus—as with any figure of the past—is to suggest hypotheses. We cannot provide unalloyed "truths" or unalloyed "facts." A given historical hypothesis is but one way, among other contending ways, of accounting for certain events or phenomena. Whenever a particular hypothesis appears capable of explaining a gestalt of events, it becomes worthy of consideration. Very often, two or more hypotheses will compete with each other and even manage to survive side by side.)

My hypothesis may be developed with the aid of two considerations.

(1) The hypothesis is not unsupported by Mark, which remains in all probability the earliest of the Gospels.[40] For all his self-doubt, the Jesus of that Gospel at least succeeds in being self-assertive enough to conjoin the initiating of God's kingdom with his own personal embrace of the messianic challenge. This state of affairs helps to account for the fact that, as the end draws near, the Galilean does not deny the allegation of messiahship (Mark 15:2-5; Matt. 27:11-14; Luke 23:3). Indeed, before the high priest—though this episode has been questioned—he replies to the official's query of whether he is the Christ with a firm "I am," and he then immediately ties this answer to divine intervention: "and you will see the Son of man seated at the right hand of Power, and coming with the clouds of heaven" (Mark 14:61-62; cf. Matt. 26:63-64).[41] Much more important, it is strictly in his identification as "King of the Jews" that Jesus will die. In a real sense he is "asking for it."[42] All the Synoptic Gospels testify to this as a truth of history: "And the inscription of the charge against him read, 'The King of the Jews' " (Mark 15:26; also Matt. 27:37; Luke 23:38). Even the writer of the Fourth Gospel, for all his spiritualizing and anti-Jewish biases, cannot change this fact of history: "Pilate also wrote a title and put it on the cross; it read, 'Jesus of Nazareth, the King of the Jews.' " The succeeding Johannine verses even support Jesus' own acceptance of that identification, though such is not their immediate intention: The chief priests "said to Pilate, 'Do not write "The King of the Jews," but, "This man said I am King of the Jews." ' Pilate answered, 'What I have written I have written' " (John 19:19, 21-22).

In the matter of the *Aktion* of Jesus' death various Christologists speak with one voice: "The most certain fact about the historical Jesus is his execution as a political rebel" (Borg). "Jesus was executed by the Romans as would-be 'king of the Jews' " (Sanders). "Jesus was crucified by the Romans, on charges that he was a political insurrectionist" (Charlesworth). Jesus was put to death by the Romans as a political rebel (Fredriksen).[43]

It appears out of the question to hold that Jesus is never forced to confront, as a life-and-death question, his own relation to the messianic office. It is equally gratuitous to make him into some kind of dupe who has the kingly office foisted upon him. *There has to be some explanation of why Jesus has not fled from his Roman persecutors, as he doubtless could have done in earlier days.* Here we may especially ponder two things: the Galilean's repeated preaching of the imminent intervention of God (the one telling explanation we have for Jesus' refusal or failure to flee); and the socially authoritative tradition that there can be no messianic fulfillment as long as the people of God remain under oppression.

Jesus' gathering certainties about the coming kingdom will be contradicted by events—as per (2) below—but his uncertainties about the Messiahship will have two futures that are opposite to each other: the wholly understandable *nonacceptance* by most of the very people who come to know of the messianic claim he finally manages to make; and the historically momentous, revisionist *acceptance* of that claim by the primitive Christian community. The heavy price the church will come to pay for receiving Jesus as its Lord is the categorical transformation of the Messiahship into something "spiritual" and "individual," something not of this (political) world. The Messiah will be transmogrified into a "religious" figure. In this connection, the ostensibly nonconsequential translation of the Hebrew word *Mashiach* (Messiah, anointed one) into its Greek equivalent *Christos* (Christ) conveys, in fact, a world of difference, for in this act is symbolized a transmigration from the Jewish world to the Gentile world. Jesus is not the Messiah of the Jews, but he is the Christ of the church.[44] As Paul M. van Buren points out, Jesus could not have been the Messiah of Israel. Israel's Messiah was to be marked and identified "as the inaugurator of the Messianic age. The Messianic age, in turn, is marked by radical historical transformation." (In a word for today, van Buren goes farther: In the face of the destroyed Jewish children of the *Shoah,* "dare any Christian say that Jesus was or is the Messiah?")[45]

There is no other way for Jesus to become "Messiah" to the church than by his not being the anticipated Messiah of Israel—or, in other words, by the nonimplementation of the kingdom of God. No kingdom, no Messiah; no Messiah, no kingdom. All this has a consequence that is weighty: In and through the very nonarrival of the kingdom, the nagging reticence of Jesus as King Messiah is granted some degree of exculpation. But here is a final (conjectural) paradox: The really unacceptable combination would have been, not Jesus' certainty of the kingdom and his uncertainty as King Messiah, but instead his certainty of the kingdom and his (potential) self-assurance as Messiah. "Had the latter combination proved to be the actualized one, the factual nonrealization of the kingdom would have shown Jesus to be not merely a failed Messiah but also a false one—in everyone's eyes. His diffidence toward the Messianic office goes some way to excuse, so to speak, his pretension respecting the kingdom. But even the latter pretension is qualified, and perhaps made somewhat forgivable, by his constant directing of people's hearts and minds away from himself to fix upon the acts of God."[46]

(2) We have to live—and die—with the fact that the whole foundation-hope of Jesus turns out to be an illusion. Correspondingly, he is to be eliminated. The failure is his, yet, for him, it is God's failure as well.

In order to make concrete the failure shared by son and Father, we have to finish out, as positively as we can, the drama of Jesus' life and fate. The factor that is the most crucial here is also the most rudimentary: Jesus is other than just one more apocalypticist. For instance, while he and the apostle Paul equally err in their imminent-eschatological expectations, Jesus' mistake is infinitely more egregious. For in contrast to Paul, the Nazarene comes to presume, however gradually and haltingly, an isochronism between his own person/history and the about-to-be-realized eschatology of his Father's kingdom. This state of affairs can be elucidated in two ways, the one philological-historical and the other "political"-historical.

(a) Can we perhaps contribute something to veracity of language vis-à-vis the relation between Jesus' person and the hoped-for intervention of God?

By having Jesus solicit "faith in himself" in the process of introducing the divine kingdom, Michael Grant overweights the scales on the one side. According to Grant, Jesus believes "that the actual inauguration of God's kingdom had been placed in his own hands." It is "by his agency" that the kingdom has "already started happening."[47] Grant is not correct. He greatly exaggerates the actual place of Jesus in the coming of the *eschaton—from Jesus' own point of view*. For Jesus is not some sovereign, self-appointed agent provocateur—however much his message of the imminent kingdom of God is "indissolubly bound up with the liberation of Israel."[48] The fact is that Jesus has no interest in collecting "faith in himself"; he only demands/hopes for faith in his Father, who is the sole instigator of the kingdom and sole liberator of his people. As we have earlier cited: "Fear not, little flock, for it is your Father's good pleasure to give you the kingdom" (Luke 12:32). Would-be participants in the kingdom are to pray only to the Father—"Thy kingdom come"—as in all urgency they prepare themselves for the day: "Let your loins be girded and your lamps burning" (Luke 12:35).

Just here, however, we must note how tempting it is to overweight the scales on the other side, in a way that robs Jesus' vocation of its singularity. True, the *Aktion* that takes place in between the lines of the Synoptic Gospels extends to Jesus' entirely human predicament as he sweats out what he is to do next. But his behavior is of exactly the kind we should expect from someone who is being specially used by God. To reduce Jesus to just one of many representatives or spokespersons of God's kingdom is to deprive the actual relationship of its authenticity, indeed of its splendor. For among many possible sons of God, this son of God is uniquely chosen (or humanly put, comes to believe himself uniquely chosen), if not actually to usher in God's reign, at least to announce its coming, to risk everything by virtue of his Father's believed promise, *and to stake his life upon the about-to-be-established kingdom*—yet never apart from a hoped-for interposition of the revived political independence and integrity of his people. This life-and-death state of mind and heart—the inner aspect of objective-historical truth—carries us over into the "political"-historical dimension. We must first ask, however, what philological conclusion is suggested by the above weighing upon the scales?

We have noted that among the titles of Jesus, *Son of God* may reflect his special filial consciousness. The point is that this son is distinguished from other sons. (I continue to speak historically.) For at a number of places in the record a heavenly voice calls Jesus "my *beloved* Son" (Mark 1:11; 9:7; Matt. 3:17; 17:5; Luke 3:22; cf. 2 Pet. 1:17).[49] Until Jesus' final disillusionment —upon the cross he no longer calls God "Father" but *Eloi,* "my God" (Mark 15:34)—he had evidently come to some such self-understanding in relation to God. Most probably, he had come to look upon himself as the decisive *human occasion* of the now-burgeoning reign of God, the special instrument through whom God is about to act eschatologically. But since he "turned out to be wrong,"[50] and the kingdom never came off, it is necessary to modify his self-understanding as "beloved" of God—otherwise there is a lack of historical explanation, completeness, and accuracy, and there are planted the seeds of theological error and even heresy. In his presumed role of "beloved Son" Jesus is simply thwarted. In different language—to be more conclusive respecting an earlier point—he is a failed Messiah. He is *not* a false Messiah—never once does he betray the messianic imperative—but he is a woefully mistaken Messiah.

(b) As in the question of philology, the "political"-historical question may be approached through calling attention to extreme positions. But first a word of explanation is in order upon the use of quotation marks in the wording "political"-historical. This usage is to caution us that historical expositions dealing with primitive Christian times have to respect the truth that in those days no hard-and-fast division obtained between politics and religion or between politics and other dimensions of culture (as against the dominating practice in the West today). With respect to the days of Jesus, the category *political* must simply stand for collective human life as such. Modern, sophisticated understandings of the kingdom of God that sharply differentiate worldly political-military-material affairs from otherworldly nonpolitical-pacifist-spiritual realities would not be possible in first-century Palestine. The kingdom of God means God's reign (*basileia*) over the totality of life and nature. There is a notable tendency in the Gospels to depoliticize the life of Jesus;[51] this compounds the difficulty of the historian's task. A failure to be aware of such depoliticization may help explain Martin Hengel's inability to comprehend the reasons for Jesus' death at the hands of the Romans. Following Rudolf Bultmann, Hengel tries to account for Jesus' execution by saying that the Nazarene's activity was *misunderstood* "as something political."[52] But John H. Yoder points out that "the kingdom of God is a social order and not a hidden one."[53] Yet were it then declared that *social* is the right concept, we should have to respond that such a substitution for *political* only supports, perhaps inadvertently, a religious ideology that wrongly subtracts from the praxis of Jesus, or even obliterates, the interests of political power and liberation.

Two extreme interpretations offer themselves; both are reductionist. According to the one view, Jesus is, in effect, made over into a purely soldierly figure, a first-century Che Guevara, a guerrilla fighter, a revolutionary soldier of (his own) fortune, who dreams that he and a heavenly army that is (supposedly) gathering somewhere will dispatch the Roman oppressor and substitute a reign of justice and freedom. "Power to the people!" The fatal difficulty in this view is Jesus' unyielding theocentrism. There is just no way to remove the divinely apocalyptic element from his praxis, with special reference to his struggle against Rome. In this connection, a revealing rhetorical query is voiced by Jesus, who, upon being captured by certain opponents, says to a follower who has just been putting his sword to use, "Do you think that I cannot appeal to my Father, and he will at once send me more than twelve legions of angels?" (Matt. 26:53). Such an eventuality presupposes a categorical certainty of divine intervention.

Across the Christian centuries a second, different form of reductionism has been put forward repeatedly: Jesus is transmuted into a purely "religious" leader, a wholly nonpolitical and even antipolitical figure. Accordingly, he is allowed no interest whatever in the Roman overlordship and the "worldly" fortunes of his people. His "kingship is not of this world" (John 18:36). This second case of reductionism is refuted, like the first, by authentic scriptural passages and available historical data. To transform Jesus' struggle into something called "pure spirituality" is to betray that struggle. Any such "religious" hypothesis is negated by Jesus himself as pretender to the throne of David, the one who comes to read the advent of God's kingdom through apocalyptic glasses (thus refuting preveniently the notion of John Riches that Jesus rules out the "militaristic" connotations of the kingdom).[54]

I suggest that Jesus' actual "political" destiny moves or belongs somewhere between the two above forms of reductionism. The very label *reductionism* conveys to us that neither extreme is totally incorrect. To maintain that Jesus is *only* such-and-such goes too far. But to conclude that he is this *and also* something more may point the way to the truth. Thus, Jesus cannot be just a soldierly figure or resistance fighter, not because he is not at all a soldierly figure or resistance fighter, but because his whole commitment is to the realization of the kingdom of God, which is greater than and the transformation of every earthly or soldierly kingdom. In the same way, Jesus cannot be just a religious figure, not because he is not at all a religious figure, but because he is devoted to the coming of the reign of God *upon earth*, which means anything but a purely "heavenly" or "spiritual" affair. *Either to politicize or to religionize Jesus is to give offense to him.* That he is dedicated to God's kingdom means that he is not a politician in today's usage of that word. But in the last reckoning Jesus *is* a politician, or he finally becomes one, viz., he is a man who concerns himself with the total welfare and power of his people, and in the end he gives his life for their sake. S. G. F. Brandon interprets Jesus' counsel, "Render to Caesar the things that are Caesar's and to God the things that are God's" (Mark 12:17; cf. Luke 20:25), to mean, "Let Caesar go back to Rome where he belongs, and leave God's land to the people of God."[55] In this interpretation, Jesus forbids payments of tribute to Rome (as Luke 23:2 bears out).

As Joel Carmichael writes,

> The only way to make the career of Jesus comprehensible is to see its organic linkage to the simmering mutiny that had gripped Palestine for generations. Jesus' occupation of the Temple, his turning over of the money-changers' tables, his "preaching" in the Temple for days, the charge of King of the Jews, his execution by means of the Roman sentence of crucifixion, reserved for the vilest criminals and for political insurrectionists, were all part and parcel of a political upheaval against the Romans that while insignificant, apparently, compared with the later explosions in 66 and 132, was important enough to make its mark.

That mark was Christianity, a faith that was to profit immeasurably from Rome's defeat of the Jewish people in c.e. 70.[56]

There is strong evidence, as Brandon and others argue, that Jesus actively supported the cause of independence for his people.[57]

The historical analyst has little choice but to do some reading between the lines of the Gospels. Yet it would seem that an equal or even greater burden of proof lies with the skeptic or dissenter, who as someone no different from the rest of us must somehow account for at least two stubborn, inseparable historical facts: Jesus' eventual death in the office of "King of the Jews"; and Jesus' tireless insistence that the divine/kingly power of God is about to establish itself in massive, world-determining form.

The pioneering contribution of S. G. F. Brandon has sometimes been cited as maintaining that Jesus was a Zealot. Brandon contends the virtual opposite of this, concluding that in all probability Jesus was *not* a Zealot (even if as many as half of his twelve disciples may have come from that element).[58] "The Zealots were the militant activist wing of the Pharisee party, sharing all religious viewpoints with their fellow-Pharisees and differing from the majority . . . only on the question of the timing of active resistance against the Romans. . . . [From] first to last, the Resistance against Rome came from the Pharisee party." We have already emphasized Jesus' place within Pharisee life and conviction. Despite their yearning for liberation from the Romans, however, the Zealots had evidently surrendered belief in the Messiah.[59] As things were to turn out, this last is clearly what separates Jesus from the Zealots, rather than the issue of rebellion against Rome. Evidently Jesus came to the conviction—held also by the Zealots—that God would go to his people's aid against the foreign enemy. (This helps account for the consideration that superior Roman military might did not seem to deter Jewish rebellion, including Jesus' behavior.) But at the same time the Zealots did not believe that God would come to the rescue of his people unless they did their part in fighting for their deliverance.[60] The really significant factor, from the standpoint of the history of Jesus, is that his special version of apocalypticism and his latter-day messianic self-acceptance closely correspond to the two all-decisive elements just mentioned: the required intervention of God, and the required action of human beings.

John T. Townsend observes that the oldest extant Christian literature (the Pauline correspondence) substantiates the finding that Jesus is disposed of by the Romans as a political rebel. Having proclaimed himself King of the Jews, Townsend goes on, Jesus has been endeavoring to free his people and *Eretz Yisrael* from the foreign occupiers. And the picture in the Gospels matches closely what we learn from Paul.[61] Somewhere along the way, our own hypothesis continues, Jesus must have persuaded himself that in the world after the Fall the only responsible way to battle the collective suffering of the people of God, a suffering made unavoidable by powerlessness, is via the weight and authority of physical/political power. Jesus must have convinced himself that the idolatrous principalities and powers of this world have to be fought, not just with the sword of the spirit (cf. Zech. 4:6), but with real swords, in the prayerful expectation of corresponding intrusion "by the hand of God."[62]

Jesus of Nazareth gave himself to the historicization of the eschatological hope of the liberation of the people of God from the yoke of the nations; this is the vital (= eschatological) finding to which we are drawn. Accordingly, Jesus effectively identifies himself "with his people's cause against the government of heathen," yet strictly from the vantage point of "an uncompromising emphasis upon the sovereignty of Yahweh." If Jesus is King of the Jews, it is the Father, and only the Father, who can bring and is bringing his kingdom to earth. The very affirmation of King Messiah, however, is in itself a world-changing, revolutionary act. For its introduction means that *in principle,* i.e., even apart from its "worldly [cosmic] success" (or for that matter its "worldly [cosmic] failure"), the foreign occupation of *Eretz Yisrael,* the Land of Israel and therefore the Land of God—for Israel is the one who strives with God (Gen. 32:28)—is brought to its end, to its *eschaton (finis/telos;* finish/goal). Within this affirmation, as in his particular version of apocalypticism, Jesus lives in the line of the sectaries of Qumran, as well as of the Pharisees, both of which groupings envision a final, real-life battle with the hated Romans, leading to the latter's defeat and the establishing of the kingdom of God upon earth.[63] *But Jesus is a thoroughgoing presentist.* The time for action is *now,* this moment. Jesus is to carry out his part in and through the claim (as "beloved Son" of God) to the throne of David. And God is to do God's part (so Jesus is convinced, or, better, fervently hopes) through the judging yet grace-full descent of God's reign. Has not Jesus' Father *already* made clear the promises of his imminent coming? Are not the demons *already* being cast out and individual children of God *already* being healed of their maladies?[64]

Relentlessly, the drama moves to its denouement. All the roads of culpability lead to Rome. This miracle-working prophet, lord of his band of followers, Messiah of Israel, Galilean *hasid,* "beloved Son" of God in the establishing of the kingdom, and apocalypticist now fully become an activist figure—this man is to be found guilty as a seditionary.[65] And guilty he is—as charged. (Within the uninterpreted, bare Gospel explanation, Jesus is innocent of sedition and is put to death in consequence of a trumped-up charge brought by Jewish leaders. To mention this datum is not to agree that the Apostolic Writings do not support our historical hypothesis. They do support it, once they are subjected to careful analysis.) There is no way to reconcile the absolute claims of the City of God and the idolatrous claims of the city of humankind. It will be remembered that when, according to Mark, Jesus is asked which commandment is "first of all," he answers with the great antipolytheist *Sh'ma* of Judaism, "Hear, O Israel: The Lord our God, the Lord is one; and you shall love the Lord your God with all your heart, and with all your soul, and with all your mind, and with all your strength" (12:29-30). And now, as Jesus draws near to Jerusalem, the city of David, the "multitude of the disciples" cries out, "Blessed is the King who comes in the name of the Lord! Peace in heaven and glory to the highest!" (Luke 19:37-38). Down almost to the very end, the holy man assures his friends (at the "last supper"), "I shall not drink again of the fruit of the vine until that day when I drink it new in the kingdom of God" (Mark 14:25). According to Luke, after the meal Jesus issues an order to the disciples to see to it that they are armed before proceeding on to Gethsemane: "And let him who has no sword sell his mantle and buy one" (22:36). Brandon suggests that Mark may have "deemed it politic" to suppress this event. It may be asked why so many studies of Jesus (not excluding those of Borg and Sanders) pass over this revealing passage. But significantly, every one of the Gospels records that in Gethsemane the arrest of Jesus is met by armed resistance (Mark 14:47; Matt. 26:51; Luke 22:38, 49-50; John 18:10-11).[66] That the spiritualizing Gospel of John does not exclude itself here is most noteworthy of all.

Luke also preserves the fateful charges that are entered against Jesus: "We found this man perverting our nation, and forbidding us to give tribute to Caesar, and saying that he himself is Christ a king" (23:2). The facts involved, fully allowing for Gospel distortions respecting responsibility for Jesus' death, are listed herewith: "Every item in this indictment was true. Jesus *was* 'perverting the nation,' in the sense of turning them away from allegiance to Rome. He *was* 'forbidding to give tribute to Caesar.' He *was* saying that he himself was 'Christ, a King.' The charge was subversion and rebellion, not blasphemy."[67]

I am not convinced that E. P. Sanders's explanation of Jesus' death meets the question of why the Nazarene should be executed as a seditionary. Allied difficulties obtain in the attempt to make the cause of Jesus' death something "religious." Among many similar Christian efforts, we have Jürgen Moltmann's endeavor to turn Jesus into a "blasphemer," guilty of the blasphemy of self-deification and of placing himself "above" God's "Law."[68] This accounting does not stand. Moltmann's attempt cannot be dissociated from the centuries-old effort within the churches to shift culpability for Jesus' death from the Romans to "the Jews." For example, any claim to be Messiah had nothing to do with blasphemy,[69] and the same would be the case with any consent to being God's "beloved Son." The high priest's alleged response to Jesus' self-affirmation of Messiah, "you have heard his blasphemy" (Mark 14:64; cf. Matt. 26:65) is historically impossible.

The Roman penalty for the crime of high treason is, of course, death by crucifixion. At Golgotha the taunt is heard, "Let the Christ, the King of Israel, come down from the cross, that we may see and believe" (Mark 15:32; cf. Luke 23:37). Upon the cross the Davidic pretender demands to know why his Father has abandoned him: "My God, my God, why hast thou forsaken me?" (Mark 15:34; Matt. 27:46, echoing Ps. 22:1). No answer is given, and none shall be given. True, Jesus is not a Zealot, yet for him—a shattering point often missed—there is a sense in which *God* is. Yet his Father "betrays" him; i.e., God does not come to deliver him and his people.

Whether Jesus will be "saved" in and through his resurrection must await our later attention. It may be appropriate, however, to remind ourselves at this juncture that the apostle Paul never identifies Jesus as Messiah during the Nazarene's earthly life. Together with the disciples, Paul evidently came to believe that Jesus is made the Christ by virtue of the resurrection (cf. Acts 2:36). But this belief demanded, of course, a complete change in the traditional expectation of Messiah.

In the very moment when the heavenly legions are supposed to strike, nothing happens. No avenging hosts of heaven join the fray; no warrior angels come to Jesus' rescue. In contrast to his patriarch Moses, Jesus is not empowered to deliver his people. Instead, he dies "a martyr's death for Israel."[70] Jesus' crucifixion represents, i.e., re-presents, the final weakness of humankind—but also of God.[71] Later on, two of the apostles en route to Emmaus will confide to the risen Jesus (whom they do not recognize), "We had been hoping that he was the man to liberate Israel" (Luke 24:21, NEB). And just before the ascension a larger company will inquire of the resurrected Messiah, "Lord, will you at this time restore the kingdom to Israel?" (Acts 1:6). The original, normative messianic hope here continues on.

We have three alternatives respecting that messianic hope. First, we are offered the view of Joseph Klausner: "Jesus came and thrust aside all the requirements of [Jewish] national life."[72] Klausner is entirely mistaken. Second, Jesus realized the requirements of Jewish national life. This, too, has no basis in fact—but not because Jesus did not try. Third, Jesus did his very best to meet the God-intended requirements of his nation's collective integrity. This is a truthful alternative—yet tragically Jesus could not realize the goal. The Romans killed him.

I am assured that much of the Christian failure to acknowledge that Jesus was a theocentric Jewish revolutionist (against Rome) is related to continuing influences within the church of anti-Jewishness on the one hand and a Christian ideology of "nonviolence" on the other. Both these influences get read into the Apostolic Writings, with deplorable moral-theological-historical consequences.

We have no choice but to receive Jesus' failure as a failure. (Cf. Gerd Theissen: "As a renewal movement within Judaism, the Jesus movement was a failure.")[73] It is significant that John H. Yoder's effort to make Jesus into a political pacifist also tries to make him into a success—this, from (reputedly) the very standpoint of Jesus' clear intention. Jesus' "failure," so Yoder puts it, was purely apparent. But the price for Yoder's conclusion is high indeed; it is nothing less than the abandonment of historical fact. Quixotically, Yoder is prepared to stamp with approval a radical (= counterrevolutionary) consequence: Today's followers of the Nazarene are to accept political impotence and surrender all claims to "govern history." "God's will for God's man [sic] in this world is that he should renounce legitimate defense." The use of violence is categorically forbidden to the Christian. The Christian is called to follow "Jesus' way" of the cross. Quite expectably, Yoder has Jesus refusing "to be king or to defend himself"—"not that there was anything wrong with kingship or self-defense; *he just could not have met his destined cross that way.*"[74]

A virtue of Yoder's *Politics of Jesus,* not despoiled by the book's pacifism, is its insistence that the kingdom of God means, not the transcending of time, but a new historical order. Nonetheless, Yoder's dialectic of Jesus' failure/ "success" is incongruous. Several lessons may be drawn from it: (a) The study by Yoder forcibly reminds us of how a commitment to historical activism and responsibility (such as Yoder's) can sometimes end up in an antihistorical, passivist, nonresponsible position. A resolutely Christian witness gets infiltrated and subverted by an ideology of nonviolence. (b) Even a failed endeavor to fight the oppression of one's people (Jesus' own praxis) is better, from the perspective of moral responsibility, than a successful endeavor to accede to such oppression through the way of impotence. Jesus' reputed "success"—à la Yoder—means, in fact, to desert the people of Israel. Jesus' actual failure at least battles against that betrayal. (c) A failed effort to do something to direct history is superior, morally speaking, to a successful effort to abandon history. As always, the moral question is one of whether responsibility (*Verantwortlichkeit*) is going to be taken for today and the future. (d) Only a nonspiritualizing recognition that Jesus' life-work was a failure can sustain and bless the historical truth (and thereby the theological truth) about him and his mission: Here was no success story. "God sacrifices his Son."[75]

Who, then, is more faithful to the God of history—the fabricator of Jesus' "success" or the Christian witness to his abject failure?

BEYOND THE FAILURE OF JESUS: THE TORAH OF GOD

Other questions pursue us. Does the teaching of the kingdom of God negate the quiddity of the people of God, or does it finally prove able to buttress and celebrate that reality? Does the reign of God turn out to be essentially discontinuous with the historical being of Israel, or is it yet somehow continuous with that being? How if at all can Jesus' praxis (message/mission) contribute to a life of responsible decision-making—despite the nonactualization of the kingdom of God?

Two types of response may be ventured to such questions, a largely negative type and a positive type.

(1) Jesus is marked by all the naïveté of his forebears and contemporaries; God is held to intervene in the human world in prosaic ways not unlike that of lightning striking the earth.

We may call to mind here an important strand of the biblical-prophetic tradition, according to which certain of the prophets assume the artless posture of rejecting alliances between Israel and other nations on the ground that Israel already has its sufficient and effective support in God, "a very present help in trouble" (Ps.46:1). Who needs the Egyptians or the Moabites or the Persians? Jesus inherits this tradition. It is probable that in agreement with Isaiah and Ezra, he would say that God's people are well advised to stay clear of capricious and idolatrous human friends. Although it does not follow from this that Jesus would necessarily exclude the prudence of armed protectors of his own,[76] the effective principle or presupposition nevertheless remains that the Lord and his hosts comprise Israel's real allies, and they are all-sufficient. Herein is found a companion-illusion to Jesus' grand illusion that God is about to overturn the world and institute his kingdom: the Lord of the universe is treated as, in effect, a kind of *deus ex machina.*

It is out of such illusions, however, that Jesus is able, remarkably, to convey certain truths: Human oppression is not vanquished by "deeds of lovingkindness"; such oppression is destroyed only by power *from beyond*—power that is enfleshed in things historical/physical. Surely Jesus must have known that in the fulfillment of his vocation he required massive help from his Father. The Roman legions would not be enticed into impotence by the charms of pacifism. At this point Jesus was anything but naïve. Somehow he was glimpsing the hard truth that prophetic faith can never suffice as a guarantee of effective political action. Trust in the coming of God's power must be supplemented by human deeds.

Jesus' error remains twofold: his misapprehension of the ways in which God operates—is forced to operate?—within the exigencies of the created world; and prematurity of persuasion. The tragedy of this Galilean *hasid* is made inevitable by his own particularly obdurate collaborationism with God. As is intimated above, in his finally accepted place as King Messiah, Jesus finds his own presence to be constituent—perhaps even prerequisite?—to the arrival of the kingdom. (Here lies much of his originality; as Sanders reminds us, "a Messiah is not common in material which reflects eschatological expectation.")[77] The son is convinced that the Father will intervene to support and fulfill the son's *Aktion* against Rome. Yet neither collaborator carries out— can carry out?—his side of the ostensible bargain. The blessed conspiracy only comes to a denouement—in the form of a pitiable cross against the lowering sky.

To sum up this prevailingly negative response:

The abortive eschatology of Jesus may itself be brought to terms by means of a negativistic eschatological judgment: If in fact the Egyptians or the Ethiopians are untrustworthy allies to the ends of Israel's historical deliverance and freedom, must not the same be said of God himself? In other words, there is just no way to manipulate or hasten the epiphany of the divine righteousness, not even by virtue of visible acts performed by the "beloved Son." The irony here is that Jesus seems otherwise to have been cognizant of this truth: "The kingdom of God is not coming with signs to be observed; nor will they say, 'Lo, here it is!' or 'There!' for behold the kingdom of God is [suddenly] in the midst of you" (Luke 17:20-21). "Of that day or that hour no one knows, not even the angels in heaven, nor the Son, but only the Father" (Mark 13:32). The time of the kingdom's coming is God's secret.[78]

In and through Jesus, however, a second choice is offered.

(2) A more positive response to questions such as those listed at the start of the present section of this chapter looks to the discontinuities and continuities that are adduceable among Jesus, Paul, and (to a lesser extent) the Essenes.

Is anything recoverable, despite the failure of the *eschaton* to come? A positive answer to this query is made possible through aspects of Jesus' praxis that persist quite independent of his unrealized apocalyptic expectation. Indeed, the latter failure may help throw into relief a genre of praxis that does not fail.

A most striking paradox within Jesus' vocation as a whole is that his imminent apocalypticism is never able to crowd out the observance and celebration of an authoritative Torah.[79] On the contrary, there is a strong sense in which his apocalyptic hope derives from and rests upon Torah, the original Word of God. I propose that this fealty to and representation of Torah goes far to save Jesus' message/mission from futility.

The conviction appears within some Jewish messianism that with the appearance of the Messiah, the authority of God's law comes to an end. The apostle Paul may be reflecting an early version of this general idea in his declaration, "Christ is the end of the law" (Rom. 10:4). But if, as Richard L. Rubenstein has it, Paul makes Jesus Christ both the goal toward which the law points and the one who abolishes the law's binding authority,[80] this is the last thing that could ever be said respecting Jesus' own message and behavior. The conflict with the faith of Paul's forebears that marks the one side of the apostle's reasoning is entirely absent in Jesus.[81] The conflict, however, between the faith and praxis of Jesus and the faith and praxis of Paul, a conflict that yesterday's scholarship tried to annul, is massive.

Jesus says or does nothing to separate himself from the normative Judaism of his day or from his own people. At both these points he is distinguished from the Essenes.[82] *With* the people of Qumran, however, and in some contrast to Pauline ambivalence, the man from Nazareth fully honors the Torah of God.[83] He carries forward the tradition of the Pharisees, those creative, self-critical heirs of the law and disciples of the prophets.[84] "All the arguments placed in Jesus' mouth in his supposed conflicts with the Pharisees are themselves Pharisee."[85] In Matthew's version of an injunction of Jesus, "the scribes and the Pharisees sit on Moses' seat; so practice and observe whatever they tell you ..." (23:2-3). With respect to the thesis of John Riches in *Jesus and the Transformation of Judaism,* Jesus says or does nothing to support that thesis. According to Riches, Jesus shows a "radical response to the situation of Judaism in first-century Galilee" by means of a distinctive stress upon God's love and forgiveness.[86] It is beyond question that Jesus stresses these very things. But what matters here is that the divine love and mercy have long since been part and parcel of the biblical faith that Jesus inherits. One reminder among many is Ezekiel's word from God: "Have I any pleasure in the death of the wicked, says the Lord God, and not rather that he should turn from his way and live?" (18:23). Riches is so committed to separating Jesus from the Judaism of his time[87] that he does not understand how Jesus' concentration upon the love of God and neighbor, and upon God as Creator and Father, carries ahead and revivifies the teachings of the Torah and the prophets and is thus indigenous to a Judaism that was already present and was being perpetuated and developed by the Pharisees contemporary to Jesus.[88]

Many of the same things are to be said of Marcus J. Borg's treatment of Jesus, although Borg's portrait is more nuanced and knowledgeable and hence less flagrant than that of Riches.

Is all this to call into question the singularity or originality of Jesus? No. Jesus is entirely unique. His uniqueness and power lie in his gathering up all the major strands of the Jewish tradition (Torahist, prophetic, wisdom, apocalyptic, messianic) and finally fusing these perceptions and norms distinctively within the hoped-for *kairos* (timeliness) of his own vocation and *kerygma* (proclamation).[89] The man from Nazareth remains incomparable.

Accordingly, Jesus insists, "Think not that I have come to abolish the law and the prophets; I have come not to abolish them but to fulfill [*plērōsai,* to complete] them. For truly, I say to you, till heaven and earth pass away, not an iota, not a dot, will pass from the law until all is accomplished" (Matt. 5:17-18). As A. E. Harvey suggests, "to fulfill" means here to disclose the true meaning of the law by supplying "a personal demonstration of how that meaning might be carried out in daily living."[90] In one sense, Torah-cum-prophecy is the *Interimsethik* of Jesus, an ethic for the meanwhile. It is, however, much more than this. For there is an unqualified connection between the faithful observance of Torah and the judging praxis of the reign of God: "Whoever then relaxes one of the least of these commandments and teaches men so, shall be called least in the kingdom of heaven; but he who does them and teaches them shall be called great in the kingdom of heaven" (Matt. 5:19). We see that the Torah is normative not only in the prekingdom dispensation but within the very heart of the kingdom. "Since today's honoring of Torah is determinative for life in the kingdom, the present is, in effect, treated as though the future were already here, while the future is treated as though it were present. Thus is there continuity between Jesus and that major strand within Judaism which does not sanction any hiatus between the Law and the Messianic age."[91]

In the matter of "the law" Paul of Tarsus is a Christian (of a sort) while Jesus is a Jew (though hardly of a sort). To propose to Jesus that Jews cannot be saved apart from faith in Christ or, for that matter, that Gentiles *are* saved in this way would probably produce in Jesus either puzzlement or laughter or a simple and resounding no (or all three together). For from the standpoint both of the ever-impinging reign of God and of needed moral norms, any Christian abandonment of the law is wrong and Jesus' retention of the Torah is right. Because Jesus, unlike Paul, does not have to contend against the law,[92] he can foster and celebrate unqualifiedly the abiding truth of the Torah, the Word of God, not alone in a judgmental-normative sense but also in full and joyful application to daily life.

In keeping with one aspect of the tradition of Jewish apocalypticism (the one we have examined) and together with the Qumran sectaries before him and Paul after him, Jesus' praxis is everywhere conditioned by his eschatology. Yet he is convinced as well, with his forefather David, that the Torah is "sweeter than honey" (cf. Ps. 19:7-10). Nowhere does Jesus ever doubt or qualify the integrity/absoluteness of the divine will for this world. His disciples "must be perfect, as [their] heavenly Father is perfect" (Matt. 5:48; cf. Luke 6:36). They must "seek first [God's] kingdom and his righteousness" (Matt. 6:33; cf. Luke 12:31). And they must take into their hearts the fearsome terms of the last judgment (see Matt. 25:31-46). Nevertheless: the prophet of Nazareth, with earlier prophets, never rests content with the judging character of the divine righteousness:

> Your Father ... makes his sun rise on the evil and on the good, and sends rain on the just and on the unjust. (Matt. 5:45)

> Do not be anxious about your life, what you shall eat or what you shall drink, nor about your body, what you shall put on. . . . Look at the birds of the air: they neither sow nor reap nor gather into barns, and yet your heavenly Father feeds them. Are you not of more value than they? ... And why are you anxious about clothing? Consider the lilies of the field, how they grow; they neither toil nor spin; yet I tell you, even Solomon in all his glory was not arrayed like one of these. But if God so clothes the grass of the field, which today is alive and tomorrow is thrown into the oven, will he not much more clothe you, O men of little faith? (Matt. 6:25-26, 28-30; cf. Luke 12:22-24, 26-28)

The business of God is much more diversified than acts of judgment; indeed, God's primordial obligation/vocation is to care for creation, in an accepting and loving way. God has to be a true Father: this is God's own, self-imposed duty. "[God's] mercy is not simply to the Sons of Light, but to the fallen, to the sick, the sinners. Indeed Jesus seems explicitly to deny that God sets . . . boundaries to his mercy. It may be impossible for a rich man to enter the Kingdom of Heaven, but with God all things are possible!"[93] In ways reminiscent of the people of Qumran, Jesus embodies an utter dependence upon God's grace and compassion. Thus, even in his final torment (according to Luke) the *hasid* from Galilee asks his Father to forgive those who are killing him: "Father, forgive them; for they do not know what they are doing" (23:34).

In addition, the truth that Jesus' entire eschatological worldview is isochronically out of joint says or does nothing to annul the coming of the reign of God within five minutes/five years/five hundred years/five thousand years/ five million years from now. What counts is that one day the divine righteousness will be victorious, upon earth. "The kingdom of God will be marked by the historicalness of a transformed world. In this transcendent respect the Nazarene's miscalculations are something of a mere momentary lapse. The weight of his sayings about the future 'does not lie on the time-factor so much as on the God-factor.' "[94] As we have noted, for Jesus the purpose of doing/obeying Torah in the interim before the *eschaton* is to prepare for membership in the kingdom: "Not every one who says to me, 'Lord, Lord,' shall enter the kingdom of heaven, but he who does the will of my Father who is in heaven" (Matt. 7:21; cf. Luke 6:46). It is not just speculation to anticipate that once the kingdom comes to be realized, this teleological orientation may fade from the scene, and we shall be as "angels in heaven" (Matt. 22:30; Mark 12:25; Luke 20:36)—or perhaps like God's own self. For the tale is sometimes told that one way God passes the time, now that the task of creation is rather out of the way, is in the study of God's Torah (that is, when, as another tale has it, God is not helping arrange marriages between us human children). Presumably, too, God's conduct is free of ulterior motives.

THE OPENING OF THE COVENANT

To conclude this modest effort restorative of the historical Jesus, but now in a way that underscores the grounding of faith upon history, I refer to a fairly original and focal contention of mine, long since expressed: the opening of the covenant between Yahweh and Israel to the wider world, a process that takes place in and through the event of the Jewish Jesus.[95] This affirmation takes its scriptural authentication or at least inspiration from Ephesians 2:

> Remember that at one time you Gentiles . . . were . . . separated from Christ, alienated from the commonwealth of Israel, and strangers to the covenants of promise, having no hope and without God in the world. But now in Christ Jesus you who once were far off have been brought near in the blood of Christ. For he is our

peace, who has made us both one, and has broken down the dividing wall of hostility, by abolishing in his flesh the law of commandments and ordinances, that he might create in himself one new man in place of the two, so making peace, and might reconcile us both to God in one body through the cross, thereby bringing the hostility to an end. . . . [For] through him we both have access in one Spirit to the Father. So then you are no longer strangers and sojourners, but you are fellow-citizens with the saints and members of the household of God, built upon the foundation of the apostles and prophets, Christ Jesus himself being the cornerstone, in whom the whole structure is joined together and grows into a holy temple in the Lord; in whom you also are built into it for a dwelling place of God in the Spirit (vv. 11-16, 18-22).

We shall see in chapter 10 how a covenantal Christology such as this has become central to the contribution of Paul M. van Buren.

The passage cited is not without difficulties. (The Letter to the Ephesians was probably not composed by Paul.)[96] For one thing, Jesus of Nazareth would totally disagree that he was doing anything to abolish "the law"—or to abolish his allegiance to Judaism. Ephesians 2 is markedly and wrongheadedly supersessionist vis-à-vis Judaism. "Christian" attempts to convert the Jewish people to Christianity are a veiled attack, though probably unknowingly so, upon the foundation of Christianity and hence upon the Christian faith itself.[97] Again, from the perspective of long centuries of ensuing history it is simply incorrect to maintain that, in and through Jesus, hostility between Jews and Gentiles is brought to an end. Finally, we do well to keep in mind that not all Christians are Gentiles.

Granted the seriousness of these problems, we may nevertheless affirm that it is indeed the event of Jesus that brings outsiders into God's covenant with Israel and that, strictly in this one respect, Ephesians 2 is christologically representational or authoritative. The point here is not merely one of religious confession; it is also one of historical truth. Yet in the end, faith and history are conjoined:

> We Christians have dared to speak of the exclusion of "the Jews" from the household of salvation when in plain truth we are, as Karl Barth has said, mere guests in the house of Israel. In the presence of original Israel the Gentile has no business asking, "What must the Jew do to be saved?" The rightful existential question of the Gentile is entirely different: "How is it possible that I could ever be included in the unbroken Covenant with Israel?" And the answer, with all answers that bring good news, that comprise the true story of salvation, must begin with "Once upon a time." Once upon a time there was a certain woodworker who lived in an obscure village of northern Palestine. . . . [98]

EXCURSUS: CRUCIS PERSONAE

The historical observation that the Romans did away with Jesus on the charge and finding that he was a seditionary need not mean that no other people were involved in the crucifixion. Even were partial responsibility or collaboration to be attributed to others, however, this would do nothing to silence a further question, a deeply moral question: Where is the justification in the late twentieth century of talking up this other responsibility or in keeping alive the issue as a whole? (For that matter, where is the justification in keeping alive the issue of Roman responsibility?)

It is a fact that Christian leaders and lay people continue to associate "the Jews" with blame for Jesus' death even after the passage of centuries. This takes place every Eastertide, and often during in between times (as in Christian "passion plays"), despite the stipulation of such authorities as the National Conference of Catholic Bishops that "the Jewish people never were, nor are they now, guilty of the death of Christ." The issue here goes much deeper than questions of responsibility (*Strafbarkeit*), however. For what needs to be said applies to the alternative of nonresponsibility as well as to that of responsibility.

The really fateful question, the one that matters, is why the Christian world must keep *driving itself* to raise the issue of Jewish linkage to Jesus' death (cf. the absolute impossibility of universal "American" linkage to the death of John F. Kennedy.) The psychological and moral nature of the problem suggests that expressions of Jewish "innocence" are in a sense tainted along with those of Jewish "guilt." For what is the malady that is present within the collective Christian psyche that demands repeated, unrelenting concentration upon the "place" of Jews ("guilty" or "innocent") in Jesus' trial and crucifixion?[99] Where is the moral legitimacy in keeping this kind of pot boiling? Japan attacked the United States only a half century ago, yet there bygones can wholly be bygones, and Americans can enjoy every available Japanese automobile, camera, and television set. In the same way, after two thousand years the question of culpability for Jesus' death is a nonquestion or ought to be. It ought to have been buried long ago, together with all other efforts at hostility to Jews. Rather than concentrating upon reputed Jewish (and Roman) malice in the death of Jesus, Christians could expend their time more responsibly in fighting the Christian malice toward Jews that the churches inculcate every "Holy Week."[100]

The brevity and negativity of the judgment provided here explains why I treat the topic of *crucis personae* as no more than an excursus. To be sure, the historian's task extends to a right to ask and to know that must never be censored. Yet historians do not operate in a moral vacuum. The Christian historian of today has no choice but to work within a frame of reference of many centuries of Christian derogation of the Jewish people and Judaism. (Since I myself consume time and space in this book upon the question of responsibility for Jesus' death, it follows that the counsel behind this excursus applies to me along with others.)

6

The Judaism
of Jesus, Liberator of
the Wretched

We turn now to selected elements of liberation Christology.

Earlier chapters have reminded us of Jesus' concern for "sinners," the downtrodden, the wretched. There appears no doubt of the Nazarene's identification with and commitment to the oppressed and the suffering, and of his hope of their liberation. (It is so that liberation thinking sometimes tends to lose sight of equally central elements in Jesus, particularly his expectation of a theocentric kingdom and his unquestioned fealty to God's Torah.) Chapter 5 has served to emphasize that, with respect to his beloved people Israel, Jesus filled the role of liberationist. But the implementation of Jesus' commitment — the question of whether the cause he represented could come to fruition — is quite another matter. We have been reminded of the severe sense in which Jesus failed. Among the major problematics of liberation thinking/praxis is the issue of whether its voices may sometimes confuse intention or goals or hopes with realization. Was Jesus, in fact, a liberator, or did he prove to be no more than a would-be liberator? It seems that there can be conclusive agreement only upon the second appellation.

THE QUALITY OF LIBERATION

The literature of contemporary liberation thinking is vast. All that we can hope to analyze here is a selection of representative materials. Before coming directly to our subject, we may find of some use a few orienting considerations: the apprehension of liberation theology as partisan; what may be

understood by liberation itself; the redeeming quality of praxis; and praxis
vis-à-vis history.

Liberation theology as partisan. Elisabeth Schüssler Fiorenza points
out that the various forms of liberation theology challenge "the so-called objectivity and value-neutrality of academic theology. The basic insight of all liberation theologies, including feminist theology, is the recognition that all theology, willingly or not, is by definition always engaged for or against the
oppressed. Intellectual neutrality is not possible in a world of exploitation and
oppression."[1] To this I should only add that in its committed quality, liberation
theology comprises a particular case within all theology, which entails commitment to (subjectively speaking) some form of faith or (objectively speaking) to a divine being or divine beings.

The meaning of liberation. There is considerable accord upon the
meaning of liberation as such.

David Tracy provides helpful refinements from among the related concepts of salvation, liberation, and bondage. Liberation from bondage is a central
biblical and postbiblical metaphor and hence appertains to both Jewish and
Christian understandings. "More exactly, death, suffering, and guilt-sin are fre-
quently described in terms of 'bondage,' " from which only godly liberation-
salvation can save us. Experiential liberation as such does not attain unto identity with salvation, for salvation in its ultimate reaches is *total* liberation—
"from guilt-sin, from death and transience and, in principle, from any bondage
that entraps us." On the one hand, Christian understandings of salvation must
join "wholeheartedly in the modern and post-modern journeys of political,
cultural, and social emancipation and freedom." Yet on the other hand,

> Christian salvation, as grounded in God as origin and goal of all human action, can-
> not be exhausted by any ... [claim] that our emancipation can be achieved
> through the sole use of some new emancipatory method or struggle. ... [Christian
> salvation insists] upon total liberation of the individual *and* of all those linguistic,
> psychic, social, and political structures that form individuals whether they will it
> or not. The fragmentary signs of such liberation may, therefore, be found not only
> in the salvific and social liberation of oppressed peoples. There is no individual
> freed from these structures (oppressed and alienated oppressors alike). *It is not
> adequate to speak of Christian liberation-salvation of any individual while ig-
> noring those structures of bondage which inflict themselves upon each and all.*
> ... [If] Christian salvation is appropriately described in our period as both freedom
> from all bondage and freedom for authentic existence, then there is every good
> reason to suggest that the liberation, political, and feminist theologians are correct
> to insist that "total liberation" is a most appropriate metaphor and concept for
> Christian salvation in our day.

It follows, in Tracy's view, that "Jesus Christ Liberator" is a proper model/ goal "for a contemporary Christology." And certain implications are thereby established: There is perforce a "*re-Judaizing* of Christian soteriology against some individualist, ahistorical, and apolitical traditional readings." Again, to speak as we must in a post-*Shoah* age of the "fragmentariness" of salvation means "a profound recognition by Christians of the indelibly eschatological 'not-yet' in unrelieved tension with every 'even now' and 'always-already' understanding of Christian salvation." Finally, the necessary re-Judaization of Christianity can and ought to lead to reformulations of Christology and Christian theology as such.[2]

To the above I am only able to add several corollaries.

1. Otherworldly or transworldly "salvation" cannot be permitted to depress itself into a spiritualizing ideology according to which worldly bondage (e.g., the evil of poverty) is made "inconsequential" in view of some promise or hope of heavenly salvation (bliss).

2. Human suffering is never to be assimilated to some kind of "valuable" or "esteemed" cause (such as martyrdom). The only legitimate thing to do with suffering is to condemn it and *labor* to destroy it.

3. Together with the people he oppresses, the oppressor lives under oppression. It is his acts of oppression that oppress him, along with his suffering neighbor.

4. Point 3 gets infected with ideological destructiveness once we fail to distinguish qualitatively between the sufferings of the world's downtrodden and the "sufferings" (e.g., the guilt feelings) of those of us who are prosperous and respectable and who are able *so easily*—indeed, *with no effort at all*—to "enjoy life."[3] Most human beings of the world are never enabled to "enjoy life."

5. Since the oppression against which liberation demands relief is systemic, involving objective as well as interior structures of evil, authentic liberation carries with it, in both its inner meaning and its thrust, a politics of revolution. In this connection, it is imperative, as Gustavo Gutiérrez points out, that "our reading of the Bible ... be a *militant* reading. ... It is time to open the Bible and read it from the perspective of 'those who are persecuted in the cause of right' (Matt. 5:10), from the perspective of the condemned human beings of this earth—for, after all, theirs is the kingdom of heaven. It is for them that the gospel is destined, it is to them that the gospel is preferentially addressed."[4] The meaning of revolution, however, within and for a theology of liberation must carry in plain view the warning, "Fragile: Handle with Care." For "revolution does not mean mere religious legitimation of armed or ruthless secular-political revolutionary action. True revolution involves the transformation of the social order for the sake of a universal justice and, insofar as possible, by means that are consistent with humaneness and shalom and respect for the rights of all."[5]

6. In a Christian view, liberation is not the triumph of the "autonomous ego" of liberal modernity but the blessed self-fulfillment that can blossom only when we become men and women (and children?) "for others" (Bonhoeffer), just as we already love ourselves and just as we already covet justice for ourselves.

Most comprehensively expressed, to be a liberated human being is to be granted the freedom to serve righteousness.

7. Even though liberative theology cannot be reduced to political liberation as such or to some form of social service, we must yet remind ourselves that social and political liberation is indigenous, at least in an anticipatory way, to salvation. One sometimes hears the criticism that liberation theology reduces faith to politics. No, politics is a *consequence* of faith, in principle a wholly licit consequence. The Christian faith transcends politics, as does human liberation itself. Nevertheless, in the words of Gutiérrez, the liberation of Christ is always "present in concrete historical and political liberating events."[6]

Praxis as reality, reality as praxis. Within the heart of the Hebrew Bible there beats the grace-full identity of truth and righteousness.[7] It is in concord with this fact that liberation thinking offers "praxis" as a central concept. The concept encompasses a dialectical relation between theory (or beliefs) and practice (or action).[8] This orientation stands in contrast to the usual dictionary rendering of praxis as restrictedly a matter of practice or deed. (Clark M. Williamson notes that the very concept of praxis implies that theology be self-critical.)[9] In liberative thinking the moral indispensability of praxis is again and again stressed. "When we act, reflect on the action, and then act in a new way on the basis of our reflection (or when we reflect, and then act, and then reflect in a new way on the basis of our action)," we are assigning a signal place to praxis.[10] Praxis is action *guided* by thought. As José Miguez Bonino writes, "action overflows and challenges the theory that has informed it; and thought, projecting the shape and future of reality, pushes action to new ventures. . . . This dialectical interplay seems to be the necessary presupposition for political ethics."[11] The concerns of liberation theology are here structurally and purposefully continuous, not alone with the Hebrew Bible, but also with the admonition in the Apostolic Writings to "do the truth" (John 3:21). Ordinarily we think of the truth as simple honesty or as knowledge or, more profoundly, as something "out there" to be captured or at least discovered. Significantly, the Fourth Gospel sets the doing of truth into opposition to the doing of evil (3:20). From this perspective, truth is not merely something that "is" or "is spoken"; it is a reality the doing of which means standing up for righteousness. Truth is more than simple accuracy or a certain objective, static condition. It is something that *happens*, that incarnates itself within human life. This linkage of the truth of God with praxis points up a persisting lesson of the Epistle of James:

But be doers of the word, and not hearers only, deceiving yourselves. For if anyone is a hearer of the word and not a doer, he is like a man who observes his natural face in a mirror; for he observes himself and goes away and at once forgets what he was like. But he who looks into the perfect law, the law of liberty, and perseveres, being no hearer that forgets but a doer that acts, he shall be blessed in his doing. (1:22-25).

The liberationist apprehension of praxis is readily applicable alike to Jesus and to ancient and modern Jewish thought as such because in both these instances our vaunted Western philosophic distinction and even separation between theory and practice lacks, or ought to lack, any and all normative force. Jesus' message and mission are very well categorized under the univocal heading of praxis. The ideal convergence of word and deed into praxis may somewhat temper the necessity of E. P. Sanders's finding that the "sayings material" (what Jesus taught) is secondary to "*facts* about Jesus" and that we may subsequently move "from facts to meaning or significance." The Nazarene was, of course, much more than a teacher. And it may even be, as Sanders states, that Jesus' behavior is somewhat more recoverable than are his teachings.[12] Yet in light of the flowing together of both word and deed into praxis, it may not matter substantively should one or another analyst first treat Jesus' teachings and only subsequently work these into Jesus' mission, even if the latter be recognized as primary. We should surely expect Jesus' praxis (conviction/deeds) to throw light upon his intention or purposes.

Liberative praxis and the province of history. The fundamental philosophic-theologic link between liberative thinking and the historical Jesus as hoped-for "Liberator" is that thinking's apprehension of historical (secular) life as a potentially and at least partly holy reality. For the God who hides God-self in human history is nevertheless "known and worshiped through the doing of justice."[13] To look at the historical process in all its concreteness, indeed before the fact of all its incorrigibility, is to discern/can be to discern the presence therein of God.[14] From the point of view of a theology of liberation, *history*—most especially the history of the wretched, the downtrodden—is a foundational reference point, in the theological sense that God is viewed as pledged to be forever on the side of these people and in the moral sense that human wars are to be waged against all such suffering.

For Christians, the story of liberation is manifest, however fragmentarily and heuristically, in the message and mission of Jesus, to whom we now return. As Guitérrez declares, Jesus Christ is "the Poor One, identified with the oppressed and plundered of the world."[15]

JESUS AND HUMAN LIBERATION

From out of a congeries of salient problems and available sources respecting the Jesus of history and the challenge of liberation, I limit myself to four head-

ings: liberation and the biblical Jubilee (Sharon H. Ringe); a liberationist rendering of the Synoptic Gospels (Juan Luis Segundo); a new model for recon-
structing Christian origins (Elisabeth Schüssler Fiorenza); and a conclusion to
the chapter involving three emphases: liberation and eschatology in the presence of Jesus; the morality of taking sides; and the problem of universal salvation (primarily my interpretations).

In her examination of the biblical Jubilee and the person of Jesus, Sharon
H. Ringe exemplifies the liberationist *Anschauung* that drives through the entire Hebrew Bible and continues into the Apostolic Writings. Ringe identifies
her work as demonstrating "the intimate connection between the agenda of
liberation and the core of the Christian faith."[16]

Foundational here are Leviticus 25 and Luke 4, the latter of which puts
parts of Isaiah 61 into the mouth of Jesus.

> And you shall count seven weeks [or sabbaths] of years, seven times seven years, so
> that the time of the seven weeks of years shall be to you forty-nine years. Then you
> shall send abroad the loud trumpet on the tenth day of the seventh month; on the
> day of atonement you shall send abroad the trumpet throughout all your land. And
> you shall hallow the fiftieth year, and proclaim liberty throughout the land to all its
> inhabitants; it shall be a jubilee for you, when each of you shall return to his prop-
> erty and each of you shall return to his family. A jubilee shall that fiftieth year be to
> you; in it you shall neither sow, nor reap what grows of itself, nor gather the grapes
> from the undressed vines. For it is a jubilee; it shall be holy to you; you shall eat
> what it yields out of the field. (Lev. 25:8-12)

Marking all the regulations of Leviticus 25 "is a concern for social justice,
not as charity, but as liberation." And in the Synoptic Gospels Jesus is received
and properly adored as God's own herald of liberation:[17]

> And [Jesus] came to Nazareth, where he had been brought up; and he went to the
> synagogue, as his custom was, on the sabbath day. And he stood up to read; and
> there was given to him the book of the prophet Isaiah. He opened the book and
> found the place where it was written,
>
>> "The Spirit of the Lord is upon me, because he has anointed me to preach good
>> news to the poor. He has sent me to proclaim release to the captives and recov-
>> ering of sight to the blind, to set at liberty those who are oppressed, to proclaim
>> the acceptable year of the Lord."
>
> And he closed the book, and gave it back to the attendant, and sat down. . . . And
> he began to say to them, "Today this scripture has been fulfilled in your hearing."
> (Luke 4:16-21; Isa. 61:1-2a)

Here is Ringe's beginning explication of the latter passage:

> This Word of God [as] fulfilled in the presence of Jesus of Nazareth is alive with
> images of liberation. From their origins late in Israel's exile, where they addressed
> the people's longing for political freedom and for the healing of a shattered society,

these images continued to be words of blessing and hope to people living in occupied Palestine in the first century of the Common Era. For the early church, these same images defined Jesus' public ministry. . . . The images we glimpse [here] . . . are spun out in greater detail in the stories, sayings, parables, and prayers contained in the Synoptic Gospels. Together they present Jesus as a royal messenger announcing the "good news" of liberation at the beginning of God's reign.

Both the content and the pattern of this proclamation are rooted in the Jubilee and sabbath-year traditions of Hebrew Scriptures . . . ,[18] and in the royal edicts of release found in records of societies that were Israel's neighbors. In these traditions liberty is presented in economic, social, and political terms [*not* in "religious" terms—A.R.E.]: freedom for slaves, release for captive peoples, cancellation of debts, redistribution of land, care for the poor, food for the hungry, and healing of physical ailments.

The above moral-political language becomes a source of the declaration, within the Christian apostolic tradition, of God's coming eschatological reign and also of christological language. In the latter connection, Ringe writes, "to portray Jesus as the proclaimer of the Jubilee links recognition of Jesus as the Christ with response to the Jubilee message itself: to confess Jesus as the Christ is to participate in acts of liberation." She states the continuity more concretely: "The beginning of God's eschatological reign is to be marked by the proclamation of a 'release' from all the experiences of enslavement or imprisonment that characterize human life. . . . The poor, the suffering, and the oppressed become participants in the promises of God's reign, and the promises themselves accent precisely the points at which people's present circumstances bring them pain."[19]

Many of the relevant biblical texts together with the questions they raise cannot be gone into in a detailed way here; much of this sort of analysis is undertaken in Ringe's monograph.[20] Again, in the light of repeated emphases upon "good news for the poor" elsewhere in these pages (see, e.g., the analysis of Juan Luis Segundo in the next section of the present chapter) I shall not consider Ringe's treatment of that subject in her own chapter 3. The rest of my review and appraisal of Ringe is occasioned by the remaining chapters of her book.

In her pursuit of the twin realities, release or forgiveness, Ringe concentrates upon the story of the anointing of Jesus in Luke 7:36-50.[21] She concludes that the story makes explicit the understanding that Jesus' relation to outcasts is to be understood as "an enactment of the 'forgiveness' or 'release' in which those persons are restored to their place in the community. The bonds that are broken with Jesus' advent are the bonds that deprived people of a place in their society. Such pericopes echo the Jubilee images of 'return' to God found in Leviticus 25 as well as those in Isaiah 61 that point to liberation from captivity and celebration of God's eschatological reign, now recognized as present in

Jesus." Indeed, all the healing stories of the Gospels "might be seen as manifestations of the liberation that is part of the Jubilee in that they portray release from powers inimical to the eschatological reign of God." In this regard, the healing of the paralytic (Mark 2:1-12/Matt. 9:1-8/Luke 5:17-26) entails an explicit link between physical healing or "release" from disease and "release" or "forgiveness" of sins.[22]

In the matter of the forgiveness or cancellation of debts, Ringe treats the parable of the unforgiving servant (Matt. 18:21-35) and the petition for forgiveness in the Lord's Prayer and related sayings (Matt. 6:12/Luke 11:4; Matt. 6:14-15/Mark 11:25-26). The point of the parable is that to be "willing to receive forgiveness for one's own debts, but not to forgive others in turn, is in effect to deny the new economy of mercy in favor of the old one in which the bonds and obligations leading to indebtedness still hold sway." And in summarizing her exposition of the Lord's Prayer, Ringe writes,

> While the reign prayed for is clearly God's ... its advent implies consequences for human beings and for human society ... [including] the need to participate in the rhythms of "forgiveness," and response to the "good news to the poor" symbolized in the petition for bread. While it is ... not appropriate to call the Lord's Prayer a Jubilee prayer in the strict sense of being able to trace each of its petitions to specific Jubilee texts, it is a Jubilee prayer in that it expresses, in a highly condensed and symbolic liturgical way, images in common with the Jubilee traditions of Hebrew Scriptures as elaborated elsewhere in the Synoptic Gospels.[23]

More broadly, while Jesus' eschatological message may not have been in conscious *intent* a Jubilee message, it proved to be in *fact* that. In this sense, "it had the effect of pronouncing sentence on the powers preventing the exercise of God's new reign, which would touch, transform, and redeem the whole created order." Moreover, in and through the process "by which the proclaimer became more explicitly the one proclaimed," the themes of Jubilee "were not lost, and the message of liberation became part of the proclamation of Jesus as the Christ."[24]

I introduce now a rudimentary midrash upon Ringe's exposition.

Liberative christological argumentation is confronted, or confronts itself, with a fundamental moral-theological problem, a problem brought to focus in and through Professor Ringe's analysis, yet one that engages all representations of liberative-political Christology—not exempting the endeavors of Juan Luis Segundo and Elisabeth Schüssler Fiorenza, to be considered below. The problem is intertwined with the "failure" of Jesus as elucidated in chapter 5 above; therefore, the difficulty is not confined, and cannot be confined, to liberationism alone. (For example, in our century the same problem beset the liberal Social Gospel, in a way that made inexorable, or at least highly convincing, neo-Reformation critiques by Reinhold Niebuhr and others.) Simply put, the

difficulty consists in the chasm between the proclamation of the Christian eschatological gospel (*kerygma*)—of which Jesus of Nazareth is Exemplar—and
its fulfillment/nonfulfillment. I have already made the identical point in different words at the start of this chapter: The question pursues us, Was Jesus in fact
a "liberator," or was he not much other than a "would-be liberator"?

It is readily agreed: In the name of Jesus much relief for the oppressed has
been realized again and again (e.g., today's Christian Kairos movement against
apartheid in South Africa).[25] The historical/empirical limitations of Jesus'
praxis continue to be in part overcome; accordingly, his failure cannot have
been and is not now total. He can remain as inspiration to all Christians who, in
his name as Lord, work to lessen human suffering. "Like Jesus and all those who
follow him, [martyrs] disclose the future and leave history open so that it may
nurture and produce more justice than exists at present and more love than is
now to be found in society."[26] "From the depths of the traditions of the community of faith we learn that the Christ is one in whose company the hungry
are fed, the sick healed, the outcast embraced, and the fearful comforted, and
we learn that crucial to any confession of Christ is action to free the poor from
entanglements that impoverish and enslave. Through these images of the one
who as the Christ heralds the Jubilee of God's reign, we might find the courage
to struggle for justice and peace, and to dare to yearn for the time of liberty
acceptable to God."[27] It is legitimate to say that the Christian is, in a sense,
summoned to assuage the failure of Jesus, to become in a strange but hearten-
ing way "Christ" to Jesus as to others, to enable him to become authentic
"good news" to the wretched.

The problem that remains is readily made concrete through further allusion to Sharon H. Ringe's exposition. The four beatitudes as worded in Luke—
you poor, you who weep, you who hunger, you when people hate you (6:20-
23)—form "a graphic contrast between present suffering and the blessings that
are at hand." In the occupied Palestine of Jesus' day "many people knew firsthand the pain of hunger, poverty, grief, and persecution. Such an accent on the
reversal of circumstances would reach into the midst of people's pain to make
vivid and concrete the promises to which the ancient witnesses pointed."
Query: How long are people supposed to wait? How long before a promise is
reduced to an empty promise? It is very true: "The Jubilee images point toward
God's liberating and healing *intent* wherever institutions, customs, or physical
conditions are seen to limit human life. . . . The good news of God's reign and
God's blessing" does become incarnate in "concrete acts of care for 'the poor'
associated with Jesus' own ministry, and those by means of which people confess the Christ. . . . Those acts do not simply sustain the poor in their poverty,
but instead result in substantive changes in people's circumstances, such that
they enjoy the chance for a new beginning."[28] Nevertheless, a caution from

Gerald F. Moede against a too facile rendering of Jesus' utilization of Isaiah 61 is most apropos: We must not forget the millions of people who will never see or walk, or be healed of genetic and degenerative disease.[29] And Ringe herself states, "God's reign, which was proclaimed to be 'at hand' so long ago, is still not in evidence in the institutions of society on which our human experience is based. How can the Jubilee message of Jesus continue to focus on the drama of a boundary moment of two thousand years' duration?" This question is not met by answering that human irresponsibility is the culprit, for the issue here is not human culpability but the promised reign *of God*. Ringe refers to the confession of "Jesus as the Christ who is the herald of the Jubilee, messenger and enactor of liberation."[30] We may respond that while there is no problem with Jesus as either herald or messenger, there is a great problem with what it means to confess him as "enactor of liberation." For the eschatological reign of God never came. Or at best it came only in fragmentary and partial ways within the "interior" dimension of psycho-spiritual release. Jesus gave hope to a number of people. Some distraught people proved to be no longer distraught. But the kingdom failed to come within the all-decisive "exterior" realm of political-economic deliverance. As Ringe indicates, in the Jubilee traditions "forgiveness" is "at heart a political word." Jesus' "success" in physical and spiritual healings may serve to qualify in some measure the depiction of him as "failure." Yes, the healing stories of the Gospels "might be seen as manifestations of the liberation that is part of the Jubilee in that they portray release from powers inimical to the eschatological reign of God."[31] But these exceptions only throw into sharp relief Jesus' overall messianic failure. As ever, the question of eschatological expectation stands at the center of, and indeed perpetuates, the entire problematic of Jesus. The more we study the stories and sayings upon the subject of liberation, the more we are struck by the sharpness of the gulf between Jesus' success at the subjective-individual level and his failure at the all-important political level. The shattering tragedy/irony of Jesus' message and mission to the wretched and the downtrodden is that his assurances to them were to remain largely devoid of fulfillment or even of partial fulfillment. As the bearer of a proposed "program," Jesus did very well; as the instrument for carrying out that program, he did very poorly.

SEGUNDO, JESUS, AND THE KINGDOM

We come next to the Uruguayan theologian Juan Luis Segundo and his work *The Historical Jesus of the Synoptics*.[32] Having just confronted ourselves again with the interrogation mark of Jesus as "failure," we may for the sake of both continuity and transition begin with Segundo's awareness of the identical, nagging question. Personally speaking, I am not put off by this question. For that

Jesus "was a failure" or that he "failed" may be received as a kind of test case of the incarnation: Was Jesus or was he not a fully human person who must perforce be subject to error? Segundo is in accord: Because Jesus was "perfectly human, we cannot assume he had something improper for human nature: knowledge of the future that would do away with the risk of any and every option." Nevertheless, the truth continues to cut to the bone: "The kingdom announced and prepared for did not arrive. That, at least, is the impression *history* gives us." And all the human wretchedness remains: "Those considered blessed by Jesus because of [the kingdom's] coming continued in their miserable state, whereas the rich and the satisfied continued to triumph. The hungry begot and multiplied new generations of hungry people. . . . " More structurally and hence more fatefully, the Gospel writers freely depict Jesus "as being mistaken about the end of the world" together with "the cosmic catastrophes that would precede it."[33]

As a means of doing justice to Segundo's contribution, along with weighing out a few ounces of criticism, I shall place the question of the kingdom's nonarrival within a fourfold frame of reference. In proceeding this way, I suggest that we take with all seriousness a watchword of Segundo: "If there is such a thing as a Christology, in no way can it serve as a replacement for the ongoing task of remaking the gospel message in the Christian community." Segundo is striving to talk of Jesus in a way that will "open people up to seeing him as a witness to a more humane and liberated human life."[34]

(1) The present and the future are together casting a two-sided coin. Jesus' announcement of the approaching kingdom "is the proclamation of a joyous thing, a piece of good news, an *evangelion*." But joy for the poor is only the coin's one side; the other side is woe for the rich. This bold duality reflects a particular penchant of Luke, who is "especially anxious" to emphasize the negative side: "the kingdom of God is a piece of *bad news* for the concrete groups that stand opposite the poor in the social spectrum. Its arrival sounds the death knell of the privileges that have so far been enjoyed by the rich, the satisfied, and all those who have been able to laugh in the world as it has actually been structured (see Luke 6:24-25)."

> Jesus was, and wanted to be, a sign of *joy* for the masses of Israel. From this person — whom his enemies called a glutton, a drunkard, and a friend and cohort of publicans and sinners — the masses learned that God was preparing something marvelous for them. . . .
>
> . . . As the first Beatitude tells us, the poor possess the kingdom of God. That is not due to any merit of theirs, much less to any value that poverty might have. On the contrary, the kingdom is theirs because of the inhuman nature of their situation as poor people. The kingdom is coming because God is "humane," because God cannot tolerate that situation and is coming to make sure that the divine will be done on earth. [Query: If it is so that God "cannot tolerate" the present state of

affairs, why then *does* he tolerate it? Why has he not *already* stopped it?—A.R.E.]
Poverty must cease to wreak destructive havoc on humanity. Thus the latter part of
the second and third Beatitudes spells out the import of the latter part of the first
Beatitude. The kingdom will ensure that the mournful will be able to laugh, that
the hungry will get their fill: in short, that the poor will cease to be poor. . . . If [the
socially marginalized people] do enter the bliss of the kingdom as poor people,
without any moral precondition whatsoever, they do so because of their inhuman situation that is an affront to God: because they have been left on the sidelines
in the religiously established society of Israel.[35]

Great stress is placed upon Jesus' parable of the rich man and poor Lazarus
(Luke 16:19-31). Unfortunately for Segundo's historicist liberationism, the
stated reversal of roles between the two characters does not take place in this
world but only after they have died.[36]

(2) In Segundo's view, the coming of the kingdom of God is, for Jesus, a
matter of synergism. I think Segundo is quite correct. One consequence—
should we approve a synergistic position—is that "all the blame" for the "failure" of the kingdom does not fall upon God or upon Jesus.

Segundo's rendering of Jesus' synergistic *Anschauung* is worked out in a
context of the eschatology of the kingdom: "It is certain that no image takes for
granted the here-and-now presence of the kingdom in full and complete form
on this earth, but all those that point toward the future conceive it as being
near. Its nearness, however, does not assume an apocalyptic character that
would rule out careful attention to the complex mechanisms of history." In re-
tort to Rudolf Bultmann's notorious pronunciamento that God's reign "will be
brought about by God alone without the help of men," Segundo declares that
"one would have to erase practically the whole gospel message to arrive at
such a definition." For Jesus not only announces the coming of the kingdom, he
also places "historical [i.e., human] causality in the service of the kingdom." In
this, he invests his all and "his disciples' all as well." It appears out of the question to make Jesus conceive the imminent arrival of the kingdom

> in any way that stripped all meaning and importance from the complex process
> required to manage historical mechanisms and change them over the long run. . . .
> [The] preaching of Jesus is more than a mere *announcement*. This would include
> what he entrusted to his disciples. It does not just notify people of an event that is
> bound to take place anyway. It also is the setting in motion of mechanisms that will
> be *constitutive* of the actual reign of God. . . .
>   We find confirmation of this in Jesus' warning not to be preoccupied with one's
> own necessities in life. This is the reason he gives: "Instead, *seek* his kingdom, and
> these things shall be yours as well" (Luke 12:31; Matt. 6:33). One could hardly
> seek something if the initiative behind it belongs exclusively to God. The conclu-
> sion seems to be inevitable: there is a causal connection, however small and sec-
> ondary, between the establishment of the kingdom and human activity directed
> toward it.[37]

(3) Segundo's presentation of Jesus as synergist is coherent with the "political key" that he applies throughout to the Nazarene's life, message, and resulting conflicts—a key that in turn opens into the domain of holiness. (Segundo does not claim that the political key explains everything about Jesus but rather that it is "the best code for deciphering his destiny and teaching as a whole.")

From beginning to end, our author aims to show that "*everything* said and done by Jesus of Nazareth had inherently political dimensions, not merely hypothetical applications, that he expressed his religious message in a political key and in that way manifested God. Hence it is only by grasping the political thrust of expressions (in their rightful context) that seem to be merely religious that we will comprehend the true intention of Jesus and come to an authentic (religious) interpretation of his message."

The poor, the afflicted, the sinners live at the center of a deep human paradox. On the one hand, it is to the wretched of this world that the kingdom certainly belongs. They are the *subjects* of the kingdom. Yet on the other hand, the poor are being treated as no more than *objects*: they live in an inhuman situation, *¿no es verdad?* Right here we are brought to the question: What demands does Jesus make of sinners and the poor?

> Using our basic political key, . . . we arrive at an answer that will seem strange and unaccustomed: *none*. If the poor were still subject to (moral or religious) conditions in order to enjoy the coming kingdom of God, that would mean the collapse of the original Beatitudes and their revelation of God. They could not say of the poor that the kingdom is theirs, precisely *because* of what they suffer from their inhuman situation. The God of Jesus is a good politician. God does not pass judgment on a human being who is not yet truly human. That is why God is coming with the kingdom: to restructure a society that impoverishes, marginalizes, and oppresses the vast majority of human beings, turning them into subhumans. . . .
>
> Before anything else, therefore, the poor are the *object* of the kingdom. Only the kingdom can convert them into complete and total *subjects*. This clearly gives the lie to the (ideological) misinterpretation that says that the message of Jesus, because it is religious, must give priority to the conversion of individual hearts over the change of *structures*. Hence it clearly shows that we must use a political key in order to understand Jesus' message and his revelation of God to us.[38]

All of this proves why, if nothing is asked of the poor, *everything* is asked of the rich. The rich, the privileged must undergo a "profound conversion," lest they be excluded when the kingdom comes as a thief in the night!

The placing in Jesus' hands of a political key to the reign of God—to insert a further critical word—gives no aid to Segundo in coping with the plain truth that Jesus does not implement or make use of political power to the end of redeeming the poor from their plight. I submit that one basic consideration that helps account for this latter state of affairs is provided in the previous chapter of this book: for all his synergistic presuppositions, Jesus was waiting, probably with patience but in the end with futility, for the promised intervention of God. Segundo is left only to note: "Not in terms of some other world but in terms of his insertion in this world . . . we must question Jesus' consistency insofar as he seems indifferent to the possibility of utilizing the power he has acquired in defense of the poor."[39]

(4) Segundo's employment of a political key, however, does not lead him to exclude all transpolitical resources. He turns, finally, to the resurrected Christ:

> [Jesus'] community gradually came to realize that the breakthrough [of the kingdom] did take place, despite appearances to the contrary, with Jesus' resurrection from the dead. . . .
>
> Faced with the fact of the resurrection, the disciples shift emphases. "Conversion," the key word of Jesus' prepaschal preaching, no longer has to do with understanding and pursuing his thoroughgoing criticism of an oppressive religious ideology; now it has to do with believing that Jesus is the Messiah (Acts 2:38). Now "salvation" in "the name of Jesus" takes the place of the "year of grace," that is, the realization on earth of the values of the kingdom that will transform the plight of the poorest and most exploited members of Israelite society (see Acts 2:47; 4:10-12).
>
> This new emphasis displaces the political key of Jesus in the concrete postpaschal activity of his disciples, if not in their memory. Whether we approve or not, we can at least understand the surprising differences between the preaching of Jesus and that of the early Christian church. It is not that the message of Jesus was *lost*; the Gospels themselves are the best proof that it was not. But the fact is that we can get to it only *indirectly*.[40]

In this way Segundo returns to an astonishing admission made relatively early in his study: "The kingdom preached by Jesus had nothing to do with the political independence of Israel or the restoration of its own monarchy; it had to do mainly with the appearance of an absolute power over death, made manifest in the risen one by the paschal experiences. . . ."[41] This passage comprises the surest indication, not only that Segundo turns out to be, in fact, politically nonliberationist (i.e., irresponsible) when it comes to the Israel of God, but also that he is even prepared, in effect, to take the cause of faith ("power over death") as his ultimate norm rather than to have to acknowledge or come to grips with such objective evils as the tyranny of the Romans. In the final resort he accedes to the spiritualizing viewpoint of the postpaschal Christian community and incidentally of Marcus J. Borg (and must thereby disconcert some foes of liberation theology who charge that it sacrifices faith to history). I shall leave it to readers to choose whether Segundo's transpolitical climax is a victory for faith or a defeat for his own liberationist Jesus of history.[42]

We may be reminded of a parallel case in liberationist literature. William R. Jones disagrees with James H. Cone's designation of Jesus' resurrection as *the* event of universal human liberation. Jones argues that Cone's designation is thrown into overwhelming question by the fact that black misery, slavery, and oppression are all *post*resurrection realities.[43] According to Jones's reasoning, may we not say that Segundo's resurrectionist faith begs the entire liberationist question?[44]

So much for my fourfold commentary. I have left to the last a critical point that is more serious than those I have so far indicated.

Christian liberation thinking/praxis—particularly in its Latin American and Third World versions—is often faulted for propagating elements of anti-Jewishness and anti-Judaism, a condition that undermines its pretension to stand for unqualified human liberation. This condition is not easy to explain apart from the history and continuing influence of Christian antisemitism.[45] One accompaniment of this state of affairs is a failure to restore creatively and to honor the rootage of Jesus Christ and Christianity within Israel. Instead, the proponents do their best—against the weight of history—to set Jesus against his own people. The presence of this species of ideology is exemplified in the anti-Jewish Christology of Jon Sobrino.[46]

How does Juan Luis Segundo fit the picture? Here are representative passages: Jesus "became a threat to the Jewish [*sic*] religious authorities and was put to death." It is the "Israelite authorities" who "condemn him to death."[47] The Pharisees, "embodiments of [legalistic] religious fanaticism," "are the enemies par excellence of the God that Jesus reveals to be the center of the coming kingdom." [In truth, the Pharisees were friends of the poor and champions of the oppressed—A.R.E.] Jesus sought "to topple the barriers of the law and place the latter in the service of the human being. This was not simply heresy. It could well be viewed as an incitement to subversion." [In truth, Jesus' endeavor here was neither heretical nor subversive—A.R.E.] "Jesus seriously threatened the foundations of the theocratic authority which was responsible for the marginalization of the poor in Israel, *and which certainly was not the Roman Empire*." "The poor and *politically* marginalized people in Israel were put in that position by authorities who claimed to be acting in line with God's supposed vision of the relationship between conduct and social *status*. In making a frontal assault on that vision, Jesus was certainly attacking the political structure of Israel. On the basis of divine revelation he was destroying the foundation of an authority structure that was political in the name of an idolatrous conception of God, that was conveying a false image of God." A large number of Jesus' parables constitute "attacks on the oppressive religious ideology of the Israelite majority. . . . " Under Segundo's tutelage the parable of the prodigal son (Luke 15:11-32) is transformed into a polemic "against the Israelite [religious] authorities"; the same claim is entered respecting the parable of the laborers in the vineyard (Mark 12:1-12; Matt. 21:33-46; Luke 20:9-19). Jesus fought "the ideological mechanism that turned the religion of Yahweh into an instrument of oppression in Israel." In sum, we are advised that "in one way or another the three Synoptic writers bear unmistakable witness to a politico-religious conflict that pits Jesus, the defender of sinners and the poor, against the ideological and material authorities of Israel."[48]

A few comments are in order. (a) Segundo's act of turning his back upon Roman culpability for the suffering of the Jewish people is extraordinary (though not all that unheard of). Elisabeth Schüssler Fiorenza points out that the Roman occupation of Palestine "was the greatest offense to God's rule ... established in the Covenant with Israel."[49] Segundo's own ideological condition has evidently driven him to eclipse the Roman oppressors from the Land of Israel. It is as though they scarcely existed. (b) Segundo joins other Christian biblical scholars in disregarding or hiding tendentious elements in the Apostolic Writings, with particular reference to anti-Jewishness. The only hint, if such it can be called, that Segundo may be slightly aware of the presence of those contemporary critics of liberation theology who point out that the movement does not always surmount anti-Jewishness is that *sometimes* he replaces the ideological expression "the Jews" by the terms "Israelite authorities" and/or "Israel." The second of these substitutes, however, has the ready connotation today of "State of Israel," so at this point the linguistic replacement does not relieve Segundo of all ideological taint.[50] It is ironic that self-identified foes of bad ideology (false consciousness) should themselves engage in this form of ideology. Revealingly, at one place Segundo labels those who "represent the authority of the law" as *Jews* only immediately to portray "marginalized sinners" as belonging to *Israel*.[51] (c) Segundo's documentation is conspicuous for its absence. He is not arguing from silence; he is arguing from nothing (*ex nihilo*). Or better, he is, in effect, arguing from the *Anschauung* of a contemporary Western polemic against oppressive capitalist structures. His is a historical ideology of class that has little relevance to the state of affairs in first-century Palestine. Jesus is transfigured into the herald and leader of "the class struggle." At the very least, Segundo could have recognized Roman opposition to Jesus together with (alleged) local religious "opposition."

Do these comments suggest that Professor Segundo's contribution ought to have been excluded from our purview? Of the three characteristics attributed in chapter 1 above to the general christological position we are studying, the second is undoubtedly the most problematic within liberation thinking/praxis: freedom from traditionalist Christian imperialism or triumphalism. In *The Historical Jesus of the Synoptics* there is, to be sure, evidence of a supersessionist and absolutist predisposition, e.g., "I believe that Jesus was the Word of God made human, God's very self." With the aid of two resources, however—his strong humanist commitment and his hermeneutics of suspicion in re: "religion"—Segundo is enabled to qualify his absolutism: "[I] feel much closer to many people who say they do not believe in Jesus, but are interested in the values carried by that human figure, than I am to the vast multitude of people who say that Jesus is God and think such a stand puts them in an advantageous position over the rest of humanity." Indeed, "human beings who are not ready to set up certain human values as criteria prior and superior to any specific religion are incapable of recognizing the significance and importance of Jesus. Thus, even though they may end up calling him Messiah, Son of God, or God, that will not prevent them from turning him into an idol."[52] All in all, Segundo does *not* say what Gustavo Gutiérrez says: "There is no other road to the Father but that of Jesus Christ."[53]

On the basis of Segundo's hermeneutics of suspicion, I think there is hope that one day he will be able to rid himself of his residually anti-Jewish propensities. In the meantime we are obligated to press home the truth that ideological self-destructiveness takes place whenever Christian liberationism defies the grace of antisupersessionism and antitriumphalism.

FIORENZA, CHRISTIAN ORIGINS, AND
FEMALE LIBERATION

To seek to deal adequately with the subject or cause of human liberation apart from the oppression of female human beings would be shameful. Women and female children make up the largest of all oppressed human realities (i.e., majorities). In principle, the greatest of all liberation movements is that of females, given the sheer magnitude of this grouping, together with the singular depth, breadth, and persistence of female wretchedness.

In the presence of Jesus as feminist and the feminist dimension of the Jesus movement, no Christology can ignore this kind of oppression.[54]

The present section of this chapter concentrates upon the work of Elisabeth Schüssler Fiorenza; the chapter to follow, on women and Christology, introduces other data and argumentation.

Fiorenza's magnum opus, *In Memory of Her*, offers, in the words of its subtitle, a feminist reconstruction of Christian origins. Feminist theology broaches a particular, critical theology of liberation. The goal of Fiorenza is to reconstruct Christian history as women's history not alone in order "to restore women's stories to early Christian history but also to reclaim this history as the history *of women and men*." For "as long as the stories and history of women in . . . early Christianity are not theologically conceptualized as an integral part of the proclamation of the gospel, biblical texts and traditions formulated and codified by men will remain oppressive to women. . . . [A] feminist reconstruction of early Christian history . . . aims at both cultural-religious critique and . . . reconstruction of women's history as women's story within Christianity. It seeks not just to undermine the legitimization of patriarchal religious structures but also to empower women in their struggle against such oppressive structures." The unnamed woman disciple who anointed Jesus, and of whom he said that "wherever the gospel is preached in the whole world, what she has done will be told in memory of her" (Mark 14:9), will at last be remembered. In the original story it is quite probable that the woman anointed her master's head, an act that "must have been understood immediately" as a recognition of Jesus as the Christ. Thus was it "a politically dangerous story."[55]

I cannot report in depth upon Fiorenza's long and convincing hermeneutical and methodological argumentation.[56] We face the dismal but challenging fact that all biblical texts as we have them "are products of an androcentric patriarchal culture and history." The prophetic traditions exemplify our task: "A feminist biblical hermeneutics must take seriously the historical-patriarchal elements of the prophetic traditions in order to set free their liberating social-critical impulses for the struggle for women." For however much the androcentric texts erase women from historiography, they can do nothing to remove women "from the center of patriarchal history and biblical revelation." "A feminist critical hermeneutics must therefore move from androcentric texts to their social-historical contexts. It not only has to claim the contemporary community of women struggling for liberation as its locus of revelation, it also must reclaim its foresisters as victims *and* subjects participating in patriarchal culture. It must do so not by creating a gynocentric life-center on the fringes of androcentric culture and history, but by reclaiming such androcentric human and biblical history as women's own history." This "feminist reconstitution of the world" demands a feminist hermeneutics "that shares in the critical methods and impulses of historical scholarship on the one hand and in the theological goals of liberation theologies on the other hand. . . . Feminist theology as a critical theology of liberation therefore seeks to develop not only a textual-biblical hermeneutics but also a historical-biblical hermeneutics of liberation." In the final analysis, such a comprehensive hermeneutics "is not just geared toward the liberation of women but also toward the emancipation of the Christian community from patriarchal structures and androcentric mind-sets so that the gospel can become again a 'power for the salvation' of women as well as men." For "androcentric codifications of patriarchal power and ideology cannot claim to be the revelatory Word of God. . . . [Only] those traditions and texts that critically break through patriarchal culture and 'plausibility structures' have the theological authority of revelation." Furthermore, and of signal Christian importance, authentic revelation "is found in the life and ministry of

Jesus as well as in the discipleship *community of equals called forth by him.*"
Finally,

> liberation theologies insist that revelation and biblical authority are found in the
> lives of the poor and the oppressed whose cause God, as their advocate and liber-
> ator, has adopted. A feminist critical hermeneutics of liberation shares the "advo-
> cacy stance" of liberation theologies but, at the same time, it elaborates not only
> women's oppression but also *women's power on the locus of revelation.* As the
> root model of Christian life and community the Bible reflects biblical women's
> strength as well as their victimization. Therefore, the Bible is source for women's
> religious power as well as for their religious oppression throughout the history of
> Christianity to the present. A Christian feminist theology of liberation must cease
> its attempts to rescue the Bible from its feminist critics and assert that the source
> of our power is also the source of our oppression.[57]

Fundamental within Fiorenza's "feminist model of historical reconstruction" (chap. 3) is the paradox of patriarchy: Patriarchy is the source of women's
oppression but also of women's power. Just as in the story of Jesus' life and
death some Christian biblical authorities tend to exculpate the Romans and
blame "the Jews," so too such scholars (and others) often fail to call to moral
account the *patriarchal* tendentiousness of the Apostolic Writings. Much of
the uniqueness of Fiorenza's contribution lies in the way she insists upon a
double role for the biblical writings: their patriarchal destructiveness *and* their
(grudging and unwitting) tribute to and recognition of female dignity and
rights. Accordingly, the new feminist model will integrate "both egalitarian and
patriarchal 'heretical' and 'orthodox' traditions into its own perspective." And
because such a model rests upon the equality of all Christians, it can be called
feminist.[58] This last point is crucial to Fiorenza's hermeneutics. For only a feminist model can be genuinely egalitarian, since only such a model insists upon
the equality of all.

To the end of exploring pertinent aspects of Fiorenza's liberationist gift,
we may single out three themes: Jesus as liberator of women; women's faithfulness to Jesus and the gospel; and the issue of ideology in the frame of reference of feminist reconstruction. I shall treat the first two themes more or less
descriptively; with the third theme I shall include a good deal of my own interpretation, assessment, and application.

Jesus and women.   The Christian story came into being as "the history
of the discipleship of equals" (*In Memory of Her*, Part Two). There follows the
historical-theological setting of that story, in what I think can best be identified
as its depatriarchalized and deideologized form:

> Divine Sophia is Israel's God in the language and *Gestalt* of the goddess. Sophia is
> called sister, wife, mother, beloved, and teacher. She is the leader on the way, the

preacher in Israel, the taskmaster and creator God. She seeks people, finds them on the road, invites them to dinner. She offers life, rest, knowledge, and salvation to those who accept her. She dwells in Israel and officiates in the sanctuary. She sends prophets and apostles and makes those who accept her "friends of God." Sophia is described as "all-powerful, intelligent, unique" (Wis. 7:22). She is a people-loving spirit (*philanthrōpon pneuma*, 1:6) who shares the throne of God (9:10). She is an initiate (*mystis*) of God's knowledge, an associate in God's works, an emanation of the God of light, who lives in *symbiōsis* with God (8:3-4), an image of God's goodness (7:26). One can sense here how much the language struggles to describe Sophia as divine (without falling prey to ditheism). Goddess-language is employed to speak about the *one* God of Israel whose gracious goodness is divine Sophia.[59]

In the oldest Jesus-traditions God is met as divine Sophia (Wisdom). The old saying that "Sophia is justified [or vindicated] by all her children (Luke 7:35 [Q]) probably originated in Jesus' table community of the poor, the sinners, the tax collectors, and the prostitutes.[60]

The earliest Palestinian theological remembrances and interpretations of Jesus' life and death understand him as Sophia's messenger and later as Sophia herself. The earliest Christian theology is sophialogy. It was possible to understand Jesus' ministry and death in terms of God-Sophia, because Jesus probably understood himself as the prophet and child of Sophia. As Sophia's messenger he calls "all who labor hard and are heavy laden" and promises them rest and *shalom*. . . . Sophia, the God of Jesus, wills the wholeness and humanity of everyone and therefore enables the Jesus movement to become a "discipleship of equals." They are called to one and the same praxis of inclusiveness and equality lived by Jesus-Sophia. Like Jesus, they are sent to announce to everyone in Israel the presence of the *basileia* [kingdom], as God's gracious future, among the impoverished, the starving, the tax collectors, sinners, and prostitutes. Like Jesus, his disciples are sent to make the *basileia* experientially available in their healings and exorcisms, by restoring the humanity and wholeness of Sophia-God's children.[61]

Whatever the praxis of Sophia-God and whatever emphases are to be made within Jesus' synergistic relation to Sophia, the all-decisive fact is that the discipleship of equals was initiated by Jesus.[62] The man from Nazareth hopes for and expects the "inbreaking of God's *basileia*, when death, suffering, and injustice finally will be overcome and patriarchal marriage will be no more (cf. Mark 12:18-27 and parallels)." It was "the scum of Palestinian society" that "constituted the majority of Jesus' followers. These are the last who have become the first, the starving who have been satisfied, the uninvited who have been invited. And many of these were women." "Only when we place the Jesus stories about women into the overall story of Jesus and his movement in Palestine are we able to recognize their subversive character. In the discipleship of equals the 'role' of women is not peripheral or trivial, but at the center, and thus of utmost importance to the praxis of 'solidarity from below.' "[63]

Fiorenza wholly rejects the presupposition that patriarchal structures and poverty are two different issues. In truth, they are two sides of the one coin. Most poor and starving people are females. The traditions reveal Jesus' stance on behalf of the poor *together with* his concern for women. Although Jesus does not address directly or critically the structures of oppression, he "implicitly subverts them by envisioning a different future and different human relationships on the grounds that *all* persons in Israel are created and elected by the gracious goodness of Jesus' Sophia-God. Jesus and his movement set free those who are dehumanized and in bondage to evil powers, thus implicitly subverting economic or patriarchal-androcentric structures, even though the people involved in this process might not have thought in terms of social structures."[64]

Fiorenza's one fault here is to fail to make the necessary distinction that human liberation was primarily an intention and a hope on Jesus' part, rather than something consummately realized. This difficulty is commented upon elsewhere in these pages. The failing is shared by many Christian interpreters.

As part of her documentation of Jesus' liberation of women, Fiorenza reviews at some length certain pre-Gospel texts that "already address patriarchal structures, even if indirectly." These include pre-Markan controversy stories wherein Jesus challenges patriarchal marriage structures; texts upon the a-familial ethos of the Jesus movement; and the saying about domination-free relationships among the disciples. I can take the space only for selected materials. In Mark 10:2-9 the operative passage should be translated as "two persons—man and woman—enter into a common human life and social relationships because they are created as equals." Mark 12:18-27 "critically questions patriarchal structures" with respect not to creation but to the eschatological future. Again, careful scrutiny of the Synoptic texts that enjoin leaving house and family for the kingdom or Jesus' sake shows that it is Lukan redaction (and not the Q traditions) that counts the wife among family members to be left behind. The Q and pre-Markan traditions do not limit to men membership in the radical discipleship of Jesus. "Without question the discipleship of Jesus does not respect patriarchal family bonds, and the Jesus movement in Palestine severely intrudes into the peace of the patriarchal household." We are told, "Whoever does not receive the *basileia* of God like a child (slave) shall not enter it" (Mark 10:15). Structures of domination cannot be tolerated in a discipleship of equals; "those who 'would be' great or first among the disciples must be slaves and servants of all." Finally, in the matter of Matt. 23:9,

[the] kinship relationship in the discipleship of equals does not admit of "any father" because it is sustained by the gracious goodness of God whom the disciples and Jesus call "father" (Luke 11:2-4 [Q]; 12:30; cf. Mark 11:25). The "father" God is invoked here ... precisely to reject all [patriarchal] claims, powers and struc-

tures. . . . The monotheistic fatherhood of God, elaborated in the Jesus traditions as the gracious goodness usually associated with a mother, must engender liberation from all patriarchal structures and domination if it is to be rescued from the male projection of patriarchy into heaven. Thus liberation from patriarchal structures is not only explicitly articulated by Jesus but is in fact at the heart of the proclamation of the *basileia* of God.[65]

Women's loyalty to Jesus. If Jesus was faithful to women, they responded with faithfulness to him. Fiorenza exemplifies this in, successively, the Gospels of Mark and of John. Just as, at the start of his Gospel, Mark presents four leading male disciples, so "at the end s/he presents four leading women disciples: Mary of Magdala, Mary, the daughter or wife of James the younger, the mother of Joses, and Salome. . . . Though the [male] twelve have forsaken Jesus, betrayed and denied him, the women disciples . . . are found under the cross, risking their lives and safety. That they are well aware of the danger of being arrested and executed as followers of a political insurrectionist crucified by the Romans is indicated in the remark that the women 'were looking from afar.' They are thus characterized as Jesus' true relatives." (Note Fiorenza's use of "s/he" for Mark; for the evangelist identified as John, she goes farther, concluding that this person "might have been a woman.") But it was many women disciples who came up with Jesus to Jerusalem (Mark 15:41). And at the beginning and end of the passion narrative, an "indirect polemic" against the male disciples is given voice. It is a woman who acknowledges the suffering-messiahship of Jesus, and "in a prophetic-sign action" anoints him for burial, while some of the disciples are reprimanding her. Again, a servant woman challenges Peter to honor his promise not to betray Jesus. "In doing so she unmasks and exposes him for what he is, a betrayer." Also, Mary of Magdala and Mary (mother of) Joses witness the site of Jesus' burial, and three women receive the word of Jesus' resurrection. By the end of the Gospel "the women disciples emerge as examples of suffering discipleship and true leadership. They are the apostolic eye-witnesses of Jesus' death, burial, and resurrection." In the Markan community, "those who are the farthest from the center of religious and political power, the slaves, the children, the Gentiles, the women, become the paradigms of true discipleship."[66]

The narrative of the Gospel of John assigns a highly prominent place to women: This is identified by Fiorenza as "astonishing." "That such a pre-eminence of women in the Johannine community and its apostolic tradition caused consternation among other Christians is expressed in 4:27f. where the disciples are 'shocked' that Jesus converses and reveals himself to a woman." More specifically, Martha of Bethany is charged with the primary articulation of the Johannine community's full apostolic, christological faith, and Mary of Bethany is responsible for the correct praxis of discipleship. Most likely, the evangelist seeks to portray Mary of Bethany "as the true disciple and minister in contrast to the betrayer who was one of the twelve." Furthermore, "the Johannine community seems to have an understanding similar to that of Mark, namely, that the 'new familial community' will include 'mothers' as well as brothers and sisters, but not fathers—because their father is God alone." Finally, the last woman who appears in the Gospel of John is Mary of Magdala, who was destined to become the most prominent of the Galilean disciples. She stands under the cross of Jesus; also, she discovers the empty tomb and is the first to experience a resurrection appearance (in contradistinction to Peter); thus in a double sense this Mary "becomes the *apostola apostolorum*, the apostle of the apostles," the "primary apostolic witness to the resurrection."[67]

"Therefore, wherever the gospel is preached and heard, promulgated and read, what the women have done is not totally forgotten because the Gospel story remembers that the discipleship and apostolic leadership of women are integral parts of Jesus' 'alternative' praxis of *agape* and service. The 'light shines in the darkness' of patriarchal repression and forgetfulness, and this 'darkness has never overcome it.' "[68]

The issue of ideology. I have called attention to the problem of an ideological taint in the work of Juan Luis Segundo with respect to Judaism and the Jewish people. The reader will have noted that Fiorenza's analysis is not wholly free of critical judgments upon religion and the religious practices in Jesus' land. In view of such parallels, are we to adjudge that Fiorenza's point of view carries in some way the same ideological taint? The answer is no.

An entire chapter of *In Memory of Her* insists upon the Jesus movement as a renewal movement wholly within Judaism (chap. 4). "It is . . . misleading to speak about 'Jesus and his Jewish background' as though Jesus' Judaism was not integral to his life and ministry, or to describe the behavior of Jesus' disciples over and against Jewish practice as though the first followers of Jesus were not Jews themselves." Fiorenza knows well the dangers of antisemitism *within* feminism itself—the "Christian feminist literature and popular reasoning [that perpetuate] anti-Jewish notions when extolling Jesus, the feminist, over and against patriarchal Judaism, or when pointing to the extinction of goddess religion by Israelite patriarchal religion." Yet Fiorenza knows equally well that feminists can hardly "cease to analyze critically and denounce the patriarchal structures and traditions of Christian faith and community whenever it becomes obvious that they share in the dominant patriarchal Jewish structures of the first centuries. . . . " How "can feminists relinquish their search for the liberating elements of Christian vision and praxis that are formulated over and against the dominant patriarchal structures of Judaism? Would that not mean also an abandonment of feminist Jewish roots and of our Jewish fore-sisters who entered into the movement and vision of Jesus of Nazareth?" More-over, to underline the renewal aspect of the Jesus movement need not imply anti-Judaism. "Rather, *overlooking* it would mean subtle 'downgrading' of first-century Judaism's most compelling religious areas for salvation." Christian fem-inist theology

> can reappropriate the earliest Christian beginnings of the discipleship of equals only if and when it understands and explicates that Christian roots are Jewish and that the feminist Christian foundational story is that of Jewish women and their vision.
>
> To rediscover "Jesus, the feminist," over and against these Jewish roots . . . can only lead to a further deepening of anti-Judaism. Equally, to rediscover Jesus, the feminist, over and against Jewish but not over and against Christian patriarchy would only mean a further strengthening of Western religious patriarchy. . . . The discipleship of equals called forth by Jesus was a *Jewish* discipleship. . . . [To] re-construct the Jesus movement as a Jewish movement within its dominant patriar-chal cultural and religious structures is to delineate the feminist impulse within Judaism. The issue is not whether or not Jesus overturned patriarchy but whether Judaism had elements of a critical feminist impulse that came to the fore in the vision and ministry of Jesus. . . . The praxis and vision of Jesus and his movement is best understood as an inner-Jewish renewal movement that presented an *alterna-tive* option to the dominant patriarchal structures rather than an oppositional for-mation rejecting the values and praxis of Judaism.[69]

Fiorenza stresses how greatly misleading it is "to picture Jewish women of the first century in particular, and Jewish theology in general, in predominantly negative terms." In the Book of Judith we are presented with a quite alternative situation and tradition.[70]

The simple but telling difference between our two thinkers is that Fiorenza is constantly and *self-critically* aware of the dangers of Christian ideology vis-à-vis Judaism and the Jewish people when applying liberation norms to Christian origins. Segundo gives no evidence of any such awareness. Upon this ground we may identify Fiorenza as a fully post-*Shoah* Christian thinker and Segundo as, in effect, a pre-*Shoah* thinker, i.e., someone who lives and works as though there had been no Holocaust. Segundo's outlook and his silences may serve to open up (with regard to him and other liberation think-ers) the question of a certain *Tendenz* of rapport between antifeminism (or at least nonfeminism) and antisemitism. By contrast, Fiorenza's awareness of ideological dangers helps to neutralize the potential power of feminist norms to perpetuate anti-Jewishness (in replacement of norms of "the poor"). Accordingly, whenever she speaks in opposition to the unjust social struc-tures of the first-century world, her judgments can be free of the bad ideology (false consciousness) that afflicts Segundo. In sum, Fiorenza's unflagging rejection and exposure of the destructiveness of anti-Jewishness is what empowers her to create a biblical feminism that has been liberated from ideological taints.

We may return, at the end, to a most important historical observation made by Fiorenza in her introduction: Mark "depoliticizes the story of Jesus' passion."[71] We have seen how Juan Luis Segundo ultimately does the same thing by assigning primacy to the spiritual, soteriological truth of Jesus' resurrection and subordinating (or losing) his own earlier insistence upon the centrality of Jesus' work of liberating the wretched and the oppressed. This state of affairs is of the utmost significance. By finally shifting the role of Jesus Christ to a "spiritual" one, Segundo helps open the way to various anti-Jewish and non-Jewish renderings of Jesus' message and mission. In contrast, Elisabeth Schüssler Fiorenza, by pointing up Mark's shift of blame for Jesus' death from the Romans to "the Jews," is able to sanction implicitly the historical truth of Jesus as foe of the Romans, as at the same time she works to restore women disciples to their place as "true disciples in the passion narrative,"[72] contra the abandonment of Jesus by his male followers.

A FEW WORKING REMARKS

To conclude this chapter, I submit some working remarks upon three, highly interrelated issues: liberation and eschatology in the presence of Jesus; the morality of "taking sides";[73] and the moral dilemma of nonuniversal/universal salvation.

(1) We may begin by taking note of the contrast between the socio-political status quo-ism to be found in Paul of Tarsus and its antithesis within the eschatology of Jesus. (Let us continue to have in mind the shattering question of Jesus as "failure.") In the apostle Paul a certain convergence of apocalyptic radicalism and social conservatism is manifest.[74] The nonchalance toward the social order that obtrudes in Paul serves to conflict with Jesus' (apocalypticist?) eschatology. For the Nazarene's eschatological hopes act to challenge the status quo. The power (*dynamis*) of the kingdom as imminent—so imminent as already to have begun disclosing itself—is overturning things as they are and summoning people to a very radical ethic (beyond the day-to-day demands of Torah):

> And behold, one came up to [Jesus], saying, "Teacher, what good deed must I do, to have eternal life?" And he said to him, " . . . if you would enter life, keep the commandments." He said to him, "Which?" And Jesus said, "You shall not kill, You shall not commit adultery, You shall not steal, You shall not bear false witness, Honor your father and mother, and You shall love your neighbor as yourself." The young

man said to him, "All these I have observed; what do I still lack?" Jesus said to him, "If you would be perfect, go, sell what you possess and give to the poor, and you will have treasure in heaven; and come, follow me." When the young man heard this he went away sorrowful; for he had great possessions.

And Jesus said to his disciples, "Truly, I say to you, it will be hard for a rich man to enter the kingdom of heaven. Again I tell you, it is easier for a camel to go through the eye of a needle than for a rich man to enter the kingdom of God." (Matt. 19:16-24)[75]

Sharon Ringe appropriately introduces the concomitant parable of the Great Judgment: The story of the anointing of Jesus by the woman at Bethany (Matt. 26:6-13/Mark 14:3-9) "makes it clear that to proclaim the gospel, both as Jesus' message and as the story of his life and ministry, is first of all to proclaim 'good news to the poor.' It is a short step from this story to the parable of the Great Judgment . . . , where the enthroned and sovereign Christ is explicitly identified with the hungry, the thirsty, the stranger, the naked, the sick, and the imprisoned, and where one's case before the heavenly tribunal is resolved on the basis of one's responsiveness to the human faces of Christ in the poor and oppressed":[76]

> When the Son of man comes in his glory, and all the angels with him, then he will sit on his glorious throne. Before him will be gathered all the nations, and he will separate them one from another as a shepherd separates the sheep from the goats, and he will place the sheep at his right hand, but the goats at the left. Then the King will say to those at his right hand, "Come, O blessed of my Father, inherit the kingdom prepared for you from the foundation of the world; for I was hungry and you gave me food, I was thirsty and you gave me drink, I was a stranger and you welcomed me, I was naked and you clothed me, I was sick and you visited me, I was in prison and you came to me." Then the righteous will answer him, "Lord, when did we see thee hungry and feed thee, or thirsty and give thee drink? And when did we see thee a stranger and welcome thee, or naked and clothe thee? And when did we see thee sick or in prison and visit thee?" And the King will answer them, "Truly, I say to you, as you did it to one of the least of these my brethren, you did it to me." Then he will say to those at his left hand, "Depart from me, you cursed, into the eternal fire prepared for the devil and his angels; for I was hungry and you gave me no food, I was thirsty and you gave me no drink, I was a stranger and you did not welcome me, naked and you did not clothe me, sick and in prison and you did not visit me." Then they also will answer, "Lord, when did we see thee hungry or thirsty or a stranger or naked or sick or in prison, and did not minister to thee?" Then he will answer them, "Truly, I say to you, as you did it not to one of the least of these, you did it not to me." And they will go away into eternal punishment, but the righteous into eternal life. (Matt. 25:31-46)

Critics of liberative thinking work hard to subject such passages as these to some form of religious spiritualization and/or moral individualism. Liberationists respond that to do any such thing is to open ourselves to wrongful ideology. For the revolutionary ethic of Jesus transcends (as at one and the same time it honors) individual transformation. As Gutiérrez writes, the universality and totality of Jesus' work "go to the very heart of political behavior, giving it its authentic dimension and depth. Human wretchedness and social injustice reveal 'a state of sin,' a betrayal of brotherhood [*sic*] and communion. By freeing us from sin, Jesus attacks the very roots of an unjust social order. For Jesus, the liberation of the Jewish people was just one aspect of a universal and permanent revolution."[77]

By pledging himself to the liberation of his people Israel, Jesus can also be said to stand for solidarity with all human beings who yearn for freedom from oppression. Do not the spiritual-moral lessons of the Bible again and again lead us from things particular to things universal? For, once King Messiah appears, the people Israel will be empowered to resume their vocation as "a light to the nations" (Isa. 42:6; cf. Acts 13:47), and all the downtrodden will be "set at liberty" (Luke 4:18; cf. Isa. 61:1). It is true that the grounding of Jesus' liberative ethos in the Hebrew Bible means that his ethos is not wholly unique. Nevertheless, in H. Richard Niebuhr's expression, it is an "ethos of universal responsibility." The fact that this ethos could and can appear elsewhere does nothing to alter the truth that for Christians it takes place right here: in *this man*.[78]

> Chronologically and from a doctrinal standpoint, Paul comes after Jesus. But from the vantage point of the historical unfolding of the divine righteousness, Jesus may be said to come after Paul. Jesus is in many respects an intermediate figure between the Judaism he inherited ... and the developing corpus of Pharisee and rabbinic Judaism. More broadly stated, the event of Jesus falls between a prophetic apodicticity that frets not over pragmatic perplexities, and a practicality that obligates itself to puzzle over day-to-day, even institutional prescriptions. ... For Jesus, contemporary human history lives and moves under the suasion of God's coming reign. In Jesus the balance of faith and history is subtly altered, to the profit of history. Here is no "faith against the world" in exactly the Essene or the Pauline apprehension, but instead grace digging its way into time, via the Father's/Mother's love and justice. The paradox is that the severity and the uncompromisingness of Jesus' apocalypticism can contribute to a socio-historical transformation more radical and revolutionary than in Paul (or in Qumran dualism), as at the same time the Nazarene's zeal for Torah is tempering his eschatology in ways that Paul can never provide. If Jesus acts to overturn one world, this is only in order to bring about another one. (Here is where the allegation by some scholars that he is not an apocalypticist cannot be entirely discarded. His eschatology is supremely historicist.) And if Jesus' version of the kingdom never materialized, there is yet consolation for all: his message/praxis is enabled to enter the lists of competing, normative images in ethics within the only world that we have.[79]

One may argue, then, that despite his being dead wrong respecting the historical or empirical timing (*kairos*) of the kingdom's advent, nothing has happened to negate Jesus' decisive, creative, and supportive role, wholly from inside Judaism, enabling his followers to address responsibly the life-and-death question, "What are we called to do?"

(2) What does it mean to "take sides" with the oppressed? Is there a veritable moral rationale for so doing? Let us come back to the argumentation of Gustavo Gutiérrez, now within a frame of reference of "class struggle."[80] Gutiérrez is fully cognizant of a poignant dilemma: How can the *universality* of gospel charity be reconciled with commitment to a *particular* social class? I may venture four comments.

(a) Gutiérrez and his *colegos* are persuaded that the one path to the universalization of righteousness is a "preferential option for the poor"[81] and the abolition of the class struggle. To take part in this cause "not only does not oppose universal love; such a commitment is today the necessary and inescapable means to love's concretion. Such participation leads to a society without classes, without owners or dispossessed, without oppressors or oppressed. From a dialectical perspective, reconciliation means the conquest of conflict. The communion of paschal gladness passes over confrontation and the Cross." Or as Arthur F. McGovern writes, the way to love oppressors is to liberate them "from their inhuman condition as oppressors."[82]

(b) The notion of social neutrality is a chimera. Christian praxis has only two choices: to oppose the status quo—as in the prophets and Jesus—or to bless things as they are.[83]

(c) It is the biblical persuasion that God herself "takes sides." The prophetic bias in favor of the poor and the downtrodden cannot be denied. Yahweh will punish those who "trample the heads of the poor into the dust of the earth, and turn aside the way of the afflicted" (Amos 2:7). Krister Stendahl contends that the question

> is not how one balances off mercy and judgment, but for whom is judgment mercy and for whom is it threatening doom. For God's people God's judgment is salvation. But who are God's people? Is it not consistently true in the Bible that the only time that language about "God's people" really functions, *the only time it is allowed to stand up without the lambasting critique of the prophets*, is when it stands for the little ones, the oppressed, the suppressed, the repressed? Is it not true that all language about a chosen people becomes wrong when applied outside the situation of weakness?

Jesus did not say "man shall not live by bread alone" to a hungry person; he said it to the devil (Matt. 4:1-4).[84]

A favorite passage of liberative theologians is the one attributed to Jesus' mother:

> And Mary said, . . .
> "He has shown strength with his arm,
> he has scattered the proud in the imagination of their hearts.

he has put down the mighty from their thrones,
and exalted those of low degree;
he has filled the hungry with good things,
and the rich he has sent empty away."
(Luke 1:46, 51-53; cf. 1 Sam. 2:1-10)

Jesus of Nazareth "takes after" his mother in refusing to permit any split among faith (the domain of the spirit), morality (the domain of responsible justice and love), and politics (the domain of power). Against any such split, Jesus carries forward the developing tradition of Torah-cum-prophecy Judaism: "The Lord executeth righteousness and judgment for all that are oppressed" (Ps. 103:6, kjv). In this respect, liberative theology perpetuates Jesus' hope for, and expectation of, the transformation of the world.

When God is said to take sides, the intent is that God does this provisionally—only until all the inequity and exploitation are overcome.[85] Robert McAfee Brown, interpreting Gutiérrez, shows the eminently moral quality of God's taking sides: "It is an expression of God's *universal* love that ... God will provisionally take sides with some and against others, so that present inequities may be overcome and the full possibilities of personhood opened for all. To say that God loves *all* people, means that those who thwart love must be opposed, so that their ability to perpetuate structures of oppression, which keep people separated from love of one another and of God, can be overcome."[86]

(d) Because God takes sides, Christians are summoned to do the same thing. Human responsibility to the poor is set forth in some three thousand biblical verses. Gutiérrez demonstrates how the prophet Jeremiah's theme that to know God is to do justice and righteousness (22:15-16) pervades the whole biblical story. This means "siding with the oppressed, which means opposing the oppressors, which means involvement in conflict, which means 'taking sides' in order to affirm rather than deny God. It is all of a piece." The church "has always 'taken sides,' almost invariably with the rich. What is needed now is for the church to 'change sides,' switching its allegiance from a subtle but thoroughgoing option for the rich and the status quo, to an overt and equally thoroughgoing option for the poor and the need for radical change on their behalf." Whenever Christian praxis fails to be praxis of and for the poor, Christian thinking and life are transfigured into a nonthreatening, middle-class ideology. Segundo declares, "Jesus seems to go so far as to suggest that one cannot recognize Christ, nor, therefore, know God, unless he begins with a certain commitment to the oppressed."[87]

(3) A supreme enigma of the Gospels is their double, seemingly irreconcilable character: On the one hand, those who reject God's kingdom in Jesus will themselves be rejected (cf. Mark 12:1-11). On the other hand, Jesus (and

God) are seen to be compassionate, particularly to wretched sinners. May not the latter side of things point to an open, perhaps ultimately universal, salvation? ("I came not to call the righteous but sinners" [Matt. 9:13; Mark 2:17; Luke 5:32]).

Can this enigma be resolved? Well, if the love of God and the love of neighbor are truly the first commandments of the Torah (Matt. 22:34-40; Mark 12:28-34), is it not being implied that God is as subject to the commandment of love for the neighbor as anyone else?[88] How can God be exempt from or above her own commandments? It may be that we are called to confront God with an all-decisive question: Which is to win out, justice or love? If E. P. Sanders is correct that Jesus did not make repentance a precondition to the acceptance of sinners, what are we to say of God? How can God be less accepting than Jesus was? And how can God be a lesser moral being than her children the Pharisees, to whom absolute loyalty to God went hand in hand with love of neighbor?

I close this chapter upon liberative Christology with a reconciling passage from Donald J. Goergen:

> We can picture the crowds composed of the poor, the hungry, the sad, the sick, the lame, the outcasts, the uneducated, the unclean. What could Jesus say to them that might have been a word of consolation? Nothing would have taken away their poverty, their sadness; no words were going to feed or clothe them. Yet the heart of the compassionate Jesus reached out to them. What could he have said? He knew how his heavenly Father's love reached out to them as well. And so he said all that he could say: God is yours. The message did not remove the poverty or hunger or pain. And yet it was a word of consolation. And it expressed one of the fundamental religious insights in the teaching of Jesus: GOD BELONGS TO THE PEOPLE. Nothing can separate them from God's love. They may fall outside the realm of the Law or social acceptability but they do not fall outside the realm of God. God belongs to *them*.[89]

7

The Judaism of Jesus, Redeemer of Women

We have noted Jesus' faithfulness to the women he encountered and their responding faithfulness to him. This happy truth is, unfortunately, of limited help in the presence of a stubborn datum: the maleness of Jesus. The seriousness of the moral problem here is linked to the fact that "our internalization of the male as divine" has been brought about by the "colonialization of women by men."[1] But feminism, pledged as it is to male and female integrity together, must bring its independent resources to bear upon this moral-historical issue. The cause of women is the cause of humankind. Can women possibly look to men or male figures for a savior? In Christian society, can male idolatry and its demonic structures be conquered as long as Christian saviorhood is identified with someone male?

Rita Nakashima Brock puts the matter in a nutshell: Essential to traditional dominant-male/submissive-female praxis "are the rules that give no power and authority to women except through our connections to male institutions and our relation of submission to men. In Christianity, are women therefore redeemed and legitimated by our reconciliation to the saving efficacy of a male savior? Even if we reconceive deity as goddess, what do we do with Jesus Christ? [And if] we have felt the power of that symbol called Jesus Christ, what choices do we have?"[2]

The explication to follow—our fifth major historical image of Jesus—may be of some aid in reckoning with these and kindred questions. I submit an embryonic typology: feminist positions that tend toward sanguineness, sometimes even denying that there is any essential problem in the maleness of Jesus;

points of view that are penetrated with negativity, even antagonism, respecting the male Jesus; and dialectical or transformationist views that seek after, or at least come out with, some kind of middle way between the first two extremes.

SANGUINE VIEWPOINTS

Nelly Ritchie is superintendent of the Evangelical Methodist Church in Argentina. To be met by her essay "Women and Christology" is to undergo, from one point of view, a cheering experience. Ritchie finds herself blessed by "the Word Incarnate, Jesus Christ," as by the Christian duty "to proclaim the lordship of Christ over other lords." She gives no evidence that the variables "women" and "Jesus" together present any kind of dilemma or difficulty for Christian feminists.[3] More or less, this spirit of contentment suffuses the entire anthology in which Ritchie's accounting appears, *Through Her Eyes: Women's Theology from Latin America*. This is not to suggest that the contributors are other than ardent in their feminism; on the contrary, they speak forcefully and courageously against androcentric evils within and beyond the churches—a state of affairs epitomized in Elsa Tamez's phrase, "our machistic society."[4] But the writers are clearly not perturbed at all by the maleness of Jesus and the moral and theological problems that may be posed by that fact. In some cases the Roman Catholic contributors are supported in their optimism, at least implicitly, by their devotion to Mary, Mother of Jesus Christ, by the spiritual resources Mary provides, and by the sublimity of the relation between Jesus and Mary. Thus, Ana María Bidegain (Colombia) celebrates the truth that Jesus "actually takes a woman and makes her his mother, to fulfill God's plan by taking flesh within her." Indeed, Mary is to be identified as "the model disciple for Latin American men and women" as they perform "the joint task of giving birth to a new society."[5] In her "Reflections on the Trinity" María Clara Bingemer (Brazil) attests that the

> female principle in the divinity . . . makes it possible to believe, worship, and love God not only as the strong Father who creates us and liberates us with his powerful arm, but also as a Mother, full of tenderness, grace, beauty and receptivity who accepts the seed of life and feeds it in her womb, so it may become a full being in the light of day. . . . The Christian trinitarian doctrine, and its affirmations of the Abba of Jesus as maternal Father and paternal Mother, opens the way for the formation of a community of men and women which, "in the fellowship of the Holy Spirit" (II Cor. 13:14), should proceed to overcome privilege and domination of every sort.[6]

And Consuelo del Prado (Peru) sums up what she calls "Mary's style":

> When Mary is called the first disciple, she is not resting on her laurels as the

mother of Christ, nor on the special role in the history of salvation which she was given by God. We discover her role in the Church and in our own spirituality.

Mary brings us to the Lord for in her we find the perfect model of faithfulness to the Word. She is the disciple who listens and puts the will of the Lord into practice. And in this is rooted the blessedness of her motherhood, as Jesus pointed out (Luke 8:21).

A woman of the people, a believer and mother, Mary becomes for us a companion on the road in following her Son. So it is that we are taught the piety of Mary which is so deeply rooted in our continent. We can reclaim her name for our spirituality; in the best sense of the word, our spirituality is Marian.[7]

Perhaps we may say that in ways such as these the femaleness of Mary becomes a kind of spiritual insurance policy against the protrusion of Jesus' maleness as a potentially fatal problem—granted all the difficulties in "the improbable model of a virgin-mother."[8] In a manner of speaking, Mary is a protective shield against any existential barriers that Jesus' maleness may raise—a fresh and rather intriguing role for the "Mother of God," inaugurated by none other than today's Christian feminists. Harvey Cox speculates, "What a cosmic paradox it might turn out to be if Mary, perhaps the most male-manipulated Christian symbol of them all, [proved] to be a key ingredient in the liberation of women and in the formulation of a postmodern and postsexist theology."[9]

Some feminists within our initial type tie their position to something more than "male" attributes, and they do this in behalf of a "high Christology." For example, Bingemer finds what she calls the "feminine aspects of Jesus—his tenderness, compassion, and infinite mercy," to have been "assumed eternally, definitively, and hypostatically, by the Word, the second person of the Trinity. Thus, we can say that in Jesus, in his life, words, praxis, and his person . . . that which is feminine is divinized and belongs to the most profound mystery of the love of God."[10] I think it would be somewhat more accurate to identify characteristics such as tenderness, compassion, and mercy as *human* traits, which are present or missing in either or both of the sexes, depending upon sociohistorical states of affairs. It seems to me that a "tender" man is not thereby feminine but is thereby human. To assume otherwise is to open ourselves to a new form of sexism.

Of a tenor somewhat different though related to the prevailing point of view in *Through Her Eyes*, the position of Rebecca D. Pentz answers a firm yes to her own question, Can Jesus save women? Even though her answer is the same as the (tacit) responses in *Through Her Eyes*, the difference is that Pentz is at least aware of the problem of "women and Jesus"; she proceeds, accordingly, to defend her own affirmative response.

For Pentz, there is simply nothing in "an orthodox Christology" to "contradict feminism." She considers three aspects of the subject: Jesus' revelation of a transcendent Father; Jesus as a model for humans; and Jesus as Savior. She readily agrees that "if Jesus' work is sexist, if no Christology is compatible with feminism, then there is no place for feminists in Christianity." Her answer to the question, "If God's unique self-revelation is in a male, must we conclude that God himself is male?" is an emphatic no. Even though some theologians "do slip into this error, the biblical picture of God is overwhelmingly of a being who transcends sexual categories." Some feminists, however, feel that Jesus' description of God as "transcendent Father" communicates "an oppressive patriarch, the top dog in an oppressive hierarchy." The response of Christian feminists here is to point out that Jesus himself was fully opposed to social hierarchies. Pentz herself argues the necessity of distinguishing between varied ways of exercising power. Power *over*, which God presumably has, "need not be power *against* but can be power *for*." The truth is that God exercises God's power "only for our benefit," something that Jesus again and again makes clear: "God is the loving Father who searches for the lost sheep, who welcomes home the prodigal, who bears the load of the poor, the oppressed, the outcast."

In the second place, Christianity "claims that Jesus is the perfect human and thus reveals who we ought to be." Nevertheless, some feminists ask, How can a male, who has only male experiences, serve as a perfect model for females? Pentz denies that women's need for female models excludes Jesus as a model for them. She examines three of Jesus' encounters with women—the Samaritan woman (John 4:7-30); Martha (Luke 10:38-42); and the unidentified female in a crowd (Luke 11:27-28)—and concludes that, on the one hand, Jesus proclaims the kind of *limited* self-sacrificing servanthood that is right for women.[11] On the other hand, he "calls women, just as he calls men, to focus our lives on the kingdom of God. But Jesus realizes that hearing and keeping God's word requires effort in different areas for women than it does for men."

In the third place, while Jesus may be our model, "he is more importantly our Savior." For Pentz, nothing in feminism is inconsistent with the traditional view "that Jesus' death and resurrection vanquished sin in such a way that all humans can escape from captivity to sin while being empowered to be the persons they were created to be in relationship to God eternally." Three conditions have to be met if a male Savior is to save women: His act of salvation "must be intended to cover women." It "must be effective." And "women must be able to accept his offer of salvation." Jesus meets all three of these requirements. We have already spoken to the first of these points. With the second and third points, it appears that Pentz is tending toward a combination of *via negativa* and flat edict: "I can think of no good argument for concluding that [Jesus'] salvific acts are not effective in saving women," and "I do not think that Jesus' maleness need stand in the way of us as women accepting his offer of salvation." At this juncture it seems to me that Pentz is more restating the problem than doing anything to resolve it. But at the end she does introduce a dis-

tinctive and provocative consideration: The death on the cross, the act by
which Jesus saves human beings, "is best described in human terms by the feminine metaphor of childbirth. . . . In a spiritual sense Jesus is our birth mother.
Like a birth mother, Jesus suffered in order to give us this new life." This "was
not the act of an alien patriarchal male deity."[12]

In a response to critics of her essay, Pentz contends that we "must give up
patriarchal accretions such as the exclusion of women from leadership, the
identification of women with sin, the use of exclusively male language to describe the deity, [and] the identification of a woman's relationship to God with
her sexual relationship to men, e.g., virgin mother." Positively speaking, "Christianity has much to offer feminists. Because we Christians affirm Jesus as God,
we know that God abhors oppression because Jesus abhors it, that she values a
'discipleship of equals' because Jesus [does], that the poor (who are most fre-
quently elderly women and women with dependent children) have a special
place in God's kingdom, and that everyone is accountable for how such people
are treated."[13]

I have one further evaluative remark, prompted by Pentz's call for the
abandonment of exclusively male language applied to the deity. Her own allegation that God transcends human sexual categories or limitations is acceptable only when there is this kind of insistence that female gender symbolizations of God are just as valid as male symbolizations.[14] Female identifications
remind us, along with male identifications, not so much that God is *beyond*
gender, as that God is at once divinely female and divinely male, Mother and
Father.

All in all, the initial feminist position finds no necessity for any feminist
redemption of Jesus Christ. A traditional christological status quo remains all-
sufficient and all-blessed.

NEGATIVIST VIEWS

At the opposite pole from the position just reviewed stand feminist interpreters who are anything but sanguine or happy with respect to the male Jesus.[15]
John B. Cobb, Jr., writes, "Feminists ask whether the truly salvific process, at
least for women, is really bound up with Jesus. Their questions are searching,
and many of those who pose them answer negatively."[16] In some feminist circles the androcentric religious tradition is totally repudiated and along with it
any possibility of a feminist Christology.

As a point of departure, let us introduce the apologetic claim that is forthcoming within Roman Catholic and some non-Roman Catholic circles of authority, according to which only males can be priests because when God became incarnate he chose the male being Jesus.[17] This claim seeks to associate

Christian teaching with historical fact.[18] But the trouble is that this historical fact can be called upon just as readily in the service of a struggle against patriarchalism: From the perspective of an extreme feminism, it is precisely because the reputed "incarnation" took place in a male figure that there cannot have been in him any genuine incarnation. Insofar as males are essentially (= historically) exploitive of women, how could a male ever be their Savior? In the same connection, the androcentric character of the priesthood violates the truth that all human beings are created in the image of God. (Feminists of our first type, who reject the argument that male exploitation of women rules out the saviorhood of Jesus, may come to utilize a moral distinction between "the one and the many": The man from Nazareth was just the opposite of an oppressor of women. As Diane Tennis avows, Jesus "is the one real live historical man who is reliable in the lives of many women.")[19]

J. Coert Rylaarsdam declares, "For Christians dialogue with Israel cannot really begin until they have dealt with their own problem," by which problem he means Judaism and the Jewish people.[20] But Dorothee Sölle interprets and applies Rylaarsdam's judgment in a strikingly alternative fashion. She discerns in his statement something particularly relevant to Christian women as heirs of "a religious tradition that, as part of its ethos, disinherits the female. Our relationship to a tradition that claims universalism is ambiguous because of the oppressive character of this tradition for one half of humanity." Sölle then proceeds to draw together, from a Christian reference point, the two issues (the Christian affliction of Jews and the Christian affliction of women): "In a Christology 'from above,' Jesus no longer represents only 'the word of God,' spoken to us non-Jews and mediating the covenant between God and the goyim; instead he is the exclusive savior who has fulfilled 'once and for all' what God wants us to do. The result has been, overwhelmingly, a Christological perfectionism that leads believers into what Bonhoeffer called 'cheap grace,' in which Christ elicits admiration instead of imitation and in which he is severed from both his Jewish religious tradition and his prophecy of the yet-to-be-realized messianic kingdom." Significantly, the Protestant Christian feminist Dorothee Sölle here joins forces with the post-Catholic feminist Mary Daly against what the latter calls "Christolatry," a reality apprehended and rejected as the "idolatrous worship of a supernatural, timeless divine being who has little in common with the Jewish Jesus of Nazareth."[21] Thus is given form a revolutionary Christian feminism that ranges itself against a "Savior" who does not save, one in whom, and in whose maleness, women are, in fact, victimized. This radical attack upon an allegedly "idolatrous deification of a male human being ... constitutes a unique and unprecedented" world-historical development, which

cuts not merely in one epochal moral direction but in two: It attacks the deification of not just any human being but the specific deification that created anti-Jewish supersessionism; and it attacks the world-destroying sexism that came to pen-
etrate Christianity (because of *this* male "Savior") in continuity with the sexism of
Judaism. The inner bond between Christian antisemitism and Christian antiwomanism is disclosed. The root cause of both these phenomena in the Christian
world is the triumphalism of a male "Savior." The whole of Christian history exhibits a single affliction, with two faces. There is the idolatrous divinizing of a human being, and there is the idolatrous male-izing of divinity.[22]

A further and decisive complexity here derives from a revolutionist-feminist questioning of human completeness within the male of the species. Now
the issue is not just the exploitation of women by men but whether any male
could ever be capable of an ultimate soteriological accomplishment. For men
remain, after all, incomplete human beings, i.e., they are incapable of birthing,
of bringing forth and sustaining human life. Manitonquat (Medicine Story)
speaks not just for Native Americans but for humankind: "In the heart of our
ancient teachings is the wisdom that woman is central to the creation and sustenance of life. . . . So it is that women are the best guides and teachers, in their
inner instinctive wisdom, of the preservation and sustenance of the species."[23]

The issue is thus not that of the character or message of Jesus ("Jesus was
a feminist: so what?" — Mary Daly)[24] but rather of the relation among three factors: the nature of maleness, the oppressive sexism of a male savior, and the
incarnation. The problem is well expressed by the same Mary Daly who is sure
that were Jesus here today, he would be working for female liberation: "An effect of the liberation of women will very likely be the loss of plausibility of
Christological formulas that come close to reflecting a kind of idolatry in regard to the person of Jesus. . . . Indeed, the prevalent emphasis upon the total
uniqueness and supereminence of Jesus will, I think, become less meaningful.
. . . The underlying—and often explicit—assumption in the minds of theologians down through the centuries has been that the divinity could not have
deigned to become incarnate in the 'inferior' sex, and the 'fact' that 'he' did not
do so reinforces the belief in masculine superiority."[25]

Strikingly, this passage appears to authorize travel in two opposite directions. On the one hand, we could apply a revolutionist-feminist polemic respecting inferiority/superiority and pronounce that, unbelievably enough, God
did become incarnate in the actually incomplete or inferior (= male) sex. I am
unaware of any Christian feminists who go down this path, although I suppose
that such a view is not perforce incompatible with the persuasion of God's *kenosis*, emptying (cf. Phil. 2:8).

On the other hand, we may propose that the question is not what God
could have done but instead what—in the traditional Christian attestation—

God *did*. For analytic aid here we may refer to the eucharistic prayer that identifies Jesus as "the new man for all men." While probably few disputants would still quarrel with the change of wording from *men* to *human beings*, the difficulty remains that there is no way to change *man* to something else—not unless we are prepared to sever the incarnation from history.

Once we travel in the second direction and are also prepared to find with Daly and others (as I am not) that the Christian tradition is essentially sexist, no way appears left "for surmounting the evil of sexism apart from some form of abnegation or radical re-presentation of the Incarnation."[26] Such an existential plight as this may open the way to, or impel a quest for, a third form of praxis.

TRANSFORMATIONIST POSITIONS

On the whole, I dissociate myself from our first two interpretations—from the first, because it turns its back upon a genuine problem; from the second, because it would tear down the entire edifice of Christianity. Some feminist points of view tend to mediate between sanguine and negativist outlooks respecting the maleness of Jesus. We have considered Elisabeth Schüssler Fiorenza's highly dialectical treatment of the Christian androcentric tradition. In both the exemplifications I shall next report on, those of Rita Nakashima Brock and Isabel Carter Heyward, the "redemption of Christ" is paramount—meaning, not redemption *by* Christ alone, but the need and warrant for Christ himself and the Christ tradition itself to be in some sense redeemed.

In her essay "The Feminist Redemption of Christ," Brock inveighs against patriarchalism's "unholy goodness," which stands in opposition to the "holy goodness of presence" and the "holy goodness of erotic power." Patriarchalism visits upon us a "dualistic, hierarchical Christ ... who divides the world into true believers and heretics. ... This Christ is lord over all and servant to all, perfect in any form [I take it Brock means "every form"], a judgment on humanity as sinful, and a sign of everyone's need to be saved from what is most frightening." But such "insistence upon Jesus' human perfection as evidence of a divine presence in him removes him from the human sphere." Unholy goodness "does not arise from reality in process-as-lived, nor from the ability to hold distinctions without collapsing them into absolute, fixed dualisms. Unholy goodness demands allegiance by insisting on its own reality as unalterably absolute and by rejecting everything that questions it. The dualism behind static understandings of goodness is nonrelational and destructive of persons."

In order to reclaim Christology in and for feminist visions, we must oppose "the doctrine that only a perfect male form can incarnate God fully and be salvific," for that only makes "our individual lives in female bodies a prison against God. . . . " In a judgment that is pertinent as well to our later discussion of Jesus Christ and religious pluralism, Brock declares,

> The idolatry of Jesus Christ must cease to hold us and oppress all who do not pledge allegiance to the heart of that idolatry. The demand that we give allegiance to one paradigmatic and central symbol does not do justice to our life's experiences. We live in a pluralistic universe full of complex realities that call us.
>
> The feminist Christian commitment is not to a savior who redeems us by bringing God to us. . . . Our commitment is to a divine presence with us here and now, a presence that works through the mystery of our deepest selves and our relationships, constantly healing us and nudging us toward a wholeness of existence we only fitfully know. That healed wholeness is not Christ, it is ourselves.[27]

This declaration might seem to return us to the post-Christian negativism of the second type. Another immediate response might be to discern, so to speak, a certain war within the Trinity between its second and third persons. Neither of these reactions is necessary. To remove (contra Rebecca Pentz) "the exclusive, perfect god-man Jesus Christ from the center of our Christian commitment" enables us "to claim ourselves and, then, to reclaim the historical Jesus and Jesus Christ." Furthermore, once we are able to see the christological symbol system "as part of a community self-naming process," we put ourselves in a position to reclaim that system. "The images a community creates to name itself are a combination of the events that evoke the image, of the way the original viewers see the events and pass them on, and of the consciousness of those who uphold the image in the present." The evil is that "patriarchal theologians have created a patriarchal Christ who mystifies the feminist quest for wholeness. Christ, however, is a complex relational image created by many. Within patriarchal culture, as within ourselves, are nonpatriarchal elements, and, though attentuated, they are not absent from the Christian tradition. *We redeem Christ when we refuse to let patriarchy and its death-dealing images have the final word.*"[28]

It is through an exposé of the patriarchal-necrophilic drive that Brock climaxes her disputation. (Cf. Mary Daly: The essential message of patriarchy is necrophilia.[29] Also, keep in mind here Rebecca Pentz's notion that Jesus suffered in order that we might have new life and that his death and resurrection vanquished human captivity to sin.) Brock writes,

> The patriarchal preoccupation with death and destruction, with alienation and the risking of death to produce life, gives us Christological symbols that divide and conquer. Symbols of a self-sacrificing perfect act of love; of God sending his son to die as a substitute for us; and of the supreme sacrifice to abstract truth of an ethical champion show us a savior crucified and dead who is the way to birth into a new abstract form of life eternal. The present, the arena of relationship, is denied. As in war, death is the terror risked and conquered by the coercive powers used to de-

feat its inevitability. Salvific power is the power to die. The cross of Jesus Christ gives death the power to give life in an otherworldly, alienated future.[30]

From Brock's perspective, it is possible to adjudge that Rebecca Pentz's naming of the crucified Jesus as our birth mother comprises an unwitting tribute to patriarchal necrophilia. On first consideration, Pentz's act of naming may appear to be sanguine, yet in reality it is not that; whereas Brock's thrust, for all its seeming negativism, proves itself sanguine, a sanguineness for which history supplies the authenticity. Brock continues:

> The community of Jesus' followers is empowered by his having *lived*, as prophet, healer, teacher, and friend. They give back life in remembering him with symbolic images, begetting life from life. Christ is the community remembrance of the Jesus who lived on earth. Life rejoins death, and the tension is sustained between the two because a community of living persons responds to death without defeat. Relationships give life. . . .
>   In the early church's self-naming after Jesus' death, life is given through the symbols created. Minor voices, tenuous attempts at life-giving naming, sound persistently amidst the death-defying Christologies of patriarchy. The minor voices speak of the church's experiences of their own redemptive power symbolized in the stories of Jesus Christ. The voices speak of an erotic power experienced in his living with them, not in his dying for them. The healing voices persist against other sounds and speak of images that mirror feminist visions.

To what or to whom, then, are we brought? "Feminist freedom is the ability to increase and exercise erotic power." We are brought to Jesus "as healing presence." For "healing is the living Jesus' salvific power, his erotic power. . . . People ask to be healed, and he heals them because he has an urgent eschatological vision of wholeness that opens him to concrete persons in his presence. The church's Jesus stands with God against suffering and uses erotic power to purge illness."

Here enters, I suggest, a convergence among four forces: psychosocial holism, liberationism as such, Christian feminism (at least in its third form or type), and the Judaism of Jesus (insofar as that faith is ever doing battle with necrophilia). These four are made as one by the struggle against suffering, never by obeisance to suffering. In sum:

> The healing Christological images . . . can nourish faith when they feed our power, an erotic power that helps us save the images that restore us and lead us back to each other. We redeem Christ when we recognize the images of Jesus Christ that reflect our hunger for healing wholeness and claim those images as resources for hope because we belong to a community of transformation and empowerment. Christ as healer need not be an image of exclusive power and authority. Christ is an image of shared power that works and is increased only in the sharing. . . . The feminist visions of transformation and empowerment shatter unholy goodness and re-

deem Christ with whole-making passions for healing. And healing is to be in each other, loving ourselves and each other fiercely into wholeness.[31]

The feminine image and the feminine vision, christologically speaking, are of life, in contrast to patriarchal death. Justice is power is love; love is power is justice: here is female creativity, female passion, female redemption. This finding, or confession, is also that of Isabel Carter Heyward, to whom we now turn.[32]

Heyward's *The Redemption of God: A Theology of Mutual Relation* occupies the same genre as the essay of Brock, but there are two related differences in emphasis. First, as implied by her title, what Heyward has to say christologically is handled as part of the larger issue of the redemption of God's very self or of a comprehensive theology of mutual relation, with "relation" apprehended as the "intimate and immediate power between self and other," *Ich* and *Du*, *Wir* and *Ihr*. (Heyward agrees with Elie Wiesel that moral evil is a psychosocial structure of nonrelation, born "in our fear of both power and powerlessness.")[33]

Second, while Brock directs herself to the "*feminist* redemption of Christ," Heyward's rendition, although composed by a committed feminist, is not limited to that approach. In this regard, her definition of a "feminist" is worthy of note: "one who values and attempts to relate to people as human beings irrespective of whether they are women or men."[34] Not unfittingly, therefore, Heyward's feminist christological critique as such is remanded to an appendix of her book. Moreover, her "re-imaging" of Jesus (chapter 2) is not primarily tied to the immediate obligations of a feminist polemic. "What is important is whether we can come to some better understanding of who we are in relation to God and each other. To this end, the image of Jesus is itself a tool."[35]

Nevertheless, Heyward's Christology presupposes the struggle against patriarchal idolatry. She writes:

> It is in the nature of our idol to be intolerant of ambiguity. His first and only love is Himself. He is an impassive unflappable character who represents the headship of a universal family in which men are best and women least. He is the keeper of an ethical scorecard on which "reason" gets good marks and "relation" fails. He is a master plan-maker who maps out and, by remote-control, directs our journeys before we have learned to walk. His narcissism is unquenchable. He demands that he be loved. This cold deity is the legitimating construct of the patriarchal desire to dominate and control the world. He is the eternal King, the Chairman of the board, the President of the institution, the Guru of the youth, the Husband of the wife, the General of the army, the Judge of the court, the Master of the universe, the Father of the church. He resides above us all. He is our superior, never our friend. He is a rapist, never a lover, of women and of anyone else beneath Him. He is the first and final *icon of evil* in history.

In contrast to such alienating iconism, Heyward advances authentic theological praxis. Theology "is not a cerebral exercise; it is a passionate effort to express and evoke human activity. Its appropriate focus is earth, not heaven. And it is not about God as God is in Godself, but rather about us as we experience God in this world, at this time among ourselves."[36] More specifically, Heyward follows in the lineage of Dietrich Bonhoeffer, according to whom, paradoxically, "God would have us know that we must live as men [sic] who manage our lives without him [sic]. The God who is with us is the God who forsakes us (Mark 15:34). The God who lets us live in the world without the working hypothesis of God is the God before whom we stand continually. Before God and with God we live without God."[37] (This is surely to suggest that Jesus' "failure" is as much God's problem as it is Jesus' problem—or more so.)

What feminist theology must challenge is "the passivity and powerlessness of human beings in relation to an active and omnipotent God who has no need of us." Just

> because we are human, we are able to be co-creative agents of redemption. Our vocation is to take seriously the creative character of who we are—both in relation to one another (humanity) and to the power of relation itself (God). Our evil is seated in our sin (the fear and denial of the power we share, hence of one another). The redemption of the world—of human and divine life, ourselves and the transpersonal bond among us—is dependent upon our willingness to make love/justice in the world. In so doing, we co-operate with each other and with God in a process of mutual redemption—that is, in the deliverance of both God and humanity from evil.[38]

This is no arrogant humanism that replaces God with humankind. "God is the bond which connects us in such a way that each of us is em-powered to grow, work, play, love and be loved. God makes this justice, our justice. God is not only our immediate power in relation, but is also our immediate re-source of power: that from which we draw power to realize actively who we are in relation. It is to this God that we pray." Heyward nowhere denies God as transcending, neither does she question the "eternal and transcendent dimensions of reality." At the same time, we are asked to re-image a world "in which there is no wholly other, no up-and-againstness between person and person, subject and object, but rather co-subjects, co-operating, co-creating. No more God and humanity defined by opposition: one up, the other down; one good, the other not-good; one with power, the other without; one giving, the other receiving; one in heaven, the other on earth, but rather a constellation of relation in which God is nothing other than the resource of relational *dunamis* [power], unable to be wholly contrasted or identified with any one person in any time or place."[39]

Because of the delimiting of this book to Christology, I shall not discuss at length Heyward's treatment of God's redemption as such. Humankind is "responsible for the redemption of God in history." Heyward is at one with Martin Buber's plea, "That you need God more than anything, you know at all times in your heart. But don't you also know that God needs you—in the fullness of his eternity, you?" Anthropologically speaking, Heyward proposes that "the earth creature's defiance of command was, in fact, its first liberating act from the bondage of a passivity-mistaken-for-innocence which rendered it subject, rather than friend, of God. ... Might such authors have done well to tell us about human empowerment, in which to become 'like God' (Genesis 3:22) is to claim the power to effect God and to contend with evil? ... So it is that we 'fall' into creation, ... into the likeness of God, into the possibility of on-going voluntary friendship, into our co-creative capacity," a creator "who knows her creativity in relation." Fundamental and constitutive of human being is the experience of relation; it is "good and powerful"; and "it is only within this experience—as it is happening here and now—that we may realize *that the power in relation is God*." All this justifies and even necessitates an "insistent hermeneutical bias": The love of neighbor as self is *the* norm of Christian life and theology and *not* the love of God. And yet, "to love humanity is to befriend God"; it is "our act of making God incarnate in the world."[40]

It is from inside this theological and ethical frame of reference that Heyward marshals her Christology. Foundational here is her enmity to Christolatry: "The shift on the part of Christian theologians from an image of Jesus' own knowledge of the inbreaking of God's realm among lovers of humanity to an image of Jesus himself as Lord of an otherworldly realm is tantamount to a movement from God to idolatry, or the making of Jesus into an image of all that he did not re-present in the world." Foundational as well is Heyward's advocacy of the same synergism to which we have found Jesus adhering. In a truly authentic (functional and functioning) Christology, wherein movement and relation are the things that count, acts of co-operation are "ultimately responsible for in-carnation." "*To women and men*, Jesus represents God's capacity to touch and heal and rebuke and comfort humanity. *To God*, Jesus represents humanity's capacity to co-operate in the touching and healing and teaching and rebuking and comforting of humanity—and perhaps God as well. Re-image a God who is touched, healed, instructed, rebuked, and comforted by Jesus."[41]

The trouble with most Christology is that it is "for all practical purposes, anti-female." But, of course, this is to say that Christology tends to be "fundamentally antihuman." Indeed, "the Jewish tradition of voluntary activity between God and humanity collapsed in orthodox Christianity under the weight of Greek metaphysics, in which human and divine natures were conceptualized as being so distinctly 'other' as to disallow the possibility of any voluntary cooperation between them." What was lost was "the voluntary character of a God of justice who chooses to act in relation to people who choose to act in relation to God in the world. . . . This early doctrinal development signalled a critical shift in the understanding of how justice is established and by whom: a shift from work in history to faith in that which lies beyond history; a shift from *humanity's* responsibility for creating justice to *God's* gift of a 'natural' justice; a shift from the love of one's neighbor in the world to the love of one's God above the world." In a word, "orthodox" Christology was invaded by docetism.[42]

Heyward freely concedes that

> Jesus cannot be for us what he was for the Twelve, Mary Magdalene, or Mary and Martha of Bethany. . . . The most and least we can do if Jesus is to be anything for us—other than an idol which lures us away from the world—is to re-image Jesus on the basis of what we know already about ourselves in relation to the Jesus-figure about whom we have heard, to each other, and to that which we believe to be God. Our Christology becomes an image of our relational experience, just as, I believe, incarnation was an image of Jesus' relational experience.[43]

Relational theology has to be incarnational—"between us, in the physicality of all that we do: breathe, move, feel, reach, touch." The God who is "the resource and power of relation," the one "with whom we image ourselves in relation, is in flesh (*sarx*), alive in human being, active in human life, on earth, in history. . . . The centrality of Jesus' place in Christianity has resulted from a mis-conception of Jesus as a divine person rather than as a human being who knew and loved God." "Re-image a Jesus whose *dunamis* pushed him [in a direction totally against] absolute opposition; a Jesus whose relation to God was the resource of his movement into ambiguity and tension between self and other, the law and its re-imaging, heaven and earth, *dunamis* and *exousia* [authority], past and present and future; a Jesus who was fully and only human and, as such, fully able (*dunamai*) to incarnate God in the world; a Jesus in whose acts *dunamis* was immediately human and divine." By contrast, "we expect a divine savior, because we are unable to realize that we ourselves are the saviors of God. . . . The Jesus who is caricatured as the Eternal Christ has been constructed by Christian men who have missed the point of the Jesus who knew no higher value than God's in-carnation. . . ."[44]

The objection may be heard that Heyward's position (*perhaps* together with that of Brock) falls more accurately under our second type, the point of view of negativism, or (in view of the christological denials involved) even under a non-Christian or post-Christian rubric. In the world of today the specific meaning of Christian is an elusive and difficult question. Clearly, Professor Heyward does not look upon her viewpoint as non-Christian or anti-Christian but rather, along with other feminist colleagues, thinks of it as contributing to the fulfilling and reconciling truth of the Christian faith—a position that, in accordance with its fealty to the Jesus of history, can quite conceivably be identified as orthodox Christian. It seems to me that it is precisely Heyward's insistence upon Jesus' full humanity (i.e., upon the incarnation) that makes it difficult, if not wrongheaded, to exclude her from our dialectical or transformationist type. For Heyward, the real anti-Christian position is (Christian) patriarchy or any ideology or praxis that undermines the church's commitment to the world.

A telling aspect of Heyward's contribution is her reckoning with the incarnation of God in a Jewish context. Elie Wiesel and the *Shoah* occupy a large place in her story. Of course, this sort of thing does not resolve the conflict between Judaism and Christianity vis-à-vis Jesus of Nazareth. Yet it may temper that conflict. It does move the conflict onto a rather different plane. The "old" issue could be expressed in this way. *The Jewish side*: Jesus is not God; to Jewish sensibility "the deification [or divinization] of any human being is simply unthinkable."[45] *The Christian side*: God became human (incarnate) in Jesus, but only the one time. In partial contrast, the "new" issue between Judaism and Christianity can perhaps be put in this way: *The Jewish side*: Jesus is not God, even though God may be incarnate wherever and whenever s/he chooses. (Here, of course, the failure of Jesus to link himself or to be linked to the [coming] kingdom of God is crucial.) *The Christian side*: Jesus is a special incarnation of God; in principle, this becomes possible through the overall truth that God incarnates her/himself in all kinds of ways. The strength of Heyward's Christology lies in the fact that, rather than acting as if the maleness of Jesus is not there, she makes that maleness *ultimately* nondecisive because Jesus is not some god walking around but is a fully human being with the limitations-obligations (including gender) that everyone has. To "reject Jesus solely on the basis of his 'maleness' or Jesus' 'Father' on the basis of God's bondage to patriarchal projection" is to strengthen a "tenet that is so oppressive" to woman: Biology is destiny. In other words, had Jesus been a woman, the christological challenge would remain exactly what it is: to avoid lifting Jesus "above human experience and stripping us of our responsibility to make God incarnate in the world."[46] It is within this context that an intervention of Anne E. Carr becomes pertinent: "In a profound sense, Jesus' sex does not make any difference for feminists whose cause is, finally, to emancipate sexuality from its distorted societal and religious valorization. . . . [Feminist] women in the church insist that sexuality has nothing to do with saviorhood."[47]

All in all, according to Heyward's reasoning the question of Jesus Christ as "Savior" of humankind is to be inverted: Humankind is (equally but *not* more) "savior" of Christ. Thereby may the christological problem for feminists eventually be resolved: Insofar as human beings act to redeem Jesus, and thus in a sense redeem God, the question, Can Jesus redeem women? is opened to a positive, creative response. For a mutual relation is now forged, or at least started, between the two sides. As Harvey Cox puts it, "The dangerous female element which male power has tried to eliminate from the modern world is poised and ready to return. No valid postmodern theology can ignore it."[48]

From the standpoint of the third position in our embryonic typology, there is hope for a positive feminist Christology. In the end, neither Brock nor Heyward construes the maleness of Jesus as such to be a barrier to a Christian faith for feminists, though they are both well aware of the seriousness and poignancy of that question and of the tensions it can create.

The exposition in this chapter has already carried us over into the next part of our inquiry, "From Jesus to Christ." In the meantime—a painful "meantime," an *Interimsethik* if there ever was one—the torment remains, for Isabel Carter Heyward as much as, *if not more so*, for the rest of us: God did not cooperate; the Cooperator par excellence failed to show God's face. The "theology of mutual relation" never came off. Jesus was left there, upon the cross.

What do we do now?

PART

3

From Jesus to Christ

8

Discontinuity and Continuity: The Christs of the Apostolic Writings

The title of Part Three of the present book is borrowed from Paula Fredriksen's work *From Jesus to Christ: The Origins of the New Testament Images of Jesus*. In this chapter we occupy ourselves with the plural "Christs" of the Apostolic Writings, grappling with these Christs amidst the unceasing dialectic "Jesus of history"/"Christ of faith"; then go on (chap. 9) to the discretely covenantal Christ of Paul M. van Buren; reckon (chap. 10) with the spirited current subject of Jesus Christ and extra-Christian faiths; address (chap. 11) the all-telling question of Jesus' resurrection; and offer (chap. 12) a closing commentary. These treatments will scarcely exhaust the vast subject "From Jesus to Christ"; yet each contributes materially and heuristically to that subject.

James H. Charlesworth sets the stage for this part of our study: "The search for the historical Jesus over the last two hundred years has been a rocky road with many dead ends and detours. Many scholars have served us well; and it is now obvious the journey is both possible and necessary. . . . The search for the Jesus of history does bring us closer to the historical reality of Jesus of Nazareth and does awaken us with crescending interrogatives. The search and the questions free us to perceive more clearly the *mysterium Christi*."[1]

Much more than has been the case in earlier pages, the several final chapters of this book invest us in the *mysterium Christi*, or more modestly put, in the encounter between the historical domain and that mystery.

METHODOLOGICAL AND HERMENEUTICAL
QUESTIONS

At this point I introduce, and in part reintroduce, certain methodological and hermeneutical issues.

The present study operates out of the proposition—much debated—that Christology is to be grounded upon the historical Jesus. Or better, the study approaches the christological question from a prevailingly historical perspective. Accordingly, were the analysis to have ended with the previous chapter, a certain completedness could have been felt. And yet, throughout the Christian tradition, as still today even in scholarly circles, the quite different position is defended or assumed according to which, materially and decisively, Christology is much more than or other than a historical matter; it has other intentions and requirements, and it is obliged to honor alternative claims and truths. Our study of several historical images of Jesus (chaps. 3–7) has opened up many questions of faith and of theology. For to declare that Jesus is "the Christ" is to make a statement of faith that is not provable (or disprovable) by history. Alister McGrath can provide a whole monograph upon the relevance and centrality of the cross for Christians of today without finding it necessary to enter substantially upon questions of the historical Jesus (other than, naturally, upon Jesus' death).[2] Some go so far as to deny that a valid or compelling Christology has anything substantive or decisive to do with "history"—beyond, of course, the history or story of a particular individual's or Christian community's encounter with the living Christ who transcends, judges, and redeems all things, not excepting things historical. Matters are further complicated when at one and the same time someone shows an awareness of the essential difference between historical norms and transhistorical norms, as is the case with James P. Mackey, and yet then goes on to contend that the best starting point for the quest of the historical Jesus "is that event in which the historical life of Jesus ended, his death."[3]

Wolfhart Pannenberg epitomizes the ongoing problem: "Does Christology have primarily to do with the Jesus of that past time or with the Jesus who is present today?"[4] Accordingly, it is not out of order to include in this book—the Apostolic Writings provide the source par excellence—arguments and confessions that are not purely historical but point much more in the direction of faith and the assumptions and life of faith. Indeed, chapter 11, on the resurrection of Jesus, will comprise my own Christian reflections or faith-reflections upon that teaching. (It may be agreed that Jesus' history, in the usual sense, ended when he died.) Because the primary purpose of the book, however, is to "reclaim the Jesus of history," those outlooks that are other than historical or historicist will tend, in the pages that remain, to be received critically or prob-

lematically or (less critically speaking) in ways that seek to utilize and to respect historical understanding. The question does persist: Is a given christological claim reconcilable to the historical Jesus, his message and his mission, as
one who lived for the sake of the restoration of Israel? And even where no act
of evaluation is at stake, the book's morphology and balance are still such as to
suggest that history is rightfully foundational to Christology.

We do well to keep in mind, to return to chapter 1, that, objectively speaking, any division between history and extrahistorical understanding is not absolute. For extrahistorical apprehension is itself amenable to varying measures
of historical and/or phenomenological understanding—just as historical understanding and method are ever subject to apprehensions beyond purely historical ones.

Let me see if I can make the above form of reasoning more pertinent to
our particular subject.

Together with the Hebrew Bible, the Apostolic Writings comprise the canonical foundation of Christianity. The Apostolic Writings present us at once
with the Jesus of history and the Christ of faith. Within and by means of this
canon the church holds in "creative tension the very human Jesus of Luke's
Gospel and the transcendent Jesus of the Fourth Gospel."[5] Within the Apostolic Writings there is, indeed, no way finally to separate "Jesus" and "Christ."
(This is another way of saying that the kind of preeminently historical expositions I have reported on and assessed in earlier chapters entail varying measures of abstraction or generalization from the canonical literature as it stands.)
It is the Christ of faith who provides the singularity of Christianity as a religion.
This fact, however, is accompanied and/or qualified by the highly paradoxical
declaration that a certain historical figure, Jesus of Nazareth, is the *fons et
origo*, or even the sine qua non, of the Christ of faith. That is to say, the Christian church has always insisted that the Christ who was raised from the dead
is—"essentially," not "accidentally"—the same Jesus who was crucified. In
philosophic language, "Jesus" is the necessary though not sufficient condition
of "Christ." Had there been no Jesus of history, there would be no Christ of
faith and no Christianity. Nevertheless, the Christ of faith is hardly reducible to
the Jesus of history.

Through the years various expressions of, and efforts to deal with, the relationship between the Jesus of history and the Christ of faith have stood up to
be counted. Sometimes the Jesus of history has been subordinated to the Christ
of faith; sometimes the Christ of faith has been subordinated to the Jesus of
history. I venture to suggest a model that is consanguine with the effort within
the philosophy of Thomism to describe the (ideal) relationship between reason and faith. That point of view is grounded in turn upon the abstract, alleged
truth that "the supernatural order rests upon the foundation of the natural or-

der, yet apart from the supernatural order, the natural order is incomplete." In simpler, logical form: "A rests upon B, yet apart from A, B remains incomplete." To implement this schema: Faith rests upon the foundation of historical reason, yet apart from faith, historical reason remains incomplete.[6] And to direct this way of thinking to the problem at hand: The Christ of faith rests upon the foundation of the Jesus of history and hence will not (must not?) violate that foundation; but yet apart from the Christ of faith, the Jesus of history remains incomplete.

This architectonic or two-storey christological model may be of some use during the remainder of our study. Thus, one immediate, even truistic derivation from the model is that while the Christ of faith transcends the Jesus of history, nevertheless nothing in the Christ of faith is inconsistent with or irreconcilable with the Jesus of history. To repeat James Parkes's aphorism, "Bad history cannot be the foundation for good theology." Readers will recall the suggestion in chapter 1 that theological-historical propositions may be either themselves reasonable or rise above and beyond reason, but they may not be in contradiction of reason. To give the most rudimentary illustration possible: Christ at once rests upon and transcends a male human being named Jesus, but Christ could never be identified with a Jesus turned into a female human being. In the remainder of this book the model I have described is presupposed (though, of course, not proved). That is to say, affirmations about Christ may be judged as either consistent with what we know of the historical Jesus or as going beyond what we may know of him; yet such affirmations ought not contradict the historical Jesus. This threefold way of judging is coherent, I believe, with the view that Christianity is a faith that grounds itself upon historical revelation.

For help in coming to terms with the vast problem of "From Jesus to Christ," and more exactly with "The Christs of the Apostolic Writings," I submit eight background and interrelated propositions, the first of them in interrogative form.

(1) In what substantive and existential ways is the Jesus of history indispensable/dispensable to the Christ of faith? (This question was made unavoidable for the church through Paul of Tarsus, for whose Christology the "whatness" of the Jesus of the flesh, though not his "thatness," was redundant.)

(2) The relation between the Jesus of history and the Christ of faith is our prevailing concern in this part of the study, in some contrast to Part Two, "Five Historical Images."

(3) The concept of *conflict* applies much more at the point of discrepancies between Jesus' message/mission and elements in the Apostolic Writings than it does with supposed differences between Jesus and other Jews.

When studied carefully, conflictive materials in the Apostolic Writings reflect primarily the former kind of conflict rather than the latter. It was the efforts of the evangelist-writers to establish conflictive situations between Jesus and his people that served to convey the erroneous impression that the latter kind of conflict was the telling one.

(4) "Jesus–vis-à-vis–Jesus" questions and "Jesus–vis-à-vis–Christ" questions are obviously different.

Much perplexity derives from the simultaneous presence of and competition between these two kinds of questions: the relation between historical Apostolic Writings' claims for Jesus and the point of view of Jesus himself; and the relation between the historical Jesus (in one and sometimes in both the senses just mentioned) and the Christ of faith. It is one thing to discern continuities/discontinuities between the Jesus of history as set forth in the Apostolic Writings on the one hand, and the "real" Jesus of history on the other hand. It is quite something else to claim objective identities (and nonidentities) between the Jesus of history and the Christ of faith. The latter identities are much more problematic than the continuities/discontinuities between the Jesus of the Apostolic Writings and the "actual" Jesus.

The first of the above types of discernment is often truistic, since we have no knowledge of Jesus apart from the Apostolic Writings. The question of how the Gospels can convey authentic information on the historical Jesus while at the same time they depart from historical fact concerning him will always be *the* enigma yet also *the* opportunity of Apostolic Writings scholarship. In different terminology: How much did the evangelists and the early church retroject into the actual message and mission of Jesus, and why did they do so? Still differently put: In what measure, if any, are the several Christs of the Apostolic Writings commensurate with the Jesus of Nazareth who is a faithful son of Judaism, the *hasid* who, sharing as he did the hope of Jewish restoration, confined his message and mission to Israel? The latter question, once it is theologically engineered, opens up inquiries into the promulgation of, or escape from, the Christolatry decried by Mary Daly, Isabel Carter Heyward, and others. A passage in Leonard Swidler, written in a Roman Catholic frame of reference, falls on the escape side:

> Is there not a clear logic in contemporary Christians' taking as a basic standard of the meaning of Yeshua the explanation given by the chief of the Apostles Peter (presumably his testimony would be especially weighty with his "successor," the pope, and the 800 million Catholics): "Jesus of Nazareth, a man (*andra*) attested to you by God with . . . signs which God did through him. . . . God raised him up. . . . This Jesus God raised up. . . . God has made him both lord and Christ" (Acts 2:22, 24, 32, 36)? Here it is clear that Peter thought of Yeshua as a man (*andra*) in whom God was manifested through "mighty works and wonders and signs," who was

killed and then raised to a new life as "lord and Christ" by God. If the first followers of Yeshua, after the resurrection event (led by no less a figure than Peter, according to Luke), held such a "low" Christology, should such a position not enjoy the greatest of respect? Is such a "low" Christology simply "lifted up," *aufgehoben*, by a "high" Christology which speaks of Yeshua as man and God, or is it in fact "swallowed up" and changed from a Jewish to a Hellenistic way of thinking—without being aware that the Jewish way is basically non-ontological, metaphorical, and thereby misunderstanding it?[7]

In a word, the temptation of Christolatry (and indeed of the "high Christology"?) is a form of heresy, when evaluated from a Petrine point of view.

(5) Because of the complex quality of such data as are available, it is not always possible to keep separate the two kinds of questions referred to under (4).

(6) There is no a priori incompatibility between the finding that Jesus did not seek to found a new religion (beyond the renewal of Judaism) and the assertion that historically Christianity arose from the mission, message, and person of Jesus of Nazareth.

In this connection, the bitter religious conflicts that the Apostolic Writings fabricate between Jesus and his contemporaries are unhistorical.[8]

(7) Jewish eschatological conviction extended in some way to the fate/destiny of the Gentiles. The fact that the Jesus movement came to involve a mission to the Gentiles is coherent with that universalist aspect of Jewish persuasion.

(8) Today's developing New Testament scholarship may help to take us beyond the acknowledgment made in proposition (4). There is gathering justification for declaring significant continuities between the convictions of the early church respecting Jesus and what may be at least tentatively or roughly identified as Jesus' own christological predilections.

This eighth proposition reflects an intention to go beyond assertions of continuity between the "real" historical Jesus and the reported historical Jesus. For the phrasing "Jesus' own christological predilections" is meant to open up the possibility of material consonance between the Jesus of history and the Christ of faith—a potential point of joining (*Anknüpfungspunkt*) of those two categories.

I shall first explore what this last possibility does not properly mean (the next section of the chapter) and then explore what it may legitimately or conceivably mean (the final two sections of the chapter).

DISCONTINUITIES BETWEEN THE JESUS OF HISTORY AND THE CHRIST OF FAITH

The Apostolic Writings boast a variety of christological ideas and claims. This congeries of effort is recently examined and assessed in *From Jesus to Christ* by Paula Fredriksen. Before we take up separate parts of the Apostolic Writings, it may be useful, with Fredriksen's aid, to remind ourselves of the overall or general *kerygma* (proclamation) of the primitive church.

The christological claims either conflict with what we know of claims made by the historical Jesus or are discontinuous with the latter claims or simply supplement them or in some instances manifest continuity of language and conviction (this last to be emphasized in the third and fourth sections of the chapter).

It is "very probable" that in response to the resurrection, the original disciples affirmed the message of Jesus Christ, the crucified and vindicated Son of Man (= "man"?), and/or risen Messiah, whose death expiated the sins of Israel and whose imminent second coming in glory would "defeat evil, judge, occasion the resurrection of the dead, redeem Israel, and establish the kingdom." The event of Jesus' resurrection, which exalted him to God's right hand and vindicated his message that the kingdom is coming, signaled "the nearness of the End, since at the End the dead (or perhaps only the righteous dead) were to be raised. It thus confirmed Jesus' message, and consequently his status as messenger." The Messiah everyone had anticipated was the Davidic Messiah. "Nowhere did Judaism anticipate a dying and rising Messiah; and the apostles, like Paul after them (Rom. 1:3-4), would have had no reason to infer from his resurrection that Jesus was the Messiah." The apostles' messianic interpretation of him was probably also associated with Jesus as their leader, "one who apparently claimed exceptional personal authority as the final forerunner of the kingdom." "Destroying the enemies of God, judging the nations, perhaps even renewing or rebuilding the Temple, gathering all the tribes of Israel— when Jesus came again, he would come the way the royal Messiah was supposed to come. And he was coming very soon." Again, Christian tradition took the Greek *kyrios* and turned it into a term "acclaiming Jesus' special status and unique nature as preexistent Lord." This usage of Lord began to overlap with "Son of God," another phrase that involved an Aramaic bridge to primitive tradition and came to denote "a unique, preexistent divine entity."[9] We early noted the reminder of Geza Vermes that in Jewish sources "Son of God" does not imply participation in the divine nature. All this changes in the course of the Apostolic Writings.

The Letters of Paul. The presence of conflict between Pauline christological affirmations and the historically reconstructed point of view and praxis of Jesus of Nazareth reminds us that the development of this kind of conflict did not have to wait upon late materials of the Apostolic Writings. For of the sources we have, Paul's writings are the nearest to the time of Jesus.[10] One might perhaps expect that the closer a written source is to Jesus' life, the more the document would be representative of his eminently human identity (vis-

age, status, stature). That this is not necessarily so is demonstrated in the letters of Paul (also in the somewhat later Gospel of Mark). The latest Gospel,
John, has a "high Christology," meaning a highly developed theology of Jesus as
divine Son. But so does Paul.[11] This means that the question of whether Jesus
would consent to/dissent from points of view put forward in the Apostolic Writings is much more than a function of the developing chronology of our sources.

(1) It is difficult to imagine that Jesus of Nazareth would agree that his
teachings and his overall temporal career were of no real consequence. But
about Jesus of Nazareth

> Paul evinces little interest. He reports few of his sayings and admits freely that he
> had not known Jesus "according to the flesh." Paul sees Jesus' significance and sta-
> tus as eschatological redeemer granted not in his biography (where he was born,
> what he preached, whom he called) but in his resurrection. [Paul's gospel] relates
> not Jesus' teachings, but Paul's teachings about the meaning of Christ's resurrec-
> tion, from which Paul reasons backward to Christ's divine sonship and forward to
> his imminent Parousia. Paul in his letters thus does not preach *about* Jesus; rather,
> he preaches *that* Jesus has descended, ascended, and is about to descend again in
> power.[12]

To be sure, the apostle's outlook has nothing to do with the docetic notion
that Jesus only *appeared* to exist as a human being. The resurrection would be
meaningless apart from a historically lived life. And Paul even sees the "life of
Jesus" manifest "in our mortal flesh" (2 Cor. 4:11). Yet the point stands concerning the importance/unimportance of Jesus' historical message and contribution. As for the resurrection, how Jesus may have "felt" or come to "feel"
about that experience is not open to historical judgment; it may not even make
sense as a christological question.

(2) A more crucial bone of contention between Jesus and Paul is suggested in the apostle's conception, or lack of conception, of the people Israel:

> Jewish history and the Jewish commitment to God's nature as revealed in Torah
> created the dynamics of apocalyptic eschatology. Paul retains these dynamics but
> renounces their particularity. His vision of the End is no drama of national libera-
> tion writ large. . . . What place has the land of Israel, the city of Jerusalem, the walls
> of the Temple—in brief, the *realia* of Jerusalem—in [Paul's] expansive and inclu-
> sive vision? What place has a prediction of the Temple's destruction, which would
> recall the redemption from Babylon and speak of salvation in its territorial idiom as
> return to the Land? What place has Torah, which distinguishes Israel from the na-
> tions and even (as at Antioch) divides the body of Christ? . . . In brief, *Paul dena-
> tionalizes Jewish restoration theology.*
>
> Accordingly, Paul also denationalizes Christ. . . . Christ's significant point of ori-
> gin is not the flesh (his putative Davidic descent) but the Spirit, which reveals him
> at his resurrection as the divine preexistent Son (Rom. 1:4).[13]

Paul early typifies the depoliticizing of Jesus in the Apostolic Writings (though it is probable that the man from Nazareth did not himself stress the national character of the kingdom of God). One is reminded of Franklin H. Littell's stern rebuttal of Joseph Klausner's notion that "the rest of mankind was everything to Jesus, but his own people was nothing": This is "not the Jesus who wept over Jerusalem and told his followers to avoid the Gentiles and even the Samaritans. The opening to the Gentile world came not with Jesus but through those who taught that through his death and resurrection believing Gentiles might be brought into holy history."[14]

(3) The most decisive element within the conflict of Jesus and Paul lies in the latter's general conception of the person and work of Jesus Christ. Fredriksen continues:

> The Jesus who is the focus of Paul's fierce commitment is the divine and preexistent Son of God, the agent of creation "through whom all things are" (I Cor. 8:6), who came to earth, died by crucifixion, was raised and exalted, and is about to return. This pattern of descent, ascent, and approaching return is the essential content of Paul's gospel—or, as he sees it, of *the* Gospel, the secret and hidden wisdom of God decreed before the *aiōnes* (ages) for the glorification of the believer (I Cor. 2:7). Before his life on earth, Jesus was "in the form of God" (i.e., divine), but he did not grasp at "equality with God." Instead, entering the plane of human existence, Christ "emptied himself," took on the "form of a slave," and was born in the "likeness of men," in "human form" (Phil. 2:5-10), even taking on the "likeness of sinful flesh" (Rom. 8:3), thereby "becoming sin" for the sake of humankind (II Cor. 5:21). Thus moving from the "riches" of his preincarnate state to the "poverty" of life in the body (II Cor. 8:9), Christ humbled himself even to the point of dying on a cross (Phil. 2:8; also I Cor. 2:8; Gal. 2:20; 5:24, etc.). . . . Therefore God raised Christ from the dead and exalted him, so that "every tongue should confess that Jesus is Lord, to the glory of God the Father." (Phil. 2:11)

For Paul, Christ is God's special agent for nothing less than the redemption of all humankind, in fact of all creation, which has been "subjected to futility . . . [in] bondage to decay" (Rom. 8:19ff.). The Christ of Paul is, in the final reckoning, the eschatological Deliverer without peer (Rom. 11:26), rather than the founder of a church or a moral exemplar per se (cf. Luke). In and with his resurrection, Christ "signaled the beginning of the End; with his return, he will shortly sum up the ages. The rescue mission for which God had commissioned his Son (Phil. 2:5-11) is now all but complete. . . . Soon, with Christ's defeat of the hostile cosmic powers and his final victory over Death, the sons [sic] of God, both adopted (Gentiles, Rom. 8:23) and 'natural' (Jews, 9:4), will join with the divine Son in rejoicing in God's kingdom." In sum, Paul taught the "radical divinization of the Risen Christ."[15] Paul's mission to the Gentiles contrasts sharply with Jesus' conviction of being sent "only to the lost sheep of the house of Israel" (Matt. 15:24).

In chapter 5 I make reference to Jesus' possible puzzlement, laughter, or outright disbelief before any preachment of salvation only through "faith in Christ." I should think that he, the devout Jew, would be quite baffled and/or repelled by the transcendent and hence discordant theologizing of Paul, the erstwhile Jew. Of course, no necessary logical-substantive disjunction obtains between (a) Jesus' knowledge or self-awareness and (b) the possible fact of his divineness. Indeed, Jesus' nonself-centeredness is sometimes linked paradoxically to his very identity as Son of God. For that matter, there is no way a fully human being can know whether they have preexisted—or, at the other end, whether they can somehow be made capable of surviving death. Be all these things as they may, it would seem that the reply to Paul of the teacher and *hasid* from Galilee would be somewhat along the line, "Thank you—but no thank you. My interests and purposes lie elsewhere. Let us concentrate upon the kingdom of God—and the wretched people of this world." (I will come back to Paul's teaching of *kenosis* [emptying, humbling] as a potential foundation of continuity between Jesus and Christ, if in necessarily reconceptualized form in the fourth section of this chapter.)

The Synoptic Gospels and Acts.   (1) Mark, who may have been a Gentile, represents a second-generation rendering of the Christian message. His Gospel is "both profoundly similar and profoundly different" vis-à-vis Paul's. For him, too, the death and resurrection of Jesus Christ, the Son of God, initiates the climax of history and signifies the imminence of God's redemption when Christ returns in glory. But Mark, as one who stands outside Jewish culture, relates his ideas, not through Jewish history, religion, or Scripture, but through traditions specifically about Jesus. And so he

> emphasizes the authority of Jesus' teaching, the importance of faith, the need to endure until the End. By ingeniously creating a prophetic synonymity between events circa 30 and events circa 70, between the fate of the Son of Man and the fate of the Temple, Mark preserves the authority of the threatened tradition by deploying it. He demonstrates through his Passion narrative that this prophecy had already been fulfilled exactly when Jesus had said it would be: at the end of his ministry, with his death and resurrection. And pointing to recent events, Mark also preserves the original, apocalyptic content of the prophecy. For if "destruction/rebuilding" symbolically corresponds to the crucifixion and resurrection of the suffering Son of Man, then clearly the Temple's actual, historical destruction [in 70] signals the imminent historical fulfillment of Jesus' prophecy, the advent of the kingdom—now to be ushered in ... by the glorious [returning] Son of Man.[16]

Mark is endeavoring to provide an eminently historical foundation and authentication for his Christology. He makes added claims for Jesus: God himself calls Jesus his "beloved Son" (1:11; 9:7); to a man with an unclean spirit (demon) Jesus is the "Holy One of God" (1:24; see also 5:7); to a Roman centurion he is "Son of God" (15:39). But Mark's entire Gospel is informed by the tension deriving from the impending parousia. "For Mark never concludes his Gospel: rather, and quite abruptly, it just stops (16:8). No theatrical miracles, no extended postresurrection appearances, but simply the empty tomb, the promise of a reunion in the Galilee reaffirmed, and the trembling, frightened women. Mark thus effectively creates ... the experience of the women at the tomb, leaving his reader in the same state that he had imagined for those first witnesses that first Easter morning: startled—indeed, frightened—but looking forward to the imminent manifestation of the glorious Son of Man."[17]

Discontinuities between the Jesus of history and the Gospel of Mark are patent, but due to Mark's historical stress, they are somewhat less than those between Jesus and Paul. "Through Mark's narrative, Jesus *in his lifetime* becomes the authoritative source of the Gentile rejection of Torah."[18] Central to the discontinuity is Mark's depoliticization of the story of Jesus' passion, a fateful development that was to suffuse most subsequent Christian teaching.

(2) Matthew, with Luke, is a third-generation interpreter of the Christian message (circa C.E. 90). Unlike Paul and Mark, and probably also unlike Jesus' (abortive) expectation of the kingdom, these later writers no longer anticipate the fulfillment of the promise of salvation within their own lifetime. "They affirm the coming End of the Age and the Parousia of the Risen Christ, but not as immediate possibilities. These great events loom on the edge of a receding horizon: time interposes between the present and the End." (Fredriksen observes that when Jesus' resurrection was coupled with the delay of the End, the early Christian movement was plunged "into a kind of eschatological twilight zone.") Nonetheless, for all their distinctiveness and originality, Matthew and Luke embody variations on the Markan theme. All three Gospels present a Jesus who preaches to fellow Jews about the kingdom of God and engages in "mighty works" that authenticate his authority as prophet and messenger of God. The three evangelists "see the Gospel message itself, Israel's ultimate response to it notwithstanding, as the complement or completion of the biblical promises of redemption."[19]

The Jesus of Matthew's Gospel is preeminently a preacher. Many of Jesus' parables are, in Matthew's version, directed to the last judgment. Continuities with Jesus himself are discernible. But in and through Matthew's great stress upon Jesus as Messiah we are brought back to two themes that forcibly pose the question of discontinuity: what it means to speak of "Messiah" and Jesus' affirmation/disaffirmation of himself as Messiah.

Matthew employs Scripture "to generate a theologically sophisticated definition and characterization of Jesus of Nazareth as the long-awaited Messiah of prophetic hope." In this connection, the evangelist chooses large numbers of passages that in their actual context had nothing to do with the Messiah (e.g., Isa. 7:14) but that he applies to Jesus in messianic fashion. To a degree matched by no other part of the Christian canon, Matthew offers narrative episodes that are specifically built upon biblical testimonies. Time and again, he begins or ends an episode with "This took place to fulfill what the Lord had spoken through the prophet." In the course of his Gospel, he cites Scripture more than sixty times.

Matthew's Jesus is thus first and foremost the Messiah who fulfills biblical prophecy. With respect to the relation between the "old" people of God and the "new," Christ is

> the endpoint. He is the ineluctable and unequivocal conclusion to the peculiar Messianic teleology that Matthew's strategy of prophetic citation has created. If the traditions behind our Gospels reflect the efforts of early communities to understand the career of their redeemer in terms of Scripture, then Matthew's Gospel seems to have reversed the process: now the Scriptures are to be explained in terms of Jesus. Matthew brooks no alternative interpretation, whether Jewish or Christian, and he anticipates with confidence the vindication of his views when the Son of Man returns, as eventually he must, to divide the saved from the damned. Meanwhile, the evangelist and his community could take comfort in the face of the active competition which Matthew's combative tone suggests they faced. They had ahead of them the great work of a universal mission to bring about the second coming of their Messiah (24:14). And they had the consolation that, as long as the community congregated, Christ was indeed together with them, until he should come again (28:20).[20]

Once more, discontinuity comes out ahead. (Queries: Is "saved/damned" any kind of final category for Jesus? And how would Jesus ever wish to explain Scripture in terms of himself?)

(3) In his two books the composer of Luke/Acts propounds "a history not of Jesus' career itself but of salvation, of how the Holy Spirit came into human history definitively through Jesus, and thence passed from the Risen Christ to his (and Luke's) largely Gentile church." He applies most of the critical christological titles: Savior, Lord, Christ, Son of David (= Messiah), Son of God — handling these as consonant with Israel's history. For the most part, Jesus is well received by his own people. In the Gospel, Luke's first book, the demonic powers against which Jesus ranges himself are illness and infirmity rather than "the Jews."[21] (Luke glosses over the episode in the temple.) There is stress upon continuity between Judaism and the Christian message. Yet "the church is the true Israel [cf. Jesus' point of view], hence even after Christ's resurrection Israel continues, though the Jews themselves might drop away." The chief theme of Jesus' mission is God's forgiveness of repentant sinners (e.g., 5:31-32). Basically, Jesus is a moral exemplar and teacher of his disciples and (future) followers.[22]

Luke "has those on the margins of human or spiritual society (Samaritans, Gentile God-fearers, the physically handicapped, on the one hand; Satan or his demons, on the other) declare Jesus' identity in biblical terms as Son of God (e.g., 4:3, 9, 34, 41; 8:28) and Son of David (e.g., 18:35-39). Elsewhere, [he] simply asserts that Jesus is the true subject of the writings of Moses and all the prophets (e.g., 24:27, 44)." Luke divests the term *Messiah* of any political content.[23] The kingdom of God "is not future and political but present and spiritual." By spiritualizing the kingdom

> and dissociating it both from earthly politics and from the End, Luke accomplishes much that is important apologetically and theologically. His new definition severs any link between Jesus and traditional Jewish political messianism. . . . Further, it allays many of the tensions inherent in preserving an initially apocalyptic tradition in the face of the empirical disconfirmation of its central prophecy, for the world has not ended. Finally, it indicates a particular consciousness of the future of the new community, a deeschatologized, this-worldly future. Hence Luke does not include Son of Man, a term with strong apocalyptic associations, in the narrative catena of Christological titles at the beginning of his Gospel. Christian apocalyptic hope had no place in Luke's theology, with or without Rome. The future that Luke envisions for his community rests *in* time, *on* earth, incarnate as the church.
>
> For if God's kingdom is established by his Messiah, if it is characterized by peace and righteousness (the idealized portrait of apostolic cooperation in Acts), and if those within the kingdom receive the Holy Spirit, then for Luke the kingdom of God can be understood, at least functionally, as the church. Luke's Jesus is thus the Ecclesiastical Christ, God's special messenger who came to found this unique instrument in his name (Acts 4:12). And until Jesus returns at whatever point in the very distant future, the church is his earthly surrogate, continuing his work of bringing the message of salvation through repentance to all peoples.[24]

The depoliticization and spiritualization of the Son of Man Jesus continues on in Luke/Acts, yet without a total loss of continuity with Jesus.

The Fourth Gospel.   I intimated earlier the element of incorrectness in assuming that the closer a source is to Jesus' time, the more the source tends to be true to his historical character. With the Gospel of John the other side of the picture is decisively present: When compared with Paul and with the other Gospels, John is furthest from the world, self-identity, convictions, and hopes of poor Jesus of Nazareth. As Fredriksen puts it, there is very little in this Gospel to indicate that Jesus any longer thinks of himself as a Jew.[25]

The Fourth Gospel preeminently combines Logos theology (theology of the Word, Rational Principle), with the Christology we find in Paul. John's account of "the Stranger from Heaven," the "divine redeemer who has descended and who will ascend," "begins not at the banks of the Jordan, nor in a manger in Bethlehem, but 'In the Beginning' itself, at the creation of the universe. To introduce his subject, the evangelist essentially revises Genesis: 'In the Beginning was the Logos, and the Logos was with God, and the Logos was God. He was in the beginning with God; through him were all things made' (1:1-3). This divine principle entered the cosmos that he had made, actually becoming flesh in order to bring the power to become children of God to those who received him (1:10-12, 14)." Before this prologue ends, the christological titles have accumulated (Messiah, King of Israel, Son of Man),[26] and all the Gospel's major theological themes have been established: Jesus is from above and comes down into human history; he supersedes John the Baptist and Moses; only he provides access to the Father, since only the Son has seen God, and he is rejected by his own people. "He came to his own home, and his own people received him not" (1:11). Why is that? Because their real father is the devil, not God (8:44). Their role in this Gospel is very largely demonic.[27] Even in his flesh, "Jesus is not quite human. He does not laugh; he does not appear to suffer; he remains impassive through all the confrontations that he provokes with both Jews and Romans, until he accomplishes his goal: the cross. He dies only when he knows that all has been fulfilled, expiring in complete control and saying only, 'It is finished' (19:30)." The dual context of this Gospel, "the Christological theme of descent/ascent, and the absolute distinction between believers and unbelievers converge nowhere more tellingly and with greater irony than in John's presentation of the crucifixion. Lifting up/crucifixion in the earthly context simultaneously entails lifting up/exaltation in the cosmic context: Jesus' crucifixion is his exaltation, and through it he brings about the salvation of those who believe that by his crucifixion he returns to the heavenly realm." John's Jesus is not the wandering charismatic Galilean of the Synoptics, but

> an enigmatic visitor from the cosmos above this cosmos, the preexistent, supremely divine son (e.g., 1:1-4; 8:23, 42, 58; 17:5; 20:28). . . . To those divinely chosen to receive it, Jesus brings the message of eternal life, of the glory of the Son and the Father, pronounced in the elliptical idiom of this Gospel as much by Jesus' wondrous signs as by his own mysterious speech (e.g., 3:15, 36; 4:14; 5:24; 6:35-53; 11:1-4). The topic of his address is, most frequently, himself. An image of Jesus thus does not emerge from John's Gospel: it dominates his entire presentation. . . .
>
> Other images . . . express Jesus' redemptive identity even more innovatively. He is the Lamb of God who takes away sin (1:29, 35-36), the Good Shepherd who lays down his life for his flock (10:11-18). He is the "bread of life," "from heaven," giving his flesh as bread for the life of the world (6:35ff., 48-58); the "light of the world," who opens the eyes of the blind and guides his followers in the darkness (8:12; 9:1-41). . . . [He] is the source of Living Water (4:7-15), the Sheepgate (10:7-10), the Resurrection and the Life (11:25), the Way and the Truth (14:6), the True Vine (15:1).

Fredriksen concludes: "Through his Christology, John rotates the axis of Christian tradition ninety degrees, away from the historical, horizontal poles of

Past/Future to the spiritualizing, vertical poles of Below/Above. Collapsing the distinctions between the traditional Christological titles, eschewing their originally apocalyptic connotations by using them solely to denote Jesus as inter-cosmic mediator, John suggests through these latter, allusively sacramental images the many ways that Jesus continuously nourishes, supports, protects, and redeems the community of his chosen ones who must dwell in the lower realm."[28]

Contra the Gospel of John, there is a massive moral-historical gulf between the Jesus who demands salvation through belief in him and the Jesus who opened God's heart to the acceptance of all "sinners," quite apart from what they believed or did. (As E. P. Sanders makes plain, the early church would not have invented Jesus' stance toward sinners, because the church quickly developed weighty intolerance of such people.) On the other hand, as we leave the subject of discontinuity between the Apostolic Writings and the historical Jesus, one caution to keep in mind—granted a monotheist-theological frame of reference—is that the Jesus of history cannot rightly function as sole or absolute arbiter of authentic/inauthentic christological affirmation, for that would be a form of Jesusolatry,[29] a variation upon Christolatry. The most we can do is to be as clear as possible respecting the nature and force of the discontinuities.

CONTINUITIES BETWEEN THE JESUS OF HISTORY AND THE CHRIST OF FAITH

Are there links, and if so what are they, that join the higher Christology of the Gospels and of Paul to the mission and message of the historical Jesus?

For heuristic and background purposes, and prolegomenous to our discussion, a number of observations may first be offered. In some cases these are reminders of points made earlier in our study.

(1) Overall, we should bear in mind James H. Charlesworth's judgment that the early church community functioned as a source for the faithful remembrance of its Lord. Early on we noted the incorrectness of the skeptic's conclusion that Jesus' sayings were simply invented by the evangelists. This consideration, however, never had the power to forestall the tendentiousness of the Apostolic Writings. For example, nothing in what Jesus himself said or did could have authorized the anti-Jewishness of these sources or contributed to the eventual Christian break with Judaism; such things had to be brought about via other agencies.

(2) Jesus believed in "the eternal validity of the Torah" (Borg).

(3) The most solid ground of continuity between Jesus and the Apostolic Writings is the teaching of the kingdom of God. Jesus' eschatological hopes and

expectations both had a counterpart in and gained weighty continuation in the hopes and expectations of the primitive church.

The postresurrection disciples, in transforming their Lord's conviction that the kingdom of God was at hand, proclaimed his resurrection and his parousia. E. P. Sanders emphasizes that by expecting Jesus to return and establish the kingdom, these believers could think of him as Messiah. But note the serious implication of this last point: In his "first advent" Jesus failed to satisfy traditional Jewish messianic expectations. There was no choice but to prolepticize the messianic hope.

(4) Many of the Apostolic Writings' claims for Jesus Christ have as their incentive not the sayings of Jesus but one or another happening, the most critical being Jesus' resurrection. "Jesus' followers experienced *an unexpected* eschatological event: Jesus was raised. The community could continue; disconfirmation became confirmation. For what else was Jesus' resurrection but a vindication of his message, a sign of just how close the kingdom really was?"[30]

(5) The truth remains that Jesus made no lordly claims for himself.

(6) It is the case that there is categorial discontinuity between the theme of "Suffering Servant" and Jesus' own thinking and action. That is to say, contemporary scholarship is very uneasy with the notion that Jesus "fulfilled" this teaching of the Hebrew Bible. For one thing, the "servant" of Isaiah 53 is probably the people Israel, rather than an individual. On the other hand, as Segundo puts it, the tradition of the Suffering Servant became "*the* Messianic tradition par excellence for interpreting the destiny of Jesus of Nazareth. We can see this in the Pauline school (see Rom. 3:26; 4:25; 8:31-33; Gal. 1:15; 3:13; II Cor. 5:21; Col. 2:15; Phil. 2:8, 11; Heb. 4:12; I Peter 2:22, 24-25) and in the Johannine school (see John 1:29, 32-34; 3:11; 8:12, 32, 45; Rev. 1:16; 19:15)."[31] And as Vermes attests, the identification of Jesus as *the* Messiah belongs to the earliest phase of Christian conviction.[32]

(7) There is a grain of truth in Marcus J. Borg's judgment that it does not ultimately matter whether Jesus identified himself as the Messiah. But the reason Borg gives—that whether Jesus was or was not the Messiah does not depend upon what he thought—is troublesome. I do not understand how the category of Messiah and the realm of Jesus' personal conviction or awareness can be so readily separated.

Even if Jesus finally came to tell himself that he was the Messiah, it may well have been that this self-identification had to keep on struggling with his self-doubt until the end of his days. We are apprised that at no time did Jesus proclaim himself Messiah (Charlesworth).

(8) We have no real evidence that Jesus found martyrological meaning in his death—though, as Sanders indicates, the possibility cannot be ruled out. There is no denying that in some quarters martyrological significance came to

be assigned to the event. As matters turned out, Jesus did give his life for his people Israel and for the God of Israel. In a real sense, he lost his life as representative (*Stellvertreter*) of his people. The history authorizes no other conclusion.

(9) The interpretation of the ministry and death of Jesus as atonement for sins soon took root in some parts of the early Christian movement.[33] Such an interpretation, however, "does not express the Jesus movement's understanding of God but is a later intepretation of the violent death of Jesus in cultic terms. The God of Jesus is not a God who demands atonement and whose wrath needs to be placated by human sacrifice or ritual. . . . Although such an interpretation . . . is soon found in early Christian theology, the death of Jesus was not a sacrifice and was not demanded by God but [was] brought about by the Romans" (Fiorenza).[34] Anne E. Carr adds, "The sacrificial love of Jesus on the cross requires reinterpretation in which Jesus' act is clearly seen as a free and active choice in the face of an evil that has been resisted. It is not passive victimization. Nor did God require a sacrificial death. Jesus died because of the way he lived, because of the pattern of fidelity and commitment of his life and his liberating message."[35]

I do not see, however, that the caveats of Fiorenza and Carr perforce rule out or contradict such an affirmation as "God so loved the world that he gave his only Son . . . " (John 3:16). For one thing, historical events are always open indeterminately to different kinds of subsequent theological and moral explication (just as theological confession is always open to historical comment and interpretation). More to the point, the love of God is foe rather than friend of antihuman or antihumane demands.

(10) In earlier pages we were met with the phenomenological theme of Jesus' self-understanding. That theme may have relevance for the larger question of continuity between Jesus and the *mysterium Christi*.

The appeal to Jesus' self-understanding as a possible resource for the assertion of continuity between Jesus and Christ rests upon or presupposes two historical-moral-theological judgments, which when taken together constitute a fundamental and abiding paradox, first alluded to in chapter 5: (a) Jesus *is not* and cannot be the Messiah of Israel, of the Jewish people as such;[36] and (b) Jesus *is* the Christ of the church, and it may be that (faithful) attestation to this latter fact is in certain respects not separable from Jesus' self-understanding and work (mission).

The tenth observation takes us back to E. P. Sanders and James H. Charlesworth.

With respect to Sanders, first in order is his own disclaimer: "The early church came to believe that Jesus was a transcendent being, that God sent him to save the world, that he would soon return in glory, and that all who believed in him would be saved. Historians should attempt to account for the origin and development of these and other beliefs, but it would be foolhardy—or worse—to rush to the conclusion that the historical Jesus must have corresponded to such beliefs. It seems intrinsically likely that beliefs about Jesus' relation to God and his imminent return depend very heavily on the resurrection appearances." At the same time, Sanders prefers a hypothesis that offers "a reasonable and well-grounded connection between Jesus and the Christian movement" in contrast to a hypothesis that appeals only to accident and the resurrection experiences supposedly in explanation of why Jesus' mission did not cease with his death. For no teacher and healer who was believed to have been executed and raised from the dead would be sufficient to account for a movement that "in a very short period of time starts the activity which characterizes the last act of an eschatological drama, the introduction of Gentiles. The first disciples must have been living already in the world of eschatological hope if they so readily countenanced the Gentile mission. Peter and the others ... must already have been led to see Jesus' ministry as a key event in the fulfillment of the prophecies of the restoration of Israel and the submission of the whole world to the God of Israel." In sum, could the resurrection have been the *whole* explanation of the Christian movement, or would there not have to be "a more than accidental connection between Jesus' own work and the emergence of the Christian church"?

We must be cautious here, for at least two reasons: Jesus' mission and message were clearly directed to Israel. And Jesus' mission and message *as a human being* cannot in itself abolish the (obvious) distance between Jesus and Christ. In other words, Sanders's quest for an explanation could still be fully identified as a matter of historical procedure rather than as christological affirmation. Nevertheless, Sanders argues that "there is substantial coherence between what Jesus had in mind, how he saw his relationship to his nation and his people's religion, the reason for his death, and the beginning of the Christian movement."[37] It is the intention of *Jesus and Judaism* to explore that coherence, a work that we have already reviewed in chapter 4.

I think the most that can be said for Sanders's approach is that it may be possible to utilize Jesus' message and mission as a connecting link between Jesus and Christ. It is probably better to have the Jesus of history as the sought-for link than not to have any link at all.

As we come back to Charlesworth's *Jesus Within Judaism* we find more positive and aggressive argumentation than in Sanders. For Charlesworth declares forthrightly, if only in a footnote, "Incipient Christology begins with Jesus."[38] And he devotes much space to the question of Jesus' self-understanding and its bearing upon christological avowal.

Today Charlesworth is living on the rebound from a position he "espoused for over a decade, that we can know practically nothing about who Jesus thought he was, that is, Jesus' self-understanding." Three major sections in the Gospels have made him move away from that position.

(a) Jesus' choice of the Twelve. "Is there some self-understanding behind Jesus' apparent desire to have twelve special men [sic] follow him? Is he by this act not symbolically representing a belief that the end of time is now becoming a present reality? ... Is he not exhibiting some perception of playing a part in the eschatological restoration of Israel?" In choosing the Twelve, "he had a clear intention to be involved in some way with helping to establish a *new Messianic age*."[39]

(b) Jesus' "triumphal entry" into Jerusalem. If it is true that the man from Galilee did indeed come in from the east and pass "through a gate riding upon an animal, and was saluted by the crowds at the time of Passover with some kind of Davidic recognition, then who did Jesus think he was? I am convinced that *some* kernel of history lies behind this account; if so, then we are obviously in some way confronted with Jesus' self-understanding." Even though Jesus may not have looked upon himself as the Messiah, "it does not necessarily follow that he held *no* Messianic self-understanding." For instance, he "may have thought that he was, or would be declared by God to be, the Son of Man; if so, then it is conceivable that the messianic overtones of this title [sic], as for example found in I Enoch 37-71, would shape his growing awareness of his mission." (But Charlesworth hastens to add that the traditions "certainly do not support the conclusion that Jesus proclaimed himself to be the Messiah.")[40]

(c) The passage to which Charlesworth devotes most of his attention (no less than 17 pages out of a main text of 172 pages—some 10 percent) is the parable of the wicked tenant farmers, as found in Mark 12:1-12; Matt. 21:33-46; Luke 20:9-19; *but also in* the Gospel of Thomas 65. Here is Charlesworth's translation of Mark 12:1-9:

> And he began to speak to them in parables. "A man planted a vineyard, and set a fence around it, and dug a trough (for the wine press), and built a tower, and leased it to tenants; then he went away. When the time came (for the harvest), he sent a servant to the tenants, to collect from them (his portion) of the fruits of the vineyard. But they took him, beat (him), and sent (him) away empty-handed. Again, he sent to them another servant, him they wounded in the head, and treated shamefully. And he sent another, him they killed; then many others, some they beat but some they killed. He had still one other: a beloved son (*huion agapēton*) [cf. chap. 5, sec. 2 of this book, on Jesus as God's "beloved Son"—A.R.E.]. He sent him to them last (of all, *eschaton*) saying, 'They will respect my son.' But those tenants said to one another, 'This is the heir; come, let us kill him, and the inheritance will be ours.' And seizing (him), they killed him, and cast him out of the vineyard. What

will the owner (*ho kyrios*) of the vineyard do? He will come and destroy the tenants, and give the vineyard to others."

We cannot enter into all the ins and outs of Charlesworth's exhaustive exegesis of this compelling story. Could it be that we are confronted here with Jesus' own self-understanding? Charlesworth musters evidence in favor of the widely acknowledged belief that behind the parable lies "an authentic Jesus tradition." The parable itself "reflects Galilee precisely as Jesus would have experienced it."

(i) There is the issue of Jesus' perception of his own death. Even though it is unsound to adjudge that Jesus specifically feared crucifixion, the disciples evidently thought that their master had definitely said something about facing martyrdom. Thus, for example, they urge him not to go up to Jerusalem to face the chief priest (Mark 8:31-33). Further, the Pharisees warn him to be wary, since Herod Antipas was looking for ways to get rid of him (Luke 13:31-33). Again, several reliable traditions indicate that Jesus felt a compulsion to go to Jerusalem. Luke 13:33 "may adequately catch" Jesus' own intent, "I must continue my journey, . . . for a prophet must not perish outside (*exō*, or away from) Jerusalem." It is "obvious" that the core of the parable "might ultimately derive from Jesus and reflect his premonition of a martyr's death. Jesus may have feared that, like Jeremiah and Honi, he would be *stoned*. He was not stoned; the fact that he was crucified tends to anchor this logion in authentic tradition. The evangelists and their predecessors would not have created a saying that both clashes with real history and tends to portray Jesus as ignorant."

(ii) There is the issue of the use of *son* in Early Judaism. In addressing this question, Charlesworth cites the version of the parable in the Gospel of Thomas 65, and then comments: At the point in the story where the father sends his own son,

> the story ceases to be credible, and attentive listeners would have asked themselves what kind of a father is being portrayed. The father appears foolish, even unjust and cruel. Surely the heightened allusions to the death of the servants, clearly the prophets . . . , are post-Jesus editorial expansions. . . . *The Gospel of Thomas is impressively free from these elements* [italics A.R.E.]; in it the story is true to life in Palestine before 70 C.E. Even the parable in . . . Thomas cannot be claimed to preserve the original form . . . ; because the killing of the son *within the vineyard*, which is the key to the authenticity to this saying of Jesus [since Jesus was killed outside Jerusalem—A.R.E.], is conspicuously absent and was probably dropped by the author of . . . Thomas, who deemphasized the cross and passion of Jesus, elevating his eschatological and wisdom pronouncements.
>
> Most important for us now, in the Gospel of Thomas the statement "Then the master sent his son" may be translated "Then the Lord (Yahweh) sent his son." There can be little doubt that the owner, master, or lord . . . is intended to be God himself.[41]

We are met then with the key question: Could Jesus have been referring to *himself* "as the son, or the son of God"? Many specialists in the Apostolic Writings simply assume that *Son of God* or *son* is a technical term created in the preaching and teaching of the primitive church. Charlesworth adduces no less than fifteen examples of the term as preserved in the literature *from Early Judaism*. These abundantly and persuasively prove that "Jews roughly contemporaneous with Jesus did use the technical term 'son' or 'Son of God,' " attributing the title "to paradigmatic, holy individuals, including the long-awaited Messiah." *The term* son *was not created in the church.*

Careful study of the four extant versions of the parable of the wicked tenant farmers, of the meaning of the preredacted layers of the Gospels of the Apostolic Writings, and of the theology of Early Judaism leads to the conclusion that "ultimately the core of the tradition of this parable derives from Jesus himself." It appears that Jesus "*thought of himself as a son*, and perhaps, since the owner of the vineyard is none other than God, *as God's son*. This discovery is significant and momentous," even though it does not tell us just what the noun meant to Jesus or what he thereby "perceived reflexively and introspectively about himself." It is not illegitimate, however, to suggest that he regarded himself as "the son" who would be killed, although certainly not in the sense of physical divine sonship so prevalent in the ancient Near East. He could well have had in mind "some aspect of the biblical concept of adoption as God's son" (cf. 2 Sam. 7:14; Ps. 2:7; 89:26-27; Isa. 9:1-6). Clearly, he did not *proclaim* himself "the son." Yet our conclusion "confronts us not only with Jesus' intent but also with his self-understanding." Finally, Charlesworth makes this judgment respecting the reign of God: When we encounter Jesus' proclamation of the nearness of God's rule, it "will no longer suffice to report, as some scholars (including myself) have tended to do for years, that in the kingdom of God sayings we are confronted only with a proclamation and not in any way with a proclaimer. Surely, as the proclaimer, Jesus is contending also that he will play a role in that kingdom."[42]

Insofar as some elements of Jesus' intentionality and self-understanding may be available to us, and insofar as these elements may reflect a special relation to God and the kingdom of God, it may follow that certain findings respecting the "Jesus of history" are in some way foundational for, or (more cautiously) commensurate with, the "Christ of faith." Here, at least, are the rationale and the justification of Charlesworth's aphorism that "incipient Christology begins with Jesus." And all this is in full agreement that theology (Christology) is always interpretive and assumes a faith that goes beyond history and historical analysis. In the final resort, however, a decision upon the usefulness of the contributions of such scholars as Sanders and Charlesworth in doing something to resolve the Jesus/Christ duality rests upon how much value we are permitted to assign to historical "truth" in reaching or approximating theological, and ultimately perhaps ontological "truth." After all, Jesus' self-understanding may be responded to by identifying it as a fully historical-phenomenological (human) datum — granted that in addition, and together with all human self-consciousness, it finally eludes purely historical understanding.

A NEOKENOTIC POSSIBILITY

I should like to propose one other possible resource for coping with the Jesus/Christ dialectic. I call it a neokenotic point of view.

As alluded to in our discussion of Paul, an early source for the original christological idea of *kenosis* (self-emptying) is Phil. 2:5-11:

> Have this mind among yourselves, which you have in Christ Jesus, who, though he was in the form of God, did not count equality with God a thing to be grasped, but emptied himself, taking the form of a servant, being born in the likeness of men. And being found in human form he humbled himself and became obedient unto death, even death on a cross. Therefore God has highly exalted him and bestowed on him the name which is above every name, that at the name of Jesus every knee should bow, in heaven and on earth and under the earth, and every tongue confess that Jesus Christ is Lord, to the glory of God the Father.

This original kenotic position boasts a very high Christology: Christ's "form" is that of God himself and Christ is, in principle, said to be equal to God. Again, the passage makes an absolutist claim (and, accordingly, a debatable one) on behalf of the Christian gospel: *every* tongue must confess Christ.

John Hick sums up the theory, as it was to develop: "The historical Jesus did not have the divine qualities of omniscience, omnipotence, omnipresence, eternality, self-existence, creatorship, or even — in the latest versions — the consciousness of his own deity. For the eternal Son, or Logos, divested himself of these attributes in becoming human." Professor Hick is not sold on the kenotic theory; he lists a number of problems with it.[43] Stephen T. Davis is much more optimistic: "The theory of kenosis . . . helps us grope toward an explanation of the Incarnation. It helps provide a sense in which we can . . . say: 'Jesus Christ is truly divine' [and] 'Jesus Christ is truly human.' "[44]

The neokenotic point of view I am proposing is critical of the original kenotic theory. It ventures upon the all-crucial step of reformulating Phil. 2:5-7 by replacing *Christ* with *God* (itself perhaps interpretable as a fully divine-kenotic step): "God emptied Godself, taking the form of a servant." Strikingly, this step of reconceptualization is in exact accord with Phil. 2:9 — it is *God* who "exalts" Jesus Christ. If this latter is so, it may also be held that God is the one who humbles Jesus Christ.

This neokenotic position may stand for at least eight things.

(1) The position is catholic (= universalist, though *not* thereby unqualifiedly "valid"!) in two respects: (a) It is in harmony with and readily exemplifies the three christological principles that underly this study (as explained in chap. 1): the historical-moral-theological distinctiveness/integrity of the Christian faith; a quest for deliverance from imperialism, triumphalism, and elitism; and an abiding insistence upon the centrality of the historical Jesus. (b) The neokenotic outlook affirms differing measures of continuity *with* and *among* all the christological positions we review in the present study—most especially, liberationist and feminist modes of thinking and action (and not excluding points of view still to come).[45]

(2) The neokenotic affirmation is in full accord with the hiddenness of God, the declaration of which is (as Carl Michalson declares in one of the epigraphs to this volume) "probably the most pertinent Christian witness about God for our time."

(3) We are to maintain and advance equally a fully *theocentric* understanding of the Christian faith and a fully *incarnationist* understanding of that faith.

(4) We are enabled to eschew the devastating, perhaps fatal, question (which is unavoidable within original kenotic theory) of whether Jesus would be/would not be aware of what it was that "Christ" had performed (as represented in Phil. 2:5-7).

(5) The Jesus we know is wholly in accord with Philippians 2, for in the Sermon on the Mount he holds out "the ideal of a self-emptying ... love for one's friends, one's neighbors, even one's enemies." In his *whole* person he lived and died according to this ideal. "What Yeshua 'thought, taught, and wrought,' that whole, that life (and death) is what made Yeshua special—for many, a human transparency of the divine. ... In teaching and living his life in fulfilling the Torah and beyond in kenotic love, in *hesed*, the *hasid*, proto-rabbi Yeshua indeed lived a special extraordinary life, the like of which his followers never before, or since, had experienced, but in this he was quintessentially Jewish."[46]

(6) There is an easing of the heavy dependence upon historical "truth" that is found in E. P. Sanders and James H. Charlesworth (as considered in this chapter); at the same time we are to remain aware of the danger in avowals of faith that are incompatible with history. A neokenotic view exemplifies the architectonic position that is discussed in chapter 1 and repeated toward the beginning of the present chapter: Faith rests upon reason, and it can and does transcend reason, but it is not permitted to violate reason (for it would then be inhuman—which would mean *against* the incarnation). The neokenotic viewpoint is wholly compatible with historical reason.

(7) In accord with the claim of the centrality of the historical Jesus, the neokenotic position does *not at all* "empty" Jesus of spatiotemporal or human content. For example: It is probable that Jesus finally regarded himself (after much sweat and many tears) as King-Liberator of his people. I think the least we can do in response—and to right the wrong of history—is to recognize that Jesus has *some* kind of claim upon that title, if only because God or history or both finally did grant liberation to his people, some nineteen hundred and eighteen years after Jesus' own struggle. Alternatively put, the self-sacrificing and self-fulfilling efforts of this people Israel at last helped to bring a kind of "redemption of God" (Heyward), despite all the terrible forsakenness at the cross. So it may be said that Jesus "can be" indeed King of the Jews, if only in tearful prolepsis.

(8) We attest to the paramountcy of the divine love, as itself embodied in *kenosis*, the power that is able finally to reconcile Jesus and Christ—and all other realities as well.[47]

The possibilities and challenges of continuity between the Jesus of history and the Christ of Christian faith continue as our standing ground as we turn to chapter 9.

CHAPTER
9
The Covenantal Christ

Paul M. van Buren's multivolume *Theology of the Jewish-Christian Reality* is, in comprehensiveness as in substance, the most significant systematic study to date to come out of the new Christian reformation vis-à-vis Israel, the Jewish people, and Judaism. In a review of *Discerning the Way*, the initial volume, I wrote "If good theology blends the historic wisdom of a community of faith, obligation to the contemporary world, and the theologian's own commitment, *Discerning the Way* is very good theology."[1] A like judgment is in order respecting the second part, *A Christian Theology of the People Israel* and also the specifically christological volume, *Christ in Context*, major aspects of which are to be discussed in this chapter.

VAN BUREN'S TASK

Van Buren takes as his task to build the essential Christian-Jewish relation together with essential Jewishness into the structure and meaning of Christian theology, Christology, and life. For him, any theology of the Christian faith — and, of course, any Christology — must rest upon and represent the truth of the Christian-Jewish relation. More specifically, "the reality within which the church finds itself today includes the Jewish people and their eternal Covenant with the God whom the church serves through Jesus Christ," the Jew who lived in solidarity with his people. (For van Buren, "Christ," which has become a name, ought to be retained as such.) Jesus' solidarity with his people stands in great "continuity with the witness to God's Covenant and therefore confirms the faithfulness of God. If God is faithful to his people, and Jesus was faithful to God, then his solidarity with his people would follow." A proper Christology for today's church "should free the church to affirm God and itself in Christ without having to negate others. . . . The whole history of the whole Covenant, not just the biblical beginnings of it, becomes the context in which the church will have to express in its Christology how it understands itself before the God of the Covenant."

In sum, Christology

> is the church's response to the love of the God of Israel with which it is confronted in Jesus Christ. . . . It is, consequently, the church's service to God's goal of recon- ciliation, which it owes to God and to the world.
>
> The fundamental context of the things concerning Jesus of Nazareth, according to the apostolic witness, was the Covenant between God and Israel; their continu- ing context is Israel in its enduring Covenant with God. Israel and its story is there- fore the fundamental context for developing a Christology for the Jewish-Christian reality, that is a Christology for the church today.
>
> The coming and going of Jesus Christ produced the utter novelty, within the continuing history of God's Covenant, of effecting the hidden goal of God's Torah to bring the nations into the plan that began to develop with the calling of Abraham.
>
> "And the Word happened as [or became, was made] flesh" (John 1:14). It was of course Jewish flesh, for the only God whom the church knows is just this God who has chosen to work by means of this particular people for the good of the whole. "Incarnation" cannot say less than this. The church cannot properly say "incarna- tion" without saying "Jew" at the same moment. It has no Lord but the Jew Jesus, and Jesus had no calling from and made no response to any but the God of the Jewish people. If the Incarnation comes from the heart of this God, then it points to the heart of the Covenant and so, in pointing to Israel's God, it points also to God's Israel.[2]

VAN BUREN AND OTHER CHRISTOLOGISTS

Where may we locate *Christ in Context* with reference to the theological spec- trum and to other contemporary christological work? I suggest eight points.

(1) A title for the entirety of van Buren's contribution could well be "The Covenant is the Heart." For here is covenantal theology in intense and thor- ough realization. No less determining a dimension than Christology itself is to be reckoned with and apprehended through the majesty and decisiveness of the one and only covenant. The one covenant is bifocal and hence bihistorical: the everlasting compact with Israel, and Jesus Christ as beloved Son within that single and singular compact. Thus, in his central chapter, "The Eternal Son," van Buren attests that "at stake is a claim about God's covenantal self-determi- nation, which is at the same time a claim about the seriousness with which God

takes the course of the Covenant in human history. . . . The covenantal pattern of call and response, or commandment and willing obedience" is the one appropriate means "for understanding the early church's confession that Jesus is the eternal Son of God." This attestation carries forward and implements the second of van Buren's two foundational rules: "Every proper Christological statement will make clear that it is an affirmation of the Covenant between God and Israel." His first foundational rule reflects a devout theocentrism: "Every proper Christological statement, however 'high,' will make clear that it gives the glory to God the Father." Van Buren's adjudication of the Arian controversy—with plagues upon the orthodox as well as the Arian houses—rests throughout upon convenantal norms and covenantal realities: God as capable of novelty, God as involved, God as responding, God as "thoroughly compromised," indeed God as suffering.[3]

Van Buren's affirmation of a covenantal Christology in fundamental continuity with the history and witness of Israel is carried ahead in various chapters—in every case in conversation with and appraisal of classical Christology. Here are representative citations from chapters 10 to 12. The Incarnate Word: "The Incarnation of the Word of God that has appeared for the church in Jesus Christ, full of grace and truth, is grounded in and added to the incarnate Word of God spoken anew every day to Israel in the Torah." Christ the Lord: "What has been given the church in the lordship of Christ is the freedom to start living as servants of this Lord and so as servants of all whom he served and serves: Israel first of all, then the church, and then all the poor and wretched of this earth." All in All: "The church has no cause of its own because its cause is Christ's. Christ has no cause of his own because his cause is God's. . . . 'Paul's religion' was none other than 'the religion of Jesus.' [In chap. 8 above I seriously question any such equation—A.R.E.] That is hardly a surprising agreement, seeing that they were both devoted Jews. For both of them the end of God's story could only be God the Father."[4]

(2) In accordance with covenantal teaching and in keeping with the great tradition of Judaism, van Buren pleads for a theology of synergism: the opportunities, tensions, and reconciliations between God's grace and human responsible response. From a convenantal perspective, it is "God's intention, so to speak" to "engage us in a game in which his moves depend on ours. The course of the game is mutually determined by both partners."[5] Here van Buren is at one with such worthies as Abraham Joshua Heschel, David Hartman, and Joseph B. Soloveitchik on the Jewish side and Ruth Nakashima Brock and Isabel Carter Heyward on the Christian side.

(3) There are links here to Christian process thought, as in the finding that "God cannot know ahead of time what his partners are going to do."[6]

(4) Any doubt about whether van Buren is an authentically post-*Shoah* theologian is here laid to rest.[7] I take it, however, that he would not wish in principle to link etiologically the *Shoah* with any demanded dissolution of one or another essential Christian doctrine. In one place he insists, "The task of the church's Christology is not to make it appealing to Jews." In this respect, he is a reformist post-*Shoah* Christian theologian, rather than a radically revolutionist or radically revisionist one. Nonetheless, in at least one place he equates "a Christology for today" with "a Christology after Auschwitz." And elsewhere he even goes so far as to place any *theologia crucis* under the judging scrutiny of the *Shoah*:

> Perhaps the greatest question that Auschwitz raises for the tradition of Christian teaching about the cross is whether we can continue to say with Hebrews (and perhaps with Rom. 6:10) that it happened "once for all.". . . A church that affirms the Jewish people as the continuing Israel of God cannot coherently define the authorization of Jesus so as to undercut God's authorization of the people Israel. In a world that has known Auschwitz, consequently, the cross can only be present as a world-redeeming event in more qualified terms than those of "once for all."
>
> Precisely the point of hesitation in the orthodox doctrine of the cross, the inability to go so far as to say that God was directly, personally, and immediately involved in the suffering of Jesus becomes unbearable when we reflect on the suffering of the Jewish men, women, and children in the Holocaust. If God was not there, suffering with his people, if God did not suffer a loss there at least as painful as that suffered on Golgotha, then that God is not worthy of respect by moral persons.[8]

The phrase "post-*Shoah* theologian" need not be more commendatory than certain other appellations. Robert A. Everett points out that a notable thing about James Parkes is that he did not "need" the *Shoah*: It was well *before* the Holocaust that Parkes saw "the whole demonic dimension of Christian antisemitism."[9] And, of course, neither the Holocaust nor any other event can have any finally determining word in the truth or falsity of, say, the mission and message of Jesus. Historical events that become events of faith either happen or they do not happen in ways quite independent of what may come after (or before) them. Christianity is a historical, perhaps even a historicist, faith.

(5) Van Buren's theology is a theology of liberation that avoids and castigates the antisemitisms and anti-Judaisms still present in, among various places, some of today's liberation theology and praxis. It does this by witnessing in characteristically Jewish ways to the church's challenge "to meet and serve all those who are hungry, thirsty, estranged, naked, sick, or imprisoned," for in these wretched souls the church is meeting Jesus Christ, "especially when it is not aware of this, when it serves them only in order to serve them, and when it loves them only because they need love."[10] It is not a matter of

"anonymous Christians," a term van Buren dislikes, but instead, I suggest, one of "an anonymous Christ."

(6) Here is a thoroughly untrammeled "Christian Zionism," free of the ulterior motivations (sometimes conversionist [missionary] ones) that beset much Christian Zionism. In belonging to Christ, "Christ's church belongs close to and supportive of his people and of their State. There its members may meet and serve him again."[11]

(7) "Israel and the church are together peoples of the God of Israel, but Israel is called to this task as a people, the church is called to it as a community of persons called out of many peoples."[12]

(8) It is the case that Professor van Buren does not appear to be wholly opposed to the utilization of morally pragmatic criteria when it comes to the definition and responsible propagation of Christian dogma. For example, we read that "the classical Christology of Nicea and Chalcedon . . . solidified and shaped a long history of Christian anti-Judaism, and also of pride and patriarchalism"; that Christology "*therefore* stands in need of critical analysis and correction." Again, "a Christology for today, a Christology after Auschwitz, will have to wrestle with its own origins. . . . If it [the church] reevaluates its origins in order to correct unhistorical or ahistorical interpretations of Jesus, *that is a small contribution to paying off the colossal debt that the church owes the Jewish people*. That, however, is not going to be reason enough to produce *the Christology demanded by the Jewish-Christian reality*. That reality calls on the church to say where it stands right now and where it means to go tomorrow. *It challenges the church to answer responsibly whether it lives in its past, or whether it is able to repent, to turn around and begin afresh*."[13]

TWO AREAS OF DEBATE

(1) Van Buren's overall concept, "a theology of the Jewish-Christian reality" is problematic. What does that concept mean in real life? (By contrast, the *intention* behind the multivolume study, *A Theology of the Jewish-Christian Reality*, is made perfectly clear: to contribute "to the church's understanding for the third stage of its life," viz., "*the church with Israel*."[14] It appears to me that the author of *Christ in Context* could still get across this momentous historical-moral proposition while avoiding, with help from a simple change in title, the problems I shall mention.)

(a) Van Buren retains a repeated and commendatory insistence upon coherence as an indispensable norm for Christian theology. But once this norm is properly in force, is there any way to make mutually coherent (i) the development of a Christian theology of a "Jewish-Christian reality" with (ii) the creation and constructive instrumentality of an essentially "gentile church"? For example: We are reminded that Jesus initiated a confrontation "between *his [Jewish] disciples* and the God of Israel."[15] Where is such an intra-Jewish confrontation supposed to live and to assert itself (if it is to live and assert itself anywhere) within Christian (i.e., "gentile") thinking and life? Jesus' disciples were Jews. As van Buren himself notes, Jesus "is presented as having understood himself as being sent only to the lost sheep of the house of Israel (Matt. 15:24), and as having ordered his disciples to confine their mission solely to Israel (Matt. 10:5-6)."[16] Yet on the page immediately next to page 80 as cited, we are advised that in the church Jesus Christ is met "as the one chosen by the God of Israel *to confront Gentiles* with the gift and claim of that God's unlimited love."[17] How are page 80 and page 81 to be reconciled? When did Jesus confront "the Gentiles"? If the answer is given that Jesus' confrontation of Gentiles is a postresurrection and present affair, we are left with the identical problem: How is Jesus' own restriction to Israel to be squared with the coming of its opposite, the witness to Gentiles?

The problematic, ambiguous character of the concept "Jewish-Christian reality" is thus pointed up, if inadvertently, by van Buren himself. On the one hand, we are apprised of the many ongoing continuities within the two peoples of God (Israel and the church); on the other hand, we are presented with a sharp, ongoing dichotomization (discontinuity) between the Jewish people and the gentile church. The church of Jesus Christ, we are told, "is not Jewish"; "it is itself Gentile."[18]

In a word: Is the dialectic of continuity/discontinuity between Israel and the church meant to be normative, or is it to be received as an unreckoned challenge, calling for treatment, perhaps even radical treatment and resolution?

(b) The second of van Buren's two fundamental theological-ethical rules avows, as cited above, that every rightful christological statement will affirm the covenant between God and Israel. Jews will, of course, insist that any and all affirmations of the covenant are not christological. To bring in this Jewish view is *not* to insinuate that the Christian rule ought to be abandoned. But it is to question whether the second rule is (against van Buren's claim) coherent with solidarity between Jesus and his people and supports the church's recent rejection of the anti-Judaic tradition.[19] We are assailed by the terrible truth that the Apostolic Writings—presumably a salient authority for the church—simply do not on balance authorize a rejection of the anti-Judaic tradition. Further, as van Buren himself assures us throughout, Jesus represented an unqualifiedly Jewish point of view. But meanwhile, today's anti-Judaic Christians, while readily agreeing that Christology affirms the covenant between God and Israel, nevertheless read that proposition to justify and support a replacement "new Israel."

(c) Van Buren's virtual reduction of the church of Jesus Christ to the gentile church is narrowing. I can discern neither need nor justification in this tacit rejection, this making invisible, of Christians of Jewish background and origin (also known as Hebrew Christians, or as Christian Jews). These people are already victims of serious marginalization: antisemitism at the hands of Christians, rejection at the hands of the Jewish community. (Van Buren does note their presence in passing in his second volume.[20] Another complication is that his very phrasing, "Jewish-Christian reality," tends to make for confusion with Jewish-Christians.)

Besides, why could there not be an alternative duality to that of van Buren? Or, since our author is by no means averse to thinking God's thoughts after God,[21] why would it not have been infinitely wiser for God to have arranged a duality quite different from the one God (ostensibly) chose? It seems to me that it would have been more sensible for God to have decided, not upon the duality of Jewish-people-plus-gentile-church, but upon a duality of the *Jewish people as such* plus God's church comprised of *Jewish-Christians drawn from all nations*. After all, "the original witness to Jesus was made by Jews. . . "![22] Was not God's basic blunder to go along with Paul the apostle and to agree to consort with the Gentiles? We Gentiles are very good at making trouble. Were I God, I think I would have said no to Paul. It is by no means out of the question to construe the blessed intention of convenantal universality as being better realized, and in much less ambiguous and destructive ways, by a worldwide Jewish church. In such a case, certain watchwords would joyfully come to the fore: "Down with the Gentiles!" "Down with Paul!" "Up with the original New Testament church!"

(*Ein Traum:* If only Jesus Christ could by some [impossible?] miracle have been both Jew and Christian! The entire problem and menacing incoherence of the concept "Jewish-Christian reality" would vanish before such an incarnation.)

(d) Van Buren's argumentation stands in incisive and powerful contrast to my own lifelong, and perhaps by contrast poverty-stricken, theology of a strictly Christian reality. I have never been comfortable with theologies that are contingent upon, or tied to, realities other than themselves—which is to confess that I remain uncomfortable with some of my own past work. Christians are not Jews. (Which is worse, the Marcionite heresy or integral *Judenfeindschaft*? At least poor Marcion would probably not abide the Christian [gentile] subreption of the Hebrew Scriptures.)[23] Whenever and wherever Christians have impinged upon Jewish reality they have tended to do mischief. As long ago as 1974 I wrote that I had come to believe that

part of the "coming of age" that Dietrich Bonhoeffer envisioned (though he failed to apply his own principle to a Christian understanding of the Jewish people) may entail the unconditional readiness within the Christian community to enable the Israel of God *to be whatever she will be*—even without us. Insofar as I comprehend my motivations—who ever does that, sufficiently?—I think that my erstwhile insistence upon Christian membership in the Jewish family has been determined in considerable measure by the necessary warfare against Christian supersessionism, that fantasy that the "new Israel" has somehow replaced original Israel. Hence, my insistence has been provisionally justified. But suppose that the fantasy is obliterated. Is the family to stay together? I am not entirely certain how to answer. I do know that loved ones often part from one another and go their different ways—though they need not cease their loving or their caring. Indeed, it may be that the parting will take place by the very decree of love and for the very sake of love. Love suffers.[24]

By contrast, Paul van Buren has staked out the entire world of Israel (Jewish and Christian) as his parish. He must testify again and again on behalf of the Jewish reality of Israel (always with high Christian and moral purposes). In my own current theological ruminations I find that I can say and do nothing with that Jewish reality—not only because I do not know as much about it as van Buren does, but also because I feel that Christians of today (i.e., after 1933–45) are not really entitled to offer judgments or counsel on it.

One traditional rule of intergroup dialogue is that the formulation of each partner's self-identity is the business of each party alone. As made clear in *A Christian Theology of the People Israel* and now in *Christ in Context*,[25] van Buren ignores this rule—though he does so irenically and sometimes convincingly. Of course, he is not writing for dialogic purposes. Nevertheless, the Jewish-Christian relation, in van Buren's view, is the relation that obtains between the church and Israel, identified together as "the people of God." *How can we avoid the shattering consideration that untold numbers of Jews (mostly in the State of Israel, but many elsewhere) simply reject any such identification?* Are not these people Jews? The Christian community would do well to avoid making itself pass judgment upon such questions. One ironic consequence of van Buren's perspective is that, empirically speaking, his conceptualization of Jewishness becomes, in effect, rather inaccurate; he must only succeed in losing or misidentifying several million Jews in the process. I think of the secularist multitudes who each evening come to haunt Rehov Dizengoff in Tel Aviv; I do not find that there can be much, if any, understanding between van Buren and them. The very last thing these people would ever condone is that "Israel lives as God's special possession."[26] Tacitly, our colleague is saying to them: I know who you are and you do not.

(e) A more serious, though not unrelated, consequence is the danger of a reincarnation of Christian imperialism respecting Jewry—though surely (yet ironically) in the name of anti-imperialism, an anti-imperialism that is in many ways highly credible and successful all through *Christ in Context*. But consider, for instance, these words: "The relationship between the church and the Jewish people . . . is grounded in Jesus Christ, the chosen instrument from among the chosen people. . . ."[27] What becomes here of human solidarity in and through the "Jewish-Christian reality" as such?

It is entirely clear that were van Buren to have his way, the Christian church would be throughout purged of all anti-Judaism, all antisemitism, all anti-Zionism.[28] But like many great gifts, this one is tagged with a price. The price is Christian intervention in things Jewish. True, van Buren solicits "*Israel's* testimony, not ours." Yet, unfortunately, contemporary Jewish testimony is riddled with internal controversy and even contradictions. True as well, van Buren is quite aware of the difficulties, carefully restricts the definition of the task, and proposes safeguards.[29] Nevertheless, I suggest that it is not right today—I have no idea what may be right in the year 5000—to fabricate a Christian theology of the people Israel.[30] And on the other side of the coin, I suggest that it is not right to identify the Christian church as gentile. There is nothing in the Apostolic Writings or in church dogma as a whole to warrant the latter identification.

In interrogative summary of point 1: Does not van Buren open himself to the error of incoherence by insisting at once upon a theology of the Jewish-Christian reality and a pervasively gentile church? Or again, will not Jewish-Christian reality serve to mislead nonhostile, uninformed people and needlessly estrange hostile, informed people? At the very least, it would seem better to resort to *explanation* to get across the point about the meaning of Jewish-Christian reality (as is done on page 104) rather that to expose the latter important truth to the slings and arrows of outrageous book titles. (It is interesting to note that in one place the phrasing "a Christology for the Jewish-Christian reality" is refined to read "a Christology for the church today."[31] No one can object to that.)

(2) To turn to the second of two major areas of debate: The resurrection of Jesus Christ (see primarily *Christ in Context*, chap. 5, "Christ Risen: Easter") is accepted and celebrated by van Buren, yet in a way that tends to exalt its theological-existential-convenantal meaning and truth and correspondingly to downplay questions of exactly what it was that took place on the initial Easter.

First, I offer some description and then some appraisal.

To van Buren, Christians are those who, in standing before the living presence of Jesus Christ, find themselves to be standing before God. There follows van Buren's overview or abstract of chapter 5: "The church exists in the trust that it is following God's lead in affirming the Jew Jesus as God's living way of being present to it. Easter is the ambiguous event in which the church recognizes both God's refusal to abandon his cause, which Jesus made his own, and the cross as evidence of the seriousness of the conflict between that cause and the misuse of human power." Furthermore, to understand the Easter event as covenantal is fundamental to the church and its Christology.

> It is clear that the apostolic witness to Jesus arose from the Easter conviction that God had confirmed Jesus "by raising him from the dead." The Jesus so confirmed, however, *is the same Jesus* whom his disciples understood to have been authorized by God to call them as Jews into a renewal of the Covenant. . . . God's self-confirmation in raising Jesus must therefore be seen as a confirmation of his Covenant with Israel and of Israel in its Covenant partnership with God. . . . There can be Jewish faith without Easter, but for the Gentile church, as for the original Jewish church within Israel, there is no Christian faith but Easter faith.[32]

Note the phrase I have italicized: At this juncture van Buren appears to be opposing any attempted dualism between, or separation of, the historical man who was crucified and the one who was raised from the dead. And he almost seems to be wanting to please traditionalist adherents of article 4 of the Articles of Religion of his own church, the Protestant Episcopal Church: "Christ did truly rise again from death, and took again his body, with flesh, bones, and all things appertaining to the perfection of Man's nature." Furthermore, the ambiguousness of the Easter event does *not* mean, for van Buren, a questioning of the truth that God "raised Jesus from the dead"; it means only the "ambiguity of the witness to that event." Finally, the claim of Easter faith

> concerns the present, continuing, post-crucifixion effectiveness of Jesus to confront persons with the reality of God's love and God's claim upon their lives. If this claim were invalid, it could hardly matter whether Jesus of Nazareth started breathing and talking again after his death.
>
> On the other hand, the claim that is essential for and that expresses Easter faith *does not need to specify* the physical means whereby God confirmed Jesus in his function of confronting persons with God's love and claim. The fact of Easter that matters absolutely for the church is that *Jesus* once more proved effective in standing for God and God's cause, that, in the cause in and for which he had lived before, he *was alive again.*[33]

Van Buren is himself cautious concerning the "quite modern question" of

> whether we should say that the event of Easter was a historical fact. . . . In our present linguistic circumstances, we might say that the church should not claim it to be a historical fact, precisely because the church wants to say that it was first of all an act of God—and history, by the rules generally accepted by modern historians, excludes acts of God. Bultmann was only following those rules in concluding that a modern historian cannot go behind the rise of Easter faith as the root event of Easter. For the same reason, God's Covenant with Israel and his gift of Torah at Sinai could not be called historical facts. On the other hand, the church's commitment to the importance of that election and that Covenant, with their historical manifestation in the continuing life of the Jewish people, lead it to hesitate to deny that they are realities having historical consequences. So also with Easter; it has to

do with the continuing impact within history of the Jesus of Nazareth who was certainly a figure in history. There is no reason, however, why the church cannot admit that any definition of the event of Easter, adequate for its needs and purposes, will not fit within the categories of a historical investigation that excludes speaking of God's history with his creation.

. . . [The] faith of the church is no more a response to the how and what of Easter than was the faith of the original disciples.[34]

So much for a purely descriptive accounting of van Buren's Christian outlook upon Easter. I turn now to appraisal and evaluation. In general, I think that there are two problems: moral credibility/noncredibility within the Christian enterprise; and coherence/incoherence within the context of the professedly historical quality of the Christian faith. (We recall that van Buren emphasizes the moral obligations of Christians to the oppressed and other sufferers, also that he advocates coherence as a theological norm.) The two points to follow revolve in one or another way around these two problems.

(a) It may be of some use in helping us grapple with this third category of understanding the resurrection (i.e., beyond pure "objectiveness" and pure "subjectiveness") if we introduce the philosophic duality of *form* (essence, pattern, idea, intelligible structure, etc.) and *matter* (specificness, content, "the accidents," etc.). The *form/matter* conceptualization is nowhere utilized by van Buren; he is not to be held accountable for this philosophic terminology as such. I am employing it for strictly methodological and heuristic purposes.

Van Buren is strong on the one and deliberately weak on the other. Here is his repeated *formal* declaration: "God raised Jesus from the dead." Within traditional Christian circles there is no debate upon the *form*, the "thatness" of the resurrection, taken in and for itself. But this absence of a debate does not hold with respect to the *matter* of the resurrection, its "how." Here there remains, of course, enormous controversy, a debate that has its source in the Apostolic Writings themselves.[35] What is the actual history of the resurrection-event? What was it that took place?

In assigning precedence to the *form* over the *matter*, van Buren could be getting himself into certain difficulties, simply because the Christian faith is so through-and-through historical in character. That is to say, this faith assigns ultimate significance to concrete historical events, by which is meant specific events in time and place that somehow involve the discrete will and action of God. One is given to understand that for van Buren the *matter* does not matter much. Were some kind of idealist system involved, this not-mattering would be quite acceptable. But for van Buren, Christianity is a historical faith. Historical event is of ultimate decisiveness. Therefore, the *matter* ought to matter— precisely upon his own theological reasoning. Not only is *form* deprived when it is not fed by *matter*; any fully historical Christian faith cannot accept a pri-

macy of *form* over *matter*. Christianity is anything but a collection of ideas. It
is not a philosophic system. It is covenantal life. And there can be no covenantal life apart from that life's material dimension.

Thus, my response to van Buren's exposition of the resurrection is not primarily a matter of fostering my own point of view; it arises out of *his* point of
view. Since it is he who pleads for the all-decisive cause and "course of the
Covenant in human history,"[36] is it not perforce the case that his witness to
history ought to be unexceptional and unqualified—in all of history's nitty-grit-
tiness, all its concretions, all its particularity? This is in no way to imply that any
treatment by van Buren of such specificness is to be any but his own; it is only
to say that it would seem to be incumbent upon him to deal more fully and
adequately than he does here with those who testify against subordinating the
matter of the resurrection to something else.

It may simply be that van Buren remains uncertain respecting the *matter*
of the resurrection (along with all the uncertainties present within the Apostolic Writings taken as a whole). In any case, the possibility of critical reaction
will be strictly a function of the critic's own stance: Is the *form* to take practical
precedence over the *matter*? If so, the argument may be assuaged. But if it is
held either that the *matter* is to take practical precedence over the *form* (as is
sometimes alleged respecting interpreters who affirm Jesus' "bodily resurrection"), or for that matter that the *form* and the *matter* are equally crucial, then
there will clearly be argument between van Buren and the critic. Any *form* that
is not nurtured by *matter* entails truncated reality. Easter can scarcely possess
true significance as a covenantal reality if the resurrection is not a complete
event, comprised equally of *form* and *matter*. What if, horror of horrors, there
is no *matter* to sustain the *form*? This question is obviously framed from a life-
and-death perspective that construes *matter* and *form* to be alike essential.
From an opposite point of view, there is, of course, no such "horror of horrors."

(b) I think that the potentially chief moral anguish for Christians today is
not so much the church's traditional "teaching of contempt" (Jules Isaac) in
response to the Jews' (supposed) "rejection of their Lord"—although such
teaching has by no means been vanquished. I suggest that the really world-
determining problem for the contemporary church is not the Friday before
Easter, but Easter itself, with the church's repeated proclamation of a resurrectionist truimphalism and supersessionism—a proclamation that appears, on the
surface, ever so innocent. For on the surface, there is no contempt for anybody.
Of equal or greater cruciality here is the question of "truth." Rabbi Peter
Levinson of Heidelberg has declared, "If I believed in Jesus' resurrection, I
would be baptized tomorrow."[37]

As will be developed further in chapter 11, it is van Buren's persuasion
that the Easter claim cannot itself be the root of Christian anti-Judaism and

antisemitism because the resurrection is, in a manner of speaking, a vindication of Jewishness—more precisely, a matter of fostering *continuity* with the mission of the Jewish Jesus of Nazareth.

At least two issues are involved here. One of these derives from our colleague's *Tendenz* to identify ideal with real. The historical truth is that the resurrection of Jesus became and remains a continuing source of the Christian world's anti-Judaism, entirely independent of whether the theological-moral logic van Buren musters is correct or incorrect. (I find it to be correct.) Unfortunately, in Christian history things did not turn out the way van Buren and the rest of us would have devoutly wished. Sinful life defeated innocent logic. There is, alas, no such entity as rectification-via-careful-definition.

The other issue is that despite his evident sanction of a specific resurrection of "the same Jesus," van Buren backs away from the specificness. It turns out that by "the same Jesus" he evidently does not mean the one who took again his body with flesh and bones but someone or something else. Who or what was or is this "else"? Along this line he attributes to me the objectionable view that "either the dead Jesus began to breathe and walk and talk again, or else he remains dead and there was no resurrection." Then he adds: "We shall see . . . how strange an interpretation this is of the ways in which the various apostolic witnesses speak of the event of Easter."[38] One catch in the attribution to me is that the view in question is hardly an idiosyncratic idea of mine. It could be, indeed, a majority Christian position today, particularly among nonintellectuals. It is propounded by Luke, in and through words attributed to the risen Jesus himself: "See my hands and my feet, that it is I myself; handle me, and see; for a spirit has not flesh and bones as you see I have" (24:39-40). The fact that the Apostolic Writings differ over the how and the what of Jesus' resurrection appearances—no other Gospel says what Luke says—can hardly be appealed to in order to justify a failure or refusal to reach and offer a decision today between or among these differences. Such a stance is question-begging and irresponsible. The issue of (historical) redemption is a life-and-death one that is scarcely met responsibly by shrugging one's shoulders and saying, "I'm not sure" or "It doesn't matter." Human salvation is in the balance. We hardly meet responsibly someone's "how" question by telling him, as the apostle Paul did, that he is a "foolish man" (1 Cor. 15:35-36).

Van Buren's argument on behalf of what comes across as a *sort of* resurrected Jesus is confronted by the two-sided enigma of the empty tomb and the resuscitation of Jesus. These questions do not go away through the device of impugning another scholar for being guilty of a "questionable philosophical conception of what a fact is." Van Buren's own questionable philosophic assumptions are evident all through his study. He maintains, supposedly against me, that "one gets the impression that, to Eckardt, the only event worthy of the name is one that can be recorded by photographic and electronic means. Surely the sort of resuscitation that Eckardt seems to have in mind would not of itself establish the claim of Easter faith."[39]

For numbers of years some of us, including myself, have been entirely aware that no alleged event of resuscitation could ever demonstrate the Easter claim. But some of us may even be more aware that this has nothing to do with the question now before us. On the one hand, it is perfectly correct, indeed a truism, to observe that the (reputed) emptiness of Jesus' tomb does nothing to establish the resurrection: Jesus' body could have been stolen or moved. On the other hand, van Buren and the rest of us would do well to listen to Raymond E. Brown, who points out, with piercing appropriateness, that it is most probable that the faith of the first apostles would have been so shaken by a later discovery of Jesus' skeleton that they would have looked upon their Christian preaching as being in vain. And while to be sure the empty tomb tells us nothing of what took place, nevertheless, Brown concludes, "as a negative check" the empty tomb *does* have a function "in our perception of the resurrection of Jesus."[40] So that, while the empty tomb proves nothing, a full tomb would have *dis*proved everything. A dead body that is *present* = resurrection that is *absent*. Here then, is the painful enigma, of untold significance not alone for the Christian-Jewish meeting but for the Christian theological-moral enterprise as such (cf. the Christian encounter with the world religions): (i) Those who *deny* Jesus' bodily resurrection may simply opine that the body was either moved or stolen (assuming the veracity of the empty-tomb account). (ii) Those who *affirm* Jesus' bodily resurrection cannot escape the sheer impossibilities of bodily resuscitation. And (iii) those who, like van Buren and not excepting myself, try to work with some other foundation for affirming the resurrection, have their own problems. For any effort to treat the reported event of the resurrection as a "symbol," "myth," "felt presence," "vision," "appearance," "spiritual body," "experience," "continuing impact" (van Buren's choice),[41] finds itself hard put to avoid spinning intellectualistic and psychologistic spider webs and thereby falling into vague esotericism. Of course, to contend that the first Christians did not *experience* what they identified as the resurrection of Jesus is absurd.[42] But the problem here is *not* in the first instance one of "experience"; it is a question of the ontological truth of the resurrection *behind* such experience, a reputedly special act of God within, not beyond, the dimension of human history.

To sum up a response suggested by the foregoing reference to Raymond E. Brown: The empty tomb was a necessary condition but in no way a sufficient condition *for the apostles' belief* in Jesus' resurrection. Van Buren does not seem to sense this, or he would not try to have me insist that the "event" could have been "photographed" or "recorded." Apparently, for at least *some* of the disciples of Jesus, nonresuscitation would have meant no resurrection. Van Buren does not appear to allow for the decisive relationship that the historical body of Jesus possesses to the entire question of the resurrection. He owes it to his readers and his constituents to reckon somewhere and sometime with the question of Jesus' historical body rather than holding that the question can be waived or relegated to relative unimportance.

To bring together this second part (b) of my more evaluative analysis: How is it possible, without violating the norm of a fully *historical* faith and the norm of coherence, virtually to ignore the "how" and the "what" of Jesus' reputed aliveness while yet trying to stay with the statement that is was *Jesus* who was "alive again"? What exactly is meant by the assertion that God raised *Jesus* "on the third day"?[43] Acts of God in history *are* historical facts. It appears to me that unless the resurrection was in *some* sense a historical fact,[44] it becomes incorrect (= incoherent) to affirm the resurrection as God's raising of *Jesus* from the dead. In van Buren's own view, some linguistic-theological concept other than *resurrection* would appear to be in order. In sum, I believe it would have greatly cleared the air and made unnecessary much disputation had van Buren done four things: simply indicated his own persuasion that by the "raising" of "Jesus" he does *not* mean the raising of Jesus' physical-historical body;[45] made more plain that he does not think of the "event" in terms of historical fact; substituted a concept alternative to *resurrection* (I think the concept *confirmation of Jesus*, used by van Buren at several places would better describe what he is driving at); and then done something to make sense out of his avowal that it was *Jesus* who was raised from the dead when he does not really mean this (unless we are supposed to assume that his anthropology is of the idealist sort that makes the "essence" of Jesus or of anybody else something "other than" the gestalt of their bodily life).[46] He has not (as yet) done any of these things for us.[47]

In chapter 11 we return to the prodigious question of Jesus' resurrection.

To conclude this discussion of substantive issues within van Buren's work: The major problematic of his contribution—yet also its major strength—has to do with the relation between faith and history. James F. Moore's summary word for van Buren's outlook is *ahistoricalness*.[48] I agree that the threat of ahistoricalness is present.

TWELVE QUESTIONS

(1) To E. P. Sanders, Paul the apostle insists that faith in Christ is necessary to membership in the people of God.[49] What are we to make of this finding in light of van Buren's diametrically opposed interpretation?

(2) (This is van Buren's own question.) Since it is evident that the text of the Apostolic Writings "contains both the original apostolic witness to a Jewish Jesus and also later editing that presents us with an anti-Judaic Jesus," "How can the extant text be our norm"?[50] But upon what basis is "earlier" to be regarded as "better" [A.R.E.]?

(3) "We see no conclusion consistent with the gospel of the early witness to Jesus Christ than that the church simply does not know how else God may be met apart from Jesus Christ and his context, Israel. . . . Indeed, in Israel's case, the church will have to insist that God *can* be met apart from Jesus Christ, for otherwise it would not know that it was the God of Israel whom it had met in him." How may this point of view bear upon the Christian relation to "other faiths" and to people not usually thought of as religious?[51] (The fourth volume of van Buren's study is to take up this matter.)

(4) The nagging question of the "Christian mission to Jews" (*Judenmission*) has not died. If Jesus bears "the very presence (= name) of God," why may he not do this to and for (some) Jews as well as to and for the gentile world? Consider this finding: "Israel, or rather some of Israel, discovered in Jesus' presence its need to become the Israel that God wanted." Yet the fact is that Gentiles may and do become Jews today (against van Buren's implied or apostolic stricture on page 156), and so, too, Jews may and do become Christians.[52]

(5) "[The] church is to follow Jesus Christ in the way in which it has been given Gentiles to follow him. That way is apart from circumcision and the *mitzvot* [commandments], and so, strictly speaking, not within the framework of the Covenant of Sinai. That Covenant is for Israel alone."[53] I question whether our elder brother Jesus would agree with this (also Peter, at least until he changed his mind). Does not the one covenant apply fully, through Jesus, to all Christians?

(6) "In a world that has known Auschwitz . . . the cross can only be presented as a world-redeeming event in more qualified terms than those of 'once for all.' "[54] What is it that gives such an event as the *Shoah* the right to determine or change Christian doctrine?

(7) With Neill Hamilton, van Buren finds Jesus' death to be "pure tragedy" and "a tragic accident." To be sure, that death *contained* tragic (i.e., fateful) elements. But was it *pure* tragedy? Were not Jesus' actions free and responsible, within his expectation of God's imminent reign? As van Buren himself goes on to say, in and through the resurrection the death of Jesus need not be seen as only a tragic accident; "it could become the culmination of Jesus' divine calling to speak and act in the name of the God of Abraham, and the means of drawing the nations into the story of his love affair with his beloved people Israel."[55]

(8) Van Buren writes, "Israel has remained blind to the covenantal novelty of what began with Jesus Christ primarily because of the church."[56] Has not Israel's no had, as a more powerful reason, commitment to her understanding of God's truth?

(9) It is said that "God will be Israel's God no matter what happens." How is this declaration to be reconciled with van Buren's repeated cautions respecting the future?[57] If it is the case that the covenant means free, mutual agreement, why can there not be a time when the God/Israel covenant may be ended?

(10) Our colleague thinks God's thoughts after him, and the same is the case with God's deeds.[58] Is this necessarily bad? Is it necessarily good? Personally, I think it is blessed—a revivification of an important segment of the Jewish tradition.

(11) We are advised that the covenant with Israel "means, among other things, suffering on the part of Israel and so suffering on the part of God."[59] In the presence of the *Shoah*, and particularly of the children there, is it still possible, morally speaking, to tie Israel to special suffering? (Cf. question 6 above for a possibly opposite implication.)

(12) At the last, I refer back to the second volume, *A Christian Theology of the People Israel.* (The query could as readily be dug out of *Christ in Context.*) Israel "rejects the church's claim in the name of the church's God."[60] Are both parties right? Is the one right and the other wrong? Or is it necessary here to rethink the meaning of rightness/wrongness in ways that question the aptness of either or both attributions?

These last phrasings open the way to our chapter 10. In between it may be proposed that no Christian theology of today—no Jewish theology as well?—can avoid van Buren's Christology and remain responsible. No responsible theology can try to detour around that one. We may, accordingly, await with eagerness the fourth volume of *A Theology of the Jewish-Christian Reality*—though meanwhile not having quite abandoned hope that this magisterial work may somehow still find a way to transform itself into a more lowly (kenoticist?) theology of a Christian reality. But I have left to the very end what I believe to be the momentousness of van Buren's work (for all the limitations, even incoherences, we have found in it): its essential compatibility with, and hence its truthful recapitulation of, the actual history of Jesus of Nazareth. Christological faith here rests unreservedly and compellingly upon the foundation of history, as at the same time it properly transcends it.

10

Jesus Christ
and "the Great Ways
of Humankind"

What may we say respecting the relation between christological confession and "the great ways of humankind"?[1] In the world of today every Christian point of view is confronted sooner or later by this question. Each of three interpreters puts the issue succinctly: "Can Christianity accept other religious traditions as valid ways to salvation without giving up its fundamental conviction about the absoluteness and uniqueness of Jesus Christ?" (Lucien Richard, Roman Catholic). "We live in a world in which we Christians can consider our Way only one Way among others, and yet we cannot give up the claim to a certain ultimacy and universality with respect to that Way which is Jesus Christ" (John B. Cobb, Jr., Protestant). "In our contemporary world of many religions, encountering each other as never before, can Christianity continue to be the same Christianity it has been for the past nineteen centuries? Can Christians continue to understand and present their religion as bearing the fullness and the normative expression of God's revelation? More specifically and more painfully: Can they continue to proclaim Jesus of Nazareth as the only savior and incarnation of God in human history?" (Paul F. Knitter, Roman Catholic).[2]

The theme of this chapter will be treated under three headings: rudiments (first section); contemporary expression (largely that of Paul F. Knitter) of the soteriological truth or validity of the Christian faith while opposing—paradoxically—all Christian absolutism (second and third sections); and additional allusion to my neokenotic position in consonance with an extra-absolutist Christology and with (I hope) due regard for the relative (i.e., relational) Christian authority or precedence of the Jesus of history (fourth section).

TEN PILLARS

By way of building a foundation for our *éclaircissement*, we may provide places for at least ten pillars (findings, proposals, questions):

(1) In chapter 1, as by implication in ensuing pages, I have put forward a *relationist* outlook respecting the "truth" (in contradistinction to *absolutism* and *relativism*): Humankind "has the capacity to achieve *some kind* of relation to truth, even though it cannot express or possess truth absolutely or without distortion and ambiguity. . . . Human beings are capable of achieving partial glimpses of truth from particular, limited standpoints." Relativ*ism* stands for no real truth; by contrast, *relativity* stands for relatedness, relationness. (Even though the relationist claim must lack final proof, the orientation is not incoherent with everyday human experience.)

(2) Likewise in chapter 1 I express sympathy with "a faith in the presence of God hidden behind any or all events." This point of view is of much relevance for the Christian attitude toward "the great ways of humankind." For if God is, in fact, present within such ways, these extra-Christian modes of thinking and behaving cannot be divorced from the very life and will of God's self.

(3) In chapter 3 the query is posed: "Why are we to believe that the inclusiveness of a community must do something to make it superior to another ethos?"

(4) Marcus Borg endeavors to have Jesus assimilate the kingdom of God to the power of the Spirit and life in the Spirit. "The coming of the kingdom is the coming of the Spirit, both into individual lives and into history itself." The kingdom "has an existence within history as the alternative community of Jesus, that community which lives the life of the Spirit."[3] I think that for Jesus the kingdom of God is greater than this. Borg's theological-moral problem here is suggested by the question of the spiritual status of non-Christians and of where people stand spiritually who do not or cannot grant the reality of the Spirit.

(5) The absolutist stance of Christianity was in large measure inherited from Judaism: "You shall have no other gods before me" (Exod. 20:3). Yet through the years Judaism has managed to immunize itself against an unqualified absolutism—in and through (to all intents and purposes) a restricting of its *Anschauung* to the Jewish people. Any such immunization could not prevail in the case of the church, due to the missionary command to "make disciples of all nations" (Matt. 28:19) together with subsequent universalist aspirations; also together with certain eschatological hopes for the whole of humankind:

> Zion shall be redeemed by justice,
>   and those in her who repent, by righteousness. . . .
> It shall come to pass in the latter days
>   that the mountain of the house of the Lord

shall be established as the highest of the mountains,
    and shall be raised above the hills;
and all the nations shall flow to it,
    and many peoples shall come, and say:
"Come, let us go up to the mountain of the Lord,
    to the house of the God of Jacob;
that he may teach us his ways
    and that we may walk in his paths."
For out of Zion shall go forth the law [Torah],
    and the word of the LORD from Jerusalem. . . .
nation shall not lift up sword against nation,
    neither shall they learn war any more.
                                    (Isa. 1:27; 2:2-4)

(6) I have alluded to Paul M. van Buren's judgment that an authentic Christology for our time is able to "free the church to affirm God and itself in Christ without having to negate others." But van Buren further declares that the event of Jesus Christ "produced the utter novelty . . . of effecting the hidden goal of God's Torah to bring the nations" into God's plan. When these two attestations are set side by side, a fateful query suggests itself: How is it possible to prosper "the hidden goal of God's Torah" and yet not "negate other people"? Taken in so many words, the query is Jewish; in a Christian conceptualization such phrasing might read: How is it possible to quicken the salvation embodied in Jesus Christ and yet not "negate others"? For there remains the "stubborn truth that a nonconversionist Christian viewpoint respecting Jews, however much it may aid reconciliation between Christians and Jews, does not in itself reduce obstacles to solidarity with peoples of other faiths. On the contrary, the very affirmation that, through Jesus Christ those who are outsiders are enabled to become part of the Israel of God, serves to point up an unhappy division within humanity itself: the division between Israel (Jews and Christians) and all those who remain beyond the Covenant of promise."[4]

Adherents of the Christian faith may indeed come to declare that salvation for the Jewish people can be quite independent of the Christian dispensation or achievement (chap. 9 above). But this declaration will have consequences that are rather opposite to each another. The one consequence is an unfortunate restricting of salvation or blessedness to Jews and Christians. The other consequence is an opening of the door to salvation or wholeness for non-Christians other than Jews. Yet even in the second case, the danger of absolutism may not be wholly missing: People need not be Christians, but they ought at least be Jews! In its more winsome or nonabsolutist form, however, the second of the consequences is simply a way of witnessing against the arrogance of Christian absolutism. (A difficulty in my theology through the years is its seeming implication that it would be good if everyone were Christian—except Jews.

I have never said this in so many words; as a matter of fact, I have never be-lieved it. But one could perhaps draw just that conclusion from some of my musings upon the covenant of God and her people. And I think that today Paul van Buren runs up against the very same problem.)

In point of truth, Judaism—not usually pictured as beset by the same even-tuality of exclusivism/inclusivism that is peculiar to the Christian church (also to Islam)—is met by a related challenge. On the one hand, Jewish teaching stresses that the "righteous" of all the nations of the world have a share in the world to come. On the other hand, such "righteousness" is traditionally com-prehended in and through the seven Noachic laws, which rabbinical Judaism early established as incumbent upon Gentiles: prohibitions of idolatry, murder, adultery or incest, the eating of limbs torn from a living animal, blasphemy, and theft; and the establishing of adequate systems of law and justice.[5] The stum-bling block is the first item on the list: no idolatry. While Judaism as a whole is able to handle the foibles or aberrations of the Gentiles with a kind of live-and-let-live attitude, it has never tolerated what it deems the sin of idolatry. For Judaism presupposes the one and only Holy God as alone worthy of devotion. In principle, this places the Jewish tradition and ethos in conflict with many "religions of the world" (not excepting the idolatries that afflict Christianity). To oppose this facet of the Jewish tradition and of Jewish distinctiveness would be to oppose Jewish identity, an act of injustice.

To the end of showing that "the real problem of Christology is not the problem of pluralism but the question of the relation of Christianity to its Jew-ish origins," Michael Wyschogrod reviews the "absolutism that Christianity de-rives from its Jewish origins."[6] Although the antipathies and prejudices nur-tured by the Apostolic Writings and the history of Christianity are directed primarily to the Jewish people and Judaism, such hostile outlooks and attitudes can be and have been readily transferred to other non-Christians. Wyscho-grod's judgment prompts the question: If the Christian *Judenmission* is to be ruled out upon theological and moral grounds, are there any comparable Christian theological and moral bases for opposing Christian missionizing at-tempts against the religions of the world?

(7) From within Jewish feminism a "reconstruction of monotheism" is at present given voice. Marcia Falk declaims that "any single-image monotheism is idolatrous, since all images are necessarily partial and the exclusive use of any part to represent the whole is misleading and theologically inauthentic." Authentic monotheism "entails 'an embracing unity of a multiplicity of images.' Such multiplicity not only celebrates pluralism and diversity; it diminishes the likelihood of unconscious forms of idolatry." Falk has specifically argued that "anthropocentrism in Jewish God-language is as idolatrous as sexism; that we cannot have an authentic imaging of a monotheistic Divinity that uses exclu-

sively personal terms, even if those terms include female representations."
From a feminist perspective, the definition of God as other than the world is
highly problematic. The traditional Jewish premise of a perfect God and im-
perfect world makes for a hierarchical dualism that splits the world into two
unequal halves. Whenever monotheism deviates from its primal insight of affirming unity in the world, and of serving as the source of justice and of the
passion for a single standard of justice, it supports patriarchy. And whenever

> patriarchy takes the principle of unity and splits it into two—when God is re-
> moved from the world and set above it, when Divinity is no longer inherent in us
> but exists as an ideal outside ourselves—both God and world are exiled. The prob-
> lem, in other words, is not the oneness of Divinity but the otherness of Divinity.
> The problem is in our imagery of transcendence, through which we disempower
> ourselves as we portray God as power over us.
>
> As a feminist Jew, [Falk seeks] a return to the fundamental insight of the
> religion—the perception of unity in the world. Unity of all elements of creation,
> unity of creation with creative source and power. This perception can be restored
> only through radical re-visioning, *re-imaging* that brings us back to the root of the
> monotheistic idea.

Falk yearns for "a *theology of immanence* that will both affirm the sanctity
of the world and shatter the idolatrous reign of the lord/God/king."[7] It appears
to me that her thrust may be received as implemental of the teaching of Jesus
of Nazareth, something of a feminist himself. But let us not ignore Pinchas
Lapide:

> [The] I-thou experience of immediate relationship is so powerful, singular, and
> unique that it never allows the presentation of a plurality of principles or a multi-
> ple personality of God to arise. In order to protect the oneness of God from every
> multiplication, watering down, or amalgamation with the rites of the surrounding
> world, the people of Israel chose for itself that verse of the Bible to be its credo
> which to this very day not only belongs to the daily liturgy of the synagogue but
> also is impressed as the first sentence of instruction upon the five-year-old school-
> child.
>
> This is the confession which Jesus acknowledged as the "most important of all
> the commandments," and which is spoken by every child of Israel as a final word
> in the hour of death: "Hear, O Israel! The Lord our God is One" (Deut. 6:4).[8]

I do not perceive any substantive incompatibility between Falk and
Lapide—Martin Buber was after all an archfoe of theological dualism—even
though when juxtaposed the two statements do stand as eminently paradoxical, perhaps the paradox that so often accompanies, yet may also give meaning
to, the female–vis-à-vis–male concatenation. Yet against any dogmatic coveting
of the paradox, one does well to recall that the Christian "Trinity" was essentially the fabrication of males. Meanwhile, the Jewish *laos* continued to forbid
all images.

(8) The interreligious question is far more complex than the issue of the one living God versus (reputed) false gods or even of "monotheism" versus "polytheism." The problem extends to the very nature of divineness, not excepting the exclusion or absence of divineness. Thus, the "personal" God of the Western religious tradition can hardly be equated with the "impersonal" One of the Eastern tradition. But in what sense, if any, is it right to say that the singular God of Torah and the Apostolic Writings is to be ultimately affirmed? What of other gods and other points of view? More than a few Christian adherents of a nonexclusivist persuasion want to know whether it is, in fact, God's intention to effect all human salvation in and through the Christian way.

(9) Once the soteriological power or eschatological import surrounding Jesus Christ is avowed, a judgment is thereby implicitly offered upon one or another religion of the world. The basis of this statement is that the issue of salvation or wholeness is foundational within various faiths (as given voice in and through a whole universe of concepts and teachings). A possible synonymous expression for *salvation* is found in Paul Tillich's understanding of religion: "Religion is the state of being grasped by an ultimate concern, a concern which qualifies all other concerns as preliminary and which itself contains the answer to the question of the meaning of our life." While "the predominant religious name for the content of such concern is God—a god or gods," in nontheistic faiths "divine qualities are ascribed to a sacred object or an all-pervading power or a highest principle such as the Brahma or the One. In secular quasi-religions the ultimate concern is directed towards objects like nation, science, a particular form or stage of society, or a highest ideal of humanity. . . ." Raimundo Panikkar describes the religious attitude simply as "trust in reality." All in all, religion is immerged in the sacred, and in distinguishing, in real life, the sacred from the profane.[9]

(10) Our study is representative of christological constructions that do three things: assume the validity or integrity of the Christian faith; endeavor to avoid imperialism or triumphalism vis-à-vis other faiths; and emphasize the significance of the historical Jesus for christological understanding. This threefold dedication plays a delimiting role within the theme of the present chapter as it does for other chapters, since there is no analytical need—other than perhaps for critical or historical purposes—to enter far into either extreme Christian exclusivism (only Christianity is true and other faiths are false)[10] or, for that matter, into extreme Christian latitudinarianism (the polar opposite of exclusivism). While we shall take into account argumentation critical of such positions—more particularly, of exclusivism—the positive stress will fall upon an overall christological outlook that ranges somewhere between exclusivism and latitudinarianism. This will keep us in line with the general character of the study. As it is, the available median views are very numerous and somewhat

diverse; in calling attention to some of them, and to one major one in particular, we still have plenty to do. We have to choose from within abundant materials and from among a legion of scholars. Today such median views are burgeoning and are having increasing influence within and beyond the church.

THE TYPOLOGY OF PAUL F. KNITTER

We are brought to an examination of Paul F. Knitter's position in his comprehensive and extremely useful study, *No Other Name? A Critical Survey of Christian Attitudes Toward the World Religions*. The title derives from the testimony of Luke: "there is salvation in no one else, for there is no other name under heaven given among men by which we must be saved" (Acts 4:12). Knitter speaks to all major aspects of the christological-interreligious question. I shall also respond to *No Other Name?* by marshaling and assessing the efforts of additional scholars.[11]

The "apperceptive mass" that Knitter provides for us consists of a fourfold set of Christian models for apprehending religious pluralism,[12] named and examined according to their roots in particular Christian confessions.[13]

(1) The "conservative evangelical model" (found as well in all churches, including mainline Protestant and Roman Catholic) today encompasses Fundamentalists, conservative Evangelicals, and ecumenical Evangelicals. All of these "hold to the primary authority of the Bible as the one absolute source of knowledge about God and the human condition, whether the Bible be regarded as 'inerrant' or as 'infallible.' " All three "proclaim the universal lordship of Jesus as the only savior of the world and the necessity of personal experience of his saving power." And all three "stress the necessity of mission, of witnessing the Lord Jesus to all peoples, so that all can come to salvation."

Knitter concentrates upon conservative or nonecumenical Evangelicals. For these people, to maintain that the non-Christian faiths are legitimate ways of salvation is to be taken captive by false teaching. Apart from an encounter with Jesus Christ, eternal life is out of the question. A number of pages are devoted to Karl Barth as an eloquent and sophisticated representative of the Evangelical viewpoint—for all Barth's conviction that the "Word of God" is opposed to all religion.[14] Since Christianity is the one and only true faith, all talk about the "values of pluralism" is nonsense or worse than nonsense. Such talk flouts the grim fact of a humankind mired in sin and it despoils the one saving truth of God's grace in Christ as the unqualified remedy of sin and an absolute necessity for eternal life. The pluralist "ethic" is a servant of the devil.

Knitter does not dismiss the conservative evangelical model out of hand. It would be intellectually dishonest to exclude the possibility that what these people are saying may be correct. On the other hand, these believers must con-

front another possibility, "that an embrace of the *relativity* of all truth-claims
does not necessarily force one into a universal *relativism.*" The Evangelicals
"should face the further possibility that Christians can maintain and proclaim
the particular importance of Christ—even, *perhaps*, scandalously, as a universal
truth for all religions—without having to negate the importance of universal
truth in other religions." In sum, conservative Evangelicals tend to "lose touch
with the full content of Christian tradition and with contemporary experience.
Most importantly, they raise serious roadblocks to the kind of interreligious dialogue that many Christians feel called to if they, as well as adherents of other
faiths, are to make their religious contribution to the welfare of our divided
world."[15] (Knitter's last point will cut no ice with conservative Evangelicals,
for whom truth is anything but a servant of pragmatic "values.")[16]

(2) The "mainline Protestant model" is held to be represented by such
disparate figures as Wolfhart Pannenberg, Paul Tillich, Carl Braaten, Paul Devan-
andan, and M. M. Thomas. While standing up for "salvation only in Christ," this
model differs from the conservative evangelical model in seeking "a more positive, a more dialogical, Christian approach to other faiths," a "more open attitude." On the basis of their reading of Christian Scripture and the human condition, these people argue that "Christians not only can but must recognize
that the God revealed in Jesus is truly speaking through voices other than that
of Jesus." Thus, for Pannenberg, "the history of religions is the history of the
appearing of the divine mystery which is presupposed in the structure of human existence."[17] Universal *revelation* (grounded in Scripture and tradition)
is one thing; concrete *salvation*, however, is something else. Unfortunately, followers of other religions manifest a tendency to try to effect their own salvation. In making this effort, they end up attempting to capture God.

> The overall assessment of the religions by the mainline Protestant model . . . is that
> they are bearers of authentic, divine revelation, but barren of authentic salva-
> tion. . . . Although there are many heart-warming calls for openness, respect, dia-
> logue, although it is even said that Christians can learn from other faiths and
> through them find "new expressions" for "the true identity of Jesus," still the basic
> category for the relationship between Christianity and the religions is that of "the
> law and the gospel" as understood by the [Protestant] Reformers.
>
> The law has been given not only to the Jews but to all peoples [an egregious
> misstatement of fact—by the Reformers, not by Knitter—A.R.E.] as a "preparatory
> revelation" for the full and saving revelation of the gospel of Jesus Christ. . . . [It]
> remains basically a *negative* preparation. It prepares for Christ in that its truth ul-
> timately breaks down and proves inadequate.[18]

In his critique of this second model Knitter doubts the correctness of the
charge that non-Christian faiths are necessarily ways of self-redemption; challenges the identification of a God who would offer a revelation that could

never lead to salvation; seriously questions the coherence of maintaining the ontological necessity and exclusive uniqueness of Christ for salvation amidst a profession of God's wish to save all people; and opposes the notion that nowhere in the world faiths is the meaning of salvation properly grasped. It may well be that "the Christian understanding of salvation has much more to *understand* from other religions."[19]

(3) A third type is identified as "the Catholic model: many ways, one norm." Knitter speaks of the Second Vatican Council as a watershed for Roman Catholic attitudes to the world religions and concentrates upon Karl Rahner as chief originator of this model.[20] Vatican II "clearly teaches—or at least clearly implies—that authentic 'religious experience' takes place in and through [these] religions." To Knitter, the third viewpoint may even be construed as a *mainline Christian* model, for ever since the 1960s it has been extending and evolving across confessional lines, and it represents a "growing ecumenical consensus" within such diverse ranks as Anglicanism, Eastern Orthodoxy, Third World Protestant theologians, the process theology of John B. Cobb, Jr., and others, and the World Council of Churches.[21]

Knitter's third model is sometimes identified as Christian inclusivism. As Timothy R. Stinnett writes, "the inclusivist position is that the affirmation of God's decisive revelation in Jesus Christ does not commit one to a denial of the possibility that God is also decisively revealed in non-Christian religions.[22] The decisiveness of the Christian revelation does not entail exclusiveness; rather, essential to the Christian view of God is that God is unfailingly present and at least implicitly revealed in the experience of all human beings." For the inclusivist, "God is definitively revealed in Christ," but revelation means that "God may also be definitively revealed in non-Christian religions as well."[23]

At the center of the Catholic model, and its main achievement, is the argument "that Christians not only can but must look on other religions as possible *ways of salvation.* This model takes seriously and consistently a conviction common to all Christian confessions [but implicitly abandoned or at least passed over in models 1 and 2—A.R.E.] that the God of Jesus Christ is a God of universal love." Representatives of the model "do not tie that love to an encounter with Jesus, as both the conservative evangelical and mainline Protestant models, in different ways, tend to do. For the Catholic model, both revelation *and* salvation are alive and well beyond the borders of Christianity." Nevertheless, in this model the same stumbling block is present that is evident "within all Christian models for a theology of religions." For the church as a whole continues to say that "Christ must be proclaimed as the fullest revelation, the definitive savior, the norm above all other norms for all religions"—or in the words of Vatican II's Declaration on the Relationship of the Church to Non-Christian Religions (*Nostra Aetate*; specifically, at the close of the section on the Jews), "It is . . . the duty of the Church's preaching to proclaim the cross of Christ . . . as the fountain from which every grace flows."[24]

It is perhaps noteworthy that John B. Cobb, Jr, who is known for his "high Christology" in a frame of reference of process theology and a world theology for today, should write, "The idea that Jesus is God without qualification is heresy and simply makes no sense. Orthodox teaching is that Jesus is the fully human Incarnation of the everlasting Word, or the Son, who is one with the Father." In an important sense "God is incarnate in all things." But yet the light and life of the Word of God were "embodied in him in a special way"; there is "a qualitative or structural difference." For the Word "became flesh in Jesus." Indeed, "it is God who is incarnate in Jesus and . . . this God is the Trinity in its totality. . . . Christ is not only the way and the life but also the truth."[25] It appears to me that Cobb here seriously qualifies his statement that Jesus is not God.[26] Michael Wyschogrod detects a residual supersessionism in Cobb vis-à-vis Judaism, despite Cobb's denial of supersessionism.[27] I suggest that Cobb's insistence upon retaining the symbol *Christ* for use across the boundaries of the religions serves to hinder or compromise his own goal of transcending Christian absolutism and parochialism. I think that this outcome could be precluded were Cobb to take the simple step of replacing *Christ* with *Logos*, since the theology of Wisdom is after all what he is driving for. A purely linguistic residue of Christian imperialism gets in his own way.

Professor Knitter enters searching questions: "In the light of contemporary religious pluralism and the demands of interreligious dialogue, we must ask: . . . Must Christians proclaim a final normativity for Christ? Can they? To express it more precisely, what are the conditions for the possibility of making such an affirmation?" In later pages Knitter will seek to meet these questions; for the present, he simply sharpens the import of the queries in two ways, one for each of two different orientations: (a) To those who testify to "the normativity and finality of Christ for all religions because this is what their *personal experience of Christ* tells them," he responds in this way: "What is 'felt' by those who experience and commit themselves to the power and truth of Christ? Certainly they experience that Christ is an utterly reliable and demanding expression of who God is. This includes the conviction that Christ has something crucially important to say to all peoples (universal relevance). But such a Christian faith-experience does not seem to imply that Christ is the *one and only* utterly reliable and demanding expression of God's reality. When a Christian experiences Jesus Christ to be 'my savior' and [even] 'savior for all,' that does not necessarily mean 'only savior.' " (b) To those who for support call upon "the New Testament witness and Christian tradition," Knitter responds in this way: (i) "Can such a claim be made on the authority of tradition when tradition seems to contradict our present experience?" (ii) "Is it true that belief in the normativity, finality, unsurpassability of Christ forms an essential part of the Christian message? We shall see that a careful analysis of the language and socio-cultural world of early Christianity suggests that it does not."

It is surely the case that the foregoing responses do nothing to imply that Jesus Christ is *not* the "norm above all other norms" (*norma normans non normata*). The distinctiveness of Christianity may well be precisely that "it contains a 'surprise,' an unimagined possibility." "What would be the grounds for recognizing such a possibility? What is it that would make Jesus Christ the fullest, the definitive, the normative revelation of God? Because such claims are universal, the reasons for them would have to be universally available—to all peoples. Our review of the Catholic model has not offered such evidence."[28]

(4) The "theocentric model: many ways to the center," while it is still a minority position, involves an openness that is more and more taking shape across denominational boundaries. This model entails a *paradigm shift* away from the normativity or normativism (absolutism) of Christ in favor of God-centered understanding and dedication that allows for a more "authentic interreligious dialogue" yet at the same time fully preserves Christ's distinctiveness.[29] S. Wesley Ariarajah of Sri Lanka attests, "The recovery of a theocentric theology will enable Christians, without denying their witness to Jesus Christ, to stand alongside people of other faiths as children of the one God."[30]

The theocentric model is represented by, among others, John Hick,[31] Raimundo Panikkar,[32] Stanley J. Samartha,[33] many Christian theologians of the Jewish-Christian relation,[34] and such liberation/political thinkers as Dorothee Sölle and Tom F. Driver.[35]

According to John Hick, Christians may continue to follow Jesus Christ as their unique Savior without demanding that he be normative for others. "The dogma of the unique superiority of Jesus and of the Christian religion" simply does not follow from the divine Incarnation of God in Jesus.[36] A major device of Hick, perhaps his main contribution to the theocentric model, is his persuasion that belief in the incarnation and the divinity of Jesus is mythic and thus not only allows but requires reinterpretation.[37]

Explicating the work of Samartha, Knitter writes,

> With such a theocentric model for understanding and encountering other religions, based on a nonnormative Christology, Christians . . . will still be able to hold to their personal commitment to Christ and to their belief in his universal meaning. They will still be able to tell other religions that *for them*, for Christians, "nowhere else is the victory over suffering and death manifested so decisively as in the death and resurrection of Jesus Christ." But such an announcement will be an enthusiastic *witness* to their own revealer, *not* a denigrating *judgment* about other revealers. Although Christians continue to carry out what they feel is their universal mission of witnessing to Christ, they will be able to "recognize that their neighbors too have their 'missions' in the same pluralistic world." There may be other

"universally relevant" revelations, other "norms," other saviors. To recognize this is not necessarily to jeopardize what Christians have experienced in Jesus Christ.[38]

KNITTER'S OWN CHRISTOLOGY

Paul F. Knitter himself propounds a constructive version of the Christian theocentric position; it is to a more discrete examination of his own views that we now turn. He believes that the theocentric model "both addresses the inadequacies and preserves the values" of alternative models and "holds the greatest promise for the future of interreligious dialogue and for the continued evolution of the meaning of Jesus Christ for the world."[39]

While the conservative evangelical and mainline Protestant models both assign an *exclusive uniqueness* to Jesus, and the Catholic model an *inclusive uniqueness* to him, the theocentric model offers a *relational uniqueness*, meaning a uniqueness that is able to relate to, to include, and to be included by, other unique religious figures. Such an understanding views Jesus "not as exclusive or even as normative but as *theocentric*, as a universally relevant manifestation (sacrament, Incarnation) of divine revelation and salvation."[40]

Knitter's procedure here extends to four considerations.

(1) A nonnormative, theocentric Christology is not in violation of the Apostolic Writings' proclamation of Jesus and is therefore a valid rendering of that proclamation. ("Nonnormative" Christology is not the happiest conceptual way for Knitter to represent his position, despite the fact that he again and again bespeaks a "nonnormative" Jesus. He surely believes that Jesus Christ is wholly normative for Christians. What he actually means by nonnormative, in a Christian frame of reference, is nonnormativ*ist* or nonnormativ*istic*, i.e., *nonabsolutist.*)

The theocentric point of view follows in the way of Jesus of Nazareth, for Jesus and his core message of the kingdom of God are themselves theocentric. What, then, are we to say concerning the undeniably christocentric message of the Apostolic Writings? "The Christocentrism of the New Testament does not lose hold of Jesus' original theocentrism. Jesus never takes the place of God. . . . The New Testament maintains a delicate, sometimes difficult balance between Christocentrism and theocentrism." Jesus' deep awareness of God as his Father does indicate uniqueness; "this must be respected" in all contemporary Christologies. Yet whenever Christology forgets Jesus' profound theocentrism "it opens Christian consciousness to a 'myopic Christocentrism,' to a 'Jesusology,' to a reductionism that absorbs God into Jesus. Christocentrism without theocentrism easily becomes an idolatry that violates not only Christian revelation but the revelation found in other faiths."[41]

A possible comment upon Knitter's analysis here consists in the challenge, encountered all through our study of Christology, to decide whether Jesus is the judge of the Apostolic Writings, the Apostolic Writings are the judge of Jesus, or the two authorities stand in a dialectical and paradoxical relation. It is maintained in chapter 8 that to turn the Jesus of history into the sole or absolute arbiter of authentic/inauthentic christological witness would be a form of Jesusolatry. At this point it is fitting to counter this injunction with another: To turn the Apostolic Writings into the absolute arbiter of Jesus would be a form of bibliolatry. The helpful fact remains, to continue Knitter's representation, that from the beginnings of the church, Christology has been dialogical, pluriform, and evolutionary. It is, of course, the case that as the early church developed there were gropings toward such things as preexistent sonship, the resurrection as establishing Jesus' sonship, and wisdom Christologies. In this connection Knitter offers several guidelines that he traces directly to the first two generations of Christians: (a) "The Christological trajectories and titles are not definitions but *interpretations* of who Jesus was for his early followers. . . . These images, like all mythic-symbolic language, are not to be taken literally; but they are to be taken seriously." Proponents of the theocentric model are correct in looking upon New Testament christological statements "as myth; the purpose of such language is not to define or limit our understanding of Christ but to give access to the mystery of Christ [*mysterium Christi*]." (I submit that we must be very careful here. There is no convincing historical ground for adjudging that the original purveyors of these christological images looked upon them as mythic. "Myth" is *our* idea; it would be incorrect to foist it upon the ancients.)

(b) "No single New Testament trajectory or image of Jesus should be absolutized and allowed to absorb the others."

(c) It is *not* so that "all the New Testament images of Jesus, *taken together*, say everything about who this man was and what he means for Christians and for the world."

(d) The "continuing evolution of Christology" will have to make use of a main force that moved it ahead in the apostolic time: dialogue with other cultures and religions.

(e) What we especially need in order to carry ahead the evolution of Christology is a "renewal or return to the theocentrism that marked Jesus' understanding of his mission and . . . of himself."[42] (Unless I somehow missed it, Knitter does not quite go to the point of declaring outright that the historical Jesus must serve as a normative criterion of Christology.)

A further feature of the Christology of the Apostolic Writings is its exclusivism; no one comes to the Father save through Jesus (John 14:6). Knitter's overall proposal here is that "the 'one and only' qualifiers to the various

Christological titles pertain more to the *medium* used by the New Testament than to its core *message*." I am not so sure: How can we disjoin in this way the message from its medium?

For Knitter, no less than three characteristics of the cultural milieu in which Christianity developed are able to account for the fact that "there was no other way, no other language, for them [the first Christians] to talk about what Jesus had done in their lives": First, the consciousness of the Christian community was pervaded by classicist culture (contra contemporary historical culture). In classicist culture "truth was one, certain, unchanging, normative." Second, "given the *Jewish eschatological-apocalyptic mentality* that marked especially the first generation of Christians, it was natural that they should interpret their experience of God in Jesus as final and unsurpassable." And third, the minority status of the early church within the larger Jewish community and the Roman Empire required the community "to arm itself with clear identity and total commitment." Its doctrinal language was, in a real sense, "survival language."[43]

Knitter's sociologistic explication does not quite wash. As a matter of fact, he has himself preveniently called into question his own counsel by conceding, just a few passages earlier, that it is "either dishonest or naïve to argue that the early Christians really did not mean or believe what they were saying, as if they were conscious of the 'historical relativity' or 'mythic conditioning' of [their] language. When the early Jesus-followers announced to the world that Jesus was 'one and only,' they meant it."[44] Yet he now asserts that the purpose of their language "was more to define identity and membership within the community than to define the purpose of Jesus for all time." How can this be so? Knitter further declares, "If we understand the absolute, one-and-only descriptions of Jesus as insuring the survival of the community rather than as offering a once-for-all definition of Jesus, we can today still adhere to the basic worldview of early Christianity without insisting on its absolute, exclusive adjectives. In fact, in our present pluralistic situation, this seems to be what Christians are called to do."[45] But how can it be normatively the case that the presence of pluralism rightly determines what people are "called to do"? Again, there is a serious philosophic-moral issue here, with reference to the apostolic Christian community: The social reasons why people say and do certain things cannot properly exhaust *the meaning of the content* of what they say and do. A pitfall here is that *to explain* easily becomes *to explain away*.

Knitter maintains that "all the 'one and only' adjectives used to describe Jesus belong 'not to the language of philosophy, science, or dogmatics, but rather to the language of confession and testimony' [Frances Young]." No, all this is primarily *our* interpretation of the language. In all probability, the first Christians had no idea of any distinction between metaphysical principles and personal relationships and commitments. Strangely enough, Knitter himself admits this very thing in a footnote: We cannot imply that the early Christians were conscious of any distinction between metaphysical and confessional language.[46] On this basis, Knitter's analogy between exclusivist christological language and the language that a husband would use of his wife ("You are the most beautiful woman in the world") does not hold up. For while there are a great many women in the world, there was *for the early Christians* only one Jesus. He was not *their* one-and-only; he was *the* one-and-only. In a contemporary pluralist context Knitter's marital analogy works fine; any such context is not provided by the Apostolic Writings.[47] Exclusivist christological language is precisely *not*, in the first instance, confessional language; it is, in the first instance, ontological language. It is *we* who turn it into confessional language—with purposes and consequences that may well be entirely necessary and legitimate.

All Knitter had to do to avoid this entire problem was to concede from the start that he does not agree with apostolic ontology or metaphysics—certainly a respectable and defensible form of disagreement. His disagreement can be received as a perfectly fitting and normal illustration of how modern historical understanding differs from classical understanding. It would have been far more convincing had Knitter merely utilized as the basis of his argument something that he obviously believes: Since we today do not think as the first Christians thought, their outlook is correctly subject to revisionist treatment—under, in theological terms, our guidance by the Holy Spirit.

(2) A nonnormative understanding of Christ is consistent with "contemporary methods of Christology."

Knitter here calls upon interpretations of Jesus put forward in Karl Rahner's "transcendental Christology," process thought,[48] and by liberation theologians. He shows that much of today's Christology, Catholic and Protestant, is, in fact, moving toward nonexclusivist interpretations of Jesus Christ—even if the scholars involved do not always realize it or "are reluctant to follow the momentum of their own thought." The truth is that such contemporary trends add coherence and validity to the theocentric christological position. "Rahner and the process theologians have shown that Christians can claim that incarnation *really* took place in Jesus, . . . but they have also implicitly shown that Christians can make such claims without having to add that this is true *only* of Jesus. If Christians can proclaim that 'in him [Jesus] all the fullness of God was pleased to dwell' (Col. 1:19), they must also recognize that 'you [others] may be filled with all the fullness of God' (Eph. 3:19)." Finally, it is liberation thinking that helps Christians to recognize how various beliefs—for instance, in the exclusivity of salvation in Christ—can be "nurtured more by the desire to maintain power and privilege than by the desire to promote truth and freedom." Among other lessons that the liberative outlook has for the decisive question of the uniqueness of Jesus, one is to show that normativist claims for

Jesus are not necessary—the one requirement for being a Christian is "commitment to the kingdom vision of liberating, redemptive action"—and another is to insist that "if liberating praxis is the foundation and norm for authentic divine revelation and truth, then Christians must be open to the possibility that in their dialogue with other believers they may encounter religious figures whose vision offers a liberating praxis and promise of the kingdom equal to that of Jesus. In view of their fruits of praxis, such saviors would have to be recognized and affirmed. . . . [Their] existence would in no way have to jeopardize the universal relevance of Jesus' vision or lessen one's total commitment to it. 'Anyone who is not against us, is with us' (Mark 9:40)."[49]

(3) Knitter next explores the question of whether a nonnormative, theocentric Christology is consistent with faith in Jesus' resurrection.

The starting point here is the increasing contemporary effort "to crack the dichotomy of views that hold the resurrection to be either an *objective* or a *subjective* event." For such scholars as Edward Schillebeeckx, Norman Perrin, and James Mackey, "the resurrection, one might say, happened both in and to the disciples. Faith in the risen Lord was not simply caused by an objective event taking place in front of them; neither, however, was it created or concocted by the disciples' personal convictions or wishes or hallucinations. The Easter event was caused by something outside the witnesses (objective), and yet took place within them and was dependent on their personal perceptions and response (subjective)." The scholars involved generally conclude that the resurrection belief "originated from a deeply personal faith experience," describable as a "revelation" or "conversion" experience. "Like any authentic faith or conversion experience, it was brought about by the objective reality of grace, the power of God, the Spirit. But this grace was mediated through 'psychological realities and human experiences' (Schillebeeckx)."

Knitter contends that such an interpretation "does justice not only to the nature of the New Testament accounts but to the nature of resurrection faith itself," which is a matter "of deeply personal-communitarian experience and commitment." Crucially, this understanding of the resurrection fully allows for the nonnormative Christology of the theocentric model. In doing so, it opens the way to the further eventuality that what happened "to the early Christians and to Jesus after his death might possibly have happened to other believers and their saviors. The resurrection of Jesus, in all its authentic mystery and power, does not necessarily imply 'one and only.' "[50]

Professor Knitter's inclusion of the resurrection of Jesus among the major elements of his theocentric Christology helps point the way to our next chapter.

(4) Central and climactic to his point of view is Knitter's prescription that a nonnormative, theocentric view of Jesus allows and even demands "a total personal commitment to him. Such a commitment calls for a distinctive Chris-

tian praxis within society and a distinctive Christian contribution to the new dialogue among religions." Thereby, Christians are enabled to endorse a theocentric theology of religions.

This move and orientation "need in no way diminish one's personal and full commitment to Jesus as incarnation of God's saving purpose and presence." On the contrary, such an understanding "can confirm and intensify" the commitment to Jesus "by rendering it more intellectually coherent (better theory) and more practically demanding (better praxis)."

Knitter develops this part of his argument via three emphases: (a) To acknowledge the possibility of other saviors and incarnations may seem threatening to one's Christian faith. Knitter reasons that such fears derive primarily from the residual influence upon us of classicist consciousness "or from unquestioned presuppositions of much Western philosophy to the effect that truth is always a matter of either-or, this-or-that." The psychology of faith does not demand any such outlook. "Faith in and commitment to Jesus is a transforming experience; Jesus so empowers the heart and illumines the mind that one can now feel and know and, especially, act differently. The experience of faith necessarily includes the conviction that Jesus *is* God's revelation and grace. It does not necessarily include the conviction that he *alone* is this revelation and grace." At this juncture Knitter reintroduces the marital analogy considered above, but now upon grounds where my earlier criticism no longer applies. For he is talking now, not of the apostolic Christian community, but of the spiritual life of today's Christians: "One can be totally and faithfully committed to one's spouse, even though one knows that there are other persons in this world equally as good, intelligent, beautiful. . . ." In point of fact, "absolute exclusivity, in attitude or practice, is neither honest nor healthy in any commitment." Knitter goes so far as to suggest that

> the ability to be open to others can serve as a gauge for the depth of one's commitment to Jesus. Sociologists point out that the more a group is secure in its own identity and the more it is committed to its unifying vision, the more it will be able to tolerate, even accept, other visions—what sociologists call "cognitive dissonance.". . . Again, the analogy with marriage applies: the deeper the commitment to one's spouse and the more secure the marriage relationship, the more one will be able to appreciate the truth and beauty of others. Therefore, not only does commitment to Jesus not exclude openness to others, but the greater the commitment to him, the greater will be one's openness to others.
>
> This proportionality also works in reverse: Might Christians' anxiety about the possibility of "other Christs" be a symptom of an underlying insecurity concerning their own identity and praxis?[51]

I think that Knitter rather underestimates the will-to-power (or the imperialist urge) that is present in all human collectivities, not excluding those who

are objectively secure. They may readily convince themselves that their "uni-
fying vision" ought to be the vision of everyone (cf. the diagnostic political
writings of Reinhold Niebuhr).[52] As for the marriage relationship, we can
hardly ignore the propensity, largely of males and not excepting highly secure
married men, for "playing around."

(b) The difficulty in maintaining a human dialectic of commitment and
openness is an aspect of the tension between universality and particularity that
is inherent in all authentic religious experience. Two considerations are apropos: (i) The occurrence of "particular experiences of divinity" tends to convince individuals or communities that the revelation or symbol involved is not
alone decisive for them but is universally relevant. It has something to say to all
peoples. (ii) This state of affairs creates a tension within the psychology of faith
but a condition that drives in the direction of mystery. Knitter finds

> a direct proportionality between the appropriation by a community of the power
> of its *particular* mediator and the confrontation of the community with the *uni-
> versal* reality of mystery mediated through that savior. The more the community
> realizes that its savior *really* does make God known, the more it realizes that this
> God is a mystery ever more than what has been made known—the *Deus semper
> major*, the God ever beyond. In other words, the more the particular mediator's
> efficacy is realized, the more its relativity is recognized. Such a tension is creative
> because it constantly beckons the community to hold to and remain faithful to its
> mediator, without, however, allowing this mediator to become an idol.[53]

Here, too, I think that Knitter underestimates the potentially and actually
destructive side of human belief, its proclivity for falling into ideology and idolatry. For the, at least, equal possibility obtains that "the more the particular mediator's efficacy is realized," the *less* is its relativity realized and the more the
community launches into imperialist ventures. The history of the papacy, with
all its idolatries of christological and papal absolutism, provides a ready illustration. As Paul Tillich used to stress, the greatest crimes in the history of humankind are those committed in the name of some kind of religion. In this connection, it is a pity that Knitter throughout fails to benefit from any reference
to the feminist anti-idolatrous critique and christological construction, a war
that, in alliance with the Jesus of history, is being waged against Christolatry.[54]
Knitter partially redeems himself when he counsels that "the community must
never slip into the false security of thinking it knows what its mediator has revealed; for Christianity this implies that the task of Christology . . . is never finished." In other terms, the mystery is not to be dissolved. "In our present age of
religious pluralism, the creative tension between the particular and the universal also requires that each religious community recognize that there can be,
and most likely are, other particular mediators of [the] divine mystery, a mystery that can be captured, definitively, by no one mediator."

(c) At the last, Knitter calls for a *confessional* approach to others. We are told that Christians do well to follow the proposal of H. Richard Niebuhr that "they confess and make known what they have experienced God to have done for them and the world in Jesus, *without* making any claims about Jesus' superiority or normativity over other religious figures." Knitter's reliance upon H. Richard Niebuhr is unfortunate because the latter is, in fact, inconsistent in his views. In the course of protesting against what he calls "Christomonism"—understood as the reduction of God to the figure of Jesus Christ—Niebuhr pens the words, "some imagined idol called by his name takes the place of Jesus Christ the Lord." The tragedy here is Niebuhr's ignoring of *his own insistence* that to ascribe lordship to any being other than the Creator of heaven and earth is to fall prey to idolatry.[55] Nevertheless, Knitter properly concludes the following:

> A confessional approach ... will be both certain and open-ended. It will enable Christians to take a firm position; but it will also require them to be open to and possibly learn from other positions. It will allow them to affirm the *uniqueness* and the universal significance of what God has done in Jesus; but at the same time it will require them to recognize and be challenged by the *uniqueness* and universal significance of what the divine mystery may have revealed through others. In boldly proclaiming that God has indeed been defined in Jesus, Christians will also humbly admit that God has not been confined to Jesus.[56]

In a closing chapter, "Doing before Knowing—The Challenge of Interreligious Dialogue," Knitter deals with issues of the practical application of a theocentric, nonnormative Christology in relations with adherents of other faiths. Authentic dialogue is held to rest on "a new model of truth," wherein "what is true will reveal itself mainly by its ability to *relate* to other expressions of truth and to *grow* through these relationships—truth defined not by exclusion but by relation."[57] For the most part, that chapter takes us beyond our specifically christological concerns. But I include one pertinent citation:

> The primary mission of the church ... is not the "salvation business" (making persons Christians so they can be saved), but the task of serving and promoting the kingdom of justice and love, by being sign and servant, wherever that kingdom may be forming.
>
> In order to promote the kingdom, Christians must witness to Christ. All peoples, all religions, must know of him in order to grasp the full content of God's presence in history. This need is part of the purpose and motivation for going forth to the ends of the earth. But in the new ecclesiology and in the new model for truth, one admits also that all peoples should know of Buddha, of Muhammad, of Krishna. [Would not "one affirms" be more to the point than "one admits"?—A.R.E.] This, too, is part of the goal and inspiration for missionary work: to be witnessed to, in order that Christians might deepen and expand their own grasp of God's presence

and purpose in the world. Through this mutual witnessing, this mutual growth, the work of realizing the kingdom moves on.[58]

It is obvious that a theocentric Christology such as Paul Knitter advocates in *No Other Name?* (and as I put forward in the present book) does not speak to differences and conflicts with antitheocentric and nontheistic religious positions (as examples, classical or Hinayana Buddhism and Marxism).[59]

AGAIN NEO*KENOSIS*

The final section of this chapter is directed to my own neokenotic position as sketched above in chapter 8—the persuasion that, in Jesus, *God* emptied or humbled Godself, "taking the form of a servant" (cf. Phil. 2:5-11). In that chapter I suggested a number of things for which a neokenotic position may stand or with which it is in accord: a certain catholicity; the hiddenness of God; theocentricity and incarnation as carrying equal weight; an overcoming or making redundant of the question of whether Jesus was aware of what "Christ" was doing; the Jesus of history as we know of him; an easing of the weighty dependence upon historical "truth" in E. P. Sanders and James H. Charlesworth, together with awareness of the danger in affirmations of faith that are incompatible with history; a refusal to "empty" Jesus of spatiotemporal or human content; and the paramountcy of the divine love, as itself brought forth in God's *kenosis*. In general, I hold that this neokenotic point of view is coherent with an extra-absolutist Christology and with the relative (= relational) Christian authority of the Jesus of history.

A neokenotic christological viewpoint, as consonant with and supportive of Christian theocentric confessionalism, may be further though briefly developed with aid from the ten points to follow. (I hope that readers have not been put off by my repeated recourse to enumerations. Increasing acquaintance with some contemporary biblical scholars seems to have turned me into a purveyor of lists.)

(1) The major problem with much traditional Christology is not so much that it fails to accord with a religiously pluralist world or temper—though that condition obtains all right. The real difficulty that besets us is how to foster the Christian theological task in a way that (a) avoids idolatry and (b) escapes negative attitudes toward non-Christians (exclusivism).

(2) The humbling (and hiding) of God in and through Jesus of Nazareth is coherent with Hebrew Scripture and with the Judaism of Jesus. For the revealing (and hiding) of God is essential to the Jewish historical tradition with, as the ultimate normative act, God's revealing (and hiding) of Godself in Torah.

(3) The humbling of God—not to be confused with "from above" Christo-

logies of a God-man—means that God is prepared to be a servant. One way God effects God's self-abnegation is through the man Jesus, who walked around Galilee, Samaria, and Judea proclaiming his Father's kingdom.

(4) A neokenotic orientation does its level best to be coherent with what we know of the Jesus of history, whose reclamation, or at least reaffirmation, is the aim of this book. Both historically and religiously speaking, Jesus is the special authority of Christians. He is "their rebbe." The model for Christians is the Jesus who went about doing good, incarnating the righteousness of God in deeds of justice, mercy, and love. The life and praxis of Jesus are entirely consistent with *kenosis*, with God assuming the guise of servant. But once the Jesus of divine-human history is placed in one or another (nonabsolutist, nonexclusivist, nonidolatrous) way at the center of faith, a revolutionary consequence shatters our analytic calm: The issue of *Christianity* and the world religions recedes into the shadows. Instead, there comes to the fore the question of Judaism and the world religions, since Judaism was Jesus' own faith. (Later we shall note the sense in which the question may also become Islam and the world religions.) What is the lesson of this fact for today? Well, as earlier stated, post-Jesus Judaism embodies a form of collective theocentrism according to which "we" are called to worship God and God alone, while "they" may likewise share in the world to come (the kingdom of God) on the condition that "they" satisfy certain minimal standards of goodness. The theocentrism is made a living thing in and through its practical relationism: "We see the church from the steeple" (chap. 1)—or better, "we see life from the perspective of Torah." Meanwhile, "they"—the Gentiles, the Marxists, the Buddhists, the Confucians —are entitled to their own problems. They are responsible for themselves and their salvation, according to their lights and amidst their own dignity as human beings. The Jesus-follower of today will not pass any kind of final judgment upon these people.

(5) The peculiar basis upon which Christians may oppose religious absolutism and exclusivism is Jesus' entirely Jewish commitment to the kingdom of God, which encompasses the struggle against human injustice and the realization of love. Jesus' proclamation of his Father's kingdom constitutes a historical foundation or insurance against Christian exclusivism. And since Jesus "takes history and human affairs with ultimate seriousness,"[60] the danger is forestalled that the kingdom will exert otherworldly pressures. All this is a far cry from both relativism and indifferentism,[61] since the living God of Judaism is Jesus' focus and the primary criterion of all his values and actions. Thus, while for Jesus religious absolutism would have no justification, the same would be the case with latitudinarianism and indifferentism. And the same would also apply to "our" deification of Jesus. John Hick sounds the proper warning:

Christians who seek to follow Jesus as their Lord but who believe that he would have regarded the church's deification of him as profoundly mistaken are described as having a low or reduced or defective or minimal or heretical Christology. This is like saying that those who do not subscribe to the theory of demon possession have a low, defective demonology. Such a strategy mistakes a problem for its solution. What is primarily at issue in our response to Jesus is not which theoretical apparatus we shall employ to deify him, but whether deification, relatively commonplace in the ancient world, is in our postmythic world meaningful and appropriate. Now that modern biblical scholarship has concluded that in all probability the historical Jesus did not think of himself as God, his deification requires reconsideration on its own merits.[62]

How could the Christian ever insist upon a fundamental religious tenet that his master Jesus rejects? Is Jesus some kind of heretic? In Lockean terms, is faith to be enabled to subvert reason?

(6) Is it being insinuated that Jesus is not unique? No, Jesus is entirely unique. As faithful son of Israel and faithful believer in and emissary of Judaism, Jesus is constituent to the single and singular drama that rests upon the call and blessing of God's special people Israel,[63] within the larger drama of universal redemption. Furthermore, the event, the presence, of Jesus Christ means the establishing of the Christian faith as the historical and moral continuation and outreach of Israel. (*Continuation* and *outreach* are alternative terms to *fulfillment*; to make Christianity the *fulfillment* of Judaism would be wrongly to foster Christian supersessionism.)

The unique historical quality of the event of Jesus Christ—better, its uniquely unique quality (since every historical event is after all unique)—is here based upon that event's soteriological character. This takes us into the reality of the incarnation.

(7) In the incarnation, as Stanley J. Samartha puts it, "God relativizes himself."[64] This is part of Samartha's warning against the Christomonism that in its absolutization of Jesus has invaded Christian doctrine. Respecting the Chalcedonian proclamation that in Jesus divine nature and human nature were truly united, Paul Knitter maintains that this "means that divinity 'assumed flesh' not as one puts on a coat but as wine mixed with water becomes one liquid—God *becomes* human." Knitter interposes that "all revelation and grace can be considered incarnational." I am not sure that we can go quite this far. But we can agree that all revelation and grace are directed to *humankind*: this is, after all, what revelation and grace *mean*. When pointing to the affirmation of God's grace as operative and coming to expression in the world religions, Knitter adds, "We see how vitally a Christian theology of religions is tied to Christology."[65] We may conclude that the link that binds grace in the world to christological effort is the incarnation, the humanization of God.

(8) The human world as such is open to the salvation of God. In a neokenotic view there is no hindrance to the saving presence of God among many different peoples and faiths and in many different times. There is, of course, the implication of a historicizing (i.e., a delimiting) of revelations in accordance with transitory times and seasons. (Is it possible that Christianity, and with it the Christian faith, could one day come to an end? Such a question must create anguish in the hearts of many Christians. But the answer cannot be other than affirmative. For upon what conceivable grounds could the response be negative? The world has lived most of its life without Christianity. Human history is replete with death, the death of nations, of civilizations, of human faiths. These things are not said for the primary purpose of consolation. But they do remain as facts.)

A neokenotic orientation may serve to sustain a plural quality (i.e., an eminently historical quality) within the praxis of God. For if we are in truth confronted with the kind of God who humbles Godself in and through the event of Jesus Christ, there is no reason to believe that God does not humble Godself in other revelations and deeds. Indeed, were God not a humbling God, there would be no ground for anticipating any divine-historical intervention. For God to intervene in human history is itself to empty God, to humble God, to hide God.

In sum, the "emptying" of God in Jesus the man—the incarnation—may be construed as entirely compatible with the praxis of God within other human creations and witnesses, such as the Qur'ān.

Speaking of the Qur'ān, I call attention to an essay by Hans Küng on the Christian dialogue with Islam. The reason for doing so is not alone to illustrate the present point but, more importantly, to tie the analysis as a whole to the historical Jesus as relational authority for Christians.

In the course of his exposition, Küng—in many aspects of his own Christology a highly conservative Christian[66]—raises the intriguing dual question of whether the Qur'ān may be identified as "Word of God" and of whether the portrayal of Jesus in the Qur'ān is accurate. To the first part of the question, Küng responds in this way:

> Many Christians do not realize that the Catholic Church has excluded as an error the claim that outside the church there is no salvation, no grace.[67] By implication, there is *grace* outside the church. There can be special charisms outside the church. How, then, can we deny that outside the church there also are persons who have such charisms, including prophetic gifts? *Extra ecclesiam gratia!* If we recognize Muhammad as a prophet, to be consistent we must also admit that the message of Muhammad is not of his own making; the Qur'ān is not simply the word of Muhammad, but the *Word of God.*

On the question of the Qur'ān's correctness respecting Jesus, we know that Muslim Scripture contains inaccuracies (e.g., Jesus did not die but was simply assumed into heaven), yet we have to acknowledge, significantly, that "the picture of Jesus in the Qur'ān is very analogous to the picture of Jesus" in what Küng calls "Judeo-Christianity," the earliest Christianity before the so-called high Christology or Christomonism set in, as recorded in the Apostolic Writings (cf. Samartha above). For support Küng calls upon two scholars, Adolf Schlatter and Hans-Joachim Schoeps. For the former, "Muhammad took over many of the beliefs preserved by Jewish Christians—their awareness of God, their eschatology with its proclamation of the Day of Judgment, their customs and legends—and launched a new mission as 'the one sent from God.' " For the latter, "there can be no doubt about Muhammad's indirect dependence on sectarian Judeo-Christianity. It remains one of the truly great paradoxes of world history that Jewish Christianity, cut off from the Christian church, has been preserved in Islam and so has been able, to this day, to continue its influence."

Küng concludes that

> any direct dependence of Islam on Jewish Christianity will continue to be disputed. Yet the similarities are amazing. Muhammad rejected the orthodox (and Monophysitic) Son-of-God christology, yet accepted Jesus as the great "messenger" (*rasul*) of God, indeed as the "messiah" (*masih*) who brought the gospel. . . . Thus Muhammad's "christology" (if you wish) was not far removed from that of the Judeo-Christian church. . . . We have to recognize that Muhammad himself wanted to be a witness to Jesus—not to a Jesus of the Hellenistic gentile Christians, but rather to a Jesus as seen by his first disciples, who were Jews like Jesus himself. . . . According to the Qur'ān, Muslims already see Jesus as the great prophet and messenger of the one God, designated by God to be the "Servant of God" from his birth to his exaltation, as one who, along with the message he proclaimed, was of lasting importance to Muhammad. . . . Christians need to hear Muhammad's warning against the dangerous idolatry of listening to other gods, as well as his admonition that faith and life, orthodoxy and orthopraxis, belong together, even in politics. Thus, Muhammad could provide for us Christians, not the decisive guiding norm that Jesus gives us, but a *prophetic corrective* in the name of the one and same God: "I am nothing but a distinctive warner" (sura 46:9).[68]

The consequences of Küng's disquisition are potentially world-shattering. That Muhammad should direct the Qur'ān toward the actual Jesus of history as against subsequent Christomonism may help inspire the view that the Qur'ān (at this place) is a Word of God. Could it be that the Muslims are, strictly in the context of this aspect of their canonical authority, more "Christian" in their "Christology" than many Christians? For Jesus, as the historical Word of God, judges and finds wanting the Christomonism of the Apostolic Writings as he, in effect and preveniently, also sustains the Qur'ān as Word of God where it is representing the real Jesus of history. Much of the material of the Apostolic Writings may well fall outside the "Word of God," in contradistinction to the Qur'ān's greater faithfulness to Jesus. All of this has momentous implications for the Christian-Muslim dialogue.

In a personal confession, Raimundo Panikkar declares, "I 'left' as a Christian; I 'found' myself a Hindu; and I 'return' as a Buddhist, without having ceased to be a Christian."[69] Should the astonishing exposition of Hans Küng be taken into full account, and should the Jewishness of Jesus be granted the place that his own history (story) would appear to demand, we may suggest an analogy to the experience of Panikkar, a venture of faith: "I 'left' as a Christian; I 'found' myself a Muslim; and I 'return' as a Jew, without having ceased to be a Christian." I propose further that the Christian identity that *does not cease* is securely represented by John Hick: "We want to say of Jesus that he was *totus Deus*, 'wholly God,' in the sense that his *agape* was genuinely the *agape* of God at work on earth, but not that he was *totum Dei*, 'the whole of God,' in the sense that the divine *agape* was expressed without remainder in each or even in some of his actions." God is thus *truly* encountered in Jesus but not *alone* in Jesus. On this reasoning, as Knitter writes, Christians "can announce that Jesus is the center and norm for their lives, without having to insist that he be so for all other human beings."[70]

All of this is coherent with a neokenotic Christology.

(9) How may a neokenotic view accord with opposition to androcentric hierarchicalism, an opposition insisted upon in today's feminist critique, a critique that is seriously needed not only in Christianity but in Islam and in Judaism? Monika K. Hellwig attests that compassion means "a movement towards the other to help, but also a movement into the experience of the other to be present in solidarity and communion of experience. It implies sensitivity, vulnerability to be affected by the experience of the other but it also implies remedial action against suffering and oppression. Most of all, it implies involvement in the situation. . . . [The] Word of God to us which is Jesus is a Word of Compassion, the Compassion of God become human that we might share in it both passively and actively."[71]

(10) Jesus said that the second commandment is to love the neighbor as one loves oneself (Mark 12:31). In this we may detect a certain warning against the notion that the *kenosis* of God is subject to simple translation into human morality. No, self-love is to accompany the creative and enduring love of others. An unqualifiedly self-abnegating "ethic" would threaten the justice without which love (*agape*) stays powerless. The ethic of love is to be balanced, indeed fulfilled, by the righteousness that is to be an everflowing stream (Amos 5:24). In a word, we are not God and we are not Jesus Christ.

Each of these ten considerations is offered in the interest of living with the paradoxical dialectic of redemption: its transcending quality (in Christian terms, the "Christ" side) and its historical quality (the "Jesus" side). I say "in the interest of living with" because no Christology is capable of resolving the paradox nor ought it presume to do so. That the God for others is somehow bonded to "the man for others" (Bonhoeffer) remains as the final *mysterium Christi*. As Jesus admonishes his disciples, according to the Gospel of John: "He who believes in me, believes not in me but in him who sent me. And he who sees me sees him who sent me" (12:44-45). With the aid of the testimony of John, we may move ahead toward an authentic world theology.

Do we have in Jesus Christ no more than the story of another human being (if, to be sure, a man singularly chosen and used by God)? Or is there something in and about Jesus that points to the peculiar presence of God? A word of Stephen T. Davis may be apropos: "In my opinion, Jesus is the only person in the history of the world ever to have been resurrected from the dead."[72] It seems to me, however, that any such event cannot be separated from God's abiding covenant with Israel (cf. chap. 9). It is, in that sense, an event within the history of Israel, rather than in the first instance a "Christian" event or possession. In any case, Davis's assertion takes us over into the recurrent and momentous question of the resurrection.

11

Restoring the Resurrection: "Why Do You Search among the Dead?"

This chapter continues the review of my own christological reflections as presented in chapter 5 and referred to *passim* since then.[1]

The birth, life, crucifixion, and resurrection of Jesus comprise the overall subject matter of Christology. While the crucifixion is a straight or manifest historical happening (although its Christian meaning is much more than or other than historical), there is abiding debate in Christian theological and scholarly circles at a decisive point: Should the resurrection be treated or accepted as a historical event, or should it be received or placed within some alternative category? Is the resurrection part of the worldly history of Jesus, or is it to be construed as metahistorical?[2]

Jesus' resurrection is among the more problematic and contentious of all Christian doctrines, within at least two major frames of reference: the distinctiveness of the Christian faith; and Christianity's relation to extra-Christian persuasion.

In Christian scholarship and testimony upon the resurrection of Jesus we immediately face two extreme positions, not to mention additional viewpoints that fall between the extremes. For analytical purposes, the two extremes may be identified as indicative of subjectiveness and of objectiveness.

J. K. Elliott represents the former extreme. He concludes that "whereas we can assert with conviction that the resurrection belief founded the church, we cannot readily assert as fact the resurrection itself. . . . [The] resurrection of Jesus was an event only in the minds and lives of Jesus' followers. It cannot be described as an historic event.[3] The Easter story is a faith legend, not an objective eye-witness report: but it is a myth that the Christian church through the centuries has found to be a continuing inspiration."[4] (It is somewhat ironic that Elliott's book should be published by the Student Christian Movement Press.)

At the opposite extreme is the point of view of objectiveness. This position is represented in the Gospels, wherein "the Easter stories are all told as if they were historical events on the same basis as, say, the crucifixion."[5] In the Gospel of Luke the postresurrection Jesus replicates the precrucifixion Jesus. For it is the risen Jesus himself who protests to the eleven disciples and to "those who were with them," "See my hands and my feet, that it is I myself; handle me, and see; for a spirit has not flesh and bones as you see that I have." Jesus then proceeds to eat "a piece of broiled fish" (Luke 24:33, 39-40, 42). Within the Gospels, however, as in the Apostolic Writings as a whole there are differences and conflicts respecting the form and content of the objectiveness.[6] Thus, in contrast to the Gospel of Luke, the apostle Paul maintains that when the dead are raised, the body in question differs from the body that has died: "It is sown a physical body, it is raised a spiritual body" (1 Cor. 15:35-50). The only way to reconcile Luke and Paul would be to treat the risen Jesus as a special and different case within the abstract or generic category of those people who have been dead.

Why is the claimed event of the resurrection to be singled out as *the* issue within the Christian-Jewish encounter or, more precisely, within the problem of Christian triumphalism and supersessionism? The reason is that in the Christian *Anschauung* the resurrection constitutes a class by itself. To turn for a moment to the general history of religions: Under the rubric of sacred or numinous events as such, we are apprised of certain events that concentrate univocally upon the action and power of the *divine*; certain others that emphasize the action and power of *humans* (the Hinayana Buddhist paradigm, for example); and finally those that exhibit *synergism*, a combination of the action and power of both kinds of agents (the human and the divine, perhaps with Moses and God at Sinai as an exemplar). Objectively stated, the resurrection of Jesus would seem to boast the first of the three eventualities: God alone as the agent—this upon a most rudimentary and (humanly) anxiety-inducing experiential foundation: human beings can do nothing whatever to extricate themselves from death. It is this that puts the resurrection of Jesus (or of course *any* alleged resurrection) in a singular class.

I am going to recount and assess the stages through which my own thinking and conviction upon Jesus' resurrection have passed. To this end, I shall apply a Hegelian form of dialectic:

Thesis: Pedestrian Acknowledgment
Antithesis: Critical Questioning of the Thesis upon Moral Grounds
Synthesis: Antitriumphalist Affirmation

Recall that although in Hegel's theoretical schema *thesis* is reputed to reveal one aspect of things and *antithesis* a contrasting aspect, the two are then raised (*aufgehoben*) to the higher synthesis of a third stage.[7] What I mean by this allusion when applied to my own situation—and I mean nothing else—is that I do not now wholly repudiate either the thesis of pedestrian acknowledgment or the antithesis of critical questioning upon moral grounds; each of these is—I hope—gathered up, for their partial truths, into the third stage.

THESIS: PEDESTRIAN ACKNOWLEDGMENT (1942–74)

As I look through my earlier writings, I am struck by the rather casual and unthinking way in which, over a number of years, I received and handled the resurrection. I remained quite oblivious to such moral issues as the promulgation of that doctrine might raise. In my first book I ignored the subject entirely, though in an avowal of "loyalty to Christ as the transcendent Truth who stands above the relativities of history," I was obviously giving voice to a high Christology. In another book I unabashedly equated the "incarnate and resurrected Christ" with "the Word of God," though I did add that the resurrection of Jesus "stands at the apex of the Jewish-Christian *Auseinandersetzung* [confrontation]," and I did recognize that the resurrection entails "a fundamental transformation of Messianic expectations." In a later book I continued to agree that "the uniqueness of Christianity is its faith in the resurrection of Jesus as the Christ," although I did supplement such bald statements as this with an awareness that "from a Jewish point of view the Christ has not come and was not raised from the dead." Further along in the same study I seemed to be hinting at future misgivings in and through counsel to the church "to proclaim the death of the resurrected Christ, in the name of the Christ who may one day come"—wording that strikes me today as rather incoherent.[8]

All in all, my thesis stage appears in retrospect to mirror a prosaic, unreflective attitude.

ANTITHESIS: CRITICAL QUESTIONING OF THE THESIS UPON MORAL GROUNDS (1975–86)

This second stage requires a background, autobiographical note: My personal and scholarly interest in the overall relation between Christian thinking and life and Jewish thinking and life, and more especially in the human evil and destructiveness fabricated by Christian triumphalism and absolutism, did not result from a confrontation with the *Shoah* (Holocaust) as such but preceded the latter concern, a concern that did not develop until considerably later. The *Shoah*, however, was subsequently to exercise salient influence upon me— particularly through the mediation of Elie Wiesel, Irving Greenberg, Emil L. Fackenheim, and Eliezer Berkovits—and the *Shoah* has been the single most determining element in my encounter with the resurrection of Jesus. The phenomenon that originally nurtured my interest in the Christian-Jewish relation, beginning in 1944–45, was Christian antisemitism as such. But since that phenomenon and the *Shoah* are ineluctably bound together, there is no point in disjoining the *Shoah* from my original work and its motivations. Nevertheless, it was the anti-Jewish problematic within Christianity and Christian history that finally led me, and also my wife, to the subject of the *Shoah*.[9] I speak of all this here only in order to underscore the fact that the question of Christology and its moral/immoral potentialities is much more than a contemporary issue. It has ancient and abiding and tragic roots.

By way of further clarification of my antithetical stage: The nature of the confrontation between the *Shoah* and Christian theological doctrine is elementary and transparent. It is the issue of *transhistoricalness*. For the way to try to shelter or shield Christianity as something transhistorical is to turn it into a faith that, as Alan T. Davies has maintained, "does not see history as open to God's presence in the way Judaism does." In this view, such happenings as the crucifixion and the resurrection become transhistorical events that rule out "further orienting experiences."[10] (Davies seems to be opposing here the doctrine of the Holy Spirit as present guide.) Yet to any such view the *Shoah*, as a fully historical consequence of Christian praxis (as, of course, of other influences as well), answers: No, you cannot turn your back upon such orienting experiences.

Much more than a purely personal response was involved in my antithetical stage. That stage developed at a time of shattering unrest and a searching of conscience among Christian scholars and theologians (a period that remains with us). For Jean Daniélou, among many others, had expressed the final logic of Christian anti-Jewishness: The offense of the Jews is that "they do not believe in the *risen* Christ."[11] The citations that follow may be set in polemical juxtaposition to Daniélou's claim.

The Canadian Catholic theologian Gregory G. Baum declared, "What Auschwitz has revealed to the Christian community is the deadly power of its own symbolism." The "anti-Jewish thrust of the church's preaching" is not a historical, psychological, or sociological matter; "it touches the very formulation of the Christian gospel." Baum was speaking here of Christian triumphalism and supersessionism respecting the Jews and Judaism, the sort of thing that "assigns the Jews to the darkness of history," rejected by God and all peoples, in ways that could only end in the murder camps. In the Nazi *Endlösung* "the theological negation of Judaism and the vilification of the Jewish people" within the Christian tradition were, at the last, translated into the genocide of the Jews. "The message of the Holocaust to Christian theology . . . is that at whatever cost to its own self-understanding, the church must be willing to confront the ideologies implicit in its doctrinal tradition."[12]

Baum's judgments were paralleled by the Episcopal theologian Paul M. van Buren: "The roots of Hitler's final solution are to be found in the proclamation of the very *kerygma* of the early Christians. . . . [The command out of Auschwitz] is that we accept a judgment on something false lying close to the very heart of our tradition."[13]

And the United Methodist historian-theologian Franklin H. Littell wrote,

> The cornerstone of Christian antisemitism is the superseding or displacement myth, which already rings with the genocidal note. This is the myth that the mission of the Jewish people was finished with the coming of Jesus Christ, that "the old Israel" was written off with the appearance of "the new Israel." To teach that a people's mission in God's providence is finished, that they have been relegated to the limbo of history, has murderous implications which murderers will in time spell out. The murder of six million Jews by baptized Christians, from whom membership in good standing was not (and has not yet been) withdrawn, raises the most insistent question about the credibility of Christianity.[14]

To all these colleagues, there is a common foe: supersessionist elitism. Before the fact of the *Shoah* the question emerges, Is the Christian message morally credible? In the post-*Shoah* world many Christian spokespersons have expressed a readiness to rethink Christian teaching, to avoid Christian imperialism. Yet such expressions of concern often appear as no more than nice or pleasing sentiments lacking any concreteness. When a demand is made for specifics, the reformer may back off. And whenever a critic from within the Christian community raises the moral question concerning *specific* Christian teachings (viz., christological teachings), he or she may be dismissed as a radical who is undermining the faith. It is as if the *critic* were on trial and not the Christian message.[15] Until the self-identified reformer does something concrete to reconcile the resurrection of Jesus and the apodictic requirements of human morality, he or she can hardly take refuge in objections respecting what is or is not the *conditio sine qua non* of the Christian faith. Because the demand for revolutionary changes in Christian teaching and praxis is strictly moral in character, there is no way to meet that demand responsibly through reducing it or changing it into a "religious" or "theological" question. Unless calls for post-*Shoah* Christian reform are implemented in specific proposals and specific measures, the calls remain mere words—noisy gongs and clanging cymbals.

In the frame of reference of the resurrection, the overall moral-psychoan-alytic issue may be formulated as follows: On the one hand, a consummated resurrection of Jesus may be said to constitute a basic theological (christolo-gical) threat to or indictment of Judaism and the Jewish people; on the other hand, any denial of Jesus' resurrection may be said to comprise a life-and-death threat to the Christian faith and the Christian community. On the one hand, "once the resurrection is identified as a special act of God, a divine event or divine fact, how can Christian vilification, imperialism, and supersessionism vis-à-vis Judaism and the Jewish people ever be vanquished? For the issue be-tween the two sides is seen to be, not a relatively harmless disparity of mere human symbolism, spiritual conviction, or 'religious experience'—probably amenable to the soothings of 'relativization' or 'confessionalism'—but a matter of saying Yes or No to God himself, Sovereign of all things."[16] Yet on the other hand, are we then compelled to identify the Christian as visited by forlornness, as lost and without hope in this world? (Cf. Eph. 2:11-22.)

In checking over my own writings I note that, back in 1976 in a critical analysis entitled "Jürgen Moltmann, the Jewish People, and the Holocaust," I first made more than passing reference to the problematic of the resurrection. The context of the passage that follows is Moltmann's explanation that, while his book *Theology of Hope* begins with "the *resurrection* of the crucified Christ," his succeeding work *The Crucified God* turns back "to look at the *cross* of the risen Christ."[17] Here is my response:

> We may have the temerity to envisage a next step: the nonresurrection of the cru-cified Jesus, and the crucifixion of the nonresurrected Christ. This potential de-velopment may be formulated in at least two alternative ways: (i) Absolute God-forsakenness (until the still-future resurrection, which means the future resurrection of Jesus, as of others). (ii) The pure faith of Christian Judaism (not to be confused with Jewish Christianity, which is the faith of Jews and not of Gen-tiles). If we are to "turn back" with radical and total resoluteness, then we must really turn back: to the crucified Jew, and thereby to the suffering Jews (of whom Jesus remains, to be sure, in a real sense the *Stellvertreter*).[18]

In the remainder of the above source, however, I did not follow up on the subject of the resurrection but concentrated instead on the issue of the cruci-fixion and the *Shoah*[19]—although at the end I did suggest that ultimate Chris-tian liberation from complicity in the Nazi *Endlösung der Judenfrage*, "Final Deliverance from the Jews," necessitates "the total secularization, demytholo-gization, and humanization" of Christian theology.[20]

In 1977 I gave a paper that may clarify a little—though hardly do anything to authenticate—the above-cited materials vis-à-vis Moltmann. My presenta-tion took as its point of departure the historical-moral finding, for some time now a truism of scholarship, that Christian teachings and ideology helped prepare the way for the coming of the *Shoah*. (None of this is to forget that the Christian gospel, insofar as it incarnates the love of God and neighbor, also retains an opposite consequence of fostering human solidarity and justice.) In the 1977 piece I declared that "the all-decisive avowal of Christianity is the resurrection of Jesus Christ," citing Paul's word to the church in Corinth, "if Christ has not been raised, . . . your faith is vain" (1 Cor. 15:14), and adding that to my knowledge the possible vainness of the Christian faith has never been linked to the denial of any other church doctrine.[21] I continued that some in the Christian community assume that they can oppose anti-Jewishness "while holding fast to the central Christian dogma, the consummated resurrection of Jesus Christ." In a word, I was maintaining that the teaching of Jesus' resurrection cannot be separated from other Christian doctrines that Jules Isaac gathers under the rubric of the "teaching of contempt."[22] But then I concluded on a note of faith or trust or hope—falling, as I now look back upon the essay, into something of a *non sequitur* or at least a superfluity—by affirming a resurrection yet in the future:

> The man from the Galilee sleeps now. [I wonder how I knew that.][23] He sleeps with the other Jewish dead, with all the distraught and scattered dead of the murder camps, and with the infinite dead of the human and nonhuman family. But Jesus of Nazareth shall be raised. So too the young Hungarian children of Auschwitz shall be raised. Once upon a coming time, they shall again play and laugh. The little ones of Terezín shall see another butterfly.[24] "The wolf shall dwell with the lamb, and the leopard shall lie down with the kid, and the calf and the lion and the fatling together. . . . They shall not hurt or destroy in all my holy mountain; for the earth shall be full of the knowledge of the Lord as the waters cover the sea" (Isa. 11:6, 9). The last enemy, death, shall be sentenced to death (I Cor. 15:26; Rev. 21:3, 4). One day we shall be together in the regnancy of God, so hope tells us, the hope that lives upon faith and love. We shall sing and we shall dance. And we shall love one another. Accordingly, it is not assured that we shall read and write theological papers to each other.[25]

I have not completely given up the above stress upon the future. Here is a comment of mine on Ulrich E. Simon's declaration that without the resurrection, the *Shoah* is pure hell:[26] "He is right—in principle. But for the sufferers, as for the survivors and descendants, the only way that hell can be defeated is through a future resurrection, when God will be victorious over every satanic and evil power, including death itself. *For no past event, however holy or divine, could ever redeem the terror of the present; only a future happening can do this.*"[27]

Shattering questions remain: How can the resurrection of Jesus be proclaimed as a special act of God without the Christian triumphalism that paved the way to Belzec and Sobibor? Is not the resurrection in and of itself a form of Christian supersessionism? How can the Christian church escape supersessionism and triumphalism while continuing to proclaim as a realized fact the resurrection of Jesus Christ? In its claim that the resurrection of Jesus concretely means God's triumph over death, is not the church inevitably implying its own triumph over non-Christian faith? In the resurrection does not God (reputedly) *confirm* the Christian gospel in the sense of a definitive embodiment of objective truth? Does not the resurrection appear as a divinely wrought displacement event? Is it possible, or how is it possible, to proclaim Jesus' resurrection in a nontriumphalist way?

The above questions come forcibly to mind as one consults many Christian advocacies of the resurrection. One example is a study of John Frederick Jansen: "In the resurrection and vindication of Jesus the earliest church saw the completion and goal of Israel's faith in God." That faith "finds its ultimate expression" in the Easter faith of Christianity. "The whole of God's story with his people" is "fulfilled in the resurrection of Jesus. . . . All people do not yet accept Easter's pledge, but one day 'every eye will see him, every one who pierced him' (Rev. 1:7). . . . Ultimate vindication includes ultimate judgment. The risen Jesus 'is the one ordained of God to be judge of the living and the dead' (Acts 10:42)." The New Testament message "sees in Easter the surety of the future of Jesus Christ as Lord of all and Lord forever." The Easter faith reminds us that "the future of Jesus includes the future of Israel. . . . Israel's future is bound up with the future of Christ."[28]

Subsequent writings by me carry forward the moral critique of the proclamation of a consummated or triumphalist resurrection of Jesus. For example, in 1978 I developed that critique in an assessment of Wolfhart Pannenberg. Pannenberg contends that "through the cross of Jesus, the Jewish legal tradition as a whole has been set aside in its claim to contain the eternal will of God in its final formulation."[29] The "law" is consummated and fulfilled in Jesus. For support, Pannenberg calls upon Jesus' resurrection: Jesus came into basic conflict "with the law itself, that is with the positive Israelite legal tradition which had become calcified as 'the law' after the exile." But through the resurrection "the emancipation from this law" takes place. Jesus' claim to authority, in replacement of the "law" and through which he put himself in God's place, "has been visibly and unambiguously confirmed by the God of Israel. . . ." In a word, the resurrection of Jesus Christ serves to abolish Judaism.[30]

Pannenberg's exposition points up the way in which

> the teaching of an achieved resurrection can lie at the center of Christian opposition and hostility to Judaism and the Jewish people. For only with that teaching does Christian triumphalism reach fulfillment. Only here are the various human and divine-human claims making up the church's dogmatic structure furnished with the capstone of an event that is said to be exclusively God's and that in this way vindicates every other claim. The representative of this ideology declares, in effect: "It is not the Christian theologian to whom you Jews are to listen. The theo-

logian is, after all, a fallible and sinful human being. Rather, let us have God decide the matter. But God's decision proves to be on the Christian side, not yours. *God raised Jesus from the dead.* Thus is the Christian shown to be right and you are shown to be wrong. In the resurrection God himself *confirms* the Christian gospel, the Christian cause."[31]

Those who affirm the resurrection of Jesus but who oppose Wolfhart Pannenberg's assimilation of that event to Christian imperialism are challenged to make clear how, if at all, their own affirmation avoids supersessionism.[32]

In our joint work, *Long Night's Journey into Day*, first published in 1982 and revised by Alice L. Eckardt for publication in 1988, my wife and I included an intensive critique of Christian supersessionist elitism. The integrity of the Christian faith was avowed, but it was also characterized as problematic: "Through the continuous and contemporaneous asserted truth that in Jesus Christ the eschatological domain entered into human history in definitive, salvational form, Christianity has legitimized historically-theologically its supersessionism and triumphalism over Judaism and the Jewish people, as well as its exclusivism toward other faiths." If Rosemary Ruether is right that "the Christian historicizing of eschatological reality is the foundation of Christian antisemitism, and if we are correct that the center and proof of Christianity is the event of the resurrection, then any continued advocacy of the resurrection appears to represent in clear and authoritative form the fateful, culpable union of the Christian message and the murder camps."[33]

To conclude this review of my antithetical stage, during that period (in 1986) I referred in at least two places to the hope that a nontriumphalist apprehension of the resurrection might yet gain a place in Christian teaching.[34] These references may perhaps be looked upon as a kind of transition to stage three of my thinking.

SYNTHESIS: ANTITRIUMPHALIST AFFIRMATION (1987ff.)

To recall a point made early in this chapter: A synthesis beyond both the thesis of pedestrian acknowledgment and the antithesis of critical questioning upon moral grounds need not abandon or wholly repudiate the other alternatives. The synthesis may gather up, assimilate, but also subject to critical judgment the thesis and the antithesis.

I have come at least tentatively to the view that a moral-theological remedy for Christian resurrectionist supersessionism, elitism, and triumphalism is to apprehend the resurrection of Jesus in the frame of reference "Spirit of God" (cf. the discussion of Marcus J. Borg's viewpoint in chap. 3) within the special and continuing history of Judaism and the Jewish people.[35] (This affirmation may also be compared with the analysis in chap. 9.) It is within the reality of Israel that the all-decisive meeting or convergence of religious faith and historical event takes place. Once Christian confessions are deideologized,[36] i.e., monotheized, they may be enabled to become the spiritual implementation of what might be called "Jesus-historicity." A primary Christian challenge in the shadow of the *Shoah* is not just to demythologize the Christian tradition but to deideologize it (viz., to wage war upon its supersessionist elitism).

The above "remedy" is not a mere pragmatic or political move calculated to make the Jewish people or other people happy. Its character as, I hope, a responsible position derives from its grounding in historical experience. The resurrection, part and parcel of the nascent world of Christian faith, is yet continuous with, even integral to, the social world of Judaism—or, in theological phrasing and following Paul M. van Buren, to the covenant with Israel. Accordingly, against John Frederick Jansen's conclusion that "Israel's future is bound up with the future of Christ," we may propose that Christ's future is bound up with the future of Israel.

A few current illustrations may be adduced. Each of these can be treated as tacitly rejecting the triumphalist view of such spokespersons as Jansen and Pannenberg.

If only to get it out of the way I reproduce first my own, somewhat mischievous midrash upon a spiritual (= Spirit of God) rendering of the resurrection, the date 1987:

> We are given to understand that the Sadducees insisted that there is no resurrection (e.g., Matt. 22:23)—contra Pharisee teaching. To introduce a light note (and perhaps therefore an especially serious one): We are advised that the One who sits in the heavens is not above laughing certain parties to scorn (Ps. 2:4). What would be a better joke on those reactionary Sadducees than for God to raise her own Pharisee-liberal Son from the dead! She would be having a go at one of her dearest truths, and would also be giving at least a few of her people a foretaste of the things that are to come. Maybe best of all, she would be reminding the Sadducees exactly what she thought of them, meanwhile assuring her good friends the Pharisees that she was on their side.[37]

The Dutch Protestant theologian Jacobus Schoneveld provides broader and deeper conceptualization:

> The resurrection means the vindication of Jesus as a Jew, as a person who was faithful to the Torah, as a martyr who participated in Jewish martyrdom for the sanctification of God's name. What else can this mean than the validation of Torah and vindication of the Jewish people as God's beloved people? The resurrection of Jesus confirms God's promises as well as God's commandments to the people Israel. . . . I see the Jewish people's survival throughout the centuries in the light of what the resurrection means: the affirmation of the Torah, of the people of Israel, and of Jewish existence. . . .

It is not true that the church has replaced Israel or taken over its vocation. Both Israel and the church await the fulfillment of the Torah, when the image of God will be visible in the whole of humanity. The Jews await this final Day incorporated in the people of Israel, the Christians incorporated in the body of Christ. . . . Jews have expressed their faithfulness in a "no" to Jesus as his church tried to take the Torah away from them. Christians may express their faithfulness in their "yes" to Jesus who embodies the Torah, and therefore also in a "yes" to his brothers and, sisters, the Jewish people.[38]

From a point of view such as that of Schoneveld, the resurrection may be legitimately and morally restored to Christianity once the poison of victimization is drained from it.

Paul M. van Buren is at one with Schoneveld in construing the resurrection (and perforce each and every authentic christological attestation) as indigenous to God's unbroken (unbreakable?) covenant with Israel. In this connection van Buren works to counteract (at least upon a theoretical level) the linkage between Christian resurrection doctrine and anti-Jewishness:

The fact of Easter that matters absolutely for the church is that Jesus once more proved effective in standing for God and God's cause, that, in the cause in and for which he had lived before, he was alive again. . . .[This] claim of Easter faith cannot be itself the root of the church's anti-Judaism. [I should want to qualify this: "cannot be allowed to remain the root . . . ," since the declaration here is not a factual one but a normative one—A.R.E.] That root we have seen to consist of the subtle and not-so-subtle transformation of the original witness to Jesus as a Jew committed to the renewal of his people in their Covenant with God, into a witness to an anti-Judaic Jesus in deepest conflict with his people. If Easter faith concerns this one who, as Paul wrote, became a servant of the Jewish people (Rom. 15:8), if the event of Easter is preached, as Paul claimed he had both learned and practiced, "in accordance with the Scriptures" (I Cor. 15:3-4), then it undercuts the anti-Judaism that developed in the church. . . . Indeed, the resurrection only stands in the way of anti-Judaism, since it underscores the continuity of the risen one with the Jew from Nazareth.[39]

With acknowledgment to Paul van Buren and others, I rather think now that a refusal to entertain the option of an extrabodily or spiritual resurrection of Jesus, together with a failure to insist upon the Jewishness of the resurrection (as in *Long Night's Journey into Day*),[40] are overdrawn and probably not right. Furthermore, I now recognize a substantive discrepancy between triumphalist resurrectionism and nontriumphalist or antitriumphalist resurrectionism. Can the Christian church achieve the latter? I believe so. Or at least I hope so.[41]

I submit a concluding comment upon the resurrection in its place as an ongoing challenge but also an enigma to Christians.

We know that among the earliest followers of Jesus, as represented in the Apostolic Writings, doubt of his resurrection was present. "The resurrection is

impossible"—Is not that the shattering conclusion to which especially ratio-
nalistic and/or burdensomely despairing moments sometimes drive the Christian? The rationalist and the cynic join hands in propagating the grim proposition that within the rules with which this world is run, dead people do not
become living people. Against such a conclusion, advocates of a strictly or minimally somatic resurrection continue to array themselves. John 20:27 is among
their proof texts: "Then he [the risen Jesus] said to Thomas, 'Reach your finger
here; see my hands. Reach your hand here and put it into my side. Be unbelieving no longer, but believe' "(*NEB*). Yet we moderns—or postmoderns—
tend to turn aside from somaticist explications of the resurrection. The
Christology of many Christians (including the Christology under review) also
has problems with these explications. But at the same time many such people
are not happy with modernist reductionism, which restricts the resurrection to
the moral and religious influence of a "great teacher" as continuing on in the
world. A new and increasingly influential Christology appears to be seeking out
a resurrectionist position that navigates between and thence beyond both the
Scylla of somaticism and the Charybdis of modernism. Thus does Paul van Buren proffer a synergist-covenantal viewpoint that involves a living parallel between the resurrection and the event of Sinai. To some, the resurrection

> was a pure act of God; the recipients of the act were purely recipients. Or, on the
> contrary, it has seemed to others that the appearances were the subjective expe-
> riences of believers, so that it could be said that Jesus rose into the *kerygma*, the
> preached faith of the disciples. Each of these conclusions misses the covenantal
> character of Easter: it was at once an act of God and an act of the disciples, of the
> nascent church. Without a doubt the witness to Easter, consistent with the witness
> to Sinai, insisted on the priority of God's initiative but, as in the case of Sinai, the
> action of those who bore witness to it was [also] constitutive to the event.[42]

To return to a distinction made at the beginning of the chapter: From van
Buren's standpoint the resurrection partakes at once of objectiveness and subjectiveness.[43] In the vocabulary of our own day, the expression "resurrection of
Jesus" may become, if you will, a spiritual—*not* spiritualized—metaphor or a
transcending-historicist metaphor that presents us with a particularly epochal
renewal of God's covenant with Israel. I suggest that van Buren's proposal may
be buttressed through the Pauline persuasion of a transformed risen body (1
Cor. 15:35-44), since in that case the historically discrete aspect of the resurrection is retained as at the same time literalist-somaticist difficulties are
avoided. For to separate the resurrected one from all somatic identity would be
to divorce the risen Christ from Jesus of Nazareth.

The sum and substance of this position of synthesis is that the imperiali-
zation of the resurrection is definitely opposable from within the Christian
community by those Christians who, just because they will to live and die in

historical-moral solidarity with the Jewish people to whom the resurrection in the first instance belongs, are thereby allowed to witness to the resurrection themselves.

At the last, there is the assurance that if the God of Israel has defeated death in God's Son Jesus, God may will to do the same again and again—for Christians, in and through the Body of Christ; for others, in and through God's, Spirit as it blows wherever God wills (John 3:8). In either case, the question to Mary of Magdala and the other women—the first Christian believers were evidently women—is fitting: "Why do you search among the dead?" (Luke 24:5). For is not Jesus, the Jewish *hasid* from the town of Nazareth, loose (again) in the social world, amidst all the anguish and all the joy of human events?

CHAPTER

12

For the Sake
of Rachel and for the
Sake of Sarah

The problem this book has raised is how to affirm the salvational power of the event of the Jesus of history without permitting the Christian faith to nurture idolatry (by, e.g., transmuting Jesus into the "center" of all human history).[1] We have seen how different Christologists of today, either implicitly, or explicitly, or both, are grappling with this problem.

TOWARD A POSTMODERN CHRISTOLOGY:
JESUS-ISRAEL-LIBERATION-SALVATION

Behind my reflections and hopes is a search for "a theology [read: Christology] forged by those who have been inspired and abused, both touched and trampled on by the religion of the modern age." For, as Harvey Cox also declares, "a viable postmodern theology will be created neither by those who have completely withdrawn from the modern world nor by those who have affirmed it unconditionally. It will come from those who have lived within it but have never been fully part of it, like the women in Adrienne Rich's poem who, though they dived into the wreck, have not found their names inscribed within it."[2]

One constructive and normative way to cope with the christological question is to continue to search for the historical Jesus within the frame of reference of the history, faith, and theology of his Judaism. People who are as far apart as Christian liberals and Christian fundamentalists nevertheless base their *Anschauungen* "upon a message whose inspiration is taken from the life and teachings of Jesus,"[3] from the Jesus of history, the Jewish man who worked to free the wretched of this world, the Son of a God whom we may identify and cherish as *dios pobre*. Today's reformation is sparked by a

> powerful biblical idea, . . . lost for years but recently rediscovered. The idea is that of resurrection: God alive in the world, life defeating death. But in liberation theology, especially in its Latin American version, the idea carries a more specific edge. It is that the special locus of God's presence is the poor and that therefore the poor have a singular and privileged role to play in the divine intention for human history. The poor are those through whom God chooses to mediate the coming of the divine reign. If anything, [the] idea of the *dios pobre* is even more central to the Bible and is repeated more frequently than the idea of justification by faith. . . . [And] like the *sola fide* of the sixteenth century, the idea of *dios pobre* has always been there. Smoldering, it has now been fanned into flames and become the central religious idea of the new reformation.[4]

But the poor and wretched of the world remain for the most part women, together with their children. Thus is Elisabeth Schüssler Fiorenza entirely right that women are the peculiar "people of God," and therefore, in a Christian frame of reference, they are the *ekklēsia*, the "body of Christ." "As in the past so still today men fight their wars on the battlefields of our bodies, making us the targets of their physical or spiritual violence. Therefore, the *ekklēsia* of women must reclaim women's bodies as the 'image and body of Christ.' "[5]

Within the context of a liberationist, feminist Christology, my own thinking tends, as I have tried to show, to exhibit two foci: (1) Jesus as "champion of Israel" (chap. 5) and (2) Jesus as the one through whom God humbles Godself (chaps. 8 and 10). Within their dialectical tension, these two foci may help to flesh out that continuity between the Jesus of history and the Christ of faith that is the aim of Christology as a whole: the dialectic between Israel and human salvation. The point of view I represent, however, has much continuity with other christological views examined in this book. This is not to ignore the many discontinuities; by means of critical commentary throughout the study I have sought to indicate what some of these discontinuities and differences are.

A DIALECTIC OF TWO WORLDS

In bringing my work to its end I set in apposition two midrashim: Abraham Joshua Heschel's aphorism that what the prophets of Israel discovered is that human history is a nightmare, and H. Richard Niebuhr's dictum that the present moment remains as the time of decision. For we are not granted a place to flee from history, neither to some heaven sublime nor even to some hell irresponsible.

To be more concrete, the particular meaning I give to my vocational task as a Christian moral philosopher and historian is to conjoin, if only in a heu-

ristic way, an inaugural way, two worlds: the world of Christian belief and behavior, and the postmodern world of the *Shoah* and the *Shoah's* aftermath.[6] In
this connection I refer again to a scholar of my ancestral land of Germany,
Johann Baptist Metz (in chap. 1 I mention a collateral passage from him): There
is no Christian truth that I could defend "with my back turned toward Auschwitz. . . . [The] problem, with a view toward Auschwitz, is not merely a revision
of the Christian theology of Judaism, but of *a revision of Christian theology
altogether.*"[7]

In a certain Belgian film, *As If It Were Yesterday* (1980), a little Jewish boy
who had been spirited away from the German Nazis is accused of stealing. His
reply: "I didn't steal anything. I took the baby Jesus out of the crèche to hide
him from the Nazis."

When my wife and I were conducting research at Yad Vashem, Jerusalem,
we saw the children. They came in busloads. In front of the library where we
were working stands the sculpture of a man clutching lifeless little ones. Of
course, we saw that as well. But our eyes and hearts were taken with the living
children. They were all over the place, beneath and around the sculpture: playing, shouting, running, calling, laughing, singing. I do not wish to make myself
misunderstood. There is no balancing of the scales. There is no quid pro quo.
There is no consolation for the *Shoah*—not even the State of Israel with all its
moral-political rightness and all its contribution to Jewry and the life of the
world. For it is without surcease that Rachel weeps for her children, as the
prophet Jeremiah tells:

> Thus says the LORD:
> "A voice is heard in Ramah,
>   lamentation and bitter weeping.
> Rachel is weeping for her children;
>   she refuses to be comforted for her children,
>   because they are not."
>   (Jer. 31:15)

What does it mean to "remember for the future"? It means to remember
for the children. The writing of this book may be construed as no more than a
brief chapter of a children's story, a story for the children: the children who
were murdered (before the eyes of other children who saw thereby that the
very same fate was to be theirs); the children who are with us now; and in the
premier instance, the children who are yet to be. *We* remember for *their* future.

I do this for the sake of Rachel. I do it as well for the sake of Sarah. I refer
now not to the *Tanak's* famous Sarah but instead to a twelve-year-old prosti-
tute who appears in Elie Wiesel's early work, *The Accident.*

Sarah was allowed to live—for the enjoyment of German officers. And she
somehow managed to retain enough humanity to offer herself to a pitiable sur-

vivor boy, with no money. He said to her, "You are a saint." She replied, "You are mad." But she was a saint. And the boy had grasped that truth. For he was enabled to testify, "Whoever listens to Sarah and doesn't change, whoever enters Sarah's world and doesn't invent new gods and new religions, deserves death and destruction. Sarah alone has the right to decide what is good and what is evil, the right to differentiate what is true from what usurps the appearance of truth."[8]

In Minneapolis a clergyperson, Ernest O'Neill, has said that the Jews were killed in the Holocaust because, having rejected Jesus Christ, they were rejected by God. One fateful difficulty for this minister is that, according to Jesus, the prostitutes go into the kingdom of God ahead of the clergy (Matt. 21:31). Today such a passage may seem to smack of sacrilege. But in this century of Auschwitz-Birkenau and Belzec, of Chelmno and Maidanek, of Sobibor and Treblinka, how can religious thinking and praxis not come across as sacrilege? Thus may this Minneapolis clergyperson and others of his ilk be consigned to perdition. The twelve-year-old saint would spit in his face, as we bid welcome to Sarah in his place. Why? Because Sarah "alone has the right to decide what is good and what is evil, the right to differentiate what is true from what usurps the appearance of truth."

THE HIDING AND THE GIVING

One other thing might be said. Emil L. Fackenheim ends his study, *What is Judaism?* by alluding to a Talmudic ambiguity on the hiding of God. "Does [God] hide in wrath against, or punishment of, His people? God forbid that He should do so at such a time [as ours]! Does He hide for reasons unknown? God forbid that He should, in this of all times, be a *deus absconditus* [a secretive or obscuring God]! Then why does He hide?" It is his weeping that He hides. "He hides His weeping in the inner chamber, for *just as God is infinite so His pain is infinite, and this, were it to touch the world, would destroy it. . . . God so loved the world that He hid the infinity of His pain from it lest it be destroyed.*"[9]

The final reality of the Jewish-Christian *Auseinandersetzung* shows itself (and hides itself) just at this place, in all its starkness. For as Christians read the words of Fackenheim, how can they escape the remembrance, "God so loved the world that he gave his only Son, that whoever believes in him should not perish but have eternal life" (John 3:16)?

The chasm appears uncrossable, does it not? And yet the chasm is crossed, from both directions—but only by the love of God. It is in the hiding that the love of God is given (the witness of Israel); and it is in the giving that the love of God is hidden (the witness of the church). "Let the children come to me, and do not hinder them; for to such belongs the kingdom of heaven" (Matt. 19:14). "What really matters is the children" (John F. Kennedy). Were the infinity of God's pain to touch the world, the world would indeed be destroyed. And so God must empty Godself, continuing to weep within the inner chamber (as God once wept hiddenly behind the cross). In the meantime, God addresses us, *kiveyachol* (in a manner of speaking), through the children who come to visit Yad Vashem. This is *only* to say, In the long run, however guilty God appears, God must be innocent, as the children are innocent. God does not willfully sin. Therefore, it is fitting that, in the Wiesel work *Twilight*, Raphael should at the end reject the idea that God could be cruel.[10] It follows that whenever we approach the weeping God, we have no other gift to bring, no other consolation, than our own tears. Julian Green was right: After the *Shoah*, "only tears have meaning." Whenever we follow this counsel, we know that if Christology is to continue it can only be a Christology that itself weeps—in simple truthfulness, and for the sake of truth, and thereby for the sake of Rachel and for the sake of Sarah.

Epilogue
John Macquarrie's
Jesus Christ
in Modern Thought

John Macquarrie's new study (1990) appeared too late for treatment within the main body of this book. But I do not want to let his large and important work in Christology go unnoticed.[1]

Although the greater part of *Jesus Christ in Modern Thought* comprises a more or less historical analysis of the sources and the rise of classical Christology and of the critique of that Christology within modern and contemporary times, Macquarrie makes room for his own position in a third section, "Who Really Is Jesus Christ For Us Today?" What are we to make of Jesus Christ in our time?

For present purposes these questions may be approached by discerning what Macquarrie's responses would be to our own three measuring rods: the historical-moral-theological distinctiveness/integrity of the Christian faith; an alternative or alternatives to Christian traditionalistic imperialism and triumphalism; and the historical, Jewish Jesus as crucial within christological affirmation.

(1) Professor Macquarrie seeks for a Christology that "will both remain loyal to the traditional faith in Christ and will be respectful toward the canons of modern thought." Yet one is from time to time given the impression that modernist-Enlightenment criteria of truth may be permitted to judge and perhaps even to take precedence over historic Christian claims. The overall thrust of my own book is postmodernist, i.e., it derives its normative impulses not from the modern would but from certain abiding tenets of the Christian faith, as that faith rests upon and moves from a Jewish foundation. Again, within the

bounds of church doctrine itself, Macquarrie avers that the Pauline effort to make the Christian faith stand or fall upon Jesus Christ's resurrection is simplistic. Macquarrie further questions (with many scholars) whether Jesus "thought of himself as messiah or under any of the other titles that came to be applied to him."[2]

Macquarrie, however, does hope that the Christology set forth in his study, "though it does not use the traditional language and categories [this expressed qualification does not always apply in Macquarrie—A.R.E.], stays within the parameters of the catholic tradition and is entirely compatible with the 'governing intention' of Chalcedon and other classic Christian pronouncements." In this connection, Macquarrie is quite ready to speak of Jesus Christ as "the mediator between God and the human race" and "the Word made flesh" and indeed to adjudge that in Jesus Christ "we are confronted with both the deification of a man and the inhumanization (incarnation) of God." With respect to the Hebrew and Jewish inheritance and the revelation in Jesus Christ, "only the inherited understanding of God permitted the disciples to say Christ had come from God, yet as soon as this was said, it meant that God must be understood anew in the light of Christ, as his own self-communication." In and through the cross of Christ Christians definitely experience salvation or at least the beginning of salvation. To believe or have faith in the cross is authentically to turn away "with Christ from the temptations of the world, the temptations of power, wealth, sensual indulgence and so on, to the things of the kingdom of God." In sum, "the two great distinctive Christian affirmations" are "God is love, and God is revealed in Jesus Christ."[3]

(2) As we have seen, for Paul F. Knitter among others the Christian faith entails the conviction that Jesus *is* indeed God's revelation and grace, but this faith need not thereby say that Jesus *alone* is God's revelation and grace. Where does John Macquarrie stand on the issue of Christian supersessionism, triumphalism, and exclusivism? In his own wording: Does Jesus Christ "provide the only way to a right relation to God, so that other ways and those who have taught them must be accounted mistaken?"[4]

Any explicit avowal of or allowance for Israel as the ongoing, convenanted people of God (as in Paul M. van Buren) does not gain a place in *Jesus Christ in Modern Thought.*[5] In his closing chapter, however, "Christ and the Saviour Figures," Macquarrie is not unsympathetic toward non-Christian faiths. (He has earlier denied that Judaism is no more than a prelude to Christianity.)[6] "Today I think our attitude to other faiths would be much more affirmative than it has been in the past. . . . [We] must respect these other teachers of the human race who have brought enhancement of life in other traditions." Macquarrie goes so far as to identify these "saviour figures" as "mediators of grace," figures who "had received in some measure the Word or Logos of God and had been to that extent vehicles of God's self-communication and agents of his in the salvation or making whole of mankind. . . ."[7]

Feminists and others will note Macquarrie's use of *his* in application to God. Of pertinence here is the fact that just about all Macquarrie's theological authorities are males. It is as though there were no such thing as contemporary feminist Christology.

(3) Upon nothing is Macquarrie more repeatedly insistent than the complete humanity of Jesus Christ—"a genuine human being in the fullest sense" and "of the same constitution as ourselves." Such humanity is absolutely essential because any doubt of it would at a stroke "render him irrelevant to human beings." "Only one who has lived as a truly human person, has known the weaknesses and temptations of such a life, but has also known its possibilities for transcendence—only such a one can be a saviour and can push forward the frontiers of the human spirit. . . . The difference between Jesus Christ and other human beings, including the saviour figures, is a difference *within* humanity." Jesus "differs from other human beings in degree, not in kind." Were we to make the difference one of kind, we would "have fallen into docetism, whatsoever we may say," or we "would turn him [Jesus] into an alien supernatural being."[8]

In keeping with the above point of view, Macquarrie maintains that those today who exclude the findings of critical, historical research from Christology are "willing to live with a split mind."[9]

A difficulty within Macquarrie's treatment of the humanness of Jesus is that he does not push the matter to its required historical and analytic conclusion. There is, after all, no such reality as a human being apart from the specificity that distinguishes him or her from all other human beings: sex, race, physical features, time and place of birth, national belongingness, personal convictions and commitments, etc. In one place Macquarrie seems aware of this requirement within historiography as within Christology; he objects to making Jesus " 'man' in a generic sense without being 'a man,' a human person or individual human being."[10] But Macquarrie does not always stay with the requirement and its logic. Had he remained wholly consistent and coherent with it, he would have entered unreservedly, exhaustively, and indeed decisively into such all-important considerations as Jesus' maleness (cf. chap. 7 above)[11] and Jesus' Jewishness and Judaism (as I have emphasized throughout this book). He does neither of these things. His references to the Jewishness of Jesus are few and far between.[12] The proper foundation of Jesus as a restorationist figure within the people Israel and Judaism tends to be undercut by Macquarrie's silences as by his positive emphases in alternative directions. For example, he does nothing to emphasize Jesus' central persuasion of "the eternal validity of the Torah" (Marcus J. Borg). Thus is his own dedication to the human historicity of Jesus, in effect, qualified. In this regard Macquarrie stands in contrast to such scholars as James H. Charlesworth, E. P. Sanders, and Paul M. van Buren.[13] Nevertheless, the differences remain those of emphasis.

All in all, John Macquarrie's *Jesus Christ in Modern Thought* maintains, in differing degrees, the three qualities within current Christology that we have identified and pursued. He exhibits the first characteristic in a very solid way. He represents the second characteristic as well, though without any great fervency. And he supports the third characteristic, though his adherence to it could benefit from a more fulfilled historical logic.

Notes

1. JOURNEY INTO THE APOSTOLIC PAST

1. Consult Donald J. Goergen, *The Mission and Ministry of Jesus* (Wilmington, Del.: Michael Glazier, 1986), chap. 1, "Christology: An Invitation to an Encounter."

2. Charlesworth employs the phrase "Jesus Research" as a way of distinguishing this enterprise "from the former 'Quest for the Historical Jesus,' which was characterized by dogmatic or theological interests. Even the so-called 'New Quest for the Historical Jesus,' which began in the fifties, was grounded in theological concerns" (James H. Charlesworth, *Jesus Within Judaism*, Anchor Bible Reference Library [Garden City, N.Y.: Doubleday, 1988], p. 26).

3. A possible further corollary of the third characteristic is that the "religion" *of* Jesus may come to be regarded as normative for a "religion" *about* Jesus.

4. Emil L. Fackenheim, *The Jewish Return into History: Reflections in the Age of Auschwitz and a New Jerusalem* (New York: Schocken Books, 1978). More than a one-way street is involved. Recent Jewish interest in the historical Jesus appears related— apart from its own independent rationale or purposes—to Christian attention to the Jesus of history. Consult, e.g., Eugene B. Borowitz, *Contemporary Christologies: A Jewish Response* (New York: Paulist, 1980); David R. Catchpole, *The Trial of Jesus* (Leiden: E. J. Brill, 1971); David Flusser, *Jesus*, trans. Ronald Walls (New York: Herder and Herder, 1969); Pinchas Lapide, *Israelis, Jews, and Jesus*, trans. Peter Heinegg (Garden City, N.Y.: Doubleday, 1979); *The Resurrection of Jesus: A Jewish Perspective*, trans. Wilhelm C. Linss (Minneapolis: Augsburg, 1983). See also Trude Weiss Rosmarin, ed., *Jewish Expressions on Jesus: An Anthology* (New York: Ktav, 1977).

5. Emil L. Fackenheim, *To Mend the World: Foundations of Future Jewish Thought* (New York: Schocken Books, 1982), p. 158.

6. Cf. A. Roy Eckardt, *For Righteousness' Sake* (Bloomington: Indiana University Press, 1987), p. 247.

7. Luke Timothy Johnson, *The Writings of the New Testament* (Philadelphia: Fortress, 1986), p. 532. Cf. Charlesworth: "New Testament theology and Jesus Research must both be built upon a thorough and appreciative examination of *all* early Jewish phenomena. This one emphasis unites all my work; it alone legitimates the integrity of my research" (*Jesus Within Judaism*, p. 192).

8. Michael L. Cook, *The Jesus of Faith* (New York: Paulist, 1981), p. 2.

9. Van A. Harvey, as interpreted by Cook, *Jesus of Faith*, p. 20.

10. Eckardt, *For Righteousness' Sake*, p. 53.

11. Leonardo Boff, *Pasión de Cristo y sufrimiento humano*, p. 11, trans. and cited in Juan Luis Segundo, *The Historical Jesus of the Synoptics*, trans. John Drury, vol. 2 of *Jesus of Nazareth Yesterday and Today* (Maryknoll, N.Y.: Orbis, 1985), p. 193 n. 6.

12. Cook, *Jesus of Faith*, p. 16.

13. Charlesworth, *Jesus Within Judaism*, p. 166.

14. Paula Fredriksen, *From Jesus to Christ* (New Haven, Conn.: Yale University Press, 1988), p. xi.

15. Marcus J. Borg, *Jesus: A New Vision* (San Francisco: Harper & Row, 1987), p. 15; E. P. Sanders, *Jesus and Judaism* (Philadelphia: Fortress, 1985), pp. 2, 3; Johnson, *Writings of the New Testament*, p. 146. Cf. Borg: "Every story and word of Jesus has been shaped by the eyes and hands of the early church" (*Jesus*, p. 9). Charlesworth observes, "To talk about the 'dominant view today' as a return to considerable confidence in our knowledge about the historical Jesus is an exaggeration; what Sanders and I are observing is a marked turn in scholarly research, a paradigm shift in Jesus Research" (*Jesus Within Judaism*, p. 2). Cf. Bruce Chilton: The Gospels "generally attest, not 'the historical Jesus,' but a faith in Jesus which happens to have a historical coordinate" ("Silver Blaze Rides Again," *Reflections* [Yale Divinity School] 84 [Winter 1987]: 11).

16. Sanders, *Jesus and Judaism*, pp. 11, 326–27; cf. Charlesworth, *Jesus Within Judaism*, p. 169. Norman Perrin lists as *minimally* authentic Jesus-material recognized within scholarly opinion: kingdom sayings, the Lord's Prayer, proverbial sayings (e.g., the Beatitudes), and major parables (*Jesus and the Language of the Kingdom* [Philadelphia: Fortress, 1976], p. 41).

17. Q, from the German *Quelle*, is an early, now-lost collection of Jesus' sayings utilized by Matthew and Luke, along with their own shared utilizations of Mark.

18. There are some 40–70 years between Jesus and the Gospels.

19. Charlesworth, *Jesus Within Judaism*, pp. 19–21. Shortly therafter, in speaking to the claim that New Testament scholars are obliged to provide answers to questions emanating from the New Testament, Charlesworth lists four requisites (New Testament people seem to be heavy on *lists* these days): the recognition that New Testament scholars do not study "the New Testament" but instead biblical *passages*; the acknowledgment that "some generative force unites these documents"; the knowledge that the proclamation (*kerygma*) and explanation of Jesus' death and resurrection are buttressed by the *remembrance* of Jesus' life and work; and the understanding that "portions of the Jesus phenomena represent historical facts that lie behind the New Testament authors and their compositions." There remains, however, a "vast difference between the *edited* documents in the New Testament and the earlier traditions" behind them (*Jesus Within Judaism*, pp. 24–25, 59).

20. Fredriksen, *From Jesus to Christ*, p. 5. The Bible of the early Christians was, of course, not the "New Testament" but the "Old Testament," translated from Hebrew into Greek and known as the Septuagint.

21. Ibid., p. 6.

22. Charlesworth, *Jesus Within Judaism*, pp. 6, 7.

23. In the book *For Righteousness' Sake* I identify this point of view as "faith for the world" (chap. 6 and *passim* in that study). For Harvey Cox, modernity at its core is "the world view of the entrepreneurial class which seized the tiller of history from the weakened grip of its feudal forerunner" (*Religion in the Secular City* [New York: Simon and Schuster, 1984], p. 82).

24. The German Nazi destruction of the Jews of Europe (1933–45) has come to be identified by the Hebrew concept *Ha'Shoah*.

25. Consult Cox, *Religion in the Secular City*, fittingly subtitled *Toward a Postmodern Theology*.

26. "Postpatriarchal" can hardly mean that patriarchal horrors are matters of the past. But the cause of women's rights is today fully out in the open, and its guns are securely in place. Already many signs of phallocentric retreat reveal themselves; consult A. Roy Eckardt, *Black-Women-Jew: Three Wars for Human Liberation* (Bloomington: Indiana University Press, 1989), chaps. 7–13.

27. It remains so that much religious thinking after the *Shoah* proceeds as though that event had never happened. For example, in John Macquarrie's survey covering eighty years, there is not a single mention of the *Shoah* (*Twentieth-Century Religious Thought: The Frontiers of Philosophy and Theology, 1900–1980*, rev. ed. [New York: Scribner, 1981]).

28. Calvin O. Shrag, "Liberal Learning in the Postmodern World," *The Key Reporter* 54 (Autumn 1988): 2; Cox, *Religion in the Secular City*, p. 20.

29. Mary Daly, *Gyn/Ecology: The Metaethics of Radical Feminism* (Boston: Beacon, 1978), p. 298.

30. Johann Baptist Metz, *The Emergent Church* (New York: Crossroad, 1981), p. 29.

31. Michael McGarry, "Emil Fackenheim and Christianity After the Holocaust," *American Journal of Theology & Philosophy* 9 (January-May 1988): 131.

32. Beverly Wildung Harrison, *Making the Connections* (Boston: Beacon Press, 1985), p. 217.

33. Tom F. Driver, "Jesus: God, Man, and Movie," *Christianity and Crisis* 48 (1988): 339.

34. I use the term *ideology* in the now-familiar connotation of collective self-interest and self-justification. But the phenomena described by the definition are not viewed as necessarily or always bad or wrong.

35. Thus does Donald J. Goergen relate the three elements of history, humanness, and existential questioning: "The issues of the humanity of Jesus and his identity with us really come down to one question. We want to know whether it was really as tough for him as for us, whether his search and struggle were real, whether he really knew what it is like to be one of us" (*Mission and Ministry of Jesus*, p. 45).

36. To say "hidden behind" is not the same as to say "causally behind." It is one thing to affirm that God was hiddenly present in, say, the *Shoah* and quite something else to affirm that God caused the *Shoah*.

37. Cook, *Jesus of Faith*, p. 5; Borg, *Jesus*, p. 2.

38. A. Roy Eckardt, "Christian Faith and the Jews," *The Journal of Religion* 30 (1950): 238, slightly emended. The reference to Arnold Nash is to his study *The University and the Modern World* (New York: Macmillan, 1944), pp. 243–44.

39. This final section of the present chapter follows the argument of Eckardt, *For Righteousness' Sake*, pp. 270–71.

40. Cook, *Jesus of Faith*, p. 13.

41. For an application of this point to the world(s) of social symbol and myth, with emphasis on the dynamics of human experience and interpretation, see Johnson, *Writings of the New Testament*, pp. 11–18.

42. Franz Rosenzweig saw Jewish existence as transhistorical. In this, he was not alone. But historicalness remains a foremost attestation within Jewish life, markedly since the *Shoah*.

43. James Parkes, *Prelude to Dialogue: Jewish-Christian Relationships* (London: Vallentine, Mitchell, 1969), p. 193.

44. Jürgen Moltmann, "Dieu dans la révolution," in *Discussion sur "la théologie de la révolution"* (Paris: Cerf-Mame, 1972), p. 72.

2. SYNOPTIC TITLES

1. A fine overview of the historical-social-religious background for dealing with and understanding the historical Jesus is found in Donald J. Goergen, *The Mission and Ministry of Jesus* (Wilmington, Del.: Michael Glazier, 1986), chaps. 2, 3. An excellent and particularly lively introductory interpretation of the Apostolic Writings as a whole is Luke Timothy Johnson, *The Writings of the New Testament* (Philadelphia: Fortress, 1986), especially part 2, "The Christian Experience." Johnson's approach is close to that of literary criticism. *Apostolic Writings* means the *New Testament*. The term *Old Testament* has long been subjected to the criticism that it is implicitly anti-Judaic. In its place we are to speak of the *Hebrew Bible* or the *Tanak*. Because *New Testament* is the obverse of *Old Testament* and is a similarly loaded term, this book utilizes (apart from quoted materials) the description *Apostolic Writings*.

2. Gerard S. Sloyan, *Is Christ the End of the Law?* (Philadelphia: Westminster, 1978), pp. 27–28.

3. Recent materials of relevance to problems of procedure and methodology include Johnson, *Writings of the New Testament*, introduction; James H. Charlesworth, *Jesus Within Judaism*, Anchor Bible Reference Library (Garden City, N.Y.: Doubleday, 1988), chap. 1 and app. 5; Paula Fredriksen, *From Jesus to Christ* (New Haven, Conn.: Yale University Press, 1988), pp. 3–8; Juan Luis Segundo, *The Historical Jesus of the Synoptics*, trans. John Drury, vol. 2 of *Jesus of Nazareth Yesterday and Today* (Maryknoll, N.Y.: Orbis, 1988), pp. 3–70; Marcus J. Borg, *Conflict, Holiness and Politics in the Teaching of Jesus* (New York–Toronto: Edward Mellen, 1984), chap. 1; *Jesus* (San Francisco: Harper & Row, 1987), chap.1; Michael L. Cook, *The Jesus of Faith* (New York: Paulist, 1981), pp. 28–34; Bernard J. Lee, *The Galilean Jewishness of Jesus* (New York: Paulist, 1988), chap. 1; A. E. Harvey, *Jesus and the Constraints of History* (London: Duckworth, 1982), chap. 1; James P. Mackey, *Jesus the Man and the Myth* (New York: Paulist, 1979), chap. 1; E. P. Sanders, *Jesus and Judaism* (Philadelphia: Fortress, 1985), introduction; and Goergen, *Mission and Ministry of Jesus*, introduction. Goergen discerns four moments or tasks in the work of Christology: Jesus research; historical retrieval; hermeneutical reconstruction of who Jesus is today; and grappling with the social implications of Christology.

4. E. P. Sanders is not enthused by such a procedure: "The question of titles should be de-emphasized." Two reasons are given: No term that we today think of as a

"title" had a single meaning in Jesus' time; and probably Jesus did not think of himself in terms of titles (*Jesus and Judaism*, p. 411 n. 8).

5. Charlesworth's study *Jesus Within Judaism* seeks to follow after the light shone upon Jesus by "the Old Testament Pseudepigrapha, the Dead Sea Scrolls, the Nag Hammadi Codices [which preserve some sayings of Jesus], an Arabic manuscript that contains a version of the testimony to Jesus by the Jewish historian Josephus, and archaeological excavations in Palestine, especially in Capernaum and Jerusalem." One consequence of this scholarly revolution is that it is very difficult to separate Jewish writers from Christian writings. Thus, many of the Pseudepigrapha are roughly contemporary with Jesus and are Palestinian. The Gospel of Thomas, highly significant for the sayings of the historical Jesus, evidently derives from Syrian Christianity, which rested heavily on Judaism. All in all, it must be stressed that "Jesus research is emphatically linked with an improved view of the origins of the Gospels within first-century Judaism" (pp. ix, 31, 32, 77, 81, 89, 204, and throughout).

6. The analysis of Jesus' titles here follows the outline in A. Roy Eckardt, *For Righteousness' Sake* (Bloomington: Indiana University Press, 1987), pp. 55–58; that sequence is in turn grounded in the outline-exposition of Geza Vermes, *Jesus the Jew* (London: Fontana/Collins, 1976), pp. 83–225.

7. Consult Goergen, *Mission and Ministry of Jesus*, chap. 5, "A Prophet from Nazareth." Jesus was "akin to the prophets of old, preaching faith and justice, and in this was essentially and radically conservative, as prophets were: going back to their roots in the Yahwistic faith and choosing to live according to the covenant" (p. 178).

8. In this book the Revised Standard Version of the Bible is utilized in most instances.

9. Cook, *Jesus of Faith*, pp. 37–40. See also Goergen, *Mission and Ministry of Jesus*, chap. 5, "The Origins of a Mission."

10. Sanders, *Jesus and Judaism*, p. 239. Consult Goergen, *Mission and Ministry of Jesus*, pp. 170–76.

11. Vermes, *Jesus the Jew*, pp. 88–90; Harvey, *Jesus*, p. 6; see also pp. 57–65, 135; Cook, *Jesus of Faith*, p. 38.

12. Cf. Gustavo Gutiérrez, *Teología de la Liberación*, 8th ed. (Salamanca: Ediciones Sigueme, 1977), chap. 13, "Pobreza: solidaridad y protesta."

13. Albert Nolan, *Jesus Before Christianity* (London: Darton, Longman and Todd, 1977), p. 21; Goergen, *Mission and Ministry of Jesus*, p. 222.

14. Fundamentally, a charismatic "is a person who is in touch with the power of the Spirit and who becomes a channel for the power of the Spirit to enter the world of ordinary experience" (Borg, *Jesus*, p. 16).

15. Vermes, *Jesus the Jew*, pp. 103, 127, 121, 126, 123, 125; Martin Hengel, *The Charismatic Leader and His Followers*, trans. James Greig (New York: Crossroad, 1981), but with awareness of difficulties that Hengel stresses in the accustomed reference to Jesus as "teacher" or "rabbi" (pp. 46–51).

16. Vermes, *Jesus the Jew*, p. 129.

17. Sanders cautions that a Davidic Messiah "is one of the least frequent themes" in the Jewish literature of the time (*Jesus and Judaism*, p. 117).

18. Ibid., pp. 130–40.

19. Cf. the later, pre-ascension query of the apostles, "Lord, will you at this time restore the kingdom to Israel?" (Acts 1:6). This would seem to reflect the persistence of messianic hope among the early followers of Jesus despite his crucifixion.

20. Eckardt, *For Righteousness' Sake*, p. 57; Vermes, *Jesus the Jew*, pp. 140–43, 149; see also Borg, *Jesus*, pp. 10–11; and in general Harvey, *Jesus*, chap. 6. Charlesworth declares straightforwardly, Jesus "did not proclaim himself the Messiah." Nor did he look upon himself as "the suffering servant" (*Jesus Within Judaism*, pp. 153–54).

21. See especially chaps. 4, 5.

22. Eckardt, *For Righteousness' Sake*, p. 57; Vermes, *Jesus the Jew*, chap. 7.

23. Goergen, *Mission and Ministry of Jesus*, pp. 180–202; see also Borg, *Conflict*, pp. 221–27.

24. Charlesworth, *Jesus Within Judaism*, pp. 3, 40, 235.

25. Consult Harvey, *Jesus*, chap. 7, "Son of God: the Constraint of Monotheism."

26. Geza Vermes, "Jewish Studies and New Testament Interpretation," *Journal of Jewish Studies* 31 (1980): 15–16.

27. Vermes, *Jesus the Jew*, p. 211.

28. Eckardt, *For Righteousness' Sake*, p. 58 (slightly emended); cf. Vermes, *Jesus the Jew*, pp. 202–11. Also cf. Goergen: The notion of Jesus' sonship ought "to be seen in a Semitic, Hebrew, Jewish context. In the Scriptures the Hebrew *ben* (Aramaic *bar*) is primarily an expression of subordination, in contrast to the Greek *huios* which denotes physical descent. … The son of God is a servant of God" (*Mission and Ministry of Jesus*, p. 145).

29. Vermes, *Jesus the Jew*, p. 209.

30. Harvey, *Jesus*, p. 157 and n. 26.

31. Borg, *Jesus*, p. 49.

3. THE JUDAISM OF JESUS, COUNTERCULTURAL SPIRITUALIZER

1. The theme of Marcus J. Borg's *Conflict, Holiness and Politics in the Teachings of Jesus* (New York–Toronto: Edwin Mellen, 1984) is the conflict that occurred between Jesus and his contemporaries concerning the shape and purpose of the people of God, but—we must not forget—a conflict that took place within the frame of reference of Israel's conflict with Rome (pp. 4, 20).

2. Marcus J. Borg, *Jesus* (San Francisco: Harper & Row, 1987), pp. x, 190, ix, 2, 7, 5 (italics added).

3. Ibid., pp. ix, 15, 25–26.

4. Ibid., pp. 25, 29, 27, 32, 34.

5. Ibid., pp. 43, 48, 45. The presence of the Spirit in Jesus is accentuated more in Luke than in the other Gospels.

6. Ibid., pp. 45–48, 63, 51. On Jesus as sage, see Donald J. Goergen, *The Mission and Ministry of Jesus* (Wilmington; Del.: Michael Glazier, 1986), pp. 267–77; also Borg, *Conflict*, pp. 237–47.

7. Borg, *Jesus*, pp. 62, 66, 70–71; in general, chap. 4.

8. A new emphasis has emerged in New Testament studies that, "rather than tending to exclude politics, highlights the social and political factors shaping the emergence of the Christian movement and the ministry of the historical Jesus" (Borg, *Conflict*, p. 17).

9. Borg, *Jesus*, pp. ix–x, 16, 79.

10. *Torah* is much more accurately translated as "teaching" or "guidance." To translate it as "law" is to help perpetuate the old "law/gospel" dichotomy.

11. Borg, *Jesus*, pp. 86–87 (italics added); *Conflict*, pp. 51, 53; in general, *Conflict*, chap. 3, "The Dynamics of Jewish Resistance to Rome; The Quest for Holiness."

12. Borg, *Jesus*, p. 89.

13. As James Parkes points out, *Spätjudentum* implied that the Judaism of Jesus' time had already passed its zenith, whereas, from the standpoint of its actual development, Judaism was in fact still in its early stages. "It would be just as accurate to describe the Elizabethan Age as 'Bas Moyen-age,' or the early north-Italian renascence as 'spät-Lombardisch.' Bad history cannot be the foundation for good theology" (*Prelude to Dialogue* [London: Vallentine, Mitchell, 1969], pp. 6, 7; *The Foundations of Judaism and Christianity* [London: Vallentine, Mitchell, 1960], p. x). Of course, Borg does not resort to the polemic description *Spätjudentum*, late Judaism. James H. Charlesworth is eminently right in consistently using the term Early Judaism. That term applies to the entire period from 250 B.C.E. to C.E. 200 (*Jesus Within Judaism*, Anchor Bible Reference Library [Garden City, N.Y.: Doubleday, 1988], p. 3).

14. Borg, *Jesus*, p. 91.

15. Ibid., pp. 93, 97, 100, 116.

16. Ibid., pp. 101, 92, 101–2, 132, 104, 106; see also pp. 131–33, 145 n. 28. E. P. Sanders regards this parable as a Lucan (or pre-Lucan) creation (*Jesus and Judaism* [Philadelphia: Fortress, 1985], p. 175).

17. Leonard Swidler, *Yeshua* [Kansas City: Sheed & Ward, 1988], p. 66.

18. For Donald Goergen, Jesus was a man who *lived* the *Shema* (*Mission and Ministry of Jesus*, pp. 131–32).

19. Borg, *Jesus*, pp. 108, 109, 110, 111.

20. Ibid., pp. 111–15. The "way of death" is a major structural element in Mark and Luke (p. 122). See also Borg, *Conflict*, pp. 242–47.

21. Borg, *Jesus*, p. 116.

22. "Though the movement's charismatic character is often underemphasized within both contemporary scholarship and the mainstream church, it was one of its most remarkable features" (ibid., p. 127).

23. The term *Jesus movement* now quite widely refers to Jesus' own lifetime as well as to the time between his death and the destruction of Jerusalem. "The relationship between a renewal or revitalization movement and a social world is one of both affirmation and advocacy of change." Were the movement only for change it would be called a *new* movement. Revitalization movements claim the need for a radical response to present conditions (ibid., pp. 142, 125–26). On the reasons why Christianity came into separate existence, see p. 126. On the basis of his own definition of the Jesus movement, it is somewhat inaccurate of Borg to apply that term to gentile Christianity outside Palestine (p. 126).

24. Ibid., pp. 125, 126–27. Cf. Matt. 15:24: "I was sent only to the lost sheep of the house of Israel." The (Christian) mission to the Gentiles did not begin until after Easter; it was the *risen* Lord who commanded, "Go therefore and make disciples of all nations . . . " (Matt. 28:19).

25. Ibid., pp. 128, 129–30, 118, 131.

26. See Goergen, *Mission and Ministry of Jesus*, chap. 7, "The Compassionate Sage."

27. Inclusion of a reference to the duality of Jew and Gentile is somewhat puzzling here, since there were probably no Gentiles in the original Jesus movement.

28. Borg, *Jesus*, p. 131.

29. Borg argues that the command later in Leviticus (19:34) to love the "sojourner," meaning the foreigner in the land, referred by the first century to the Gentile who had become a Jew (ibid., p. 147 n. 56). This is *very* debatable.

30. Ibid., pp. 137–39.

31. Ibid., pp. 139–40.

32. Ibid., pp. 141–42.

33. Ibid., pp. 152–58.

34. See Borg, *Conflict*, pp. 103–6.

35. Ibid., pp. 74, 99, 102, 115. See in general chaps. 4–7 and especially pp. 139–43. Chapter 6 deals with the (alleged) conflict over the Sabbath and chap. 7 with the question of the temple. "Controversy between Jesus and his opponents concerning the sabbath is one of the best attested features in the Gospels." Jesus' paradigm was that the Sabbath "was a day for works of compassion" or even of "killing" *for the sake of Israel* (pp. 148, 151, 155ff.). Concerning the temple, Borg argues that, since it "had become a center of exclusiveness," its coming destruction was evident—as against the historic notion that Yahweh would always protect the temple. The threatened destruction was "the consequence of a historical choice: continued commitment to the quest for holiness." Borg reads Luke 13:1–5 to mean, "If you do not repent (i.e., change your course by responding to the teaching of Jesus), you, like the Galileans, will be slain by the sword of Rome." Throughout, Jesus is held to stand in the prophetic tradition of Israel (pp. 195, 164–70, 196–97, 191–92, 198). Respecting the temple, Borg denies any *vaticinium ex eventu*.

36. Borg, *Jesus*, p. 158; *Conflict*, p. 58.

37. Borg, *Jesus*, pp. 161–65.

38. Cf. Borg, *Conflict*, chap. 8, "Jesus and the Future."

39. Borg, *Jesus*, pp. 172–73.

40. Ibid., p. 174; Sanders, *Jesus and Judaism*, pp. 306–8.

41. In a reference to one of his own writings Borg maintains unqualifiedly that Jesus was noneschatological (*Jesus*, p. 203 n. 20). On the issue of eschatology, see also Goergen, *Mission and Ministry of Jesus*, pp. 68–83 (on eschatology within Judaism), pp. 229–48 (on the eschatological teaching of Jesus).

42. According to Sanders, the temple controversy gives a good "point of entry for the study of Jesus' career" and also opens "the way to re-examine the question of 'Jesus and the Kingdom'" (*Jesus and Judaism*, pp. 11–12).

43. Borg, *Jesus*, pp. 174–75; Sanders, *Jesus and Judaism*, p. 62. Borg notes that "robbers" ought to read "violent ones," since the evangelist is quoting Jeremiah. In Jeremiah "violent ones" refers to men who believe that the temple afforded security despite any of their violations of the covenant (*Jesus*, pp. 175–76).

44. Sanders, *Jesus and Judaism*, pp. 62–65, 68, 90.

45. Ibid., pp. 61, 66–69, 364, 365.

46. Ibid., pp. 69, 70–76. Fittingly, the early apostles did not believe that Jesus considered the temple worship impure (Acts 2:46; 3:1; 21:26) but only that the present temple's days were numbered (p. 76).

47. Borg, *Conflict*, pp. 202, 226, 211; *Jesus*, pp. 177–84. See *Conflict*, pp. 265–76, "Appendix: The Threat/Warrant Tradition of the Synoptic Gospels."

48. For a convenient review of all but one of these figures, see Sanders, *Jesus and Judaism*, pp. 23–51. On Wolfhart Pannenberg, consult that theologian's *Jesus—God*

and Man, trans. Lewis L. Wilkins and Duane A. Priebe, 2d ed. (Philadelphia: Westminster, 1977).

49. Joachim Jeremias, *The Proclamation of Jesus*, as cited in Sanders, *Jesus and Judaism*, p. 44.

50. Borg, *Jesus*, pp. 110, 115, 142.

51. Ibid., p. 160.

52. Sanders, *Jesus and Judaism*, p. 276. Another, textbook case of traditionalist distortions of the Pharisees is Albert Nolan, *Jesus Before Christianity* (London: Darton, Longman and Todd, 1977). Sometimes Nolan's argumentation verges on out-and-out anti-Jewishness, e.g., "the struggles of the Zealots had nothing whatsoever to do with genuine liberation. They were fighting for Jewish nationalism, Jewish superiority, and Jewish religious prejudice" (p. 97).

53. Charlesworth, *Jesus Within Judaism*, p. 46.

54. Sanders, *Jesus and Judaism*, pp. 264, 265.

55. Because of the derogatory connotation that *Pharisaic* has come to have, it is better to use *Pharisee* as the adjectival form. This practice is adhered to in scholarly Jewish literature of today.

56. "The notion of resurrection constituted the Pharisees' ultimate statement about the utter dignity and uniqueness of each human person" (John T. Pawlikowski, *Christ in the Light of the Christian-Jewish Dialogue* [New York: Paulist, 1982], p. 89).

57. Clark M. Williamson, *Has God Rejected His People?* (Nashville: Abingdon, 1982), pp. 13, 14, 15. The wording that the Pharisees "were the grand internalizers" is from Ellis Rivkin, *A Hidden Revolution: The Pharisees' Search for the Kingdom Within* (Nashville: Abingdon, 1978), p. 297. The oral Torah was the Pharisees' way of opposing attempts by the Sadducees "to freeze the Torah in its written form" (Williamson, p. 20).

58. Pawlikowski, *Christ*, p. 83. Borg does concede that along with what "distinguishes" the Pharisees from first-century Judaism, they were also devoted to what was common to Judaism: "absolute loyalty to God, love of neighbor, the joy of the sabbath, the richness of the Jewish festivals, religious disciplines such as prayer and fasting" (*Conflict*, p. 59).

59. Jesus was "a part of the general [Pharisee] movement, even though in many areas he held a distinctive viewpoint" (Pawlikowski, *Christ*, p. 92; see also pp. 102–7). His "eating of the Last Supper with his disciples indicates his function as leader of a Pharisaic brotherhood and table fellowship. He was rightly called rabbi" (Williamson, *Has God Rejected His People?* p. 22). Additional materials on Jesus and the Pharisees include Philip Culbertson, "Changing Christian Images of the Pharisees," *Anglican Theological Review* 44 (1982): 539–61; "The Pharisaic Jesus and His Gospel Parallels," *The Christian Century* 102 (1985): 74–77; Leonard Swidler, *Yeshua* (Kansas City: Sheed & Ward, 1988), pp. 55–64; Pawlikowski, *Christ*, chap. 4; Rivkin, *A Hidden Revolution*; Harvey Falk, *Jesus the Pharisee: A New Look at the Jewishness of Jesus* (New York: Paulist, 1985); but cf. John Bowker, *Jesus and the Pharisees* (Cambridge: Cambridge University Press, 1973).

60. Sanders, *Jesus and Judaism*, p. 261.

61. Cf. the analysis of Harvey Falk: Jesus' debates with the Pharisees were, in fact, talmudic disputes between two schools, Bet Shammai and Bet Hillel, with Jesus subscribing to the latter view (*Jesus the Pharisee*).

62. Williamson, *Has God Rejected His People?* pp. 16–17; in general on the Pharisees, pp. 12–28. Cf. Goergen: "Much of the anti-Jewish and anti-Pharisaic language of

the Gospels flows from a post-resurrection church uneasy about its relationship to Judaism and from Jewish-Christian conflict after 70 c.e. . . . Essenes and Sadducees did not survive the war and the future of Judaism was in the hands of the rabbis and Pharisees. Thus Christian anti-Jewish polemic was at that time anti-Pharisaic polemic" (*Mission and Ministry of Jesus*, pp. 250, 104).

63. Sanders, *Jesus and Judaism*, p. 10 and throughout. Goergen holds that "Jesus consistently spoke of himself in eschatological terms," citing Mark 2:18-22 in support (*Mission and Ministry of Jesus*, p. 235).

64. Borg, *Conflict*, p. 12.

65. Borg offers the somewhat curious judgment that "it does not matter whether [Jesus] thought of himself as Messiah . . . , for whether or not he was does not depend on whether he thought so" (*Jesus*, p. 50).

66. Ibid., p. 60.

4. THE JUDAISM OF JESUS, REJECTED ADVOCATE OF ISRAEL'S RESTORATION

1. E. P. Sanders, *Jesus and Judaism* (Philadelphia: Fortress, 1985), pp. 17, 18, 22.

2. Ibid., pp. 97, 58, 77, 86. In chap. 2 of *Jesus and Judaism* Sanders deals with what Jewish literature of the time has to say of a positive nature about a destroyed and restored temple. In consequence, Jesus' temple eschatology could be believable in some circles. Bruce Chilton asks why, if Jesus subscribed to the hope of a restored temple, he did not openly voice it ("Silver Blaze Rides Again," *Reflections* 84 [Winter 1987]: p. 10).

3. Sanders, *Jesus and Judaism*, pp. 98, 106; in general, pp. 98–106. Cf. James H. Charlesworth: In choosing twelve disciples, Jesus manifested "a clear intention to be involved in some way with helping to establish a *new messianic age*" (*Jesus Within Judaism*, Anchor Bible Reference Library [Garden City, N.Y.: Doubleday, 1988], p. 155). Luke Timothy Johnson completely deeschatologizes the phenomenon of the Twelve, at least with respect to Luke-Acts: "Despite receiving a beating . . . the apostles continue to preach Jesus as the Messiah (Acts 5:42). Luke has made his essential point clear. Whatever political manipulations might still be available to the Sanhedrin, effective religious authority over Israel, considered as God's people, has passed to the apostles. They rule over the Twelve Tribes of the restored Israel in Jerusalem." For Luke, in Johnson's view, "the primitive Jerusalem church is the restored people of Israel" (*The Writings of the New Testament* [Philadelphia: Fortress, 1986], pp. 227, 228).

4. Sanders claims that most of the passages that depict Jesus as calling for national repentance are inauthentic, on the ground that they either conform his message to the Baptist or prompt a suspicion that they reflect later church activity (*Jesus and Judaism*, p. 117). Chilton comments, "Even if we allow that a number of Jesus' demands for repentance are secondary, it is surely odd to claim that, because Jesus did not *emphasize* repentance in his parable of the lost sheep (for example), he did not require it. . . . Sanders has Jesus openly predict a new Temple because that expectation was characteristic of early Judaism, even though the Gospels do not have it so, while he refuses to admit Jesus preached repentance, despite the prevalence of the concept both in the Gospels and early Judaism. It is difficult to avoid forming the impression that theological taste plays a determinative role here, in deciding when Jesus will be por-

trayed as similar to his contemporaries, and when he will be presented as differing radically from them" ("Silver Blaze Rides Again," pp. 10–11).

5. In forgiving sins, Jesus is often said to have put himself in the place of God. For Sanders, this is overdone. We must note that Jesus "only pronounced forgiveness, which is not the prerogative of God, but of the priesthood" (*Jesus and Judaism*, p. 240).

6. Ibid., pp. 108–13.

7. Ibid., pp. 115–16.

8. Ibid., p. 119.

9. Ibid., pp. 376, 133, 136, 138, 126, 127, 139–40. Sanders offers four reasons for dubbing only "conceivable" Jesus' view that his exorcisms indicated that the kingdom of God was present (pp. 140–41).

10. Ibid., pp. 141–50.

11. Ibid., pp. 151, 152, 376 n. 3.

12. Ibid., pp. 155, 153, 156.

13. Ibid., pp. 157–73, 383 n. 31.

14. Ibid., pp. 174–80, 183, 199, 187, 189, 198, 202–4; italics added to sentence, "It is a mistake . . . " One is made "wicked" by the *intention* not to be observant; "the wickedness comes not from impurity as such, but from the attitude that the commandments of the Bible need not be heeded" (pp. 184–85). On the purity laws, see especially pp. 186–87. A particularly decisive argument against the notion that the *ḥaberim* and/or the Pharisees excluded the *'amme ha-erets* from the social and religious community is that these groupings simply had no control over that community (p. 193; cf. pp. 195–98).

15. In the conclusion to *Jesus and Judaism* Sanders states it as just *probable* that Jesus "thought that the wicked who accepted his message would share in the kingdom even though they did not do the things customary in Judaism for the atonement of sin" (p. 326). *If* Jesus did take this view, we may be provided with a primordial basis in his thinking for the Christian teaching of justification by faith.

16. Ibid., pp. 206–7. The sole passage that "might count against the view proposed here is Mark 1:44 and parr., where Jesus tells the cleansed leper to show himself to the priest and to make the required offering. This curious passage—which in any case does not deal with a transgression—actually highlights the lack of any such statement to the tax collectors and other sinners who accepted him. Even in the Lucan story of Zacchaeus the tax collector was not required by Jesus to makes restitution, and no sacrifice is mentioned" (p. 207).

17. Ibid., pp. 207–8, 210.

18. Ibid., pp. 263, 274.

19. Ibid., pp. 223–24, 231.

20. There is *no* reason to suppose that the *ḥaberim*, whether before or after c.e. 70, "thought of themselves as 'the righteous' and of the rest of Israel—the *'amme ha-arets*—as 'the wicked.' The supposition, so often held by New Testament scholars, that the *ḥaberim* considered all others to be 'cut off' from God, Israel and salvation, is totally without foundation" (ibid., p. 181; see also p. 192). Much more significantly, Sanders would argue in the identical way regarding the Pharisees. Further to Jesus and the Pharisees, see pp. 191ff. The Dead Sea sectarians did consider everyone else as outside the truly elect; but in this they contrasted with the *ḥaberim*, the Pharisees, and later the rabbis (p. 193).

21. Further to the issue of table-fellowship, see ibid., pp 208-10. Sanders does not doubt that "Jesus ate with people who were ritually impure, both by the standards of the priesthood and those of the *ḥaberim*," people especially concerned with ritual purity. But the issue of such purity could not possibly be a source of conflict with the religious leaders (p. 210).

22. But Sanders points out that "the closer one puts the Pharisees to the *ḥaberim*, the less significance attaches to any possible conflict between Jesus and the Pharisees" (ibid., p. 389 n. 59). Sanders adjudges that "it is more reasonable to equate Pharisees and scribes than Pharisees and *ḥaberim* (p. 390 n. 91).

23. Ibid., pp. 209, 266.

24. Sanders lists six discernible prophetic predictions about the Gentiles in the end time, all of which are repeated in later Jewish literature (ibid., pp. 213–14).

25. Ibid., pp. 212, 117, 218, 217, 220–21.

26. Cf. Marcus J. Borg, *Jesus, A New Vision* (San Francisco: Harper & Row, 1987), pp. 202–3, wherein reasons are adduced for not focusing on the kingdom of God in Jesus' message.

27. Sanders, *Jesus and Judaism*, pp. 237, 153, 229, 232, 227.

28. I suggest we keep in mind that *apolitical* is not the same as *antipolitical*.

29. Ibid., pp. 230–33.

30. Ibid., pp. 152, 234.

31. Ibid., pp. 249, 250, 397 n. 17, 252.

32. Sanders contends that the statements in the Sermon on the Mount that bear on the law are, save for the pericope on divorce, "of dubious authenticity" (ibid., p. 263).

33. Ibid., pp. 255, 256, 260, 267, 269.

34. Ibid., pp. 270, 271. Cf. Charlesworth: "It seems much clearer today than it did a few years ago that at least in some ways Jesus' arrest resulted from his anger in the Temple" (*Jesus Within Judaism*, p. 118).

35. Sanders, *Jesus and Judaism*, pp. 288, 289, 310–17; see also Sanders's contribution to the symposium, "Who Killed Jesus and Why?" *Manna* (London) 12 (Summer 1986): 5. "The first obligation of the Jewish leadership, *both to Rome and to the populace*, was to prevent the outbreak of signs of insurrection, which would lead the Romans to intercede directly and bloodily" (ibid.). Cf. also Charlesworth: Jesus "was rejected by the ruling priests in Jerusalem" (*Jesus Within Judaism*, p. x).

36. Sanders, *Jesus and Judaism*, pp. 292, 271, 272. Sanders dismisses the accusation that Jesus put himself in God's place by forgiving sins. "If Jesus actually said to a paralytic, 'My son, your sins are forgiven' (Mark 2:5; cf. Luke 7:47-48), he was presumably speaking for God (note the passive), not claiming to be God" (ibid, p. 273).

37. Ibid., pp. 276–81.

38. Ibid., pp. 296–301, 317. Must we not ask what historical evidence there is of a link between the temple episode and Jesus' execution—this despite Sanders's argumentation in *Jesus and Judaism* (e.g., p. 302)?

39. Ibid., pp. 331–32, 333. Sanders admits as *perhaps possible* that Jesus saw his death as one of "a martyr who would be vindicated" (p. 332).

40. "The Gospels are all influenced by the desire to incriminate the Jews and exculpate the Romans" (ibid., p. 298).

41. Ibid., pp. 118, 129, 20, 307.

42. In *Jesus and Judaism* relevant parallel materials to Sanders's symposium contribution include the following: "At least in Judea, the Romans played no role in the persecution of the movement after the death of Jesus." It was the chief priests who had pressed Jesus' execution. Anyone such as Jesus "who claimed to speak for God and who attracted a following would alarm those who wanted to maintain the somewhat precarious *status quo* with Rome. . . . Talk of a 'kingdom' might excite a crowd, and mass excitement could be dangerous" (pp. 285, 286, 288).

43. Sanders, contribution to symposium, "Who Killed Jesus and Why?" p. 4. There are also brief contributions by Hyam Maccoby, Hugh J. Schonfield, and A. Roy Eckardt. "Jewish scholars like Geza Vermes have recognized for some time that there is no substantial transgression of the law attributed to Jesus in the Gospels, and that the supposed *conflict with the Pharisees* must be dropped as a substantial cause of his death, and of recent years they have been joined by many Christian scholars" (pp. 4–5).

44. Sanders, *Jesus and Judaism*, p. 265.

45. Ibid., p. 329.

46. Ibid., p. 232.

47. Ibid., p. 289.

48. Ibid., p. 329 (italics in original).

49. Hyam Maccoby, contribution to symposium, "Who Killed Jesus and Why?" p. 3. But Maccoby does not reject all non-Roman involvement: Jesus "was tried in the police-court of the High Priest, who was a quisling appointee of the Romans" (ibid.). Maccoby's point of view is developed at length in *Revolution in Judaea* (New York: Taplinger, 1980).

5. THE JUDAISM OF JESUS, CHAMPION OF ISRAEL

1. This chapter reapplies the morphology and content of A. Roy Eckardt, *For Righteousness' Sake* (Bloomington: Indiana University Press, 1987), pp. 59–78. I have rewritten and updated that exposition, adding considerable factual and analytic material. Unemended passages that are reproduced are assigned quotation marks.

2. Ibid., p. 35. On relations between the Essenes and Jesus, see James H. Charlesworth, *Jesus Within Judaism*, Anchor Bible Reference Library (Garden City, N.Y.: Doubleday, 1988), pp. 59, 64, 71–72. "Like the Essenes, Jesus' theology was categorically eschatological" (ibid., p. 71). According to Mark, Jesus denied the possibility of divorce, and a prohibition of divorce is "apparently found" in the Temple Scroll of the Dead Sea Scrolls (ibid., p. 72).

3. Burton Mack remarks disdainfully that a century of scholarship has been unfortunately bewitched by Mark 1:14, regarding it as historically authentic rather than as the Marcan redaction it, in fact, is ("The Kingdom Sayings in Mark," *Foundations and Facets Forum* 3 [March 1987], as cited in Marcus J. Borg, *Jesus, A New Vision* [San Francisco: Harper & Row, 1987], p. 203 n. 20). Contra Mack's dismissal, Charlesworth writes, "Despite the objections by R. Bultmann long ago and E. P. Sanders recently, Mark 1:14b-15 is an accurate summary of Jesus' message, even though the words employed to articulate this summary derive from Mark and his community" (*Jesus Within Judaism*, p. 44).

4. Juan Luis Segundo, *The Historical Jesus of the Synoptics*, trans. John Drury,

vol. 2 of *Jesus of Nazareth Yesterday and Today* (Maryknoll, N.Y.: Orbis, 1985), pp. 194 n. 14, 63.

5. As an example, in October 1988 a group of biblical scholars known as the "Jesus Seminar" noted that this prayer was not originated by Jesus but was instead the effort of early Christians who composed it years after the crucifixion. The group agreed that the Lord's Prayer originated with the Gospel writer identified earlier in the twentieth century as Q (Gustav Niebuhr, "The Jesus Seminar Courts Notoriety," *The Christian Century* 105 [1988]: 1060–61). Borg suggests that Jesus' use of *Abba* reflects the intimacy and intensity of his experience of Spirit (God). The term is found in reported traditions upon Jewish charismatics of Jesus' day (*Jesus*, p. 45; cf. Charlesworth, *Jesus Within Judaism*, pp. 132–35). Charlesworth submits that Jesus "probably taught his disciples a special prayer, which is recognizable in the Lord's Prayer ... [and] is strikingly similar to Jewish prayers, especially the Qaddish, and his appeal to God to 'forgive our debts as we also forgive our debtors' is not a 'Christian' invention, but a Jewish tradition reflected, for example, in the Prayer of Manasseh" (ibid., p. 50). Further to the origins of the Lord's Prayer, perhaps including pre-Christian Judaism, consult Sharon H. Ringe, *Jesus, Liberation, and the Biblical Jubilee* (Philadelphia: Fortress, 1985), pp. 115–16 n. 1

6. Hyam Maccoby, *Revolution in Judaea* (New York: Taplinger, 1980), p. 206. See Donald J. Goergen's discussion of the Lord's Prayer, *Mission and Ministry of Jesus* (Wilmington, Del.: Michael Glazier, 1986), pp. 132–45.

7. Consult Charlesworth, *Jesus Within Judaism*, pp. 84–90, for an extended analysis of the relation between Luke 14:26/Matt. 10:37-38 and parallel passages in the Gospel of Thomas.

8. Geza Vermes, *Jesus and the World of Judaism* (Philadelphia: Fortress, 1984), p. 53.

9. Clark M. Williamson, *Has God Rejected His People?* (Nashville: Abingdon, 1982), p. 14.

10. Michael Grant, *Jesus* (London: Weidenfeld & Nicolson, 1977), pp. 30, 33, 26, 45, 76. Grant's semipopular study has to be used with caution. For he retains much of the anti-Jewishness of the Gospels (in their later materials) and of the ongoing Christian tradition (cf. his uncritical treatment of John 8:41-44). Grant is among the many who prejudicially identify the people of Jesus as "the Jews" or as "Jewish" in the same breath with references to Jesus himself—as if Jesus were somehow not himself a Jew.

11. As examples: Vermes, *Jesus and the World of Judaism*, chap. 3; John Riches, *Jesus and the Transformation of Judaism* (London: Darton, Longman & Todd, 1980), p. 87; in general, pp. 87–111; A. E. Harvey, *Jesus and the Constraints of History* (London: Duckworth, 1982), pp. 66-97; Martin Hengel, *The Charismatic Leader and His Followers*, trans. James Greig (New York: Crossroad, 1981), p. 53. See also Marcus J. Borg, *Conflict, Holiness and Politics in the Teachings of Jesus* (New York–Toronto: Edwin Mellen, 1984), pp. 248–63, wherein are included difficulties Borg discerns within the practice of beginning an approach to Jesus' teachings via the "kingdom of God."

12. Charlesworth, *Jesus Within Judaism*, p. 38; Goergen, *Mission and Ministry of Jesus*, p. 229.

13. Marcus J. Borg, "A Renaissance in Jesus Studies," *Theology Today* 45 (1988): 280–92; *Jesus*, pp. 157, 168 n. 28, 2, 14, 20 n. 25.

14. Borg, "Renaissance in Jesus Studies," pp. 286–87. Elsewhere, Borg refers to a scholarly consensus of an earlier time: "To say that Jesus was the eschatological prophet

is to say that he saw himself as the prophet of the end who proclaimed the end of the world *in his own time* and the urgency of repentance before it was too late" (*Jesus*, p. 11). For Charlesworth's identifications of the meaning of the relevant concept *apocalypticism*, together with *apocalyptic thought* and *apocalypse*, consult *Jesus Within Judaism*, pp. 33–42.

15. Goergen, *Mission and Ministry of Jesus*, p. 203. The following passage from Vermes seeks also to preserve the kingdom of God as both this-worldly and as something else: The kingdom was "to ensue from the victory on earth of heavenly angelic armies over the hosts of Satan. Israel's final glorious triumph was to be the corollary in this world of God's total dominion over the world of the spirits. Such a kingdom was of course not to be built. It was to irrupt into the world here below, annihilate it, and set itself up in a new heaven on a new earth" (*Jesus and the World of Judaism*, p. 34).

16. Borg, *Jesus*, pp. 137–40.

17. Borg, "Renaissance in Jesus Studies," p. 286.

18. See John T. Pawlikowski, *Christ in the Light of the Christian-Jewish Dialogue* (New York: Paulist, 1982), pp. 89–92; and cf. Ellis Rivkin, *A Hidden Revolution* (Nashville: Abingdon, 1978).

19. Leonard Swidler, *Yeshua* (Kansas City: Sheed & Ward, 1988), p. 84; in general, chap. 3.

20. Phillip Sigal, *The Halakhah of Jesus of Nazareth according to the Gospel of Matthew* (Lanham, Md.: University Press of America, 1987), p. 6; Williamson, *Has God Rejected His People?* chap. 1. The several callings and roles of Jesus are summarized in Swidler, *Yeshua*, chaps. 2, 3.

21. "Today almost all scholars maintain that the reign of God in the teaching of Jesus is both present and future, both already here but not yet consummated" (Goergen, *Mission and Ministry of Jesus*, p. 235). In one place Goergen declares that in Jesus' time the reign of God "was envisioned as an eschatological reign, the coming times when God would rule as sovereign on earth." Elsewhere he writes that in Jesus' usage " 'reign of God' was not an apocalyptic or eschatological concept; it was *a way of speaking about God. The reign of God is God.* . . . Understanding Jesus' usage properly makes outmoded many of the discussions about whether the kingdom was present or future in the teaching of Jesus, for God is both here and coming. . . . God's reign is his rule, his power, his presence, his glory; it is *God as present* to his people" (ibid., pp. 230, 225, 226). (In the presence of women's rights, the word *his* five times in a row here is rather daunting.)

22. Probably the woman sought to touch the fringes or tassels attached to his outer garment (*tzitziot*, singular *tzitzit*). These were worn by Jewish men in keeping with the commandment of Num. 15:38-41.

23. Borg, *Jesus*, p. 165.

24. Harvey, *Jesus*, pp. 112–13; Grant, *Jesus*, pp. 20–21, 40.

25. See Goergen's analysis of the parables (*Mission and Ministry of Jesus*, pp. 211–18); also Brad H. Young, *Jesus and His Jewish Parables* (New York: Paulist, 1989).

26. Geza Vermes, *Jesus the Jew* (London: Fontana/Collins, 1976), p. 224; see also Grant, *Jesus*, pp. 52ff.

27. See Charlesworth's analysis of *poor* and *poor in spirit* as Essene technical terms of self-description (*Jesus Within Judaism*, pp. 68–70).

28. Goergen, *Mission and Ministry of Jesus*, p. 225.

29. Grant, *Jesus*, pp. 22–23.

30. Ibid., p. 24.

31. Eckardt, *For Righteousness' Sake*, p. 63 (slightly emended). Cf. Goergen's discussion of Jesus and messianism (*Mission and Ministry of Jesus*, pp. 157–70). Goergen argues "that it is better to describe Jesus' consciousness neither as messianic nor as unmessianic" (pp. 168ff.).

32. For a comprehensive account, see Borg, *Conflict*, chaps. 2–3 and *passim*. "The common view of the Sadducees as collaborators, Pharisees as quietists, and Zealots as Galilean militants needs substantial revision. . . . Jewish resistance to Rome had its sources not in a single sect operating underground as a guerrilla movement . . . but in loyalties embraced by diverse groups" (ibid., p. 48).

33. "It may even be wondered whether or not the entire 'trial' before the high priest and others is largely fictional" (E. P. Sanders, *Jesus and Judaism* [Philadelphia: Fortress, 1985], p. 71).

34. Joel Carmichael, "The Jesus Story and the Jewish War," *Midstream* 25 (1979): 63. It is estimated that in the time of Jesus, taxation levied upon the Jewish people reached as high as 40 percent or perhaps even more.

35. Consult, e.g., Paula Fredriksen, *From Jesus to Christ* (New Haven, Conn.: Yale University Press, 1988), pp. 120–25 and *passim*; S. G. F. Brandon, "Jesus and the Zealots: Aftermath," *Bulletin of the John Rylands Library* 44 (1971): 53–55; *Jesus and the Zealots* (Manchester: Manchester University Press, 1967), especially chaps. 1, 5; *The Trial of Jesus of Nazareth* (London: B. T. Batsford, 1968); Carmichael, "The Jesus Story and the Jewish War," pp. 62ff.; Haim Cohn, *The Trial and Death of Jesus* (New York: Harper & Row, 1971); Paul Winter, *On the Trial of Jesus* (Berlin: Gruyter, 1961); and cf. Borg, *Jesus*, pp. 178–84; Sanders, *Jesus and Judaism*, chaps. 10, 11; and Paul M. van Buren, *Christ in Context*, chap. 7, part 3 of *A Theology of the Jewish-Christian Reality* (San Francisco: Harper & Row, 1988). Anti-Jewish elements within the Apostolic Writings are exemplified in Acts 3:14-15; 14:2; John 5:18; 7:13; 8:39-59; and 1 Thess. 2:14-16. For an analysis of antisemitic aspects of the Apostolic Writings, consult A. Roy Eckardt, *Your People, My People* (New York: Quadrangle/New York Times, 1974), pp. 8–13, 29–30. A brief, useful accounting is Michael J. Cook, "Anti-Judaism in the New Testament," *Union Seminary Quarterly Review* 38 (1983): 125–37.

36. Cf. Sanders: There "is not a shred of evidence . . . that Jesus had military/ political ambitions, and the same applies to the disciples. . . . They expected *something*, but not a conquest. . . . *[Their] expectation throughout must have been for a miraculous event which would so transform the world that arms would not be needed in the new kingdom*" (*Jesus and Judaism*, p. 231).

37. Brandon, *Jesus and the Zealots*, p. 20. Examples include Matt. 5:9, 39; 26:52; Luke 6:27-29; Matt. 10:34f.; 21:12-13; Luke 12:51f.; 19:45-46; 22:36; and Mark 11:15-16.

38. John T. Pawlikowski, *Christ in the Light of the Christian-Jewish Dialogue* (New York, Paulist, 1982), p. 95.

39. Vermes, *Jesus and the World of Judaism*, pp. 35, 156.

40. Cf. William R. Farmer, "Is Mark Really the First Gospel?" *Circuit Rider* (Nashville) 5 (October 1981): 6–7; Hans-Herbert Stoldt, *History and Criticism of the Marcan Hypothesis* (Macon, Ga.: Macon University Press, 1980).

41. Marcus Borg comments that the high priest virtually had to drag the response out of Jesus, plus the fact that "I am" can be equally translated as "Am I?" It remains true that "there is no human proclamation of Jesus' identity in Mark's Gospel, either by Jesus or others" (*Jesus*, pp. 17–18).

42. By contrast, had Jesus been alive in Europe at the time of the *Shoah*, it is possible that he would have been put to death not for making an issue of himself (see Luke 9:51) but instead with total fatefulness: He was one of those *Untermenschen* of which the Nazis pledged to rid the world.

43. Borg, *Jesus*, p. 179; Sanders, *Jesus and Judaism*, p. 294; Charlesworth, *Jesus Within Judaism*, p. 90; Fredriksen, *From Jesus to Christ*, p. 122.

44. A. Roy Eckardt, "Christians and Jews: Along a Theological Frontier," *Encounter* 40 (1979): 112.

45. Paul M. van Buren, "Affirmation of the Jewish People: a condition of theological coherence," Supplement to *Journal of the American Academy of Religion* 45 (1977): 1090. Cf. Paul Tillich: "How can someone be the Christ when he has not fulfilled the function of the Christ?" ("The Jewish Question: Christian and German Problem," *Jewish Social Studies* 33 [1971]: 270). Involved here is the serious question of whether the first Christians were wrong in their acceptance of Jesus as the Christ. Cf. Eckardt, *Jews and Christians* (Bloomington: Indiana University Press, 1986): "The Christian faith is . . . tied to and indeed made possible only by the history of Jesus. . . . Once the claim is made that God acted to bring non-Jews into the family of Israel, the affirmation/disaffirmation and interpretation of these exact events, while very important, are not of final importance. We are advised that 'the wrath of men shall praise' God (Ps. 76:10). The same conviction may be applied to human errors and limitations of various sorts—not excluding the error of the small number of first-century Jews who, against Judaism, saw in Jesus the Messiah and Redeemer" (p. 88). Cf. Swidler: "The Messiah, the Christ, expected by Peter and the other disciples was first thought to be a Jewish royal figure in David's mold who would eject the Roman occupiers of the land of Israel and reestablish kingship in Israel. Clearly this did not happen; hence, most Jews had no grounds for assuming that Yeshua was the promised Messiah" (*Yeshua*, p. 4).

46. Eckardt, *For Righteousness' Sake*, pp. 65–66 (slightly emended).

47. Grant, *Jesus*, pp. 43, 88, 10; see also pp. 11, 34, 41, 44, 48.

48. Gustavo Gutiérrez, *Teología de la Liberación*, 8th ed. (Salamanca: Ediciones Sigueme, 1977), pp. 236–41; Carmichael, "Jesus Story and the Jewish War," p. 68.

49. A stronger phrasing is "only Son" (John 1:14, 18; 3:16, 18; 1 John 4:9).

50. Grant, *Jesus*, p. 21; also Riches, *Jesus and the Transformation of Judaism*, p. 160.

51. See Brandon, *Jesus and the Zealots*, pp. 17–18, 280–82; Gutiérrez, *Teología de la Liberación*, pp. 297ff.

52. Hengel, *Charismatic Leader*, pp. 38ff. On this matter consult Sanders, *Jesus and Judaism*, pp. 224–26.

53. John H. Yoder, *The Politics of Jesus: Vicit Agnus Noster* (Grand Rapids, Mich.: Eerdmans, 1972), p. 108.

54. Riches, *Jesus and the Transformation of Judaism*, p. 100.

55. S. G. F. Brandon, as cited in Maccoby, *Revolution in Judaea*, p. 100; cf. Borg, *Jesus*, p. 138.

56. Carmichael, "Jesus Story and the Jewish War," p. 67.

57. Eckardt, *Your People, My People*, p. 59; Brandon, *Jesus and the Zealots*; *Trial of Jesus of Nazareth*. See the important review-article by Walter Wink, "Jesus and Revolution: Reflections on S. G. F. Brandon's Jesus and the Zealots," *Union Seminary Quarterly Review* 25 (1969): 37–59. For all his serious criticisms of Brandon's work, Wink acknowledges that Brandon has succeeded "in reviving the prospect that Jesus' escha-

tological convictions were really fleshed out in the form of Jewish nationalistic long-ings" (p. 54). A. E. Harvey goes so far as to adjudge that for Jesus to be executed as pretender-king, "he must have had an army" (*Jesus on Trial*, p. 3, as quoted in Sanders, *Jesus and Judaism*, p. 294).

58. Brandon, *Jesus and the Zealots*, p. 355. Sanders is skeptical respecting knowl-edge of the disciples' individual activities (*Jesus and Judaism*, p. 103). Bruce Chilton wholly rules out the designation *Zealot*, arguing on behalf of a consensus that the term was used in a partisan sense only after Jesus' death, in conjunction with the Jewish re-volt against the Romans ("Silver Blaze Rides Again," *Reflections* 84 [Winter 1987]: p. 9).

59. But Brandon points out that Zealotism was still closely linked to messianic expectation (*Jesus and the Zealots*, pp. 112–13).

60. Maccoby, *Revolution in Judaea*, pp. 56, 78–79, 66.

61. John T. Townsend, "Jesus, Land, Temple" (unpublished paper at Princeton University, 1981). Cf. 1 Cor. 1:23 and the many other passages where Paul refers to Jesus' death by crucifixion.

62. Maccoby, *Revolution in Judaea*, p. 145.

63. Brandon, "Jesus and the Zealots: Aftermath," pp. 64, 65–66; Maccoby, *Revo-lution in Judaea*, pp. 69, 90.

64. Cf. Sanders: "I see no evidence that the sign of the coming kingdom was gen-erally thought to be exorcism; for one thing, there were too many exorcists" (*Jesus and Judaism*, p. 378 n. 56). Cf. also Borg: "In the clearly authentic sayings of Jesus, the phrase Kingdom of God never pointed unmistakably to a temporally-conceived future, though it may allude to that in a few. Rather, when spoken of as coming, it was a symbol for the power or presence of the numinous breaking into ordinary reality, either sub-jectively or objectively, as in the case of the exorcisms. . . . The eschatological mysticism [N.B.] of Jesus did not turn him away from the world, but instead was the basis for his passionate involvement in the corporate life and direction of his people. Thus the King-dom of God is connected to history, not as a future historical event, but as the source of Jesus' paradigm for historical life: compassion" (*Conflict*, pp. 260–61, 262).

65. Yoder, *Politics of Jesus*, p. 50. "What roles the Roman and Jewish administra-tions played in the trial [of Jesus], and whether or not Pilate found any fault in Jesus, both the mode of death and the titulus indicate that Jesus was executed as a 'brigand chief' on the charge of sedition" (Borg, *Conflict*, p. 360 n. 152).

66. Brandon, *Jesus and the Zealots*, pp. 16, 203; see also pp. 20, 316, 317, 340–41.

67. Maccoby, *Revolution in Judaea*, p. 157.

68. Jürgen Moltmann, *The Crucified God*, trans. R. A. Wilson and John Bowden (New York: Harper & Row, 1974), pp. 128–35. For a full critique of Moltmann here, consult Alice L. Eckardt and A. Roy Eckardt, *Long Night's Journey into Day*, rev. ed. (Detroit: Wayne State University Press; Oxford: Pergamon Press, 1988), pp. 103–6.

69. James P. Mackey, *Jesus the Man and the Myth* (New York: Paulist, 1979), p. 65.

70. Brandon, "Jesus and the Zealots: Aftermath," p. 66.

71. Cf. David Tracy, *Blessed Rage for Order: The New Pluralism in Theology* (New York: Seabury, 1978), p. 220.

72. Joseph Klausner, *Jesus of Nazareth: His Life, Times, and Teaching*, trans. Her-bert Danby (New York: Macmillan, 1946), p. 370.

73. Gerd Theissen, *The First Followers of Jesus*, p. 112, as cited in Sanders, *Jesus and Judaism*, p. 395 n. 12.

74. Yoder, *Politics of Jesus*, pp. 242, 100, 102 (emphasis added).

75. J. C. O'Neill, *Messiah* (Cambridge, U.K.: Cochrane, 1980), p. 58.

76. Cf. Brandon, *Jesus and the Zealots*, pp. 316, 340–42, 355.

77. Sanders, *Jesus and Judaism*, p. 124.

78. Eckardt, *For Righteousness' Sake*, pp. 74–75. The phrase "God's secret" is taken from Vermes, *Jesus and the World of Judaism*, p. 38.

79. Marcus Borg concedes that Matt. 5:17-18 "on the eternal validity of the Torah reflects the posture of the Jesus movement and probably the attitude of Jesus himself" (*Conflict*, p. 138).

80. Richard L. Rubenstein, *My Brother Paul* (New York: Harper Torchbooks, 1972), p. 39.

81. E. P. Sanders, *Paul, the Law, and the Jewish People* (Philadelphia: Fortress, 1983); *Paul and Palestinian Judaism: A Comparison of Patterns of Religion* (Philadelphia: Fortress, 1977); and cf. A. Roy Eckardt, *Elder and Younger Brothers* (New York: Scribner, 1967; Schocken, 1973), pp, 54–58, 66–70.

82. Geza Vermes, *The Dead Sea Scrolls: Qumran in Perspective*, rev. ed. (Philadelphia: Fortress, 1981), pp. 220–21.

83. On Jesus, the Deuteronomic tradition, and the Torah; also on the closeness of the Sermon on the Mount to the Decalogue, see Walter Harrelson, *The Ten Commandments and Human Rights* (Philadelphia: Fortress, 1980), pp. 161–64; also "Law and Gospel," pp. 164–72. In addition, consult O'Neill, *Messiah*, pp. 27–43; Gerard S. Sloyan, *Is Christ the End of the Law?* (Philadelphia: Westminster, 1978), pp. 38–69; and Vermes, *Jesus and the World of Judaism*, pp. 46–48. On the general problem of Jesus' relation to the law, see Harvey, *Jesus*, pp. 36–65.

84. Williamson, *Has God Rejected His People?* pp. 13–16.

85. Carmichael, "Jesus Story and the Jewish War," p. 64. In no way would the Pharisees object to Jesus' cures on the Sabbath; his method of healing "involved no breach of the Sabbath law" (Maccoby, *Revolution in Judaea*, pp. 63–64).

86. Riches, *Jesus and the Transformation of Judaism*, pp. 97, 168, and *passim*.

87. See, e.g., ibid., chap. 6, "Jesus and the Law of Purity." Throughout, Riches represents the highly dubious methodological assumption that where Synoptic materials are close to other Jewish materials, they are secondary (cf., e.g., p. 151).

88. Cf., e.g., Harrelson, *Ten Commandments*, pp. 161–64.

89. Harvey, *Jesus*, p. 93.

90. Ibid., p. 56.

91. Eckardt, *For Righteousness' Sake*, p. 76. Consult Salo W. Baron, *A Social and Religious History of the Jews*, 2d rev. ed., vol. 2, part 2 (New York: Columbia University Press, 1952), pp. 73–75.

92. For an intensive accounting of Paul, consult Eckardt, *For Righteousness' Sake*, pp. 36–50.

93. Riches, *Jesus and the Transformation of Judaism*, p. 159; Matt. 19:26; Mark 10:27.

94. Eckardt, *For Righteousness' Sake*, p. 78, in turn citing H. Richard Niebuhr, *The Responsible Self: An Essay in Christian Moral Philosophy* (San Francisco: Harper & Row, 1978), p. 167.

95. Eckardt, *Elder and Younger Brothers*, pp. 23, 158–59; in general, chap. 8.

96. The point of view of Ephesians 2, however, is not inconsistent with Paul himself; cf., e.g., 2 Cor. 5:19; more controversially, Romans 9–11.

97. I refer again to Romans 11 where Paul identifies the church as a wild olive shoot grafted onto the root of Israel. "Remember it is not you that support the root, but the root that supports you" (v. 18).

98. Eckardt, *Elder and Younger Brothers*, p. 158.

99. Cf. ibid., pp. 116–19.

100. This excursus adapts a letter by the author in the *New York Times*, April 16, 1985.

6. THE JUDAISM OF JESUS, LIBERATOR OF THE WRETCHED

1. Elisabeth Schüssler Fiorenza, *In Memory of Her* (New York: Crossroad, 1983), p. 6.

2. David Tracy, "The Christian Understanding of Salvation-Liberation," *Face to Face* (New York) 14 (Spring 1988): 39–40; italics added to sentence beginning, "It is not adequate to speak ... "

3. For possible differentiation between "good ideology" and "bad ideology" (= false consciousness), see A. Roy Eckardt, *For Righteousness' Sake* (Bloomington: Indiana University Press, 1987), pp. 205–6. Of course, insofar as Christian theology and theological ethics force themselves into captivity to "bad ideology," the theology of liberation thereby becomes "internally contradictory and impossible of application" (ibid., p. 205). It is the expectation of Juan Luis Segundo that ideology, when construed as a "historical system of means and ends" in its relation to real-life challenges, helps very much to construct a bridge between our conception of God and concrete historical realities. Without ideologies—of necessity, provisional in character—faith becomes dead due to its complete impracticality (*Liberación de la teología* [Buenos Aires: Ediciones Carlos Lohlé, 1975], pp. 175, 133, 189, 139, 146).

4. Gustavo Gutiérrez, *The Power of the Poor in History: Selected Writings*, trans. Robert R. Barr (Maryknoll, N.Y.: Orbis, 1983), p. 4.

5. Eckardt, *For Righteousness' Sake*, p. 204.

6. Consult Robert McAfee Brown, *Gustavo Gutiérrez* (Atlanta: John Knox, 1980), p. 52; Gustavo Gutiérrez, *Teología de la liberación*, 8th ed. (Salamanca: Ediciones Sigueme, 1977), pp. 68–69; *Power of the Poor in History*, pp. 68, 73; "Terrorism, Liberation, and Sexuality," *The Witness* (April 1977): 10, as cited in Brown, *op. cit.*, p. 53; Eckardt, *For Righteousness' Sake*, pp. 204–5.

7. Eckardt, *For Righteousness' Sake*, chap. 2. Parts of the next few paragraphs are adapted from ibid., pp. 201–2.

8. David Tracy, *Blessed Rage for Order* (New York: Seabury, 1978), p. 243.

9. Clark M. Williamson, "Christ Against the Jews: A Review of Jon Sobrino's Christology," *Encounter* 40 (1979): 403.

10. Brown, *Gutiérrez*, p. 34.

11. José Miguez Bonino, *Toward a Christian Political Ethics* (Philadelphia: Fortress, 1983), p. 39.

12. E. P. Sanders, *Jesus and Judaism* (Philadelphia: Fortress, 1985), pp. 4–5, 10, 35.

13. Eckardt, *For Righteousness' Sake*, pp. 200, 238.

14. Gutiérrez, *Teología de la liberación*, p. 178; in general, chap. 10. Cf. Gutiérrez, *Power of the Poor in History*, chap. 1.

15. Gutiérrez, *Power of the Poor in History*, p. 211.

16. Sharon H. Ringe, *Jesus, Liberation, and the Biblical Jubilee* (Philadelphia: Fortress, 1985), p. xv.

17. Ibid., p. 16; in general, chap. 3.

18. See Exod. 21:2-6; 23:10-11; Deut. 15:1-18; and Jer. 34:8-22. The oldest biblical laws that underlie the Jubilee fall within the covenant code (Exod. 21–23).

19. Ringe, *Jesus*, pp. xiv–xv, 30, 58.

20. As examples, Ringe analyzes at some length Jesus' "rejection" at Nazareth (Luke 4:16-30) and the query from John the Baptist (Matt. 11:2-6/Luke 7:18-23): *Jesus*, pp. 36–48. On the first of these: If E. P. Sanders is right, the Jubilee images of Isaiah 61 "were understood by Jesus' contemporaries as referring to blessings promised particularly to Israel at the time of God's eschatological reign. The prophetic reading of that text . . . challenged that assumption of privilege, but left the socially revelatory implications of the Jubilee imagery intact. In that way, the text of promise was turned into a threat: the poor to whom the good news would come and the captives who would be set free might be any of God's children" (ibid., p. 44).

21. Luke's version of this story resembles the story in Mark 14:3-9/Matt. 26:6-13 and John 12:1-8.

22. Ringe, *Jesus*, pp. 71, 72–74.

23. Ibid., pp. 76, 84.

24. Ibid., p. 89.

25. A. Roy Eckardt, *Black-Woman-Jew* (Bloomington: Indiana University Press, 1989), pp. 43–45; *The Kairos Document: Challenge to the Church*, 2d rev. ed. (Grand Rapids, Mich.: Eerdmans, 1986). To be sure, the power of South African apartheid remains. But if, as many believe, that phenomenon is doomed, the Kairos movement will have been among the causes that helped bring about the doom.

26. Leonardo Boff, *Pasión de Cristo*, as cited in Juan Luis Segundo, *The Historical Jesus of the Synoptics*, trans. John Drury, vol. 2 of *Jesus of Nazareth Yesterday and Today* (Maryknoll, N.Y.: Orbis, 1985), p. 3.

27. Ringe, *Jesus*, p. 15.

28. Ibid., pp. 51–52, 92, 93–94 (italics added).

29. Gerald F. Moede, as reported by J. Robert Nelson, "Challenging 'Disabled Theology,'" *The Christian Century* 98 (1981): 1245.

30. Ringe, *Jesus*, pp. 97, 98.

31. Ibid., pp. 94, 71.

32. *The Historical Jesus of the Synoptics* is part of a five-volume study titled *Jesus of Nazareth Yesterday and Today*.

33. Segundo, *Historical Jesus*, pp. 182, 150, 164 (italics added). In our midrash on Sharon Ringe we noted the senses in which Jesus *did* help human beings. Segundo fully celebrates this as well, e.g., there is "the *transcendent datum* that the cross of Jesus is not a closed but an open door, through which life, justice, and love are already filtering and beginning to transform historical reality" (ibid., p. 9; also pp. 87, 117).

34. Ibid., pp. 12, 16.

35. Ibid., pp. 153, 91, 147, 107, 122–23; see more generally pp. 108–14. The gospel can become good news for privileged people only through their conversion (p. 120).

36. Ibid., pp. 113–14. Segundo maintains that the parable does not focus "on the different destinies of two human beings as they move from life in this world to eternal reward or punishment, as later theology would claim." His reading is not accurate.

37. Ibid., pp. 155, 149, 154, 158.

38. Ibid., pp. 178, 160, 104–5, 139–40.

39. Ibid., pp. 178–79.

40. Ibid., pp. 165, 185–86; see also p. 164.

41. Ibid., p. 56.

42. It is significant that in one place Segundo has Jesus regarding *eternal life* and the *kingdom of God* as synonyms. "Both are expressions of eschatological well-being" (p. 208 n. 20).

43. Eckardt, *Black-Woman-Jew*, p. 24.

44. Segundo had opened himself to this problem when he said, "Only one kind of Christology is valid and dovetails with the way Jesus himself posed issues. It is a Christology that starts off from the historical data about Jesus and *multiplies* the readings of his message, each time *modifying* the *preunderstanding* that is brought to the next reading" (*Historical Jesus*, p. 39).

45. See Leon Klenicki's treatment of the phenomenon within a Latin American context: "Facing History: Redemption and Salvation After Auschwitz," *Face to Face* (New York) 14 (Spring 1988): 44. See also Eckardt, *For Righteousness' Sake*, pp. 314, 302.

46. Consult Williamson, "Christ Against the Jews," pp. 403–12, regarding Jon Sobrino's *Christology at the Crossroads: A Latin American Approach*, trans. John Drury (Maryknoll, N.Y.: Orbis, 1978). Williamson calls attention to the anti-Judaic and anti-Jewish character of German biblical scholarship (especially Joachim Jeremias) upon which Sobrino leans heavily (something we have also noted in the work of Marcus J. Borg). Typical of Sobrino's historical travesties are these claims: Jesus stood in opposition to the oppression that Jewish society visited upon the sick, lepers, women, Roman centurions, sinners, and people possessed by demons. Jesus forgave all sinners but *not* the Pharisees. Jesus hurled anathemas at the Pharisees for paying no attention to justice. Jesus set the grace of God into opposition to "the law." "The law" is the Jewish means of saying no to God's kingdom. Judaism was a "religion of orthodoxy" (!). "Jesus is condemned to death for blasphemy." Williamson concludes, "Sobrino's whole project of a Christology for liberation theology is jeopardized critically by his way of approaching the historical Jesus. . . . [His] anti-Judaism violates the criterion of *praxis*. It is an inherited theory that is not brought under critical review by the pressing concern for liberation. It undermines the concern for liberation, which has been at the heart of Judaism since the Exodus" (Williamson, "Christ Against the Jews," pp. 408, 411, 412, 404). Since Sobrino's work violates the second of the three characteristics of the christological positions I am reviewing (as indicated in chap. 1 of the present study), I decided not to utilize that book. Largely through its anti-Pharisee deportment, Albert Nolan's *Jesus Before Christianity* (London: Darton, Longman and Todd, 1977) parallels Segundo's anti-Judaism. In *The Practice of Jesus* (trans. Matthew J. O'Connell [Maryknoll, N.Y.: Orbis, 1984]), Hugo Echegaray does the same thing by trying to set Jesus against various "Jewish" parties (see especially chap. 3) though hardly at all against the Romans.

47. Segundo does nothing to make this claim compatible with his statement that "Jesus of Nazareth died, after having been condemned by the Roman authorities, as a *political agitator*." On the very same page Segundo writes, "If Jesus of Nazareth was a

threat, if he agitated anything (politically, so as to merit a political sanction), it was vis-à-vis the religio-political authorities *of Judaism*. In some way . . . he hurt their interests, or so they believed. That gave rise to envy and fear at first, then conspiratorial plotting and the capture of Jesus, then sentencing, and ultimately a successful effort to put the Roman procurator on the spot publicly so that he had no choice but to accede to their desire to have Jesus legally executed" (*Historical Jesus*, p. 72). The attempt to say that "the Jews" manipulated Pilate—a claim that is incredible from everything we know of him—is typical in Christian anti-Jewish scholarship.

    48. Ibid., pp. 33, 65, 99, 98, 64 (italics added), 85, 120, 124, 127, 146, 135; see also pp. 77, 94, 128, 136.

    49. Fiorenza, *In Memory of Her*, p. 111.

    50. No expression or advocacy of Christian faith is entirely free of ideology. Everything depends, therefore, upon whether our ideological taints are self-critical or not self-critical.

    51. Ibid., p. 130.

    52. Ibid., pp. 22, 13; see also pp. 104, 130.

    53. Gutiérrez, *Power of the Poor in History*, pp, 15–16; cf. pp. 60–61, 12–13.

    54. See Leonard Swidler, *Yeshua* (Kansas City: Sheed & Ward, 1988), chap. 3. "A feminist is a person who is in favor of, and who promotes, the equality of women with men, . . . who advocates and practices treating women primarily as human persons (as men are so treated) and willingly contravenes social customs in so acting" (ibid., p. 78).

    55. Fiorenza, *In Memory of Her*, pp. xiv (italics added), xv, xx, xiii; see also pp. 152–54.

    56. Ibid., chaps. 1–3. See also Elisabeth Schüssler Fiorenza, *Bread Not Stone* (Boston: Beacon, 1984); and Letty M. Russell, *Household of Freedom* (Philadephia: Westminster, 1988).

    57. Fiorenza, *In Memory of Her*, pp. xv, 18, 29–33, 34–35 (italics added).

    58. Ibid., pp. 85, 83. "Since gender dimorphism is generated by . . . patriarchal oppression, it is not 'natural' but social. Therefore, feminist historians reject heuristic concepts such as 'biological caste' or 'women's experience as essentially different from that of men' because these categories render women passive objects of mere biological differences or male dominance. They seek instead for heuristic models that explore women's historical participation in social-public development and their efforts to comprehend and transform social structures" (ibid., p. 86; see also p. 92).

    59. Ibid., pp. 133–34.

    60. "Truly, I say to you, the tax collectors and the harlots go into the *basileia* of God before you" (Matt. 21:31). It is essential to know "that in a patriarchal society prostitution is the worst form of 'pollution' (sin) for a woman, although prostitution is an essential function of patriarchy. . . . That the harlots will enter into the *basileia* ahead of the faithful and righteous Israelite is outrageous, to say the least." The recurrent phrase, "tax collectors, sinners, and prostitutes," refers not just to "a morally reprehensible group of people but even more [to] a class so destitute that they must engage in 'dishonorable' professions in order to survive" (Fiorenza, *In Memory of Her*, p. 127; see also p. 128).

    61. Ibid., pp. 132, 134, 135; see also pp. 130, 131. For a parallel way of reasoning, consult James M. Robinson, "Very Goddess and Very Man: Jesus' Better Self," in Stephen T. Davis, ed., *Encountering Jesus: A Debate on Christology* (Atlanta: John Knox, 1988), pp. 111–22, plus commentaries on same, pp. 122–40. In partial contrast to Marcus J.

Borg, Fiorenza points out that the countercultural element has to do with the Christian movement rather than the Jesus movement. In the Greco-Roman world the Christian movement engaged in countercultural praxis. "As as alternative Jewish renewal movement, the Jesus movement was in tension with the dominant patriarchal ethos of its own culture." But "as an inner-Jewish renewal movement, the Jesus movement could presuppose a common cultural-religious milieu" (*In Memory of Her*, pp. 100–101).

62. When Fiorenza speaks of Jesus she is referring to him "as his life and ministry is available to historical-critical reading of the earliest interpretations of the first Christians" (ibid., p. 103).

63. Ibid., pp. 102, 121, 129–30, 152.

64. Ibid., pp. 140–42.

65. Ibid., pp. 143–51.

66. Ibid., pp. 320, 333, 321, 322–23. For Fiorenza's refutation of the objection that Mark 16:8 prohibits a positive interpretation of the emerging women disciples, see pp. 321–22.

67. Ibid., pp. 326, 329–30, 331, 332, 139, 333.

68. Ibid., p. 334. The place of women in the postpaschal Christian missionary enterprise is beyond our province here; see, e.g., ibid., pp. 138–39, 183–84, 198–99; in general, chap. 5; also pp. 235–36, 279, 309–10. Chapter 6 in its entirety considers Gal. 3:28.

69. Ibid., pp. 105–7, 141.

70. Ibid., p. 118.

71. Ibid., p. xiv.

72. Ibid.

73. Points 1 and 2 only are adapted from Eckardt, *For Righteousness' Sake*, pp. 78–80, 207–10.

74. See ibid., pp. 39–40.

75. For Sharon Ringe's exegesis of this story, consult her *Jesus*, pp. 60–61.

76. Ibid., p. 64.

77. Gutiérrez, *Teología de la liberación*, p. 307.

78. H. Richard Niebuhr, *The Responsible Self* (San Francisco: Harper & Row, 1978), pp. 167, 178.

79. Eckardt, *For Righteousness' Sake*, pp. 79–80 (slightly emended). Cf. chap. 2, "Human History and the Divine Righteousness." On Essene-Qumran ethics, see ibid., pp. 34–36.

80. I am helped here by Brown, *Gutiérrez*, pp. 56–59, 65, 68.

81. A long section of the declaration of a 1979 conference of Latin American bishops in Puebla, Mexico, is devoted to a "preferential option for the poor." For Gutiérrez's appraisal of Puebla, consult *Power of the Poor in History*, chaps. 5, 6.

82. Gutiérrez, *Teología de la liberación*, p. 358; Arthur F. McGovern, *Marxism: An American Christian Perspective* (Maryknoll, N.Y.: Orbis, 1980), p. 199.

83. Segundo, *Liberación de la teología*, pp. 36, 67.

84. Krister Stendahl, *Paul Among Jews and Gentiles and Other Essays* (Philadelphia: Fortress, 1976), pp. 102, 106 (italics added).

85. Eckardt, *Black-Woman-Jew*, p. 190.

86. Brown, *Gutiérrez*, p. 56.

87. Ibid., pp. 58–59, 65, 35; Segundo, *Liberación de la teología,* p. 95.

88. I pass over the excruciating question of whether God is also required to love God. I will only say that if human self-love is in some way authorized—"love thy neighbor *as thyself* "—may it not be the case that divine self-love is in order as well? If I were God I think I should be extremely tempted (?) to love myself—because of what Godness means (unless, of course, it means something entirely different from what we humans think it means).

89. Donald J. Goergen, *Mission and Ministry of Jesus* (Wilmington, Del.: Michael Glazier, 1986), p. 227.

7. THE JUDAISM OF JESUS, REDEEMER
OF WOMEN

1. Elisabeth Schüssler Fiorenza, *In Memory of Her* (New York: Crossroad, 1983), p. 347.

2. Rita Nakashima Brock, "The Feminist Redemption of Christ," in Judith L. Weidman, ed., *Christian Feminism* (San Francisco: Harper & Row, 1984), p. 56. Consult also Anne E. Carr, *Transforming Grace* (San Francisco: Harper & Row, 1988), chap. 8, "Feminism and Christology"; and see extensive bibliography (pp. 245–66).

3. Nelly Ritchie, "Women and Christology," in Elsa Tamez, ed., *Through Her Eyes* (Maryknoll, N.Y.: Orbis, 1989), pp. 81–95.

4. Elsa Tamez, "Introduction: The Power of the Naked," in Tamez, ed., *Through Her Eyes*, p. 2.

5. Ana María Bidegain, "Women and the Theology of Liberation," in Tamez, ed., *Through Her Eyes*, pp. 34, 35.

6. María Clara Bingemer, "Reflections on the Trinity," in Tamez, ed., *Through Her Eyes*, pp. 67, 77.

7. Consuelo del Prado, "I Sense God in Another way," in Tamez, ed., *Through Her Eyes*, p. 148.

8. Harvey Cox, *Religion in the Secular City* (New York: Simon and Schuster, 1984), p. 256.

9. Ibid. See Cox's contemporary accounting of Our Lady of Guadalupe: "A dark-skinned *mastiza*, she personifies the anger and persistent dignity of people of color everywhere. A woman, she embodies the never-completely-dominated *jouissance* of the second sex. A poor person, she inspires the hopes of all those who believe that God is preferentially present in the lives of the disinherited" (ibid., pp. 256–61). Cf. Carr, *Transforming Grace*, chap. 9, "The Salvation of Women: Christ, Mary, and the Church."

10. Bingemer, "Reflections on the Trinity," p. 73.

11. Pentz is aware of Valerie Saiving's contention that total self-abnegation for women is not a virtue but a vice.

12. Rebecca D. Pentz, "Can Jesus Save Women?" in Stephen T. Davis, ed., *Encountering Jesus* (Atlanta: John Knox, 1988), pp. 77–91. Cf. Mary Condren: It is *patriarchal* birthing that "takes place primarily through death" (as cited in Brock, "Feminist Redemption of Christ," p. 182 n. 2).

13. Rebecca D. Pentz, "Response to Critiques," in Davis, ed., *Encountering Jesus*, p. 107.

14. A. Roy Eckardt, *Black-Woman-Jew* (Bloomington: Indiana University Press, 1989), p. 93. "It" forms of identification have as a consequence the depersonalization of God.

15. The analysis here follows A. Roy Eckardt, *Jews and Christians* (Bloomington: Indiana University Press, 1986), pp. 129–30; *Black-Woman-Jew*, pp. 80, 95–96.

16. John B. Cobb, Jr., "Christ Beyond Creative Transformation," in Davis, ed., *Encountering Jesus*, p. 154.

17. Stephen T. Davis maintains that it would have been much harder for God to accomplish his purposes had Jesus been female: "Sadly, even fewer would have listened to her message" (critique of Rebecca D. Pentz, in Davis, ed., *Encountering Jesus*, p. 97). It appears to me that in light of the dreadful tale of male oppression of women, it would have made more sense in the long run for God to have sent a woman. (Was this possible? That is a problem for God rather than for us.)

18. Historical truths about Jesus are nevertheless handled selectively: his maleness is concentrated on but not, e.g., his Jewishness or his alleged vocation of carpenter.

19. Diane Tennis, "The Loss of the Father God: Why Women Rage and Grieve," *Christianity and Crisis* 41 (1981): 169.

20. J. Coert Rylaarsdam, "Judaism: the Christian Problem," *Face to Face* 11 (1984): 5.

21. Dorothee Sölle, "Christianity and the Jewish Request for Signs: A Reflection on I Corinthians 1:22," *Face to Face* 11 (1984): 20.

22. Eckardt, *Jews and Christians*, p. 130 (slightly emended).

23. Manitonquet, "Daughters of Creation," *Theology Today* 39 (1982): 46, 47.

24. Mary Daly, *Beyond God the Father: Toward a Philosophy of Women's Liberation* (Boston: Beacon, 1974), pp. 73–75.

25. Mary Daly, "After the Death of God the Father," in Carol P. Christ and Judith Plaskow, eds., *Womanspirit Rising* (San Francisco: Harper & Row, 1979), pp. 59–60, 58–59.

26. Eckardt, *Black-Woman-Jew*, p. 96 (slightly emended).

27. Brock, "Feminist Redemption of Christ," pp. 57, 58, 60ff., 68–69.

28. Ibid., pp. 69–70 (italics added).

29. Mary Daly, *Gyn/Ecology* (Boston: Beacon, 1978), p. 39.

30. Brock, "Feminist Redemption of Christ," p. 70.

31. Ibid., pp. 64, 70–74. Healing does not belong exclusively to Jesus (p. 73).

32. For Isabel Carter Heyward, love and justice are one. "Love does not come first, justice later. Love is not a 'feeling' that precedes right-relationship among the persons in a family or the people of the world. We do not feel our way into right-relationship: with other races, other people. We do not feel our way into doing what is just. We act our way into feeling" (*The Redemption of God* [Washington: University Press of America, 1982], p. 219).

33. Ibid., pp. 152, 155, 180; see especially chap. 3 on Wiesel and the Holocaust.

34. Ibid., p. 196.

35. Ibid., p. 34.

36. Ibid., pp. 156, 20.

37. Dietrich Bonhoeffer, *Letters and Papers from Prison*, ed. Eberhard Bethge (New York: Macmillan, 1953), p. 360. The resurrection of Jesus in no way justifies or nullifies the injustice of his death on the cross. Any theology that assumes that Christians "must welcome pain and death as a sign of faith is constructed upon a faulty hermeneutic. . . . The notion of welcoming, or submitting oneself gladly to, injustice flies in the face of Jesus' own refusal to make concessions to unjust relation" (Heyward, *Redemption of God*, p. 58).

38. Ibid., pp. 197, 2.

39. Ibid., pp. 6, 19, 43.

40. Ibid., pp. 207, 7, 151, 152, 1–2, 9. The Buber citation is from *I and Thou*, trans. Walter Kaufmann (New York: Scribner, 1970), p. 130.

41. Heyward, *Redemption of God*, pp. 49, 34, 40 (italics added). It is essential to remember that Jesus "was not attempting to undo Judaism, but rather to re-image it." In Judaism, "God's capacity to act and human *dunamis*, or human capacity" are "necessary correlates." Jesus "was not trying to negate the covenant, but rather to radicalize it." What was new in Jesus "was the intimacy and immediacy of God's activity through human *dunamis*" (p. 42).

42. Ibid., pp. 196, 4, 5, 39.

43. Ibid., pp. 30–31.

44. Ibid., pp. 31–32, 43, 166, 167.

45. Michael Wyschogrod, "A Jewish Postscript," in Davis, ed., *Encountering Jesus*, p. 180.

46. Heyward, *Redemption of God*, pp. 201, 33–34.

47. Carr, *Transforming Grace*, pp. 112, 187.

48. Cox, *Religion in the Secular City,* p. 260.

8. DISCONTINUITY AND CONTINUITY:
THE CHRISTS OF THE APOSTOLIC WRITINGS

1. James H. Charlesworth, "Research on the Historical Jesus Today: Jesus and the Pseudepigrapha, the Dead Sea Scrolls, the Nag Hammadi Codices, Josephus and Archaeology," *Princeton Seminary Bulletin* 6 (1985): 113–15.

2. Alister McGrath, *The Enigma of the Cross* (London: Hodder and Stoughton, 1987). See also Leon Morris, *The Cross of Jesus* (Grand Rapids, Mich.: Eerdmans, 1988).

3. James P. Mackey, *Jesus the Man and the Myth* (New York: Paulist, 1979), p. 52. Cf. also Jürgen Moltmann, *The Trinity and the Kingdom* (San Francisco: Harper & Row, 1981), chap. 3, "The History of the Son."

4. Wolfhart Pannenberg, *Jesus—God and Man*, trans. Lewis L. Wilkins and Duane A. Friebe (Philadelphia: Westminster Press, 1968), p. 21.

5. Luke Timothy Johnson, *The Writings of the New Testament* (Philadelphia: Fortress, 1986), p. 544.

6. A. Roy Eckardt, *For Righteousness' Sake* (Bloomington: Indiana University Press, 1987), p. 143.

7. Leonard Swidler, *Yeshua* (Kansas City: Sheed & Ward, 1988), pp. 18–19.

8. Paula Fredriksen, *From Jesus to Christ* (New Haven, Conn.: Yale University Press, 1988), p. 110.

9. Fredriksen, *From Jesus to Christ*, pp. 139, 180, 141, 142, 140.

10. Paul's call to join the Jesus movement is dated circa c.e. 33, his extant letters in and around c.e. 50. The causes, foundation, and authority of his gospel were, for him, a special revelation of God, the experience of the risen Christ (Fredriksen, *From Jesus to Christ*, pp. 52, 174; Gal. 1:1, 16; 1 Cor. 11:23; 15:3. For Luke's account, see Acts 9:1-22).

11. Fredriksen, *From Jesus to Christ*, p. 62.

12. Ibid., p. 174. Paul employs the Greek *Christos* more as a name than as a messianic title: Jesus Christ, rather than Jesus *the* Christ (p. 56). "So soon after his death, and so definitely, did the original apostles identify the crucified Jesus as the Messiah that

within two decades the equivalent Greek term, *Christ*, functioned as part of his name" (p. 136).

13. Ibid., p. 172; see also p. 175.

14. Franklin H. Littell, contribution to symposium, "How Jewish Was Early Christianity?" *Midstream* 28 (December 1982): 35.

15. Fredriksen, *From Jesus to Christ*, pp. 56, 61, 159; in general, pp. 52–64, 136, 156–76.

16. Ibid., pp. 205–6, 184 (slightly emended), 48; in general, pp. 44–52, 177–85.

17. Ibid., p. 52.

18. Ibid., p. 182.

19. Ibid., pp. 186, 167, 198.

20. Ibid., pp. 40, 42, 37–38, 36–37, 43 (slightly emended); in general, pp. 36–43, 186–91.

21. The issue of the rejection/partial acceptance of the early Christian gospel among Jews is outside our immediate purview but by no means irrelevant to it. Fredriksen's *From Jesus to Christ* is very helpful on this matter. It is clear from Mark that the anti-Jewishness (antisemitism?) of the Apostolic Writings did not have to wait upon the later Gospels (see pp. 184–85). In Acts the "theme of universal and corporate Jewish guilt in the death of Jesus figures prominently in every summary of the early *kerygma* (3:13; 4:14; 7:52; 10:39, etc.)" (p. 34). See also pp. 210–12.

22. Ibid., pp. 27, 28, 29, 33, 43, 30.

23. But Luke's text "hints at an originally political understanding of Jesus' messiahship. Entering Jerusalem, Jesus is hailed as king by his disciples; when the Pharisees request that he disavow the title, he declines (19:38-40). Later, before Pilate, he stands accused of sedition. . . . Shortly thereafter, he dies as an insurrectionist (23:38ff.)" (ibid., p. 35).

24. Ibid., pp. 32, 34–36; in general, pp. 27–36, 186–87, 191–98.

25. Ibid., p. 25.

26. Chapter 2 above maintains that *Son of Man* was not really a title of Jesus. The expression "figures prominently in John, where it is utterly reinterpreted and given cosmic rather than apocalyptic significance" (ibid., p. 62; further to the "Son of Man," see pp. 138–39, 178ff.).

27. See ibid., pp. 19, 20–26, 43, 49, 201, 202, 211.

28. Ibid., pp. 20, 19, 23, 22, 199, 200; in general, pp. 19–26, 198–204.

29. In an important essay, "Christology Without Jesusolatry," Robert Kysar defines Jesusolatry as "veneration of the Jesus figure as a kind of naïve substitute for God" (*The Christian Century* 87 [1970]: 1035).

30. Fredriksen, *From Jesus to Christ*, p. 134.

31. Juan Luis Segundo, *The Historical Jesus of the Synoptics*, trans. John Drury, vol. 2 of *Jesus of Nazareth Yesterday and Today* (Maryknoll, N.Y.: Orbis, 1985), p. 51.

32. James H. Charlesworth points out that there is no convincing evidence that Jesus thought of himself as the "suffering servant" or as "the Messiah who was to suffer and die for the people of God" (*Jesus Within Judaism*, Anchor Bible Reference Library [Garden City, N.Y.: Doubleday, 1988], pp. 153–54).

33. A helpful study is Martin Hengel, *The Atonement: The Origins of the Doctrine in the New Testament*, trans. John Bowden (Philadelphia: Fortress, 1981). See also Leander S. Harding, Jr., "A Unique and Final Work: The Atonement as a Saving Act of Transformative Obedience," *Journal of Ecumenical Studies* 24 (Winter 1987): 80–92.

34. Elisabeth Schüssler Fiorenza, *In Memory of Her* (New York: Crossroad, 1983), p. 130.

35. Anne E. Carr, *Transforming Grace* (San Francisco: Harper & Row, 1988), p. 174.

36. Cf. Johnson: "Ultimately, it was not the confession of Jesus as Messiah that divided Christians from other Jews, for it was possible for Jews to make such confessions—as Rabbi Akiba did in the case of Bar Kochba—without apostasizing from Torah. It was the confession of a crucified sinner as resurrected Lord that was divisive" (*Writings of the New Testament*, p. 109).

37. E. P. Sanders, *Jesus and Judaism* (Philadelphia: Fortress, 1985), pp. 21, 22, 95, 19.

38. Charlesworth, *Jesus Within Judaism*, p. 164 n. 62.

39. Ibid., pp. 136, 138, 155.

40. Ibid., pp. 138, 139.

41. Ibid., p. 148.

42. Ibid., pp. 139–55. See Michael L. Cook, *The Jesus of Faith* (New York: Paulist, 1981), chap. 4, "The Proclaimer as Proclaimed." That the parable of the wicked tenant farmers is interpretable in ways diametrically opposite to that of Charlesworth is exemplified by Philip Culbertson: "Because Jesus' listeners would have been familiar with the vineyard as a symbol for the people Israel ... they would have given an altogether different meaning to the story than the one traditionally preached by Christians. They might have heard it this way: God chose Israel as the vineyard and entrusted it to various tenants: Babylonians, Persians, Greeks. From time to time God would send someone to collect the fruits of Israel's faithfulness—that is, God would inspire some sort of Covenant renewal with Israel—but each time, the overlords' oppression became stronger; they beat and treated shamefully those in Covenant relationship with God. Finally, God inspired the long-expected new Covenant, an incredible vitality in Judaism that produced the Pharisees' wisdom and charity, the Sadducees' liturgical enthusiasm, the Zealots' deep commitment to social action, and the Essenes' mystical purity. But this charismatic renewal was treated most harshly of all, for the Roman overlords at the time of Jesus persecuted Judaism with vehemence, putting to death anyone who challenged the state's control over Jewish expression. In the face of this horrible oppression, Jesus holds out a message of hope to his people Israel: God will liberate Israel from oppression, placing the vineyard into the hands of tenants who know how to care for it lovingly, and who will enable it to fulfill its mission ... " ("The Pharisaic Jesus and His Gospel Parables," *The Christian Century* 102 [1985]: 76).

43. John Hick, "An Inspiration Christology for a Religiously Plural World," in Stephen T. Davis, ed., *Encountering Jesus* (Atlanta: John Knox, 1988), p. 18.

44. Stephen T. Davis, "Jesus Christ: Savior or Guru?" in Davis, ed., *Encountering Jesus*, p. 57.

45. But some liberationist and feminist thinkers warn of the danger that a "self-emptying" image of God can perpetuate "a concept of condescension in which all the inherent dignity is on the divine side and none on the human side. God stoops to the essentially worthless human condition to bring salvation; but the idea of an inherent human powerlessness and dependency continues" (Harvey Cox, *Religion in the Secular City* [New York: Simon and Schuster, 1984], p. 142).

46. Swidler, *Yeshua*, pp. 52–54. "The living and dying according to the Torah and beyond did not in any way place Yeshua outside of Judaism. The Rabbis described this

kenotic love with the biblical term *hesed*, often simply translated as 'loving kindness' " (p. 53).

47. Additional writings of particular relevance to this chapter include A. E. Harvey, ed., *God Incarnate: Story and Belief* (London: SPCK, 1981); John Hick, *The Center of Christianity* (San Francisco: Harper & Row, 1978); Hick, ed., *The Myth of God Incarnate* (Philadelphia: Westminster, 1977) (challenges to the doctrine of incarnation); S. Mark Heim, "Thinking About Theocentric Christology," and responses by Carl E. Braaten, John B. Cobb, Jr., Thomas Dean, Elouise Renich Fraser, Kosuke Koyama, and Paul F. Knitter, *Journal of Ecumenical Studies* 24 (Winter 1987): 1–52; Bernard J. Lee, *The Galilean Jewishness of Jesus* (New York: Paulist, 1988); Gerald O'Collins, *What Are They Saying about Jesus?*, rev. ed. (New York: Paulist, 1983); and Jaroslav Pelikan, *Jesus Through the Centuries* (New Haven, Conn.: Yale University Press, 1985).

9. THE COVENANTAL CHRIST

1. A. Roy Eckardt, review of Paul M. van Buren, *Discerning the Way*, in *The Christian Century* 97 (1980): 922.

2. Paul M. van Buren, *Christ in Context*, part 3 of *A Theology of the Jewish-Christian Reality* (San Francisco: Harper & Row, 1988), pp. xvii–xix, 25, 68, 29, 54, 183, 250 (hereafter cited as *CIC*). There are solid links to Karl Barth in van Buren's work— including more than a little of Barth's turgidness—though criticisms of Barth are also found. For a penetrating criticism of the latter in regard to the proper criterion of theology, consult Paul M. van Buren, *A Christian Theology of the People Israel*, part 2 of *A Theology of the Jewish-Christian Reality* (New York: Seabury, 1983), pp. 5–9.

3. Van Buren, *CIC*, pp. 145–47, 207, xviii, xix, 213–25. Readers do not always read forewords. It would have been better had van Buren placed his two all-crucial, fundamental rules, together with his all-important accompanying explanations of same (pp. xviii–xix) in his main text. Or better, the foreword could have been presented as his initial main chapter. For it is not a "fore-word" in the usual or literal sense. It is substantive and decisive.

4. Ibid., pp. 252, 278, 284, 285.

5. Ibid., p. 185; see also pp. 271–73, 281–82.

6. Ibid., p. 194.

7. See, e.g., ibid., pp. 160–67, "The Cross and Auschwitz," especially p. 164, and, in general, chap. 7, "The Crucified One." The continued restriction to the name *Auschwitz* by van Buren, as by many Christian and Jewish writers, in equation with the *Shoah* is an (unintended) affront to Jews of the many other concentration and death camps.

8. Ibid., pp. 200, 46, 164, 165.

9. Robert A. Everett, "Christian Theology After the Holocaust (2)," *Christian Attitudes on Jews and Judaism* (London) 51 (December 1976): 11.

10. Van Buren, *CIC*, p. 84.

11. Ibid.

12. Ibid., p. 145.

13. Ibid., pp. 38, 46 (italics added).

14. Ibid., p. 104.

15. Ibid., p. 80 (italics added).

16. Ibid., p. 50.

17. Ibid., p. 81 (italics added).

18. Ibid., p. 171.

19. Ibid., pp. xviii, xix.

20. Van Buren, *Christian Theology of the People Israel*, pp. 35–36, 328, 340–41.

21. Van Buren, *CIC*, pp. 192–93.

22. Ibid., p. 58 (exclamation point added).

23. See ibid., p. 59.

24. A. Roy Eckardt, *Your People, My People* (New York: Quadrangle/New York Times, 1974), p. 245 (slightly emended).

25. The problem of the title of volume 2, *A Christian Theology of the People Israel*, carries over immediately into volume 3 (see, e.g., pp. 30ff.) and continues throughout the latter volume.

26. Van Buren, *CIC*, p. 4.

27. Ibid., p. 103.

28. On anti-Zionism, see, e.g., ibid., pp. 65, 84, 179.

29. See van Buren, *Christian Theology of the People Israel*, pp. 11–21.

30. In one place in *A Christian Theology of the People Israel* van Buren speaks of the essentiality of Christian prayer "that Israel become for it what God has promised: a kingdom of priests of the most high God, a light in our darkness, a blessing for all peoples, ourselves included" (p. 20). This rather stacks the deck. I do not in any way question the work of Christian (or other) historians who provide essential phenomenological representations of Jewish theology and life.

31. Van Buren, *CIC*, p. 54.

32. Ibid., pp. 79, 107–8, 109 (italics added).

33. Ibid., pp. 117, 110 (italics added); in general, pp. 116–19.

34. Ibid., pp. 117–18.

35. See ibid., pp. 113–17, "The diversity of the witness."

36. Ibid., p. 207.

37. Peter Levinson, as cited in *Time*, May 7, 1979.

38. Van Buren, *CIC*, p. 109.

39. Ibid., pp. 109–10.

40. Raymond E. Brown, in a review-symposium on Pheme Perkins's *Resurrection*, in *Horizons* 12 (Fall 1985): 366.

41. Van Buren, *CIC*, p. 118. In *The Burden of Freedom* (New York: Seabury, 1976), pp. 90ff., van Buren affirms an extrabodily resurrection of Jesus.

42. The unqualified historical certainty that the effective engine of the Christian movement was the resurrection of Jesus Christ is in no way incompatible with the possibility that no resurrection, in fact, took place. For, as van Buren himself reminds us, none of the witnesses to the resurrection claims to have seen the resurrection (*CIC*, pp. 11, 116).

43. Ibid., pp. 110, 120.

44. The question of what happened in the resurrection-event is not made to go away by van Buren's assertion that this is to speak of the resurrection "as an event in the past" (ibid., p. 204). If the resurrection is not an event in the past, the historicity of Christianity is denied.

45. In one place van Buren does concede that "*the risen one was not even returned to the land of the living* to bring to fruition the work he had begun" (ibid., p. 122, italics added).

46. Van Buren himself insists that to call Easter "spiritual" in the sense of "immaterial" or "unworldly" is wrongheaded (ibid., p. 129).

47. Nothing in my analysis of van Buren and the resurrection is in any way contingent upon or related to my belief/disbelief in the resurrection. A comment is required, however: Some critics of a questioning of Jesus' resurrection enter the objection, Does not such questioning threaten the central teaching of Christianity and thereby Christianity itself? To respond this way is to fail to face the issue. The critics are, in effect, changing the subject. The question is not whether a particular Christian dogma is theologically correct or incorrect. The vital and only question is whether the teaching of the resurrection can be justified in light of the evil of Christian supersessionism. Until or unless the critic succeeds in making compatible the resurrection and the demands of human morality—I make some preliminary stabs in this direction in chap. 11—he or she can hardly take refuge in objections respecting what is or is not the sine qua non of Christianity.

48. Consult James F. Moore, "The Holocaust and Christian Theology: A Spectrum of Views on the Crucifixion and the Resurrection in Light of the Holocaust," *Remembering for the Future: Working Papers and Addenda* (International Scholars' Conference on the Holocaust, Oxford, U.K., 10–13 July 1988), vol. 1 (Oxford: Pergamon Press, 1989), pp. 844–57.

49. E. P. Sanders, *Paul, the Law, and the Jewish People* (Philadelphia: Fortress, 1983), pp. 207–8.

50. Van Buren, *CIC*, p. 56.

51. Ibid., p. 86; see also p. 93.

52. Ibid., pp. 91, 136. Consult on this question van Buren, *A Christian Theology of the People Israel*, pp. 320–34.

53. Van Buren, *CIC*, p. 145.

54. Ibid., p. 165.

55. Ibid., pp. 169, 173.

56. Ibid., p. 196.

57. Ibid., p. 222; cf. pp. 286–88, and in general chap. 12.

58. E.g., ibid., pp. 222–23.

59. Ibid., p. 223.

60. Van Buren, *Christian Theology of the People Israel*, p. 33.

10. JESUS CHRIST AND "THE GREAT WAYS OF HUMANKIND"

1. The quoted phrase is from John B. Cobb, Jr., "Toward a Christocentric Catholic Theology," in Leonard Swidler, ed., *Toward a Universal Theology of Religion* (Maryknoll, N.Y.: Orbis, 1987), p. 93. Cobb has objections to the usage of *religion* and *faiths*; I think such terms are too customary and entrenched to be subject to discard.

2. Lucien Richard, *What Are They Saying about Christ and World Religions?* (New York: Paulist, 1981), p. 3; John B. Cobb, Jr., "A Critical View of Inherited Theology," *The Christian Century* 97 (1980): 196; Paul F. Knitter, *No Other Name?* (Maryknoll, N.Y.: Orbis, 1985), p. 73.

3. Marcus J. Borg, *Jesus, A New Vision* (San Francisco: Harper & Row, 1987), pp. 198–99.

4. Alice L. Eckardt and A. Roy Eckardt, *Long Night's Journey into Day*, rev. ed. (Detroit: Wayne State University Press; Oxford: Pergamon Press, 1988), pp. 136–37 (slightly emended).

5. Cf. Anthony Bayfield, "Judaism and Religious Pluralism," *European Judaism* 22 (Spring 1989): 5–6.

6. Michael Wyschogrod, "A Jewish Postscript," in Stephen T. Davis, ed., *Encountering Jesus* (Atlanta: John Knox, 1988), pp. 182–83.

7. Marcia Falk, "Toward a Feminist Jewish Reconstruction of Monotheism," *Tikkun* 4 (July/August 1989): 53–56.

8. Pinchas Lapide, "Jewish Monotheism," in Pinchas Lapide and Jürgen Moltmann, *Jewish Monotheism and Christian Trinitarian Doctrine*, trans. Leonard Swidler (Philadelphia: Fortress, 1981), p. 27.

9. Paul Tillich, *Christianity and the Encounter of the World Religions* (New York: Columbia University Press, 1963), pp. 4–5; Raimundo Panikkar, "The Invisible Harmony: A Universal Theory of Religion or a Cosmic Confidence in Reality," in Leonard Swidler, ed., *Toward a Universal Theology of Religion*, p. 137; Mircea Eliade, *The Sacred and the Profane: The Nature of Religion* (New York: Harcourt, Brace, 1959).

10. Cf. Emil Brunner: "From the standpoint of Jesus Christ, all religious systems appear untrue, unbelieving and indeed godless" (as cited in Alan Race, *Christians and Religious Pluralism* [London: SCM Press, 1983], p. 20).

11. The following works are of particular relevance to the subject of this chapter: S. Wesley Ariarajah, *The Bible and People of Other Faiths* (Maryknoll, N.Y.: Orbis, 1989); John Bowden, *Jesus: The Unanswered Questions* (Nashville, Abingdon, 1989), especially chaps. 2, 11, 12; John B. Cobb, Jr., "Christ Beyond Creative Transformation," plus critiques by John Hick, Stephen T. Davis, James M. Robinson, and Rebecca D. Pentz, and response by Cobb, in Stephen T. Davis, ed., *Encountering Jesus*, pp. 141–78; Harvey Cox, *Many Mansions* (Boston: Beacon, 1988) and *Religion in the Secular City* (New York: Simon and Schuster, 1984), especially chap. 20; Stephen T. Davis, "Jesus Christ: Savior or Guru?" plus critiques by James M. Robinson, Rebecca D. Pentz, John B. Cobb., Jr., and John Hick, and response by Davis, in Davis, ed., *Encountering Jesus*, pp. 39–76; Tom F. Driver, *Christ in a Changing World* (New York: Crossroad, 1981); A. Roy Eckardt, *Elder and Younger Brothers* (New York: Scribner, 1967; Schocken, 1973); *For Righteousness' Sake* (Bloomington: Indiana University Press, 1987); *Jews and Christians* (Bloomington: Indiana University Press, 1986); Falk, "Toward a Feminist Jewish Reconstruction of Monotheism"; John Hick, "An Inspiration Christology for a Religiously Plural World," plus critiques by Stephen T. Davis, James M. Robinson, John B. Cobb, Jr., and Rebecca D. Pentz, and response by Hick, in Davis, ed., *Encountering Jesus*, pp. 5–38; John Hick, *Center of Christianity* (San Francisco: Harper & Row, 1978); John Hick and Brian Hebblethwaite, eds., *Christianity and Other Religions* (Philadelphia: Fortress, 1980); John Hick and Paul F. Knitter, eds., *The Myth of Christian Uniqueness* (Maryknoll, N.Y.: Orbis, 1987); Eugene Hillman, *Many Paths* (Maryknoll, N.Y.: Orbis, 1989); Lapide and Moltmann, *Jewish Monotheism and Christian Trinitarian Doctrine*; Lesslie Newbigin, *Christian Witness in a Plural Society* (London: British Council of Churches, 1977); Jaroslav Pelikan, *Jesus Through the Centuries* (New Haven, Conn.: Yale University Press, 1985); Race, *Christians and Religious Pluralism*; Richard, *What Are They Saying about Christ and World Religions?*; Leroy S. Rouner, ed., *Religious Pluralism* (Notre Dame, Ind.: University of Notre Dame Press, 1984); Wilfred Cantwell

Smith, *Towards a World Theology* (Maryknoll, N.Y.: Orbis, 1989); Swidler, ed., *Toward a Universal Theology of Religion*; Mark Kline Taylor, "In Praise of Shaky Ground: The Liminal Christ and Cultural Pluralism," *Theology Today* 43 (April 1986): 36–51; Paul Tillich, *Christianity and the Encounter of the World Religions*; and David Tracy, *Blessed Rage for Order* (New York: Seabury, 1978).

12. Michael Wyschogrod epitomizes religious pluralism as "the condition in which diverse religions make competing and partly incompatible truth claims" ("Jewish Postscript," p. 182). Luke Timothy Johnson points out that "the confrontation of pluralism is threatening to a group's identity, and the group can respond in different ways: it can close up, communicate, or convert" (*The Writings of the New Testament* [Philadelphia: Fortress, 1986], p. 15). Consult also John Hick, "Religious Pluralism and Absolute Claims," in Rouner, ed., *Religious Pluralism*, pp. 193–213; Cox, *Many Mansions*, chap. 7, "Beyond Dialogue: Liberation Theology and Religious Pluralism"; and the following essays in Hick and Knitter, eds., *Myth of Christian Uniqueness*: Gordon D. Kaufman, "Religious Diversity, Historical Consciousness, and Christian Theology"; Langdon Gilkey, "Plurality and Its Theological Implications"; and Tom F. Driver, "The Case For Pluralism."

13. Paul F. Knitter, *No Other Name?*, p. 73 (hereafter identified as *NON?*). Knitter is entirely aware of, and takes fully into account, the danger that theoretical or generalizing models can act to blur differences within each confessional type and overlook areas of agreement across confessional lines (ibid., p. 74). Attention to the historical development of the several models points to certain continuities among them. Typologies of religious pluralism naturally vary from scholar to scholar; cf. the sixfold schema of Raimundo Panikkar, "Religious Pluralism: The Metaphysical Challenge," in Rouner, ed., *Religious Pluralism*, p. 98. On the shortcomings in typologies, see Tillich, *Christianity and the Encounter of the World Religions*, pp. 54–56.

14. Knitter, *NON?* pp. 75, 77, 79, 80–87.

15. Ibid., pp. 89, 93, 95–96.

16. Knitter's first model is exemplified not alone among conservatives but among liberals, at least as these latter are portrayed by radical Catholic thinker Thomas Sheehan. Sheehan labels as "Christian tribalism" the belief that "everyone has to be saved through Jesus and that Christianity is the final and only true religion." Real plurality is not to be confused with "the liberal theologian's condescending plurality, which looks like a wheel with a hub—the Jew, the Muslim, the Buddhist, they all seek salvation—but Christ is still at the hub, the only source of that salvation, and non-Christians are really, though unwittingly, anonymous Christians. That's the liberal's way of saying there still is only one Savior who founded the one true church, but we just don't burn heretics and infidels anymore. Liberals are more benign, more open. They dialogue with Hindus and Marxists, but they still believe Jesus is the only way to God" (Thomas Sheehan, as cited in Robert McClory, "The Gospel According to Thomas Sheehan," *Reader* [Chicago] 18 [April 21, 1989]: 26). Sheehan irresponsibly ignores the multitudes of liberals who *refuse* to believe that Jesus is the only way to God.

17. Knitter, *NON?* pp. 97–99; Wolfhart Pannenberg, *Basic Questions in Theology*, vol. 2 (Philadelphia: Fortress, 1971), p. 112.

18. Knitter, *NON?* pp. 102, 103, 107–8.

19. Ibid., pp. 115–19.

20. Hans Küng provides an influential variation upon the Catholic model (ibid., pp. 131–34; Küng, *Christsein* [München: R. Pieper & Co. Verlag, 1974]).

21. Knitter, *NON?* pp. 120–24, 135–39.

22. Note the (unproved) assumption here that the God who is reputedly revealed in the non-Christian religions is the same God who is revealed in Jesus Christ.

23. Timothy R. Stinnett, review of Gavin D'Costa, *John Hick's Theology of Religion,* in *Perkins Journal* 41 (October 1988): 25–26.

24. Knitter, *NON?* pp. 140–42; *The Documents of Vatican II,* ed. Walter M. Abbott (New York: Guild-America-Association Presses, 1966), p. 667.

25. Cobb, "Christ Beyond Creative Transformation," pp. 142, 144–45, 147, 153.

26. Cf. John Hick's critique of Cobb, pp. 158–61, following Cobb's essay, ibid. In his response to Hick, Cobb denies the charge (p.173).

27. Wyschogrod, "A Jewish Postscript," p. 186.

28. Knitter, *NON?* pp. 142–43.

29. Ibid., pp. 145, 73, 146. Those who affirm Jesus as the unique "Son of God" may or may not be claiming that there are no other comparable sons of God. It depends upon the interpreter.

30. Ariarajah, *Bible and People of Other Faiths,* p. 65.

31. See Knitter, *NON?* pp. 146–52; Hick, *Center of Christianity; God and the Universe of Faiths* (New York: St. Martin's Press, 1973); "Jesus and the World Religions," in John Hick, ed., *The Myth of God Incarnate* (Philadelphia: Westminster, 1977), pp. 167–85; " 'Whatever Path Men Choose is Mine,' " in Hicks and Hebblethwaite, eds., *Christianity and Other Religions,* pp. 171–90; and "The Non-Absoluteness of Christianity," in Hick and Knitter, eds., *Myth of Christian Uniqueness,* pp. 16–36.

32. In the revised and enlarged edition of *The Unknown Christ of Hinduism* (Maryknoll, N.Y.: Orbis, 1981) Panikkar rejects his earlier normativistic interpretation of Christ. See Knitter, *NON?* pp. 152–57.

33. Stanley J. Samartha identifies as patronizing the label of "anonymous Christians" applied to non-Christians (as in Karl Rahner) and the notion of the "cosmic Christ" as a means of including "principalities and powers" under Christ's domain ("The Lordship of Jesus Christ and Religious Pluralism," in Gerald H. Anderson and Thomas F. Stransky, eds., *Christ's Lordship and Religious Pluralism* [Maryknoll, N.Y.: Orbis, 1981], p. 35). See Knitter, *NON?* pp. 157–59.

34. These include Gregory Baum, James Parkes, John T. Pawlikowski, Alice L. Eckardt, A. Roy Eckardt, Monika K. Hellwig, E. P. Sanders, Clark M. Williamson, and Paul M. van Buren. See Knitter, *NON?* pp. 159–63.

35. See especially Driver, *Christ in a Changing World.*

36. In his recent statements, Hick takes pains to avoid calling the (allegedly) common content of all religions *God;* he now prefers such terms as *the Real, the True,* and *Reality* (Knitter, *NON?* p. 254 n. 9).

37. Knitter, *NON?* pp. 149–50; Hick, "An Inspiration Christology," p. 21.

38. Knitter, *NON?* pp. 158–59. The quoted words in the Knitter passage are from Samartha's essay, "The Lordship of Jesus Christ and Religious Pluralism."

39. Knitter, *NON?* pp. 166–67. For an analysis and critique of Knitter's position see S. Mark Heim, "Thinking About Theocentric Christology," with responses by Carl E. Braaten, John B. Cobb, Jr., Thomas Dean, Elouise Renich Fraser, Kosuke Koyama, and Paul F. Knitter, *Journal of Ecumenical Studies* 24 (Winter 1987): 1–52.

40. Knitter, *NON?* pp. 171–72.

41. Ibid., pp. 173–75.

42. Ibid., pp. 177–81.

43. Ibid., pp. 182–84.

44. Ibid., p. 182.

45. Ibid., p. 184.

46. Ibid., pp. 184–85, 261 n. 43.

47. Another point at which the marital analogy breaks down is that Christian theology and teaching are public affairs and entail publicly made claims. Marital language is in essence a private affair, though, of course, with public implications.

48. Knitter shows how within process thinking, as within Rahner and his followers, there is nevertheless "a uniqueness of Jesus that, though not exclusive, is definitely inclusive and normative for other revelations and religions." Knitter distinguishes between what these thinkers *say* and what they *imply*. They say much about how "belief in the Incarnation resonates with human experience. Yet they hold back from facing . . . the clear *implications* of what they are saying: that there can be *other incarnations*, other individuals who achieved (or were granted) the same fullness of god-human unity realized in Jesus." Knitter's cross-examination is right on target: "For truth to be truth, for truth to call forth total commitment, must it be the *only* truth?" (ibid., pp. 188, 190–92).

49. Ibid., pp. 186–97.

50. Ibid., pp. 197–200. Knitter alludes to the Trikaya myth in Mahayana Buddhism, according to which the Buddha came to be "deified," with a "glorified body" through which he is really present to believers.

51. Ibid., pp. 201–2.

52. Consult, e.g., Reinhold Niebuhr, *The Children of Light and the Children of Darkness* (New York: Scribner, 1946); *Christianity and Power Politics* (New York: Scribner, 1940); *Christian Realism and Political Problems* (New York: Scribner, 1953); and *Moral Man and Immoral Society* (New York: Scribner, 1941). In the last mentioned, Niebuhr observes that "perhaps the most significant moral characteristic of a nation is its hypocrisy" (p. 95).

53. Knitter, *NON?* p. 202.

54. Cf. Marjorie Hewitt Suchocki, "In Search of Justice: Religious Pluralism from a Feminist Perspective," in Hick and Knitter, eds., *Myth of Christian Uniqueness*, pp. 149–61.

55. Eckardt, *For Righteousness' Sake*, p. 236. The words cited from H. Richard Niebuhr are in *Christ and Culture* (New York: Harper, 1951), p. 68.

56. Knitter, *NON?* pp. 172, 200–204.

57. Ibid., p. 219.

58. Ibid., p. 222. Consult also Paul F. Knitter, "Toward a Liberation Theology of Religions," in Hick and Knitter, eds., *Myth of Christian Uniqueness*, pp. 178–200.

59. Langdon Gilkey comments upon the view exemplified in John Hick: "One is left with God the creator, moral ruler, and, presumably, redeemer as well; and unfortunately such a classic theism is as particular as is any orthodox theology; it is Semitic and Western in form, strikingly different from Hindu, Buddhist, or Confucian conceptions" ("Plurality and Its Theological Implications," p. 41). For Gilkey's attempt to reckon with the dilemma of conceding relativity while having to take an absolutist personal stand, see ibid., pp. 44–50. His proposed solution centers in the concept of *relative absolute-*

ness. I believe that an essentially insoluble problem is present here, both theoretically and existentially speaking.

60. Monika K. Hellwig, *Jesus: The Compassion of God* (Wilmington, Del.: Michael Glazier, 1983), p. 130.

61. For indifferentists, it never really matters what people believe.

62. John Hick, critique of James M. Robinson, in Davis, ed., *Encountering Jesus*, p. 127. See also Hick, "The Non-Absoluteness of Christianity," pp. 16–36.

63. A danger in this affirmation is one that we found in Paul M. van Buren: the imperialism in defining a collectivity other than one's own. Perhaps the intention of the statement here helps meliorate this danger: The definition involved is not primarily that of Israel but of the collectivity to which *Jesus* belongs, the Jewish people.

64. Stanley J. Samartha, as cited in Knitter, *NON?* p. 158. Consult also Samartha, "The Cross and the Rainbow: Christ in a Multireligious Culture," in Hick and Knitter, eds., *Myth of Christian Uniqueness*, pp. 69–88.

65. Knitter, *NON?* pp. 94, 95.

66. See Paul F. Knitter, "Hans Küng's Theological Rubicon," in Swidler, ed., *Toward a Universal Theology of Religion*, pp. 224–30.

67. Küng points out that the traditional Catholic view of *extra ecclesiam nulla salus*, no salvation outside the church, is no longer—at least since Vatican II—the official position. He comments (caustically), "We cannot change the words, because the conciliar statement [Florence, 1442] was, indeed, an infallible definition, but we are allowed to say the contrary!"

68. Hans Küng, "Christianity and World Religions: Dialogue with Islam," in Swidler, ed., *Toward a Universal Theology of Religion*, pp. 196, 200, 203–9. The citations by Küng are from Adolf Schlatter, *Die Geschichte der ersten Christenheit* (1926), pp. 367f.; and Hans-Joachim Schoeps, *Theologie und Geschichte des Judenchristentums* (1949), p. 342. See also Cox, *Many Mansions*, chap. 2, "The Gospel and the Koran."

69. Raimundo Panikkar, "Faith and Belief: A Multireligious Experience," *Anglican Theological Review* 53 (1971): 220.

70. Hick, *God and the Universe of Faiths*, p. 159; Knitter, *NON?* p. 152.

71. Hellwig, *Jesus*, pp. 121, 131.

72. Davis, "Jesus Christ: Savior or Guru?" p. 59.

11. RESTORING THE RESURRECTION: "WHY DO YOU SEARCH AMONG THE DEAD?"

1. This chapter is based on a paper read at the Annual Scholars Conference on the Church Struggle and the Holocaust, Philadelphia, March 5–7, 1989; and at the Graduate Theological Union, Berkeley, April 4, 1989. The substance of the material appeared in *Encounter* (Christian Theological Seminary) 51 (Winter 1990): 1–17. Pertinent sources on the subject of Jesus' resurrection include Murray J. Harris, *Easter in Durham: Bishop Jenkins and the Resurrection of Jesus* (Exeter, U.K.: Paternoster Press, 1985), a defense "of the actual revival of the buried Jesus of Nazareth," p. 31; Monika K. Hellwig, *Jesus, The Compassion of God* (Wilmington, Del.: Michael Glazier, 1983), chap. 7, the resurrection viewed as "a transformation, a breakthrough, to a wholly new mode of existence," p. 103; Luke Timothy Johnson, *The Writings of the New Testament* (Philadelphia: Fortress, 1986), chap. 5; Willi Marxsen, *The Resurrection of Jesus of Nazareth* (Philadelphia: Fortress, 1970), the declaration of Jesus' resurrection interpreted

as an inference derived from personal faith, p. 138; cf. Gerald O'Collins's critique of Marxsen in *What Are They Saying about the Resurrection?* (New York: Paulist, 1978), pp. 106–15; Richard R. Niebuhr, *Resurrection and Historical Reason* (New York: Scribner, 1957), the risen Christ as recognizable only by "those who acknowledged his part in their own past, and their part in his past of rejection, suffering and death," p. 181; Gerald O'Collins, *Interpreting the Resurrection* (New York: Paulist, 1988), Easter viewed as "the story of the risen Savior who holds out to us the full and final answers in our triple quest for what we can know, what we ought to do, and what we may hope for," p. 4; O'Collins, *What Are They Saying about the Resurrection?*; and Juan Luis Segundo, *The Historical Jesus of the Synoptics,* trans. John Drury, vol. 2 of *Jesus of Nazareth Yesterday and Today* (Maryknoll, N.Y.: Orbis, 1985), app. 1.

2. For an analysis of this issue, see Paul M. van Buren, *Christ in Context,* part 3 of *A Theology of the Jewish-Christian Reality* (San Francisco: Harper & Row, 1988), chap. 5.

3. By *historic* Elliott means *historical;* he does not deny the historic, i.e., significant, quality of the resurrection.

4. J. K. Elliott, *Questioning Christian Origins* (London: SCM, 1982), pp. 78, 92. Elliott's equation of *legend* and *myth* is careless. Legends are suffused by falsehood in a way that is not perforce the case with myths.

5. Ibid., p. 77.

6. Mark (chap. 16) and Matthew (chap. 28) are not as somaticist as Luke and John.

7. See William Kelley Wright, *A History of Modern Philosophy* (New York: Macmillan, 1941), pp. 327ff.

8. A. Roy Eckardt, *Christianity and the Children of Israel* (New York: King's Crown Press, Columbia University, 1948), p. 149; *Elder and Younger Brothers* (New York: Scribner, 1967; Schocken, 1973), pp. 127, 88, 140; but cf. pp. 139–40; *Your People, My People* (New York: Quadrangle/New York Times, 1974), pp. 225, 238, 248.

9. Alice u. Roy Eckardt, "Christentum und Judentum: Die theologische und moralische Problematik der Vernichtung des europäischen Judentums," *Evangelische Theologie* 36 (1976): 408.

10. Alan T. Davies, as reported in David Glanz, "The Holocaust as a Question," *Worldview* 17 (September 1974): 37.

11. Jean Daniélou, *Dialogue With Israel* (Baltimore: Helicon, 1966), p. 99 (italics added).

12. Gregory Baum, *Christian Theology After Auschwitz* (London: Council of Christians and Jews, 1976), pp. 8, 9, 11, 12; introduction to Rosemary Radford Ruether, *Faith and Fratricide: The Theological Roots of Anti-Semitism* (New York: Seabury, 1974), p. 8.

13. Paul M. van Buren, "The Status and Prospects for Theology," address to the Theology Section, American Academy of Religion, Chicago, Nov. 1, 1975, as cited in A. Roy Eckardt, "Christians and Jews: Along a Theological Frontier," *Encounter* 40 (1979): 93.

14. Franklin H. Littell, *The Crucifixion of the Jews* (New York: Harper & Row, 1975), p. 2.

15. An illustration of this attempt to dismiss one or another Christian post-*Shoah* theologian for "going too far" or being "too radical" is Michael B. McGarry's review of *Jews and Christians* in the journal *America* (May 23, 1987): 428–29.

16. A. Roy Eckardt, *For Righteousness' Sake* (Bloomington: Indiana University Press, 1987), pp. 304–5.

17. Jürgen Moltmann, *The Crucified God*, trans. R. A. Wilson and John Bowden (New York: Harper & Row, 1974), p. 5.

18. A. Roy Eckardt, "Jürgen Moltmann, The Jewish People, and the Holocaust," *Journal of the American Academy of Religion* 44 (1976): 686.

19. Subsequent paragraphs of the appraisal of Moltmann question whether his attribution of absolute evil to the crucifixion, "the very torment of hell," can stand up in the presence of the *Shoah* (ibid., p. 687). The analysis concludes with a recognition and critique of change in Moltmann's thinking in his subsequent volume, *Kirche in der Kraft des Geistes* (München: Chr. Kaiser Verlag, 1975).

20. Eckardt, "Jürgen Moltmann," p. 691.

21. Some of those who are loudest in their zeal for the resurrection are sometimes prepared to pass over and tacitly to cast aside other elements that are equally indigenous to the Apostolic Writings, e.g., Satan or Jesus' birth by parthenogenesis. In actuality, most of us pick and choose between beliefs. We practice a selective Christianity.

22. Jules Isaac, *The Teaching of Contempt: Christian Roots of Anti-Semitism*, trans. Helen Weaver (New York: Holt, Rinehart, and Winston, 1964).

23. There is no absolute guarantee against a bodily resurrection of Jesus. Cf. Eckardt, *For Righteousness' Sake:* "How could we ever dub [any] supposed event 'impossible' when we remain in the vulnerable position of not being able to establish final criteria for adjudging what can and cannot occur in history as in nature? In point of truth, no human being can say absolutely what is possible and impossible in our world" (pp. 306–7).

24. Cf. ... *I never saw another butterfly* ... : *Children's Drawings and Poems from Terezín Concentration Camp 1942–44*, ed. Hana Volavková, trans. Jeanne Němcová (New York: McGraw-Hill, 1971).

25. A. Roy Eckardt, "Covenant-Resurrection-Holocaust," *Proceedings of the 2nd Philadelphia Conference on the Holocaust, Feb. 16–18, 1977*, ed. Josephine Knopp (Philadelphia: National Institute on the Holocaust, 1977), pp. 39–45 (slightly emended).

26. Conversation with Ulrich E. Simon, London, 20 February 1976.

27. Eckardt, "Christians and Jews," p. 125.

28. John Frederick Jansen, *The Resurrection of Jesus Christ in New Testament Theology* (Philadelphia: Westminster, 1980), pp. 22, 84–85, 89, 92, 91.

29. Pannenberg here misrepresents the Jewish claim. The majority, ongoing point of view of Jewish scholars and rabbis is that the legal tradition must be continually rethought and reformulated.

30. Wolfhart Pannenberg, *Jesus—God and Man*, trans. Lewis L. Wilkens and Duane A. Friebe (Philadelphia: Westminster, 1968), pp. 67, 257, 258. The second English edition of this study by Pannenberg published in 1977 (translation from the 5th German edition) differs from the 1968 English-language edition only in the inclusion of an eleven-page afterword taking note of Pannenberg's critics. His strictures against Judaism and "the Jewish Law" remain.

31. Eckardt, "Christians and Jews," pp. 106–8. Other writings of mine in this period that bear upon the issue of a supersessionist or triumphalist resurrection include *"Ha'Shoah* as Christian Revolution: Toward the Liberation of the Divine Righteousness," *Quarterly Review* 2 (1982): 52–67; "Contemporary Christian Theology and a Protes-

tant Witness for the *Shoah*," *Union Seminary Quarterly Review* 38 (1983): 139–45; and "Antisemitism is the Heart," *Theology Today* 41 (1984): 301–8.

32. Eckardt, *For Righteousness' Sake*, p. 305.

33. Alice L. Eckardt and A. Roy Eckardt, *Long Night's Journey into Day*, rev. ed. (Detroit: Wayne State University Press; Oxford: Pergamon Press, 1988), pp. 136, 139, 140 (slightly emended).

34. A. Roy Eckardt, "Is There a Way Out of the Christian Crime? The Philosophic Question of the Holocaust," *Holocaust and Genocide Studies* 1 (1986): 121–26; *Jews and Christians* (Bloomington: Indiana University Press, 1986), p. 156.

35. Gerald O'Collins counsels that we pick our way "between two extremes: the reductionism of *underbelief*, which denies the reality of the resurrection, and the literalism of an *overbelief*, which woodenly takes certain vivid details to be strictly 'accurate' and thereby misses their true function in the stories" (*What Are They Saying about the Resurrection?* p. 51, italics added).

36. If "Christian ideology" means recourse to certain ideas and idea-systems in the service of collective Christian self-interest, deideologization is the Christian struggle against ideology.

37. Eckardt, *For Righteousness' Sake*, p. 310.

38. Jacobus (Coos) Schoneveld, "The Jewish 'No' to Jesus and the Christian 'Yes' to Jews," *Quarterly Review* 4 (Winter 1984): 60, 63 (slightly emended).

39. Paul van Buren, *Christ in Context*, part 3 of *A Theology of the Jewish-Christian Reality* (San Francisco: Harper & Row, 1988), p. 110.

40. Eckardt and Eckardt, *Long Night's Journey into Day*, pp. 142–43. The effort is made in the original edition of that book to limit the possibilities to either a fully somatic resurrection or no resurrection at all. In the revised edition, the possibility of other alternatives is raised (pp. 140–41). Marcus J. Borg writes that the resurrection is not bodily resuscitation but "entry into another mode of being. . . . In Jesus' case, to use the language of the church, it meant being 'raised to God's right hand' " (*Jesus, A New Vision* [San Francisco: Harper & Row, 1987], p. 185).

41. Criticisms by me still applicable to my new position on the resurrection—written, of course, before my shift—are to be found in *For Righteousness' Sake*, pp. 313–15.

42. Van Buren, *Christ in Context*, p. 111; see also Tom F. Driver, *Christ in a Changing World* (New York: Crossroad, 1981), p. 8.

43. A response of subjectiveness to the resurrection is still, in a sense, an objective datum of human history.

12. FOR THE SAKE OF RACHEL AND FOR THE SAKE OF SARAH

1. Consult Tom F. Driver, *Christ in a Changing World* (New York: Crossroad, 1981), chap. 3, "Critique of Christ as Center, Model, and Norm"; also James B. Nelson, *The Intimate Connection* (Philadelphia: Westminster, 1988), p. 105–11, "Jesus as Sexual Man and Man of Power."

2. Harvey Cox, *Religion in the Secular City* (New York: Simon and Schuster, 1984), p. 209.

3. Donald E. Miller, *The Case for Liberal Christianity* (San Francisco: Harper &

Row, 1981), p. 36; in general, John Hick, *The Center of Christianity* (San Francisco: Harper & Row, 1978).

4. Cox, *Religion in the Secular City*, p. 263; see also Cox, *Many Mansions* (Boston: Beacon, 1988), chap. 9, "The Future of Religion."

5. Elisabeth Schüssler Fiorenza, *In Memory of Her* (New York: Crossroad, 1983), pp. 349–51.

6. Much of the balance of this closing chapter is adapted from selected parts of my plenary address at the Oxford, U.K., Conference on the Impact of the Holocaust and Genocide on Jews and Christians, "Remembering for the Future," 10–13 July 1988, in *Remembering For the Future: Working Papers and Addenda*, vol. 3 (Oxford: Pergamon Press, 1989), pp. 3074–83.

7. Johann Baptist Metz, "Facing the Jews: Christian Theology After Auschwitz," in Elisabeth Schüssler Fiorenza and David Tracy, eds., *The Holocaust as Interruption*, *Concilium* 175 (Edinburgh: T. & T. Clark, 1984), pp. 28–30 (italics added).

8. Elie Wiesel, *The Accident*, trans. Anne Borchardt (New York: Hill and Wang, 1962), p. 91.

9. Emil L. Fackenheim, *What Is Judaism?* (New York: Summit, 1987), p. 291.

10. Elie Wiesel, *Twilight*, trans. Marion Wiesel (New York: Summit, 1988), p. 211.

EPILOGUE: JOHN MACQUARRIE'S *JESUS CHRIST IN MODERN THOUGHT*

1. John Macquarrie, *Jesus Christ in Modern Thought* (London: SCM Press; Philadelphia: Trinity Press International, 1990).

2. Ibid., pp. 265, 405–6, 353. Macquarrie fully acknowledges, however, that "only a belief in the resurrection provides anything like a sufficient reason for the rise of Christianity after the death of Jesus" (p. 406).

3. Ibid., pp. 383, 355, 374, 376, 378, 402, 412. See especially Macquarrie, chap. 18, "The Divinity of Jesus Christ." Macquarrie sees the great majority of Christian theologians teaching that "Christ is God," but "understanding the 'is' in the sense of predication rather than identity." The opposite wording, "God is Jesus," would be rejected by most theologians as unduly restrictive of "God" (ibid., p. 258).

4. Ibid., p. 415.

5. Macquarrie makes an unsupported (and unsupportable) reference to "Jesus' polemic against Jewish legalism" (ibid., p. 350).

6. Ibid., p. 28.

7. Ibid., pp. 417, 419, 420, 421.

8. Ibid., pp. 358, 359, 397, 419, 420, 346, 375–76. See especially Macquarrie, chap. 17, "The Humanity of Jesus Christ."

9. Ibid., p. 70.

10. Ibid., p. 345.

11. At one point Macquarrie makes the curious statement—on his very own terms a highly problematic one—"Being human was essential to Jesus as the Christ, being male was, as far as I can see, contingent" (ibid., p. 360). The end consequence of such reasoning can only be abstractness. History and historiography can hardly concede any ultimate dualism between contingency and noncontingency. Napoleon was not just a man; he was a *short* man—with what are often felt to be fateful human consequences. No self-respecting Christian feminist would ever settle for Jesus' maleness as merely

"contingent"; his maleness poses highly problematic and salient christological questions.

12. See, e.g., ibid., pp. 28, 33. Consult, in general, Macquarrie, chap. 2, "The Prehistory of Christology."

13. Macquarrie's chapter, "Christologies of the Late Twentieth Century" (14), ignores such important figures as John Hick, Paul F. Knitter, and Paul M. van Buren.

SELECTED
RECENT LITERATURE

Asterisked items are particularly germane to the development of this study. Remaining entries are of collateral aid. Some additional sources appear in the notes to each chapter.

*Ariarajah, S. Wesley. *The Bible and People of Other Faiths.* Maryknoll, N.Y.: Orbis, 1989.

*Borg, Marcus J. *Conflict, Holiness and Politics in the Teachings of Jesus.* New York–Toronto: Edwin Mellen, 1984.

*_____ . *Jesus, A New Vision: Spirit, Culture, and the Life of Discipleship.* San Francisco: Harper & Row, 1987.

Bowden, John. *Jesus: The Unanswered Questions.* Nashville: Abingdon, 1989.

*Brandon, S. G. F. *Jesus and the Zealots: A Study of the Political Factor in Primitive Christianity.* Manchester: Manchester University Press, 1967.

*_____ . *The Trial of Jesus of Nazareth.* London: B. T. Batsford, 1968.

Bright, John. *A History of Israel,* 3rd ed. Philadelphia: Westminster, 1981.

*Brock, Rita Nakashima. *Journeys by Heart: A Christology of Erotic Power.* New York: Crossroad, 1988.

Brown, Robert McAfee. *Theology in a New Key: Responding to Liberation Themes.* Philadelphia: Westminster, 1978.

Carnley, Peter. *The Structure of Resurrection Belief.* New York: Oxford University Press, 1987.

*Carr, Anne E. *Transforming Grace: Christian Tradition and Women's Experience.* San Francisco: Harper & Row, 1988.

*Charlesworth, James H. *Jesus Within Judaism: New Light from Exciting Archaeological Discoveries.* Anchor Bible Reference Library. Garden City, N.Y.: Doubleday, 1988.

_____ , ed. *The Old Testament Pseudepigrapha,* 2 vols. Garden City, N.Y.: Doubleday, 1983, 1985.

Collins, Raymond F. *Introduction to the New Testament*. Garden City, N.Y.: Doubleday, 1983.

*Cook, Michael L. *The Jesus of Faith: A Study in Christology*. New York: Paulist, 1981.

*Cox, Harvey. *Many Mansions: A Christian's Encounter with Other Faiths*. Boston: Beacon, 1988.

*_____. *Religion in the Secular City: Toward a Postmodern Theology*. New York: Simon and Schuster, 1984.

*Davis, Stephen T., ed. *Encountering Jesus: A Debate on Christology*. Atlanta: John Knox, 1988.

*Driver, Tom F. *Christ in a Changing World: Toward an Ethical Christology*. New York: Crossroad, 1981.

*Dunn, James D. G. *Christology in the Making: A New Testament Inquiry into the Origins of the Doctrine of the Incarnation*. Philadelphia: Westminster, 1980.

Echegaray, Hugo. *The Practice of Jesus*. Translated by Matthew J. O'Connell. Maryknoll, N.Y.: Orbis, 1984.

*Eckardt, Alice L., and A. Roy Eckardt. *Long Night's Journey into Day: A Revised Retrospective on the Holocaust*. Revised and enlarged. Detroit: Wayne State University Press; Oxford: Pergamon Press, 1988.

*Eckardt, A. Roy. *Black-Woman-Jew: Three Wars for Human Liberation*. Bloomington: Indiana University Press, 1989.

*_____. *Elder and Younger Brothers: The Encounter of Jews and Christians*. New York: Scribner, 1967; Schocken, 1973.

*_____. *For Righteousness' Sake: Contemporary Moral Philosophies*. Bloomington: Indiana University Press, 1987.

_____. *Jews and Christians: The Contemporary Meeting*. Bloomington: Indiana University Press, 1986.

*Elliott, J. K. *Questioning Christian Origins*. London: SCM, 1982.

*Fackenheim, Emil L. *What Is Judaism? An Interpretation for the Present Age*. New York: Summit, 1987.

*Fiorenza, Elisabeth Schüssler. *Bread Not Stone: The Challenge of Feminist Biblical Interpretation*. Boston: Beacon, 1984.

*_____. *In Memory of Her: A Feminist Theological Reconstruction of Christian Origins*. New York, Crossroad, 1983.

*Fredriksen, Paula. *From Jesus to Christ: The Origins of the New Testament Images of Jesus*. New Haven, Conn.: Yale University Press, 1988.

*Goergen, Donald J. *The Mission and Ministry of Jesus*. Wilmington, Del.: Michael Glazier, 1986.

*Gutiérrez, Gustavo. *Teología de la liberación*. 8th ed. Salamanca: Ediciones Sigueme, 1977.

*Harvey, A. E. *Jesus and the Constraints of History*. London: Duckworth, 1982.

*_____, ed. *God Incarnate: Story and Belief*. London SPCK, 1981.

*Hellwig, Monika K. *Jesus: The Compassion of God, New Perspectives on the Tradition of Christianity*. Wilmington, Del.: Michael Glazier, 1983.

Hengel, Martin. *The Atonement: The Origins of the Doctrine in the New Testament*. Translated by John Bowden. Philadelphia: Fortress, 1981.

*_____. *The Charismatic Leader and His Followers*. Translated by James Greig. New York: Crossroad, 1981.

*Heyward, Isabel Carter. *The Redemption of God: A Theology of Mutual Relation*. Washington: University Press of America, 1982.

*Hick, John. *The Center of Christianity*. San Francisco: Harper & Row, 1978.

_____ , ed. *The Myth of God Incarnate*. Philadelphia: Westminster, 1977.

*Hick, John, and Brian Hebblethwaite, eds. *Christianity and Other Religions: Selected Readings*. Philadelphia: Fortress, 1980.

*Hick, John, and Paul F. Knitter, eds. *The Myth of Christian Uniqueness: Toward a Pluralistic Theology of Religions*. Maryknoll, N.Y.: Orbis, 1987.

*Hillman, Eugene, *Many Paths: A Catholic Approach to Religious Pluralism*. Maryknoll, N.Y.: Orbis, 1989.

Hilton, Michael, with Gordian Marshall. *The Gospels and Rabbinic Judaism: A Study Guide*. Hoboken, N.J.: Ktav, 1988.

*Jansen, John Frederick. *The Resurrection of Jesus Christ in New Testament Theology*. Philadelphia: Westminster, 1980.

*Johnson, Luke Timothy. *The Writings of the New Testament: An Interpretation*. Philadelphia: Fortress, 1986.

*Knitter, Paul F. *No Other Name? A Critical Survey of Christian Attitudes Toward the World Religions*. Maryknoll, N.Y.: Orbis, 1985.

Lapide, Pinchas, and Jürgen Moltmann. *Jewish Monotheism and Christian Trinitarian Doctrine: A Dialogue*. Translated by Leonard Swidler. Philadelphia: Fortress, 1981.

*Lee, Bernard J. *The Galilean Jewishness of Jesus: Retrieving the Jewish Origins of Christianity*. New York: Paulist, 1988.

*Maccoby, Hyam. *Revolution in Judaea: Jesus and the Jewish Resistance*. New York: Taplinger, 1980.

*McGarry, Michael. *Christology After Auschwitz*. New York: Paulist, 1977.

*McGrath, Alister. *The Enigma of the Cross*. London: Hodder and Stoughton, 1987.

*Mackey, James P. *Jesus the Man and the Myth: A Contemporary Christology*. New York: Paulist, 1979.

*Macquarrie, John, *Jesus Christ in Modern Thought*. London: SCM Press; Philadelphia: Trinity Press International, 1990.

_____ . *Principles of Christian Theology*. 2d ed. New York: Scribner, 1977.

*Marxsen, Willi. *The Resurrection of Jesus of Nazareth*. Philadelphia: Fortress, 1970.

*Metz, Johann Baptist. *The Emergent Church: The Future of Christianity in a Postbourgeois World*. Translated by Peter Mann. New York: Crossroad, 1981.

Moltmann, Jürgen. *The Crucified God: The Cross of Christ as the Foundation and Criticism of Christian Theology*. Translated by R. A. Wilson and John Bowden. New York: Harper & Row, 1974.

_____ . *The Trinity and the Kingdom: The Doctrine of God*. Translated by Margaret Kohl. San Francisco: Harper & Row, 1981.

*Mowinckel, Sigmund. *He That Cometh: The Messiah Concept in the Old Testament and Later Judaism*. Translated by G. W. Anderson. Nashville: Abingdon, 1954.

Nelson, James B. *The Intimate Connection: Male Sexuality, Masculine Spirituality*. Philadelphia: Westminster, 1988.

*Niebuhr, Richard R. *Resurrection and Historical Reason: A Study of Theological Method*. New York: Scribner, 1957.

*O'Collins, Gerald. *Interpreting the Resurrection: Examining the Major Problems in the Stories of Jesus' Resurrection*. New York: Paulist, 1988.

*_____ . *What Are They Saying about Jesus?* Rev. ed. New York: Paulist, 1983.

*_____ . *What Are They Saying about the Resurrection?* New York: Paulist, 1978.

O'Neill, J. C. *Messiah: Six Lectures on the Ministry of Jesus.* Cambridge, U.K.: Cochrane, 1980.

*Parkes, James. *The Foundations of Judaism and Christianity.* London: Vallentine, Mitchell, 1960.

*Pawlikowski, John T. *Christ in the Light of the Christian-Jewish Dialogue.* New York: Paulist, 1982.

Pelikan, Jaroslav. *Jesus Through the Centuries.* New Haven, Conn.: Yale University Press, 1985.

*Richard, Lucien. *What Are They Saying about Christ and World Religions?* New York: Paulist, 1981.

*Ringe, Sharon H. *Jesus, Liberation, and the Biblical Jubilee: Images for Ethics and Christology.* Philadephia: Fortress, 1985.

*Rouner, Leroy S., ed. *Religious Pluralism.* Notre Dame, Ind.: University of Notre Dame Press, 1984.

*Russell, Letty M. *Household of Freedom: Authority in Feminist Theology.* Philadelphia: Westminster, 1988.

*Sanders, E. P. *Jesus and Judaism.* Philadelphia: Fortress, 1985.

*_____ . *Paul, the Law, and the Jewish People.* Philadelphia: Fortress, 1983.

*_____ . *Paul and Palestinian Judaism: A Comparison of Patterns of Religion.* Philadelphia: Fortress, 1977.

Scholem, Gershom. *The Messianic Idea in Judaism and Other Essays on Jewish Spirituality.* New York: Schocken, 1971.

Scott, Joan Wallach. *Gender and the Politics of History.* New York: Columbia University Press, 1988.

Segundo, Juan Luis. *An Evolutionary Approach to Jesus of Nazareth.* Edited and translated by John Drury. Vol. 5 of *Jesus of Nazareth Yesterday and Today.* Maryknoll, N.Y.: Orbis, 1988.

*_____ . *The Historical Jesus of the Synoptics.* Translated by John Drury. Vol. 2 of *Jesus of Nazareth Yesterday and Today.* Maryknoll, N.Y.: Orbis, 1985.

*_____ . *Liberación de la teología.* Buenos Aires: Ediciones Carlos Lohlé, 1975.

Selby, Peter. *Look for the Living: The Corporate Nature of Resurrection Faith.* Philadelphia: Fortress, 1976.

Sloyan, Gerard S. *Is Christ the End of the Law?* Philadelphia: Westminster, 1978.

Smith, Wilfred Cantwell. *Towards a World Theology: Faith and the Comparative History of Religion.* Maryknoll, N.Y.: Orbis, 1989.

*Swidler, Leonard. *Yeshua: A Model for Moderns.* Kansas City: Sheed & Ward, 1988.

*_____ , ed. *Toward a Universal Theology of Religion.* Maryknoll, N.Y.: Orbis, 1987.

*Tamez, Elsa, ed. *Through Her Eyes: Women's Theology from Latin America.* Maryknoll, N.Y.: Orbis, 1989.

Theissen, Gerd. *Sociology of Early Palestinian Christianity.* Translated by John Bowden. Philadelphia: Fortress, 1978.

*Tillich, Paul. *Christianity and the Encounter of the World Religions.* New York: Columbia University Press, 1963.

*Tracy, David. *Blessed Rage for Order: The New Pluralism in Theology.* New York: Seabury, 1978.

*Van Buren, Paul M. *A Christian Theology of the People Israel.* Part 2 of *A Theology of the Jewish-Christian Reality.* New York: Seabury, 1983.

*_____ . *Christ in Context*. Part 3 of *A Theology of the Jewish-Christian Reality*. San Francisco: Harper & Row, 1988.

*Vermes, Geza. *The Gospel of Jesus the Jew*. Newcastle upon Tyne: University of Newcastle Upon Tyne, 1981.

*_____ . *Jesus the Jew: A Historian's Reading of the Gospels*. London: Fontana/Collins, 1976.

*_____ . *Jesus and the World of Judaism*. Philadelphia: Fortress, 1984.

Weber, Christin Lore. *WomanChrist: A New Vision of Feminist Spirituality*. San Francisco: Harper & Row, 1987.

*Weidman, Judith L., ed. *Christian Feminism: Visions of a New Humanity*. San Francisco: Harper & Row, 1984.

Wiles, Maurice. *The Remaking of Christian Doctrine*. Philadelphia: Westminster, 1978.

*Williamson, Clark M. *Has God Rejected His People? Anti-Judaism in the Christian Church*. Nashville: Abingdon, 1982.

*Wilson, Marvin R. *Our Father Abraham: Jewish Roots of the Christian Faith*. Grand Rapids: Eerdmans; Dayton: Center for Judaic-Christian Studies, 1989.

Wilson-Kastner, Patricia. *Faith, Feminism, and the Christ*. Philadelphia: Fortress, 1983.

*Young, Brad H. *Jesus and His Jewish Parables: Rediscovering the Roots of Jesus' Teaching*. New York: Paulist, 1989.

Index of
Scriptural Passages

General Index

Abraham, call of, 162
Absolutism, 104; Christian, 158, 179,
181, 184, 189, 207; and Jesus, 200;
and Judaism, 180; opposition to, 199;
and papacy, 196; and truth, 11-12, 180
Acts, Book of, anti-Jewishness of, 256
Akiba, Rabbi, 257
'Amme ha-arets (common people), 53,
239; and Jesus, 51
Andrew, apostle, 64
Androcentrism, 9, 120; of biblical texts,
106ff.; critique of, 203; and
priesthood,124. *See also* Patriarchalism
Angels, 44; warrior, 80
Anglicanism, 187
Antifeminism, and antisemitism, 112-13
Antisemitism, and antiwomanism, 125;
Christian, 208, 209; theological, 41
Anti-Zionism, 259
Apocalypticism, Jewish, 85
"Apolitical," as not same as
"antipolitical," 240
Apostolic Writings, 15, 19, 27, 69, 70,
78, 80, 94, 169, 202, 267; anti-
Jewishness of, 104, 151, 166, 244;
authority of vis-à-vis Jesus' authority,
191ff.; Christomonism in, 202; Christs

of, 137-60; and discrepancies with
Jesus' message/mission, 140-41; and
"doing the truth," 92; doubt of
resurrection in, 215-16; exclusivism
in, 191-93; fabrications in, 69, 70; God
of, 184; and Jewish people, 182; and
knowledge of Jesus, 141;minimization
of Roman occupation in, 70;
patriarchal tendentiousness of, 107;
question of as norm, 176; and
resurrection of Jesus, 171, 172, 173,
206; shifting of culpability from
Romans to Jews in, 70; silences of,
69ff.; tendentiousness in, 70, 104, 151;
as term for "New Testament," 232;
and theocentric Christology, 190-93;
Word of God and, 202-203
Aramaic, 8, 17, 143
Arian controversy, 163
Ariarajah, S. Wesley, 189
As If It Were Yesterday, 221
Auschwitz, 221; children of, 211; as
incorrectly equated with *Shoah*, 258
Auschwitz-Birkenau, 222

Bar Kochba, 257

Perrin, Norman, 230; on resurrection of Jesus, 194
Person and work of Jesus Christ, conflict between Jesus and Paul on, 145-46
Peter, 18, 27, 64, 110, 141-42, 154, 176
"Pharisee," as adjective, 237
Pharisees, 51, 53, 70, 84, 156, 237, 239, 247, 256; alleged fault of, 30; Gospels and, 237-38; liturgy of, 64; and love, 65, 118; and oppressed, 68, 103; and resistance to Rome, 77; and resurrection of dead, 214. *See also* Jesus: and Pharisees
"Political"-historical question, meaning of, 74-75
Politics, as consequence of faith, 92
Pontius Pilate, 19, 58, 251, 256
Postmodernism, postmoderns, 9, 216; and Christian belief, 220-21; and Christology, 219ff.; and the sacred, 44; and thrust of present book, 225
Postmodern world, and Christian belief, 220-21
Post-neo-orthodoxy, 9
Postpatriarchalism, 9
Post-*Shoah* age, 91
Post-*Shoah* thinking, 9-10, 266
Praxis, as equated with reality, 92-93; and holiness of history, 93; and Jesus, 93; and Jewish thought, 93; meaning of term, 92
"Preferential option for the poor," and universalization of righteousness, 116
Priesthood, Jewish, 70
Priestly aristocracy, 57
Process thought, 193; Christian, 163
Prophet, as equal to miracle-worker, 17. *See also* Jesus: as prophet
Prophetic faith, and political action, 82
Prophets, prophetic tradition, 64, 65-66, 81-82, 83, 84, 85, 116; patriarchal elements in, 106ff.
Protestant churches, mainline, 185, 186-87
Protestant Episcopal Church, Articles of Religion of, 170
Proverbs, Book of, 39
Psalms, Book of, 39

Psychosocial holism, 128-29
Purity laws, 239

Q-source, 7, 108, 109, 230, 242
Qur'ān, and Jesus, 201-203; as Word of God, 201-203

Rachel, 221, 223
Rahner, Karl, 187, 193, 263, 264
Raphael, 223
Reason, 12, 26; and faith, 139-40, 200
Redemption, dialectic of, 203-204; as universal, 200
Reformers, Protestant, 186
Relational theology, as incarnational, 132
Relationism, 199; and authority of Jesus, 179; in Christology, 190ff.; and relativity, 179, 180; and truth, 11-12, 180
Relativism, 186; opposition to, 199; and truth, 11-12, 179, 180
Religion, and inseparability from politics, 71; and the sacred, 184
Religious pluralism, 185, 192, 193; and devil, 185; and divine mystery, 196; typologies of, 262
"Remembering for the Future," 269
Resurrection of dead, 42, 237
Resurrection of Jesus, 7, 55, 66-67, 79-80, 102-103, 137, 138, 139, 144, 152, 154, 191, chap. 11, 254, 255, 259, 260, 267, 268; antitriumphalist affirmation of, 213ff.; and Christian-Jewish encounter, 206; and Christian triumphalism, 211; in continuity with Judaism, 214ff.; and denial of Christian faith, 210; disciples and, 143; as dividing Christians and Jews, 257; and End, 147; as event within history of Israel, 204; as future, 210, 211; and hostility to Judaism/Jews, 211, 212-13; Jewishness of, 215; and Jewish people, 210; and Messianic expectations, 207; moral/critical questioning of, 207-13; and moral demands, 209, 260; moral-psychoanalytic issue of, 210; objectivist view of, 206, 216;